ABOUT THE AUTHORS

KATHARINE ANNE OMMANNEY is a pioneer in educational dramatics, having selected the high school as her chosen field in the early twenties. She has been fortunate in combining her quarter century as dramatics teacher at North High School, Denver, with extensive teaching, lecturing at the university level, acting on the stage and in radio, and professional directing of all types of productions. Her advanced specialized training has included an M. A. from Stanford, and study at the Royal Academy of Dramatic Art and the Oxford Summer School of Speech in England and at the American Academy of Dramatic Art. She was *Billboard* correspondent for several years and has contributed numerous articles to *Theater Arts* and other drama and educational magazines.

She has received widespread recognition, including listing in *Who's Who of American Women* and *Leaders in Education*, honorary membership in Zeta Phi Eta and Alpha Phi Gamma, and service on such boards as those of ATA, WPA Federal Theater (Colorado), and drama sections of NEA conventions. She was a delegate to the 1970 Governor's Conference of the Year 2000 in Honolulu.

Since her early retirement and marriage, she has been active in the theater of Hawaii, where she has taught at Maunaolu College, Maui, and produced various types of current plays and productions featuring the many racial types available. She has "pursued the drama around the world" all her life seeing plays and theater festivals, lecturing and directing on all the continents. At present she is on the Executive Board of the Hawaii State Theater Council under the State Foundation on Culture and the Arts and is active with the long standing Maui Community Theater.

HARRY H. SCHANKER is a dedicated teacher-director of high school dramatics with a wide background of training and experience in all phases of classroom and production activities, and is a devoted student of the drama.

He earned the B.S. degree in Language Arts from Kansas University, and the M. A. degree in Secondary Education from the University of Colorado. He has taught English, Speech, Drama, and Stagecraft in the Denver Public Schools for almost two decades, and is on the K-12 English Committee there as drama representative. He is the editor of *Dramatic Comedy*, an anthology of "classic" comedies and a part of the McGraw-Hill "Patterns in Literary Arts" series.

Mr. Schanker originated the Summer High School Theater in Denver and served as its first director; he has produced its summer musicals with great success. He has also planned and supervised the auditorium and backstage areas and equipment in the Thomas Jefferson High School, where he has made an enviable reputation as teacher and producer, having directed over a hundred productions and handled the technical work for at least that many.

Fourth Edition

The Stage and the School

KATHARINE ANNE OMMANNEY

HARRY H. SCHANKER

WEBSTER DIVISION, McGRAW-HILL BOOK COMPANY
St. Louis, New York, San Francisco, Dallas, Atlanta, Toronto

The authors wish to thank those publishers, authors, and friends who have permitted the reprinting of copyrighted material in this book. For a list of credits, see page 509. For information about pictures without captions, see page 508.

Editorial Development:	John Rothermich
	Evalyn Kinkead
Editing and Styling:	Barbara McDonough
	Betty Martin
Design:	Ted Smith
	John Keithley
Layout:	Richard O'Leary
Production:	Bert Henke
	Dick Shaw
Photo Consultant:	F. L. Orkin, New York

ISBN 07-047657-8
1 2 3 4 5 6 7 8 9-MAMM-7 6 5 4 3
Library of Congress Catalogue Card Number: 73-150665

TABLE OF CONTENTS

SCENES FOR CLASSROOM USE

PROLOGUE

The theater of the United States is in a period of transition which is strongly affecting the stage of the school. This latest edition of the first dramatics textbook to be used extensively at the secondary level is designed to meet the changing needs of high school students without losing the fundamental values of the earlier editions. It has been almost completely rewritten, but many features which have proved especially useful remain intact. The subject matter has been expanded and curtailed in order to include developments which show promise of becoming permanent phases of both theater and educational dramatics. Throughout the book, current trends have been presented as they are related to the secondary school.

The treatment is essentially the same as before, covering all phases of drama and including emphasis on personality development and technical skill in using the tools of interpretative art — the voice and the body — as effective means of communication. A chief consideration has been to encourage a love of the theater through an intelligent appreciation of the drama of the past and an understanding of the best of the present forms.

Both Mr. Schanker and I feel that at this period, when old standards in all the arts are being discarded and ever-changing patterns are being tried out, dramatics students should not be deprived of the knowledge and appreciation of the enduring values which have brought entertainment, inspiration, and enlightenment for 2500 years to countless generations of men and women in theaters around the world.

Therefore, the book has been reorganized to offer an even more logical and efficient presentation than in previous editions. The five-part structure of the third edition has been reduced to four, with three of the four being greatly expanded to accommodate new material.

In this new edition, we feel that "Part One: Understanding the Drama" pulls together and modernizes Parts One and Two and Chapter 14 of the third edition. "Part Two: Interpreting the Drama" (Part Three in the third edition) now has five chapters, with two new ones: "Improvisation" and "The Platform Reading of Plays." The other three chapters, "Pantomime," "Voice and Diction," and "Acting" have been updated and expanded. Now Part Two alone presents a complete introductory course in dramatic interpretation.

"Part Three: Appreciating the Drama" updates two chapters which have proved particularly popular, "History of Drama" and "Shakespearean Drama." "Part Four: Producing the Drama" has been greatly expanded to provide a complete introductory course in play production. Stage settings, lighting, costuming, and makeup have all been given full chapter status. The "Epilogue," new to this edition, offers the student valuable advice about considering a career in drama. It is the condensation of many interviews with distinguished directors, actors, and key people in the current theatrical scene and my personal experience in the world of the theater and the stage of the school.

The book has a new size, and a completely new and more attractive design. There are more technical drawings for the play production chapters, and new and up-to-date photographs keyed in provocatively with the text. Also there are about twice as many scenes from worthwhile plays for interpretative practice.

Pertinent information concerning a great many contemporary movements of importance in theater today have been emphasized. Among them are included the following: the burgeoning of the regional and repertory theaters across the country, which produce the great dramas of the past, the best plays of the present, and experimental performances anticipating those of the future; the phenomenal growth of university departments of drama; the initiation of the Federal government into financial and aesthetic patronage of the arts and artists; the opening of opportunities for training and experience in theatrical centers in all parts of the country as the influence of Broadway and Hollywood diminishes; and the internationalization of the drama of the stage, screen, and television as electronic means of communication multiply.

Futurists are stressing the values of creative leisure to prepare for living in the tomorrow rushing upon us in this electronic age. High school dramatics offers young people a meaningful opportunity to use their talents and enthusiasm for plays and motion pictures and television in relevant activity in play production and film making. In their search for identity, young people can find themselves in the understanding of contrasted roles and in their interpretation of plays and scenes dealing with fundamental human problems.

My own high school students inspired me to write this book originally to put into concrete form the joyous activities of our classes and productions. In each edition since the first in 1932 I have included current trends which I have encountered in a pursuit of the drama around the world. Recently I have centered my attention on the regional and repertory theaters here and abroad because in them lie the future opportunities for high school graduates.

It is my sincere hope that this latest edition will continue to encourage young people to reach their full potentialities as individuals, and as performers and spectators, and to find permanent satisfaction in all phases of the drama, the most universal of the arts.

Here let me express my appreciation of the interviews granted me in relation to this edition by leaders in all phases of theater here and abroad; in addition to those mentioned in the text, Ernest V. Theiss continued his invaluable assistance at NBC, Radio City, New York. Directors and actors in the regional and repertory theaters in England and across this country have been most helpful, and public relations directors in motion pictures — especially Quinn Donoghue of Mirish Productions — and in television studios have been of great service. Young actresses at the Rehearsal Club in New York graciously discussed their experiences and also current trends in theater opportunities. I especially wish to thank my personal friends for the masses of information they have continuously forwarded to me from theatrical centers. I wish to reemphasize my gratitude to my instructors in speech and drama, listed in earlier editions, whose influence permeates this one as well. My inexpressible thanks for their dedicated service in this edition go to my coauthor, Harry Schanker, my editor, John Rothermich, and my husband, Henry Vincent.

Katharine Anne Ommanney

Kula, Maui, Hawaii
August, 1970

PART

Understanding the Drama

THE STUDENT
OF DRAMA

Whether its setting has been the marble columns of ancient Greece, the crude carts of the Middle Ages, the cobbled innyards of Elizabethan England, the glittering showboat on the Mississippi, the ornate theaters and picture palaces of our commercial productions, or the intimate, contrived showplaces for our experimental theater, the stage has always had a remarkable fascination for the average individual. Radio and television have brought the drama into our homes and the school has brought it to the student.

RELATION BETWEEN THE STAGE AND SCHOOL

As a student approaching dramatics in the high school, you have a background no other young people have had. As a child you spent hours before your home TV watching, fascinated, the lives of other people involved in exciting happenings. You grew up in the days of the wide screen and stereophonic sound of the motion picture. In school probably you have already enjoyed creative dramatics, with simple improvisations freeing your mind and body for expressive action. In Junior High you may have appeared in public performances

2

of plays and musicals. You are now prepared to approach drama as a composite art form which has had a universal appeal for countless generations.

Therefore the classwork and public performances will open the world of the theater to you. You will experience the delights of both the actor and the spectator without suffering the limitations of either. At the same time you will develop yourself as an individual. The search for identity is the urgent need of young people. The acting of a role in a scene or a play demands an understanding of your own internal resources and those of the character. Also in the reading and the witnessing of plays, you involve yourself with the problems of other people empathically. Empathy is a vital phase of theater, as well as of all the arts, because it means that a person identifies with an object, situation, or individual outside of himself. Thus through empathy you gain a sympathy and sensitivity for the emotions and attitudes of other people which carries over into your daily life. The study of the techniques of acting — the effective use of the tools of your voice and body — is the practical means by which you improve your physical and emotional expressiveness. This experience in self-development and social adjustment is a reasonable means of finding the individual identity so sought after today.

Thus you can take advantage of the three phases of this course: a study of the theater as one of the chief divisions of art and literature; the actual acting and producing of plays; and the development of your personality, a natural outcome of a wholehearted absorption in the other two phases.

The world of the theater also fosters a delightful use of the leisure time which modern affluence and shorter working hours will bring into your adult life. As an avocation, a multitude of experimental and community groups are welcoming enthusiastic amateurs, the lovers of the drama, into active participation. Then, since most successful plays are immediately published, even in paperback, you can spend many hours in imaginative and fascinating reading of the most exciting form of literature. There is also a wealth of interesting reading in biographies and magazine articles about the personalities of the dramatic world of the past as well as the present. As a result of this intimate study of the theater you are about to undertake, you will keep yourself alive to current movements; and you will develop a critical judgment and enjoyment of plays you are seeing on the stage, motion-picture screen, and TV.

In this course you will be brought into contact with the finest examples of the old and new theater. You must take advantage of the opportunities afforded present-day students to attend the repertory, roadshow, summer stock, and amateur productions available, and to judge them intelligently. Perhaps you will have the invaluable experience of appearing in your school's public productions. Today high school standards are as professional as the age and appearance of the cast will permit.

You will, therefore, become a part of the knowledgeable theatergoing public which can affect the ever-changing drama of today. With discrimination you will seek out the best of stage, screen, and TV fare and not waste time in stupid, apathetic gazing at repetitious, worthless, and tasteless offerings. More important, you will face whatever life holds for you with a quickened imagination, a better developed voice and body, and a keener appreciation of art and humanity.

THE DEVELOPMENT OF THE INDIVIDUAL

The changing world of the theater is typical of the changing world you will be facing in the immediate and distant future. Never have "the changes and chances of this mortal world" been so likely to affect your attitudes and life as they are doing today, and never have so many opportunities for creative experience been afforded you. The limitless expanses of space, the new frontiers of oceanography, the "great globe itself" to its farthermost outposts are within your reach. Constant breakthroughs in every field — electronics, medicine, aviation, and all the others — are making life more meaningful and exhilarating. Consequently, the relationships of individuals and nations to each other are of utmost importance in controlling these changes and chances of modern existence.

Thus your development as an individual is of vital significance not only to you but to society. Your growth is, of course, the goal of all your subjects, but dramatics deals with you personally more than any other subject does because of your relation to the parts you play and to the other members of the class. It is distinctly a group activity where you need all the patience, sportsmanship, tact, and good nature you can muster. Nothing is more trying on the nerves and disposition than putting on a play; you may already have discovered this. Your ability to accept criticism, to get along with others, and to lose yourself in the success of class projects and productions determines your value to that success. You must be prompt, depend-

*With the help of makeup and costuming, Christopher Plummer becomes Sir Andrew
Auguecheek in* Twelfth Night *(left) and Philip the Bastard in* King John. **5**

able, and responsive if you are to gain and give all you should. If you are especially talented, you have to overcome the very grave temptation to become egotistical, arty, aggressive, and impervious to suggestion. The discipline demanded by such activity will bring you the restraint in both your public and private life that can help counteract the unreasoning violence of this latter part of the twentieth century.

In no other art is the individuality of the student so important. The actor has two persons involved in his creative experience whom he must understand — himself and the character he is portraying. The internal and external resources of these two individuals determine the response of the audience and thus the success of the performer. Your improvement mentally, emotionally, socially, and physically will give you the most enduring satisfactions of the course.

Today we are appreciating that Shakespeare knew what he was talking about when Jaques says in *As You Like It*, "All the world's a stage and all the men and women merely players." Today we use the term "role-playing." We realize that each of us plays a part as we encounter differing situations and people involved in daily living. We often seem to become divergent personalities depending on whether we are in our homes or schools or involved with jobs or social groups. Such chameleon-like personality shifts are worthy of self-analysis.

Also today the word "charisma" is heard often in association with a performer's appeal. Charisma in this context denotes that charm which Maggie has in James M. Barrie's delightful comedy *What Every Woman Knows*. Without this charm Barrie claims that nothing else matters, and it is certainly true that mere beauty is of far less importance in the theater now then ever before. Though charisma and a photogenic face, essential in success on the screen, are inherent in the lucky personalities who possess them, your character traits do determine your effect on other people. You should, therefore, cultivate traits by which you can realize your highest potentiality not only in interpreting parts, but also in becoming the person you hope to be.

Of these traits, controlled emotion is one of the most potent. Philip Barry in his fine play *Tomorrow and Tomorrow* states that emotion is the only real thing in human life. Certainly one who never experiences deep emotion never really lives. The loss of self in another individuality which comes when a person acts a part sincerely or watches a play intensely is one of the chief values of a dramatics course. This vicarious living of a life apart from one's daily experience is the chief appeal of the stage in both school and theater.

A: Here a box set is framed by a proscenium which separates actors from audience. B: The Dallas Theater Center does away with the proscenium, bringing the actors closer to the audience. Scenery is suggested rather than detailed. C: The Arena Theatre of Karamu House in Cleveland. In arena theaters the audience surrounds the playing area, and props substitute for scenery.

The fundamental character traits which are the most vital fall under such categories as mental, ethical, and altruistic. These have been the basic qualities exemplified in the great roles of the finest dramas of every age. Presented by sensitive artists of fine training and experience, they will always arouse the enthusiastic support of the great mass of theatergoers. Even during the middle years of the twentieth century, when the first interest in plays of shock, cruelty, and "involvement" were gathering a following, such dramas as *A Man for All Seasons, Becket, Man of La Mancha,* and *Luther* attracted **7** packed houses for long runs. These were dramas of outstanding value marked by fine literary style, with characters of real worth and supreme interest, and with artistic settings. Among these, too, were musicals, particularly those with lyrics by Oscar Hammerstein, and appealing characters, like those in *The King and I, The Sound of Music,* and *Carousel.* These musicals and plays drew record-breaking crowds on both the legitimate stage and the screen.

The recurring presentation of the classics, generation after generation, proves the inherent appeal of heroic characters coping with universal problems. The modern adaptations of Shakespeare, like *Your Own Thing*, the hippie *Love's Labour's Lost*, and various versions of *Hamlet* in the sixties did not dampen the glory of these classics. Today splendid productions of Shakespeare in traditional style are successfully presented the world over every season. Studying the great dramas of Greece, the Renaissance, the Restoration, and the early twentieth century — times as turbulent as our own — can give you a sense of balance and reason in meeting the last decades of the twentieth century.

Dramatics is as distinctly cultural as music and art appreciation. A cultured person has an appreciation for the finer things of life because he understands them and realizes their value. He has wide interests because all phases of life appeal to him; he has true courtesy because his sympathy for people as individuals leads him to consider others before himself; he has enthusiasm for beauty in all its forms because he understands the fundamental principles back of all artistic expression. Dramatics can be an incentive toward this understanding because it is a study of humanity and art.

Your external characteristics are obvious, and their improvement will find its greatest impetus in the technical training involved in acting and producing. By conscientiously studying and practicing the fundamental principles of dramatics, you can acquire such habits as correct breathing, upon which a good voice depends; careful articulation and enunciation, upon which good speech depends; and vocal and bodily vitality, upon which platform success depends. You should dress in better taste after studying costuming, move more expressively and effectively after studying pantomime, and communicate more persuasively after studying acting. You will be delighted to find you can measure your progress toward bettering your posture, physical responsiveness, and appearance almost daily. If you assist in the production of a play, you gain skills dependent upon rapid bodily

In Arsenic and Old Lace, *two sweet old ladies (here Dorothy Stickney and Mildred Natwick) "rescue" lonely old men from their empty lives, but give each one a private funeral. For the last curtain call on the stage, twelve earth-covered men emerged from the cellar to take a bow.*

response, physical vitality, tasteful color and line utilization, and virile leadership. When you are developing a role, your attention to the age, physical condition, hair styling, mannerisms of movement and facial expression, revealing gestures, and general appearance of the character will bring your part to life and compel immediate audience response. Actors are fascinating people largely because of their animation, originality in dress, and consciousness of the value of voice and diction and physical poise.

If you wish to get the full value of the dramatics course, you will make every play you read, in and out of class, a source of experimentation, of playing all the parts at home without an audience. As the work unfolds, establish a regular schedule for vocal, physical, and interpretation practice and follow it conscientiously. Enter into all phases of the classwork enthusiastically, whether or not the particular assignment appeals to you, and be as interested in watching the work of the other members of the class as in performing yourself. Try to catch the spirit of every scene you work up, and you will be surprised that you have acquired a keener sense of humor, a more alert interest in life, and a broader sympathy for people and their problems. **9**

As in all activity, you will get from the dramatics class only what you put into it; the very nature of the subject matter demands an intensity of effort and enthusiasm of interest few courses draw forth. In this way, in classwork or in public production, you may experience the ultimate achievement of the actor — holding an audience spellbound with your emotional appeal as you reveal the true nature of the role you are playing.

READING PLAYS FOR PERSONAL ENJOYMENT

Reading plays is one of the most satisfying ways to spend your leisure hours. Modern playwrights publish their plays as well as seek their production, and most publishing houses have excellent reissues of classics and of the most interesting dramas of the past and present. If you browse among the drama bookshelves in public libraries, you will find thousands of volumes including everything from various translations of the ancient Greek and Roman dramas to the latest Broadway and off-Broadway productions.

In addition, there are hundreds of anthologies containing national and historical plays of great current interest. The *Best Plays* of each year is a popular anthology containing excerpts which summarize the action of each play and give information about the ages of actors, the plays they have appeared in, and complete lists of all plays produced in New York and other important centers.

You should make use of the theatrical magazines. The demise of *Theatre Arts*, the finest drama magazine published in the United States, was a sad blow to theater lovers; each issue contained a complete script of a current play besides splendid photographs and articles on all phases of theater. You might find it interesting and valuable to look up some old issues. *Billboard* and *Variety* are vital to professionals, but too condensed for ordinary readers. *Show* was the first theatrical magazine to appear in the sixties; it included comments on films and theater, but was short lived, but a new *Show* appeared in 1970. In 1967 *Theatre Crafts* made its debut. It stresses the latest trends, and features excellent photographs of personalities, staging, and innovations. Sunday copies of the *New York Times* and other newspapers, as well as the theater sections of the best magazines, can also keep you informed about the latest events of special interest. Your teacher may have copies of the *Tulane Drama Review*, considered one of the best in the field, or the publications of the American Educational Theater Association. Of course, if you are a member of the International Thespians, their *Dramatics* will be of value to you. *Realities,* the English version of the elegant French magazine, has brilliant articles with magnificent colored illustrations about the world theater.

Reading plays is less time-consuming than reading novels, for the playwright must find the exact word or phrase to advance the plot, characterize his people, and bring out his theme — all through dialogue alone. He seldom has time for long descriptions or philosophical passages to explain his ideas. As the course advances, you will learn to appreciate the skills demanded in the creation of a first-class play. You will find that the secret of reading drama is to visualize the persons, settings, and action and let the development of the plot carry you along with its suspense and conflict. To help you clarify the events, it may be a good idea to begin by selecting plays you have seen on TV or in the movies. It is also interesting to note the changes frequently made, especially for films, in the sequence of events and in the ending.

As you read a play, you have time to think about what is being said without the necessity of keeping pace with rapid action on stage. You can decide what is accomplished for the plot in every situation, analyze the characters in relation to their problems, and, best of all, take time to relish the humor and enjoy the fine writing of the dialogue. The deepest satisfaction lies in the fact that you can trace the development of the theme and notice the dramatist's methods of bringing it out and pointing it up. After so many years of watching the fleeting impressions of television and motion pictures, you will thoroughly enjoy quietly living the lines and savoring them.

After you get used to the telling of a story in play form, you will enjoy reading scenes aloud and dramatizing the characters as you imagine them to be. The paperback editions of plays will encourage you to start a theater library which can be a joy the rest of your life. Rereading favorite scenes aloud is an excellent way of testing your growth in interpreting characters and their changing moods. The pleasure of picking up your own copy of a play you have seen produced and making notes about the production is an enduring reward, especially if it is a play frequently repeated, with differing casts, under various directors and scenic artists.

On the stage today physical action, psychedelic lighting, noise, confusion, and speed are tending to eliminate words. If you do not read the well-written, perfectly phrased works by our great playwrights, you are missing the most precious gift they have given us.

READING SCENES ALOUD

Group reading of scenes from plays is an excellent first step in acting, particularly for characterization. Select a scene in which people have strong feelings and express themselves convincingly. You may choose one from this chapter or from your own reading. In choosing your scene, imagine the appearances, moods, and personalities of the characters. Since this may be your first appearance before the class, your choice of scene should be the best possible introduction you can find — a scene which you really like and which you feel you can interpret effectively.

Perhaps your teacher may prefer to assign roles for this exercise. He may expect you merely to express the meaning of your character's lines and suggest the personality, or he may want a carefully rehearsed piece of work. He may want you to read from your seats and focus only on the actual reading, or he may encourage you to take several days to work up the scene to present in front of the class with considered facial expressions and movements. Perhaps, too, he will tape your first reading. At the end of the term it will be interesting to do the same scene again and compare this reading with your first.

In preparing your role, the first thing to do is to read the scene very carefully and, if possible, the entire play. Then you must visualize the character's appearance — his age, size, clothing, and vocal and bodily responses. His internal resources — his aspirations, emotions, attitudes, and inner reactions to the other persons — are even more important. Try also to understand the character's motivation in this particular scene and his changes in mood so that you can express effectively his reasons for saying and doing what he does.

Next read the entire scene aloud, including all the characters so as to appreciate their relationships and the main issues involved in their reactions. You must also determine the high point of the action and how to work up to it. Move about, if you want to, as you catch the spirit of the situation, and let your face and body express the emotions the words imply.

Analyzing Your Role

Next sit down and do some hard work on your role. Remember that sharing ideas and feelings with your audience is your only excuse for appearing before them. Before you can do this successfully, you must find out exactly what the words and lines mean. There are four vital words you should memorize at once and put into practice in every assignment involving reading aloud or acting assignments. They are *think, see, feel, speak*.

To think, you first look up the meaning and pronunciation of every unfamiliar word in the scene; have a good dictionary and Roget's *Thesaurus* at hand, preferably in your personal library. Then read the lines aloud again, thinking as you read, "What am I saying?" When you comprehend the exact significance of a sentence, you can emphasize the important words and minimize the unimportant ones. Put the words together in phrases or thought groups and breathe between them so you will not run ideas together.

In the following passage you can see one way of marking a script to be read aloud. The slashes (/) indicate phrasing (your breathing should coincide with phrasing); one check (√) indicates slight emphasis; two checks (√√) indicate moderate emphasis; three checks (√√√) great emphasis. This selection is from George Bernard Shaw's famous one-act play *The Dark Lady of the Sonnets*.

Wherefore I humbly beg Your Majesty / to give order that a / theater / be endowed out of the public revenue / for the playing of those pieces of mine which no merchant will touch / seeing that his gain / is so much greater with the worse than with the better. / Thereby you shall also encourage other men to undertake the writing of plays / who do now despise it / and leave it wholly to those whose counsels will work little good to your realm. / For this writing of plays is a great matter / forming as it does the minds and affections of men / in such sort that whatsoever they see done in show on the stage / they will presently be doing in earnest in the world / which is but a larger stage.

You break the sense of thought if you breathe just because you have to; by breathing between thought groups you can use your breath to clarify rather than confuse the meaning of the passage. Be sure you take time to make the thought clear instead of rushing through the lines.

To see, you visualize your character in detail, imagining exactly how he looks, what he is wearing, how he stands and moves. Decide what you think his past life has been like, and the resulting effects on his facial expression, mannerisms, and actions.

To feel, you can first imagine yourself in the situation and surmise how you would speak the lines. Then put yourself in the place of the character you have visualized and try to react emotionally as he would do considering his age and past experience. Be sure you put yourself into his mood when he first speaks, for those lines will set the personality for the audience. Then you must decide, if he changes that mood during the scene, at what point and why he does so. Try to empathize with him in relation to the situations and other characters.

To speak, you must remember the person farthest from you so you will be heard at all times. You must be sure you speak clearly, as the person you are portraying would under the circumstances. How to do this effectively and correctly is a phase of the technique of acting which need not bother you yet, but which will form a vital part of this course. Your inherent talent as an actor shows itself in your ability to throw yourself wholeheartedly into a role, so completely that your voice responds to every shade of feeling motivating the words spoken. If you understand your role and the situation of the moment, your voice, probably to your great surprise, will approximate the right tone for the mood.

Movement, too, is important. It should grow out of the four vital processes. To move, you react after feeling with every part of your body. In reading scenes, bodily stance, facial expression, and slight hand movements should be involved, but not too obviously. Moving about in character while you work on your lines frees your thought and feeling. When you rehearse with a group, after consulting the teacher's wishes, you can actually move about in relation to each other and to the changing situations. Usually when reading a scene you do not do so. Under many circumstances the bodily response is even more important in acting than the vocal, as you have found out in any improvisation you have done; bodily movement also is an important part of this course. The primary consideration now is that movement follows the glance and is a part of the emotional response to feeling.

Presenting The Scene

In working up a scene, it will be exciting to get the reactions of the other members of the cast to your interpretation. If they think you are all wrong, explain how you have thought the scene out and then decide whether or not to take any suggestions. You should get some ideas to carry home and try out by yourself, but do not change

Robert Bolt's A Man for All Seasons *was planned for a one-set staging. Panel changes and carry-on props "shift" the scenes. The actors: Lester Rawlins, Olga Bellin, Paul Scofield, Sarah Burton, Albert Dekker, George Rose (above).*

your interpretation unless you feel it is right to do so. After the final rehearsal, you should relax and not worry, and then come to class ready to do your best.

If you are nervous, try not to think about it. Focus on your character and concentrate on how he feels. If it is your first experience in reading a part, remember you are having the fun of doing it; you are not hunting a job or proving you are a great actor. Pick up your lines quickly on your cues, the words immediately preceding yours. Take time to read clearly and to feel the emotion before you speak. Relax, for you will want to alter your voice frequently and you cannot do this with a tight throat.

Do not be discouraged if your teacher and classmates are not satisfied with your work. Your voice may not have reacted as you hoped it would, or you may have become too excited to do yourself justice. On the other hand, with the stimulus of an audience, you may perform far better than you expect, and you will have the glorious experience of moving your audience to a definite emotional response. If they look startled, or laugh at the right places, or actually applaud, you can be really thrilled. If they don't respond at all, talk your reading over with your teacher and get his reaction so that you can improve **15** with the next assignment. Keep his suggestions in mind as you work on the part again at home, incorporating them until you are satisfied you are reading the part as well as you can.

THE FANTASTICKS

by Tom Jones and Harvey Schmidt

MATT *and* LUISA *are a young couple in love. Their fathers have built a wall between their houses, supposedly to keep them apart.*

LUISA. Matt!
MATT. Luisa!
LUISA. Shh. Be careful.
    I thought I heard a sound.
MATT. But you're trembling!
LUISA. My father loves to spy.
MATT. I know; I know.
    I had to climb out through a window.
    My father locked my room.
LUISA. Oh God, be careful!
    Suppose you were to fall!
MATT. It's on the ground floor.
LUISA. Oh.
MATT. Still, the window's very small.
    I could get stuck.
LUISA. This is madness, isn't it?
MATT. Yes, it's absolutely mad!
LUISA. And also very wicked?
MATT. Yes.
LUISA. I'm glad.
MATT. My father would be furious if he knew.
LUISA. Listen, I have had a vision.
MATT. Of disaster?
LUISA. No. Of azaleas.
    I dreamed I was picking azaleas.
    When all at once, this Duke —
    Oh, he was very old,
    I'd say he was nearly forty.
    But attractive.
    And very evil.
MATT. I hate him!
LUISA. And he had a retinue of scoundrels,
    And they were hiding behind the rhododendrons,

And then, all at once,
As I picked an azalea —
He leapt out!

MATT. God, I hate him!

LUISA. In my vision, how I struggled.
Like the Rape of the Sabine Women!
I cried "help."

MATT. And I was nearby!

LUISA. Yes. You came rushing to the rescue.
And, single-handed, you fight all his men,
And win —

MATT. And then —

LUISA. Celebration!

MATT. Fireworks!

LUISA. Fiesta!

MATT. Laughter!

LUISA. Our fathers give in!

MATT. We live happily ever after!

LUISA. There's no reason in the world why it can't happen exactly
like that. (*Suddenly she stiffens.*) Someone's coming!

MATT. It's my father.

LUISA. Kiss me!

THE FABULOUS INVALID

by Moss Hart and George S. Kaufman *

LAURENCE *and* PAULA, *a famous husband-and-wife acting team, are
dead; they have returned to haunt the theater in which they were appearing
when they died.*

PAULA. Why, Larry —

LAURENCE. Yes, darling.

PAULA. We're still in the theater.

LAURENCE. Why, yes, we are, aren't we? Curious.

THE DOORMAN. Good evening!

PAULA. Good evening.

THE DOORMAN. Don't be frightened. It's all right, I'm dead too,
you know.

PAULA. Oh!

LAURENCE. I don't think I quite understand.

THE DOORMAN. It's all right. I've been dead for years.

LAURENCE. Well — well, then what are you doing *here?* What are *we* doing here?

THE DOORMAN. Well, what it comes down to is — you're ghosts. So am I.

LAURENCE. But — why are you in this theater?

THE DOORMAN. I came around for the opening. I go to them all. You see, I used to be an actor, just like you.

LAURENCE. But — but that doesn't explain —

THE DOORMAN. I never got to be a star, exactly, but I was a good actor. I played with your father, Miss Kingsley, before you were born.

PAULA. Did you? Larry, think of that! — What was he like then? What was he playing?

LAURENCE. Paula, please! — Won't you explain all this, sir?

THE DOORMAN. There's no hurry. You'll be dead a long time. Now, let me see, what was I saying? Oh, yes — I was a good actor. — Well, this is the only way I can explain it. You see actors aren't like other people, are they? You know that yourself. As a matter of fact, they're like nothing on God's green earth. And I think God realizes that, because even when an actor dies, it's different.

PAULA. It is?

LAURENCE. How?

THE DOORMAN. Well, when anybody else dies — ordinary people — they go to heaven, don't they? I mean, if everything is all right. Well, when an actor dies, he doesn't *have* to go to heaven. Not if he dies right in the theater.

PAULA. But—why wouldn't anybody want to go to heaven?

THE DOORMAN. I'll tell you something about heaven.

PAULA. What?

THE DOORMAN. There isn't any theater there.

PAULA. Oh, Larry!

LAURENCE. Please go on.

THE DOORMAN. Oh, heaven's all right. I liked it for a while. It's restful, and — the music is good. But after a while I began to get restless. I didn't know what was the matter with me. After all, there I was in heaven — you'd think I'd be satisfied. And then suddenly I knew what it was. I missed the theater. I kept wondering what kind of season they were having, if any new stars had come along, what kind of plays they were doing now — I was downright unhappy. And of course they *noticed* it, and then they explained to me that there's a special rule for actors if they die in the theater. That I could come back here and hang around.

PAULA. Oh, Larry!

THE DOORMAN. And that's what you can do. Of course, you can go to heaven if you want to — don't let me talk you out of it — but you'd be back here in no time at all. I know real actors when I see them.

LAURENCE. Then the choice is up to us?

THE DOORMAN. That's right.

LAURENCE. Paula.

PAULA. Yes, dear?

LAURENCE. I offer you the Kingdom of Heaven — or the Theater. Which shall it be?

PAULA. Oh, Larry! The Theater.

THE DOORMAN. Good! You won't regret it — you'll have a wonderful time. You can go everywhere, see everything — all through the years. Why, I've been in a dozen theaters tonight. Saw *your* play, took a look at Bernhardt, even jumped out on the road and caught a little bit of Joe Jefferson. Heaven was never like that.

PAULA. Larry, it *is* heaven!

THE DOORMAN. Oh, I forgot to tell you one thing. There's only one chance that you might have to go up there.

LAURENCE. Oh!

PAULA. What is it?

THE DOORMAN. Now don't be frightened — it never can happen. But here it is. If the Theater ever dies, we've got to go back.

LAURENCE. I don't understand.

PAULA. There'll always be the Theater.

THE DOORMAN. Of *course* there will, but I'm just telling you what they told me. If anything ever happens so that there's no more theater — if the Theater ever dies — we go back. That's all I know.

PAULA. Then — we've got Eternity!

LAURENCE. Paula, it hasn't been taken away from us. Think of it, Paula! Think what lies ahead! Plays yet unwritten, stars that haven't been born yet. We'll see it all, Paula — we'll see it all.

THE DOORMAN. Yes, sir!

PAULA. All the magic and wonder that we love! This isn't death, Larry — it's life!

A RAISIN IN THE SUN
by Lorraine Hansberry

This is a brief scene of conflict between MAMA, *who still runs the house, and* WALTER, *who is trying to find his place in the world.*

MAMA. *(The mother and son are left alone now and the mother waits a long time, considering deeply, before she speaks.)* Son — you — you understand what I done, don't you? (WALTER *is silent and sullen.*)I — I just seen my family falling apart today . . . just falling to pieces in front of my eyes. . . We couldn't of gone on like we was today. We was going backwards 'stead of forwards — talking 'bout killing babies and wishing each other was dead . . . When it gets like that in life — you just got to do something different, push on out and do something bigger. . . . *(She waits.)* I wish you say something, son . . . I wish you'd say how deep inside you you think I done the right thing —

WALTER *(Crossing slowly to his bedroom door and finally turning there and speaking measuredly).* What you need me to say you done right for? *You* the head of this family. You run our lives like you want to. It was your money and you did what you wanted with it. So what you need for me to say it was all right for? *(Bitterly, to hurt her as deeply as he knows is possible)* So you butchered up a dream of mine — you — who always talking 'bout your children's dreams . . .

MAMA. Walter Lee —
(He just closes the door behind him. MAMA *sits alone, thinking heavily.)*

COME BLOW YOUR HORN
by Neil Simon

ALAN *has been living the life of the "man about town." His activities are interrupted by the arrival of his younger brother,* BUDDY. (BUDDY BAKER *enters with a valise in hand.* BUDDY *is the complete opposite of* ALAN. *Reserved, unsure, shy.)*

BUDDY. Hello, Alan — Are you busy? *(Enters apartment and looks around — crosses D. R. to L. of D. R. C. chair)*

ALAN *(Offstage).* No, no. Come in, kid. *(He re-enters.)* What's up? *(Crossing to L. of* BUDDY, ALAN *sees suitcase.)* What's in there?

BUDDY. Pajamas, toothbrush, the works. *(Puts suitcase down next to chair)*

Lorraine Hansberry's A Raisin in the Sun *earned the New York Drama Critics' Circle Award in 1959 cs best play of the season. Note how postures and expressions reveal emotions. Actors: Diana Sands, Claudia McNeil, Edward Hall.*

ALAN.   You're kidding?

BUDDY.   Nope.

ALAN.   You mean you left? (BUDDY *nods.*) Permanently?

BUDDY.   I took eight pairs of socks. For me that's permanently.

ALAN.   I don't believe it. You can't tell me you actually ran away from home.

BUDDY.   Well, I cheated a little. I took a taxi. (*Takes off coat and places it on suitcase*)

ALAN.   You're serious. You mean my baby brother finally broke out of prison?

BUDDY.   We planned it long enough, didn't we?

ALAN.   Yes, but every time I brought it up you said you weren't ready. Why didn't you say something to me?

BUDDY.   When? You weren't at work since Thursday.

21

ALAN.   Hey, did Dad say anything? About my being gone?

BUDDY.   Not at the office. But at home he's been slamming doors. The chandelier in the foyer fell down. Where were you?

ALAN (*Crosses L. above coffee table*). Vermont.

BUDDY.   Skiing?

ALAN.   Only during the day. (*Sits on sofa and lights cigarette*)

BUDDY   (*Crosses L. to sofa; one knee on arm*). I don't know how you do it. If I'm at work one minute after nine, he docks my pay — and I get less to eat at home.

ALAN.   Because he expects it from you. From me he says he expects nothing, so that's what I give him.

BUDDY.   You're better off. At least you're not treated like a baby. You can talk with him.

ALAN.   We don't talk. We have heart to heart threatening —

BUDDY.   That's better than the subtle treatment I get. Last night I came home at three o'clock in the morning. He didn't approve. What do you think he did? (ALAN *shakes his head.*) As I passed his door, he crowed like a rooster. Cockle-doodle-doo.

ALAN.   You're kidding? What'd you say?

BUDDY.   Nothing. I wanted to cluck back like a chicken but I didn't have the nerve.

ALAN.   Oh, he's beautiful.

BUDDY.   And then yesterday was my birthday. (*Sits on sofa R. of* ALAN) Twenty-one years old.

ALAN.   Oh, that's right. Gee, I'm sorry I wasn't there, Buddy. Happy birthday, kid. (*He shakes* BUDDY's *hand warmly.*)

BUDDY.   Thanks.

ALAN.   I even forgot to get you a present.

BUDDY.   I got one. A beaut. From Mom and Dad.

ALAN.   What was it?

BUDDY.   A surprise party. Mom, Dad and the Klingers.

ALAN.   Who are the Klingers?

BUDDY.   Oh, the Klingers are that lovely couple the folks met last summer at Lake Mahopac.

ALAN.   Why? They're not your friends.

BUDDY.   Think. Why would they have the Klingers there to meet me?

ALAN.   They've got a daughter.

BUDDY.   Oh, have they got a daughter.

ALAN.   You mean they brought her with them?

BUDDY.   In a crate.

ALAN.   Let me guess. Naomi?

BUDDY.   Close, Renee.

ALAN.   Not much on looks but brilliant.

BUDDY.   A genius. An I.Q. of 170. Same as her weight.

ALAN.   And of course they had her dressed for the kill. They figured what she couldn't do, maybe Bergdorf could.

BUDDY.   Nothing could help. So I spent the night of my twenty-first birthday watching a girl devour an entire bowl of cashew nuts.

ALAN.   Oh, I'm sorry, kid.

BUDDY (*Rises, crosses R.C. to chair*). It's been getting worse and worse. He looks in my closets, my drawers. He listens to my phone calls. I don't know what it is I've done, Alan, but I swear he's going to turn me in. (*Sits L. arm of chair*)

ALAN (*Puts out cigarette*). Well, it's simple enough. He's afraid you're going to follow in my footsteps.

BUDDY.   I did. I thought it over all day and realized I had to leave. Well — here I am.

Note the variations in postures and expressions in this scene from the Broadway production of Come Blow Your Horn, *with Karen Thorsell, Patty Jo Harmon, Warren Berlinger, Hal March, Morris Carnovsky, Henrietta Jacobson.*

ZODIAC PHOTOGRAPHERS

THE DIARY OF ANNE FRANK
by Frances Goodrich and Albert Hackett

The Frank and the Van Daan families are hiding out from the Nazis in an attic over a place of business. In this scene ANNE FRANK *and* PETER VAN DAAN *realize what young love is in war-torn Europe.*

ANNE (*Looking up through skylight*). Look, Peter, the sky. What a lovely day. Aren't the clouds beautiful? You know what I do when it seems as if I couldn't stand being cooped up for one more minute? I *think* myself out. I think myself on a walk in the park where I used to go with Pim. Where the daffodils and the crocus and the violets grow down the slopes. You know the most wonderful thing about *thinking* yourself out? You can have it any way you like. You can have roses and violets and chrysanthemums all blooming at the same time. . . . It's funny . . . I used to take it all for granted . . . and now I've gone crazy about everything to do with nature. Haven't you?

PETER (*Barely lifting his face*). I've just gone crazy. I think if something doesn't happen soon . . . if we don't get out of here . . . I can't stand much more of it!

ANNE (*Softly*). I wish you had a religion, Peter.

PETER (*Bitterly*). No, thanks. Not me.

ANNE. Oh, I don't mean you have to be Orthodox . . . or believe in heaven and hell and purgatory and things. . . . I just mean some religion . . . it doesn't matter what. Just to believe in something! When I think of all that's out there . . . the trees . . . and flowers . . . and seagulls . . . when I think of the dearness of you, Peter . . . and the goodness of the people we know . . . Mr. Kraler, Miep, Dirk, the vegetable man, all risking their lives for us every day. . . . When I think of these good things, I'm not afraid any more. . . . I find myself, and God, and I . . .

PETER (*Impatiently, as he gets to his feet*). That's fine! But when I begin to think, I get mad! Look at us, hiding out for two years. Not able to move! Caught here like . . . waiting for them to come and get us . . . and all for what?

ANNE. We're not the only people that've had to suffer. There've always been people that've had to . . . sometimes one race . . . sometimes another . . . and yet . . .

PETER (*Sitting on upstage end of bed*). That doesn't make me feel any better!

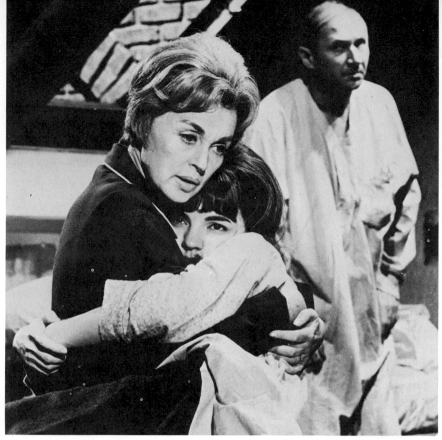

A scene from The Diary of Anne Frank, *with Lily Palmer (Mrs. Frank), Diana Davilla, and Donald Pleasence.*

ANNE.   I know it's terrible, trying to have any faith . . . when people are doing such horrible . . . (*Gently lifting his face*) but you know what I sometimes think? I think the world may be going through a phase, the way I was with Mother. It'll pass, maybe not for hundreds of years, but some day. . . . I still believe, in spite of everything, that people are really good at heart.

ORGANIZING MATERIAL AND IDEAS

Ideas, the most vital things in the world, are also the most intangible. Unless you definitely organize the material of an inspirational class like dramatics into some permanent form, many of the values will vanish. Actual facts like the who, where, when, why, and how of a play are likely to be lost in the emotional reaction to the total production. Notebooks and scrapbooks can not only give you great pleasure all your life if you keep them up, but also can be of real profit to you   **25**

Carry-on props set this casket scene in The Merchant of Venice *at the Stratford, Ontario, Festival Theatre. Frances Hyland as Portia; Donald Harron as Bassanio.*

if you continue to study drama in college or if you become a professional in any phase of theater.

These permanent records can be a source of pride, information, and pleasure whether you get class credit for them or not. They should be a distinctly personal record for your own benefit, but their value will depend upon how carefully classified and organized they are. The following suggestions may assist you in getting the most out of your classwork; of course they can be modified and expanded to suit your needs.

NOTEBOOKS

The notebooks should be the ordinary loose-leaf type, divided into 26 the following sections to be filled as the classwork develops.

Part 1: Class notes. These should be brief reports of lectures, suggestions, directions, assignments, and reviews given in class by teacher, students, and visitors.

Part 2: Reports of plays and scenes studied in class.

Part 3: Reports of plays read outside of class.

Part 4: Reports of plays seen in and out of class throughout the entire year, including holidays.

Part 5: Reviews of articles and books you have read which deal with all phases of theater activity — biography, play production, stage settings, acting, makeup, costuming, history of the drama, dramatic criticism, and kindred subjects centered about the performing arts.

Part 6: Lists of regional and repertory theaters across the country, colleges and universities featuring theater and film departments, and famous theaters here and abroad.

Part 7: Vocabulary — words, their meaning and pronunciation.

Part 8: Exercises for vocal and bodily movement.

SCRAPBOOKS

Your scrapbooks can be as simple or as elaborate as you desire, but a large loose-leaf book is recommended. When your eyes are open to all the pictures and articles pertaining to the multiplying phases of staging and acting plays, on stage and screen, you will be amazed at the amount of pertinent material you can gather from magazines, newspapers, theater programs, and advertisements. It should go without saying that you never remove pictures from library books or magazines, and never ruin a good book — even your own — for scrapbook pictures. The following sections are suggested.

Part 1: Personalities of the stage, screen, and TV. These may be pictures and clippings about actors, directors, playwrights, critics, scenic artists, dancers, and producers.

Part 2: Stage settings. This section may include not only stage settings from all over the world but also pictures that suggest possible sets, outdoor and indoor scenes of unusual beauty or interest, period furniture, stage and lighting equipment, and modern effects made of any medium.

Part 3: Costuming. This section may include a series of pictures illustrating the historical development of clothing, striking examples of various periods, appropriate clothes for all types of characters, modern clothes for definite types and occasions, examples of newly created fabrics, and suggestions for unusual combinations of line and color in stage costumes.

Part 4: Facial expression and makeup. This section may include pictures from magazine covers, advertisements, pictures in which are illustrated the lines of the face, expressions under the stress of different emotions, types of faces typical of various races and nationalities, hair styles, headdresses, and actual makeup and cosmetics.

Part 5: Color combinations. This section need not pertain to the theater but may illustrate striking or pleasing color combinations which might be useful in staging and costuming.

Part 6: Personality development. Here collect clippings, pictures, poems, slogans dealing with the improvement of character, appearance, mind and body, articles about human problems and frustrations and what to do about them; advice of famous men and women of the past and present; and future prognostications.

Part 7: Miscellaneous section. This section may include anything you care to put in it — theater programs, advertisements of plays and films, travel brochures of theater festivals here and abroad, and all material you might consider of value in your study of theater.

Part 8: Snapshots. This section may include those taken in your classrooms of interesting activities and photos of your school productions during rehearsals and performances (if permitted).

Discussion

1. Where did you first become interested in the theater?
2. What plays have you read? Have you enjoyed them as much as novels and other forms of literature?
3. Why is the use of leisure becoming a more serious problem today than ever before?
4. Why do you think the search for identity has grown to be of such concern today?
5. What are likely to be some of the best qualities of young people interested in dramatics? Some of the less admirable?
6. Do you agree that we play different roles in our social relationships?
7. How do you explain the universal appeal of the drama?

chapter

THE STRUCTURE OF DRAMA

In the historic world of Western drama, "the play's the thing." Vivified by the actors, expressed through the mediums of color, light, and movement against the background of stage and scenery, and unified by the creative genius of the director, the play itself is the nucleus about which the art of the theater is centered.

The only true test of the success of a production is the emotional response it arouses in the audience. A good play can fail to arouse that response because it is inadequately produced; a poor play may be so effectively acted and staged that it is totally successful. The great dramas of the world have survived, however, because the plays themselves are fine enough to rise above inadequate production, or can be effectively adapted to changing tastes.

Drama is the most thrilling form of literature because through it we lose ourselves in the experience of others; we sorrow or rejoice in their defeats or triumphs because the characters have become living human beings to us. The dramatist is dependent for both character portrayal and plot development solely upon dialogue condensed into swiftly **29** culminating action. He unfolds before our eyes a closely related series of events reaching a dramatic climax, working out to a logical conclusion, and bringing out a definite idea. In other words, a play has the four narrative essentials — exposition, plot, character, and theme — presented by means of dialogue and action, in which the elements of conflict and suspense arouse a definite emotional response on the part of the spectators. To build his drama, then, the dramatist must arrange the presentation of these four narrative essentials. This "arrangement" is the *structure* of the play.

TRADITION AND THE CHANGING SCENE

Since the middle of the twentieth century, playwrights have broken away from traditional rules, and most of them have modified play structure to a lesser or greater degree. For example, there was a tradition for many years that divided a play into three or five acts and sometimes added a prologue and an epilogue. The climax came at the end of the second act in three-act plays, and at the end of the third act in five-act plays. Minor plots were frequently introduced and the resolution of the plot lengthened. Now plays are more often separated into two parts or several scenes with a single intermission, the assumption being that fewer breaks in the action encourage more concentrated attention. This change affected plot structure.

Today the dramatist must adapt the play's structure to fit the theater structure, for the open stage has come into increasing use. These stages — the arena, the theater-in-the-round, the thrust stage, and the raised platform — eliminate the principle of aesthetic distance maintained by the proscenium arch, which physically and psychologically separates the spectators from the actors. The resulting intimacy and lack of realistic sets and stage curtains naturally affect the playwright's style. Improvisation and action are more and more taking the place of written dialogue. Thus, much of the glory of the written word has been dimmed as rapid-fire action discourages inspired writing. From the standpoint of structure, modern tendencies have based the play on an emotional state rather than on the development of plot, character, and theme. Clear-cut dialogue and the play of wit are frequently eliminated and ideas are obscured to produce shock and excitement.

However, since you are now studying the art of the theater, it is necessary for you to appreciate the traditional drama which has enthralled millions the world over. In your classwork and theater

A scene from Sophocles' Antigone, *presented by the Honolulu Theatre for Youth. The conflict in this play is between loyalty to the laws of man and loyalty to the laws of the gods.*

attendance in high school, you fortunately will have the opportunity of living with magnificently written plays by distinguished dramatists as well as observing the ever-changing modern innovations.

In a well-written play or movie, one of the satisfactions is seeing how the actions of people we are deeply interested in are carried to a logical conclusion. We seldom see such results in life itself, where even intimate friends drift out of our orbits and we never find out what happened to them. In a well-constructed play we see how the lives of human beings end in success or failure as the result of their own reactions during crucial events. Out of their experiences we are shown a fundamental truth which inspires and uplifts us or deepens our insights into the human experience.

The traditions which established these principles were originally expressed by the world's first literary critic, the great Greek philosopher Aristotle (384-322 B.C.). His principles have usually been applied in the great dramas of most periods. When Aristotle discussed tragedy in his *Poetics*, he stressed the theory that drama is an imitation of life, that mankind learns through imitation, and that learning something is the greatest pleasure of life. He pointed out that all human happiness or misery takes the form of action; therefore, he places plot first in his list of the parts of a play: fable or plot, characters, diction (language), thought, spectacle, and melody.

31

In Aristotle's discussion of plot, he maintains that the action must be complete in itself, with a beginning, a middle, and an end. The incidents must follow each other in logical order and reach a plausible conclusion. Out of the complications of the plot the hero does and says the things that are consistent with his character, and therefore he fails or succeeds as the result of his inherent nature. The characters must imitate reality in that they are true to life and experience happiness or misery as the result of their reactions to the episodes of the plot. The resulting impact of the action in a serious play should purge the emotions through pity and fear and bring out a universal truth.

Aristotle did not formulate the three unities of time, place, and action, but he did emphasize that the drama be restricted to one basic idea dependent upon a single incident taking place within "a single circuit of the sun." Many Greek plays do keep the action in one place, but it was the French and Italian neo-classicists of the sixteenth century who misinterpreted Aristotle and set up definite rules. You can see these rules, which they felt followed the ancient dramatic traditions, employed in the many productions of their plays being given today, plays like *Tartuffe* and *Volpone*. These rules in turn have been applied down through the years by many leading dramatists in famous plays. They require the use of the three unities, verse forms in five acts, one series of events without subplots, characters of nobility and power, and exalted themes. They also prohibit the showing of scenes of violence on the stage — the audience learns about such events in great detail from long speeches by some person who has witnessed them.

The traditions and principles, then, which have most affected playwrights down to our time have come to us from ancient Greek drama, from Aristotle's *Poetics*, and from the refinements and misinterpretations of Aristotle by the French and Italian neo-classicists. If contemporary playwrights are departing from a tradition, it is this tradition, or elements of it, which they are reacting against. Now let us look more closely at the four essential narrative elements as they have been employed traditionally in Western drama.

THE EXPOSITION

As soon as possible after the play begins, the audience must know what kind of play is being presented, where and when it is taking place, who the leading characters are, and in what situation and conflicts they find themselves. These facts constitute the literary setting, and the process of putting them before the audience is called the exposition. If skillfully written, this exposition is brief and unobtrusive, and we find out the *where, when, why,* and *who* without realizing we have been told anything.

Exposition of the Setting

Today the time and place are usually printed clearly on the program, but the text should present the complete setting in addition to such extraneous statements. Sometimes the author merely states the facts — Shakespeare did this many times because he had no scenery to show the place and no programs to supply the information. For example, in *Twelfth Night* the captain says to Viola, "This is Illyria, lady," and the entire scene which follows (Act 1, Scene 2) is the statement of what has happened to the leading characters.

Mood and Atmosphere

These qualities of the play are also established in the exposition. The spirit of the play, or mood, is brought out by the opening characters, not only through their costumes and manner of speaking and moving, but through their attitudes toward each other and their present feelings.

The atmosphere is created largely by the staging and lighting, but also by the tempo of speech and movement and by the choice of language, which show what country and class of society form the background. The type of play determines the author's style, and it is at the start of the play that the audience should settle into a responsive state of mind.

Preliminary Situation

The most important part of the exposition is the preliminary situation, sometimes referred to as the antecedent action. This is a clearly defined explanation of the events which have occurred in the lives of the leading characters before the action of the play itself begins and which place them in the situation in which we find them.

Playwrights use all sorts of devices to handle the exposition of the preliminary situation. The most common is having minor characters discuss the leading ones and gossip about their pasts. More original means are the use of prologues, telephone conversations, narrators, and ingenious scenic effects. In *The Night of January 16th, The Caine*

Caesar (Robert Christie) is stopped by a soothsayer who warns him to "beware the Ides of March." (Initial incident in Julius Caesar) *This was a 1955 production at the Stratford, Ontario, Festival Theatre.*

Mutiny Court Martial, and *The Trial of Mary Dugan*, dramas about court trials, front curtains are not used and the audience becomes a part of the courtroom action while the clerks, attorneys, and attendants casually explain the case. In *The Diary of Anne Frank* and *I Remember Mama*, the young heroines, at the opening of the play and between the scenes, are shown or heard writing about themselves and their lives in their journals.

THE PLOT

The plot is the series of related events which take place before the audience. It is the working out in action of the major conflict. A well-constructed play can be diagrammed by steps of varying heights going up to a turning point, which is then followed by steps going down. These steps are the situations involved in the problem facing the protagonist, and in the conflict between him and the antagonist arising from the problem. The conflict need not be physical as in many plays of violence, particularly in motion pictures and TV. It can be a clash of wills or wits, or a psychological struggle between phases of the hero's personality and his environment, or a battle between a group and ideological antagonisms. Whether physical, mental, or emotional, the conflicting elements must be evenly balanced so that the outcome of the struggle is in doubt — hence giving rise

34 to suspense.

The Initial Incident

The initial incident opens the plot. It is the first important event to take place on the stage after the preliminary situation, and the point from which the rest of the plot develops. All the action of the play itself starts with the initial incident, and the audience begins to ask, "What will happen next?" For example, the first scene of *Julius Caesar*, where the people and the patricians are discussing the war between Caesar and Pompey, presents the situation in Rome. The initial incident comes when the soothsayer cries out to Caesar, "Beware the Ides of March." At that point the future danger to Caesar is foreshadowed.

The Rising Action

The rising action is the series of events following the initial incident. These events take place on the stage; they are not talked about. Each situation developing out of the conflict between the protagonist and antagonist lifts the action to a higher level of interest and suspense.

In *Julius Caesar* the rising action moves from Caesar's refusal to listen to the soothsayer into the scenes in which Cassius works upon Brutus to join a conspiracy to assassinate Caesar. Cassius plays upon his close friend's democratic ideals and his loyalty to the citizens of Rome, and then he stirs others to join the conspiracy. Important steps include Brutus' decision to join the conspiracy; his resolution not to kill Antony; his wife Portia's plea to share in whatever he is undertaking; the effort Calpurnia, the wife of Caesar, makes to prevent Caesar's going to the Senate and the conspirators' persuading him to go; the assassination; the permission to Antony to deliver the funeral address; the brief remarks of Brutus calming the citizens; and the beginning of the address by Mark Antony.

The Climax

The climax is the turning point of the play toward which the rising action leads. It is the moment which determines what the outcome of the conflict will be. The dramatist often makes this event a thrilling one and the director must arrange the action to arouse the most intense interest in the audience.

There must be several important events before and after the climax to sustain the suspense and keep the interest of the audience to the end, but the climax must be the crucial event of the play as a whole.

On the steps of the Senate House, the conspirators stab Caesar to death. (Rising action in Julius Caesar) *The actors are Max Helpmann, Joseph Shaw as Caesar, Dan MacDonald, and Peter Donat at the Stratford, Ontario, Festival Theatre.*

The dramatist must build up to it in the lines and situations, and the director must use every appropriate stage technique to emphasize it. In *Julius Caesar*, the climax comes at the close of Mark Antony's funeral address when the citizens rush away to burn the houses of the conspirators with the brands from Caesar's pyre.

The Falling Action

The falling action is the series of events following the climax. It is usually shorter than the rising action, but the incidents must be of real significance and of keen interest. In five-act plays there are two acts to be filled, so there are usually entertaining or exciting subplots to be completed. In *Julius Caesar*, the mob murder of Cinna the poet and the meeting of the Triumvirate precede the final events: the quarrel between Brutus and Cassius and the decision to face battle at Philippi. The appearance of the ghost of Caesar to Brutus in his tent on the night before the battle leads into the fighting and the suicides of Cassius and of Brutus.

The Conclusion

The situation at the end of the play must be the logical outcome of all that has gone before. All the characters should receive their just deserts, thus satisfying the audience's demand for "poetic justice." The success or failure, happiness or sorrow of the characters must be the result of their inherent natures or their actual deeds, never the result of an outside force previously unrelated to them, nor a matter of luck, chance, or happy accident. In *Julius Caesar* the famous tribute of Antony above the body of Brutus is a fitting conclusion.

When the plot of a play consists of a mystery to be solved or a complicated series of interrelated events involving the leading characters, another step in the plot — the denouement — may be added in the falling action or in the actual conclusion. The denouement provides a solution of the mystery and/or the explanation of the outcome. It frequently involves an ingenious incident or exposure which not only leads to a satisfactory outcome of the plot but also to an explanation of all the secrets and puzzles connected with the complications.

CHARACTERS

Nothing in the world is as interesting as people. Since a play represents life as we know it, as it has been, or as we might like it to be, the characters, inextricably related to the plot, must be interesting people who determine the center of interest in every event. The main characters naturally hold our attention, but in a well-written play the minor ones who assist in working out the main issues — and even those in the background — are also living, individual people. Occasionally a dramatist may resort to stage "types" every audience will accept without question, but this is a dangerous practice. Shakespeare holds his position as the world's finest dramatist because even his minor characters are individually developed and live on from generation to generation as the most humorous, most tragic, most fascinating people in all literature.

Characters in a play must be vivid and varied in personality, with their dominant traits clearly brought out in their speeches and actions. Their success or failure must be the logical result of their own internal and external resources as indicated by the playwright. Actors should be able to understand the characters in order to avoid confusing them with their own personalities. For example, the heredity and environment of the protagonist and of his antagonist must be indicated so that the audience will understand their reactions at crucial moments. Subtle shades of personality add reality but must not be confusing to spectators who do not have time to analyze them.

Methods of Characterization

In presenting his characters, the playwright reveals them chiefly by what they themselves say and do. He must have them not only behave as persons of their social group would but also as their past experience would cause them to act and speak.

He also reveals his characters by what they say about each other. This is especially true of the leads. If, indeed, drama is an imitation of life, friends and enemies alike know a great deal about each other. The writer's problem is to make what a character reveals about himself consistent with what other characters reveal about him in their speeches.

Sometimes playwrights use soliloquies to reveal character. Soliloquies are speeches in which actors talk alone — "think out loud" — about themselves and their motives, or describe other people and situations. Soliloquies were accepted as a vital part of drama until the realistic play became prevalent. In real life people do not talk aloud to themselves very often. However, the soliloquy is such a simple way to reveal inner reactions and character that modern playwrights still use it effectively. Thornton Wilder does this in both *Our Town* and *The Skin of Our Teeth*, and Tennessee Williams does it in *The Glass Menagerie*. Usually today's tendency is for dramatists to avoid direct descriptions as much as possible and have their characters reveal themselves rather unconsciously through action and speech.

Motivation of Action

The most important phase of characterization is the motivation of action. Every action of a character must have a reason behind it which in turn must be the result of both his inherent nature and the situation in which he is involved at the moment. As you read or see a play, you must be able to ask, "Why did he do that?" and find a logical answer in the nature of the person as brought out by what he has done in the play. Lack of proper motivation is a fatal flaw in a

Robert Stephens as Mark Antony, after a funeral oration, shows the crowd the body of the murdered Caesar and turns the people of Rome against Brutus and the other conspirators. (*Climax in* Julius Caesar)

play or motion picture. That fact is why so many impromptu happenings in improvised productions are boring and irritating. It is equally the constructive demand of psychologically inclined actors; "Why should I do that?"

Therefore, the playwright should have asked himself constantly such questions as the following regarding all of his characters: Where did they come from and why? (on their entrances) Where are they going and why? (on their exits) Why did they make certain key statements? Are such statements in keeping with these persons in this situation? Is this fact brought out here in keeping with the characters involved in this particular situation? Are these people saying exactly what I want the audience to get from their statements?

In modern drama the terms "protagonist" and "antagonist" do not always apply to an individual hero and villain. The protagonist may be a racial group, an age category, an economic classification; and the antagonist may be another racial group, a social class like the Establishment, an ideology, or a conflict within the protagonist himself. Sometimes a situation exists against which humanity is pitted in a hopeless floundering. Sometimes the members of the audience are invited and expected to take an active part in the action among uncharacterized performers.

On the other hand, there are modern characters constantly joining the characters of the past — Saint Joan, Peter Pan, Emperor Jones, Dodsworth, Willie Loman, Sir Thomas More, Don Quixote, Oliver, and many more whom you will meet in your theatrical adventures. You should also make lasting acquaintance with such roles as Antigone, Mrs. Malaprop, Cyrano de Bergerac, Volpone, and all the famous lovers, jesters, kings, and heroes and heroines of Shakespeare.

THEME

The theme is the basic idea of a play which the author dramatizes through the conflicts of characters with one another or with life events. It expresses a special phase of the fundamental philosophy indicated by the characters. Sometimes the playwright states his theme in a sentence spoken by a character, but often he leaves it to the interpretation of the audience. The discussion of his purpose in writing the play furnishes one of the chief points of interest in a worthwhile production.

You may find it difficult to determine the theme of a play as you read or see it, but you should enjoy analyzing the plot and characters and finding what the author has expressed through them. Remember that there may be many good ideas presented in a play, but don't be misled into mistaking a minor truth for the theme of the play as a whole. The theme is the specific idea which gives unity and purpose to everything that happens; it should be an interesting phase of the particular problem, rather than a general principle which could apply to dozens of plays.

For example, two well-known plays, found in a number of collections, are Dunsany's *A Night at an Inn* and Pillot's *Two Crooks and a Lady*. Since both plays deal with the stealing of jewels and both end disastrously for the thieves, the general idea that criminals are punished for their crimes is brought out in both. However, the theme of each play is far more specific.

In *A Night at an Inn*, three sailors under the direction of the Toff have stolen the ruby eye from an idol in India and have been pursued to England by priests who have slain two of their comrades in a horrible manner. As the play begins, the sailors have sought refuge in an isolated and deserted inn on the moors of England, where they are surprised by the priests. Due to the Toff's cleverness, the sailors are able to kill the priests one by one; but in the midst of the celebration of this victory, the idol himself arrives, takes his eye, and departs. Immediately each sailor is drawn to his destruction by a magnetic force he cannot resist. Even the Toff, who has a fine intelligence, is powerless against the idol. The theme is, therefore, that human power, either physical or mental, is useless in a struggle against a supernatural force.

In *Two Crooks and a Lady*, Mrs. Simms-Vane — old, paralyzed, and ill — because of her trained intelligence, inherent refinement, emotional control, and spiritual courage, is able to play two crooks against each other, so that they not only fail to get the jewels they seek, but are taken by the police as a result of their own dishonesty. The theme of this play is that a trained mind and fine character can overcome brute strength.

Do not confuse the theme with a moral. Many plays have no moral; they are written to show how a certain type of individual would react under certain circumstances, or to portray an interesting phase of life. While it may or may not be a profound truth or teach a lesson, the theme should be an interesting idea which has wide appeal and which is clearly set forth by the characterization and plot development.

One of the difficulties facing modern audiences is that in many performances the theme of the play is either too complicated to ferret out or does not exist. Avant-garde writers frequently state that they do not care what the onlookers think is the meaning of a play as long as they are emotionally affected by the action — shocked, depressed, disturbed.

Most theatergoers like a definite statement of the theme to help them arrive at the dramatist's reason for writing the play. Sometimes, therefore, the theme is put into the title — *The Taming of the Shrew, You Can't Take It with You, Beyond the Horizon, Susan and God, There Shall Be No Night, What Every Woman Knows, Waiting for Godot, She Stoops to Conquer, Nothing But the Truth, The School for Scandal, The Imaginary Invalid*. At other times, the theme is actually stated in a key line, definitely emphasized or expressed by the leading character as his philosophy of life, and then carried out in the situations resulting from this philosophy.

DIALOGUE, ACTION, AND SITUATION

The success of a play depends upon the writer's skillful use of dialogue and action, since they are the sole means by which he can portray his characters, set forth his theme, and develop his plot.

In writing the dialogue or lines of the play, the dramatist must be sure that his characters speak as the men and women of the class, community, and experience they represent would speak in real life. At the same time, he must advance the plot, motivate the actions of the characters, and place them in exciting or amusing situations. Of course, a great writer is bound to inject his individual style into the dialogue, but a dramatist cannot always instill his own brilliance into every sentence as other authors may do. He must often sacrifice beauty of language to naturalness of speech, yet his characters cannot talk aimlessly as people do in real life, for every word must serve to develop the play.

Clever lines in themselves are valuable in a comedy, but they should be consistent with the character of the person speaking them. Sparkling dialogue may actually be injurious to the play if it is not in harmony with the overall aim of the playwright. Words, figures of speech, and epigrams, although witty in themselves, may be completely unsuited to the play. We can hardly speak of dialogue apart from action and situation. When we refer to a playwright's style, then, we mean the cleverness or beauty of his lines in relation to the mood and characterization of his plays.

Action is the lifeblood of drama: something must happen constantly to hold the undivided interest of the onlookers. Events must not only be talked about, they must occur on the stage.

As you attend films and plays, note how the situations are always presented in dialogue and action. The characters may be placed in embarrassing predicaments, melodramatic moments of great danger, tense emotional upheavals, or in any other combination of circumstances. We must see the characters solve one difficult situation after another.

The ability to place characters in exciting, tragic, comic, or pathetic situations is what makes a playwright successful. Occasionally one situation alone can be so striking that it helps to make the play a hit. The next time you are at the theater, watch especially for the opening situation, the climax, and the closing event.

Whatever the future structure of drama may be, plays must maintain the universal appeal they have had through the centuries. In the long run dramatists whose plays will survive will continue to reveal the heights and depths of human experience and to be an uplifting and creative force in civilization. Those playwrights whose plays are carelessly constructed and tasteless, and obviously cater to the lowest instincts, will not exert an influence beyond their own generation.

Brutus meditates on the coming battle with the forces of Mark Antony and Octavius. (Falling action in Julius Caesar) Lorne Greene as Brutus, William Schatner as Lucius at the Stratford Festival Theatre, Stratford, Ontario.

DON MCKAGUE

In order to keep a simple record of the plays you see and read, you can outline them briefly and use the outlines to compare plays as theatrical seasons go by. The following form may be useful for this purpose.

Title and Author

I. Exposition
    A. Time
    B. Place
    C. Mood and atmosphere
    D. Preliminary situation

II. Plot (following preliminary situation)
    A. Initial incident
    B. Rising action — summarized briefly
    C. Climax
    D. Falling action — summarized briefly
    E. Conclusion — final outcome for each major character

III. Characters — described in one sentence
    A. Protagonist
    B. Antagonist
    C. Secondary
    D. Minor — listed

43

IV. Theme — stated in one sentence

V. Personal reaction — a brief paragraph stating honestly what you think about the play

VI. Quotations — lines or passages or phrases which clearly illustrate the author's style or express ideas you wish to remember

THE ONE-ACT PLAY

The current short play, programmed alone or in connection with one or more others in an evening's performance, has aroused renewed interest for the one-act play. Dramatists today feel that the play should be as long as the central idea demands for full expression, and as a result many write both long plays and short ones not restricted by traditional standards.

One-act plays offer an ideal medium in the dramatics classroom for studying the structure of drama, for furnishing a means of seeing plays in class, and for giving all members an opportunity to appear in a good part and to share in the actual production of a play. They also serve as a means of interesting young people seldom or never exposed to seeing plays by living actors; students in other classes can be invited to class presentations and the whole school to assembly ones. Such productions illustrate the techniques of writing and acting in one class period.

The one-act play is a major structural form, and justifiably so. It demands careful writing of a compact plot centered about one dramatic incident with vividly presented characters and condensed, rapidly moving dialogue. The one main idea is today considered of paramount value, so it must be brought out without confusing sidelights. Usually the exposition is brief, the rising action short, with the climax becoming the focus of the play very near the end.

Discussion

1. Select for analysis a motion picture or televised play which the majority of the class has seen. What was the initial incident? The climax? How were suspense and interest maintained during the rising and falling action? Did the drama end as you expected it would? What was the problem presented? Did it entail mental or physical conflict? State the theme in one sentence and then tell how the actions of the protagonist emphasized the theme.

GEORGE E. JOSEPH

Mark Antony pays tribute to the dead Brutus: "This was the noblest Roman of them all." (Conclusion in Julius Caesar) *Actors in this New York Shakespeare Festival production: Garnett Smith, Richard Roat, Jack Granino, Leonard Hicks.*

2. Summarize, in not more than four sentences, the plot of a play or film with which the rest of the class is not familiar.
3. What plays or films have caused you to think deeply about their purpose? Do you like dramas that make you do this? Why?
4. Which do you prefer, plays emphasizing plot, or character, or situation? Why? Give at least one example of each kind.
5. Among the earliest plays to break away from the traditional structure were Samuel Beckett's *Waiting for Godot* and Eugene Ionesco's *The Bald Soprano* and *The Chairs*. Read them and discuss them in relation to their lack of conventional plot, theme, and characters.

Bibliography

Archer, William: *Playmaking: A Manual of Craftsmanship*, Dover, New York, 1959.

Bentley, Eric: *The Playwright as Thinker*, Harcourt Brace & World, New York, 1958.

————:*What is Theatre?*, Atheneum, New York, 1967.

Brockett, Oscar G.: *The Theatre: An Introduction*, Holt, New York 1964.

Gassner, John; *Form and Idea in Modern Theatre*, Holt, New York, 1956.

————: *Directions in Modern Theatre and Drama*, Holt, New York, 1965.

Styan, J. L.: *The Elements of Drama*, Cambridge, London, 1960.

Whiting, Frank M.: *An Introduction to the Theatre*, Harper & Row, New York, 1969.

chapter

VARIETIES OF
DRAMA

The more plays you see and read, the more you will find yourself reacting differently to each writer's style, basic themes, characters, and dialogue. You will also soon recognize that plays fall into types or categories and that your response to each kind will vary accordingly.

Tragedy and comedy are the two chief divisions. In the broad sense, all plays may arbitrarily be placed within the definitions of tragedy and comedy. Although tragedies are among the earliest of recorded dramas, most plays — fantasy, melodrama, farce, comedy of manners, sentimental comedy, and social drama — fall within the definition of comedy. None of these divisions is absolute or entirely separate, and overlapping is quite common. Some plays which have the qualities of both tragedy and comedy are called tragicomedies, and some serious plays which do not fit the qualifications of tragedy but are "heavy" in nature are simply called dramas.

Classification is further complicated by a consideration of the styles in which a play may be written. The most commonly recognized

literary styles are classicism, romanticism, realism, naturalism, symbolism, expressionism, and impressionism. In addition, there are period styles determined by theater conventions of historical eras, such as the ritualistic formalism of the Greek theater, the madcap antics of the commedia dell' arte, and the powdered wigs, fans, and coquetry of the Restoration Period.

Remember that the classification of plays is rather arbitrary. Still, the following introduction to types should challenge your critical faculties and imagination and give you some knowledge of the terms used to describe plays.

TRAGEDY

The greatest plays of all time have been tragedies. In fact, tragedy has been considered by many critics as man's highest literary achievement, because only through suffering and sacrifice can a man achieve true nobility. A tragedy is a play in which the protagonist fails to achieve his goals or is overcome by the forces opposing him. The action usually ends with the protagonist's death, but in some plays he lives on, crushed in spirit and will.

Tragedies are based upon profound emotions which, in their universal appeal, transcend time and place. It is through such strong emotions as love, hate, ambition, jealousy, and revenge that we are moved to identify empathically with tragic figures. Since emotions are the true expressions of our humanness, it is neither necessary nor desirable to "intellectualize" tragedy; instead, we should be struck by an emotional bolt of lightning that leaps through the storm of conflict. Comedies, on the other hand, often depend upon local, regional, or topical situations. They seem entertaining to us only if our cultural background, temperament, and past experience permit us to respond to them, or if the characters go beyond their particular situations and can be related to something or someone we have known.

The most important basis for judgment of tragedy is found in a critical essay, the *Poetics*, by the famous Greek critic-philosopher Aristotle. According to Aristotle, the tragic protagonist is a "better than average man" guilty of "hamartia." Hamartia has been translated as an error in judgment or a shortcoming or, by some, as the tragic flaw. The most common form of hamartia is "hubris," an act of excessive pride. However, it is quite wrong to look for a "flaw" in every tragic hero, for the greatest tragic characters do not possess a real flaw, but more frequently fail because of costly errors in judgment, or even as a result of their own almost-too-virtuous nature. During his suffering, the tragic hero usually acquires a sense of awareness — of truth, of himself, or of others. Men seem capable of seeing clearly only when under great stress.

When a man of stature, struggling mightily against dynamic forces, finally falls, the audience experiences what Aristotle termed "catharsis," a purging or cleansing which comes as a result of emotional discharge. The most forceful purgation is experienced when we realize that the doomed hero has seen life more perceptively than most men could ever hope to. Aristotle said that the catharsis comes through pity and terror — pity for the protagonist that such a great person should fall, and terror aroused by the fear that we could easily have made the same error in judgment and paid the same price.

To heighten the impact, Aristotle said writers of tragedy would use scenes of recognition — either the identifying of a loved one, kinsman, or friend from a birthmark, scar, or other means, or the awareness the hero achieves through his suffering; and reversal (peripeteia) — an ironic twist in which an action produces an effect opposite to what would at first seem probable. An example of reversal can be seen in the play *Macbeth*. The witches' prophecies concerning Birnam Wood and "man not of woman born" bring a false assurance to Macbeth. The reversal comes when the prophecies are fulfilled and security turns to catastrophe.

D'Estivet, Cauchon, the Inquisitor (John Gielgud), and the Earl of Warwick in Shaw's Saint Joan. *Many critics consider this Shaw's greatest play.*

Apart from Aristotle, the student of drama will observe certain other characteristics in tragedy. The essential quality of a tragic hero is suffering; he suffers in most instances because he has rebelled against some divine or human authority or against society. Most tragedies have a ritualistic nature and the protagonist assumes the role of a sacrifice or scapegoat — Oedipus died for Thebes, Hamlet for Denmark, John Proctor and Thomas More for the honor of being true to oneself, and Willie Loman for his dreams and for his son Biff.

Tragedies are sober, thoughtful examinations of life dealing quite often with laws of the gods and laws of man, social conflict, or the identity and sanctity of self. In all cases, a struggle exists — a struggle of dignity and value. The higher the goals toward which the protagonist reaches, the greater may be his fall and the greater the purgation for the audience. If the character is not noble in rank or stature, there must be something which elevates him above the average. Willie Loman in *Death of a Salesman* has his dreams; the weavers in Hauptmann's play *The Weavers* have a hope for a better life.

It has been said that great men all have five characteristics in common: (1) They are dogmatic or unyielding — that is, they know what they stand for and do not swerve from that stand; (2) they make no apology for their actions; (3) they set goals — goals based on their dogmatism; (4) they know the value of sacrifice — that almost everything worth having, obtaining, or keeping demands some sacrifice; and (5) they are willing to make the sacrifice themselves, never asking another to do what they alone can do. Probably one of the finest descriptions of tragedy since Aristotle is found in a speech by the Chorus in Jean Anouilh's *Antigone*.

ANTIGONE
by Jean Anouilh

CHORUS: The spring is wound up tight. It will uncoil of itself. That is what is so convenient in tragedy. The least little turn of the wrist will do the job. Anything will set it going: a glance at a girl who happens to be lifting her arms to her hair as you go by; a feeling when you wake up on a fine morning that you'd like a little respect paid to you today, as if it were as easy to order as a second cup of coffee; one question too many, idly thrown out over a friendly drink — and the tragedy is on.

A tense moment in the 1969 production of Chekhov's realistic drama Uncle Vanya *at the Tyrone Guthrie Theatre. Paul Ballantyne is Vanya; Lee Richardson, Astrov. Guthrie directed; Tanya Moiseiwitsch designed the production.*

The rest is automatic. You don't need to lift a finger. The machine is in perfect order; it has been oiled ever since time began, and it runs without friction. Death, treason, and sorrow are on the march; and they move in the wake of storm, of tears, of stillness. Every kind of stillness. The hush when the executioner's ax goes up at the end of the last act. The unbreathable silence when, at the beginning of the play, the two lovers, their hearts bared, their bodies naked, stand for the first time face to face in the darkened room, afraid to stir. The silence inside you when the roaring crowd acclaims the winner — so that you think of a film without a sound track, mouths agape and no sound coming out of them, a clamor that is no more than a picture; and you, the victor, already vanquished, alone in the desert of your silence. That is tragedy.

Tragedy is clean, it is restful, it is flawless. It has nothing to do with melodrama — with wicked villains, persecuted maidens, avengers, sudden revelations, and eleventh-hour repentances. Death, in a melodrama, is really horrible because it is never inevitable. The dear old father might so easily have been saved; the honest young man might so easily have brought in the police five minutes earlier.

In a tragedy, nothing is in doubt and everyone's destiny is known. That makes for tranquility. There is a sort of fellow-feeling among characters in a tragedy: he who kills is as innocent as he who gets killed: it's all a matter of what part you are playing. Tragedy is restful; and the reason is that hope, that foul, deceitful thing, has no part in it. There isn't any hope. You're trapped. The whole sky has fallen on you, and all you can do about it is to shout.

Don't mistake me: I said "shout": I did not say groan, whimper, complain. That, you cannot do. But you can shout aloud; you can get all those things said that you never thought you'd be able to say — or never even knew you had it in you to say. And you don't say these things because it will do any good to say them: you know better than that. You say them for their own sake; you say them because you learn a lot from them.

In melodrama you argue and struggle in the hope of escape. That is vulgar; it's practical. But in tragedy, where there is no temptation to try to escape, argument is gratuitous: it's kingly.

A MAN FOR ALL SEASONS
by Robert Bolt

This is SIR THOMAS MORE'S *final speech to the court.*

MORE. Yes. (*He rises; all others sit.*) To avoid this I have taken every path my winding wits would find. Now that the Court has determined to condemn me, God knoweth how, I will discharge my mind . . . concerning my indictment and the King's title. The indictment is grounded in an Act of Parliament which is directly repugnant to the Law of God. The King in Parliament cannot bestow the Supremacy of the Church because it is a Spiritual Supremacy! And more to this the immunity of the Church is promised both in Magna Carta and the King's own Coronation Oath!

(*He pauses, and launches, very quietly, ruminatively, into his final stock-taking.*) I am the King's true subject, and pray for him and all the realm. . . . I do none harm, I say none

harm, I think none harm. And if this be not enough to keep a
man alive, in good faith I long not to live. . . . I have, since
I came into prison, been several times in such a case that I
thought to die within the hour, and I thank Our Lord I was
never sorry for it, but rather sorry when it passed. And
therefore, my poor body is at the King's pleasure. Would God
my death might do him some good. . . . (*With a great flash of
scorn and anger*) Nevertheless, it is not for the Supremacy
that you have sought my blood — but because I would not
bend to the marriage!

ANTIGONE
by Sophocles

Translation by Dudley Fitts and Robert Fitzgerald

ANTIGONE.   Ismene, dear sister,
    You would think that we had already suffered enough
    For the curse on Oedipus:
    I cannot imagine any grief
    That you and I have not gone through. And now —
    Have they told you of the new decree of our King Creon?
ISMENE.   I have heard nothing: I know
    That two sisters lost two brothers, a double death
    In a single hour; and I know that the Argive army
    Fled in the night; but beyond this, nothing.
ANTIGONE.   I thought so. And that is why I wanted you
    To come out here with me. There is something we must do.
ISMENE.   Why do you speak so strangely?
ANTIGONE.   Listen, Ismene:
    Creon buried our brother Eteocles
    With military honors, gave him a soldier's funeral,
    And it was right that he should; but Polyneices,
    Who fought as bravely and died as miserably, —
    They say that Creon has sworn
    No one shall bury him, no one mourn for him,
    But his body must lie in the fields, a sweet treasure
    For carrion birds to find as they search for food.
    That is what they say, and our good Creon is coming here
    To announce it publicly; and the penalty —
    Stoning to death in the public square!
                        There it is,

    And now you can prove what you are:
    A true sister, or a traitor to your family.

ISMENE.   Antigone, you are mad! What could I possibly do?
ANTIGONE.   You must decide whether you will help me or not.
ISMENE.   I do not understand you. Help you in what?
ANTIGONE.   Ismene, I am going to bury him. Will you come?
ISMENE.   Bury him! You have just said the new law forbids it.
ANTIGONE.   He is my brother. And he is your brother, too.
ISMENE.   But think of the danger! Think what Creon will do!
ANTIGONE.   Creon is not strong enough to stand in my way.
ISMENE.   Ah sister!

> Oedipus died, everyone hating him
> For what his own search brought to light, his eyes
> Ripped out by his own hand; and Iocastê died,
> His mother and wife at once: she twisted the cords
> That strangled her life; and our two brothers died,
> Each killed by the other's sword. And we are left:
> But oh, Antigone,
> Think how much more terrible than these
> Our own death would be if we should go against Creon
> And do what he has forbidden! We are only women,
> We cannot fight with men, Antigone!
> The law is strong, we must give in to the law
> In this thing, and in worse. I beg the dead
> To forgive me, but I am helpless: I must yield
> To those in authority. And I think it is dangerous business
> To be always meddling.

ANTIGONE.   If that is what you think,

> I should not want you, even if you asked to come.
> You have made your choice, you can be what you want to be.
> But I will bury him; and if I must die,
> I say that this crime is holy: I shall lie down
> With him in death, and I shall be as dear
> To him as he to me.
>   It is the dead,
> Not the living, who make the longest demands:
> We die for ever . . .
>   You may do as you like,
> Since apparently the laws of the gods mean nothing to you.

ISMENE.   They mean a great deal to me; but I have no strength
> To break laws that were made for the public good.
ANTIGONE.   That must be your excuse, I suppose. But as for me,
> I will bury the brother I love.
ISMENE.   Antigone,
> I am so afraid for you!

ANTIGONE.   You need not be:
　　　You have yourself to consider, after all.
ISMENE.   But no one must hear of this, you must tell no one!
　　　I will keep it a secret, I promise!
ANTIGONE.   Oh, tell it! Tell everyone!
　　　Think how they'll hate you when it all comes out
　　　If they learn that you knew about it all the time!
ISMENE.   So fiery! You should be cold with fear.
ANTIGONE.   Perhaps. But I am doing only what I must.
ISMENE.   But can you do it? I say that you cannot.
ANTIGONE.   Very well: when my strength gives out, I shall do no more.
ISMENE.   Impossible things should not be tried at all.
ANTIGONE.   Go away, Ismene:
　　　I shall be hating you soon, and the dead will too,
　　　For your words are hateful. Leave me my foolish plan:
　　　I am not afraid of the danger; if it means death,
　　　It will not be the worst of deaths — death without honor.
ISMENE.   Go then, if you feel that you must.
　　　You are unwise,
　　　But a loyal friend indeed to those who love you.
　　　(*Exit into the Palace.* ANTIGONE *goes off, left.*)

JOAN OF LORRAINE
by Maxwell Anderson

This is JOAN's *final scene in her trial as a witch.*

JOAN.   I have an answer now. I believe in them in my heart. There
　　　is no other authority.
CAUCHON.   Do you deny the authority of the church?
JOAN.   I believe in the church from my heart. There's no other way
　　　to believe.
CAUCHON.   The church has called your Voices evil. One or the other
　　　you must deny.
JOAN.   That's your belief, Bishop Cauchon, but not mine. Each
　　　must believe for himself. Each soul chooses for itself. No
　　　other can choose for it. In all the world there is no authority
　　　for anyone save his own soul.
INQUISITOR.   Then you choose death.
JOAN.   I know you have tried to save me.
INQUISITOR.   I have never tried to save you. I have spoken only
　　　for the strict and correct application of the canon law. When
　　　the law is on your side, I am there also. When you set yourself

against the law, I must set myself against you. But I still plead with you: do not force us to abandon you. The individual soul cannot choose its own faith, cannot judge for itself!

JOAN. Yet every soul chooses for itself. Who chose your faith for you? Didn't you choose it? Don't you choose to keep it now?

COURCELLES. There's a singular logic in this.

CAUCHON. I think not.

JOAN. Yes, you did choose it. You choose to keep it. As I choose to keep mine. And, if I give my life for that choice, I know this too now: Every man gives his life for what he believes. Every woman gives her life for what she believes. Sometimes people believe in little or nothing; nevertheless they give up their lives to that little or nothing. One life is all we have, and we live it as we believe in living it, and then it's gone. But to surrender what you are, and live without belief — that's more terrible than dying — more terrible than dying young.

COMEDY

The word "comedy" is derived from a Greek word, "komos," meaning festival or revelry. Comedies are usually light, written with sparkling dialogue and peopled with amusing characters who are involved in funny situations which they solve by their wit, their charm, and sometimes by sheer good fortune. Throughout the history of the theater, the greatest and most enduring comedies have taken

Charley's "aunt" enjoys himself, much to the consternation of his Oxford chums, in a high school production of the farce Charley's Aunt.

MAXWELL STUDIO

situations and characters from life and therefore contain certain time-less human truths. Molière, Shakespeare, and Shaw are considered three of the world's best comedy writers. Their comedies have had lasting appeal because they are based on universal human experience.

When we think of comedy, we usually think of something that will make us laugh. Although that is not completely true, we may say that most comedy will amuse, delight, or please us. In any case, the protagonist in a comedy overcomes the forces opposing him, achieves his goals, or both. This hero is most often "less than an average man" in some way. He may be an idealist, a romanticist, an extreme prag-matist, or he may be a blunderer, a dreamer, or a rogue.

Comedy is built around character, situations, or dialogue. A strange character bumbling his way through life like a Don Quixote provokes laughter. The pleasure-loving but cowardly Falstaff, the linguistically confused Mrs. Malaprop, and the female-masquerading Fancourt Babberly become natural causes for mirth. Involved predicaments which seem insurmountable or improbable provide a "situation." Mistaken identities, rash promises, or a series of events where every-thing seems to go wrong focus audience attention on the solving of the problem. Trying to live one life in town and another in the country makes the situation in *The Importance of Being Earnest* ripe for amusing farce. In Noel Coward's *Blithe Spirit*, the ghost of Charles' first wife tries to murder her former husband in order that he might join her "on the other side," but by accident it is the second wife who drives off in the sabotaged car, and the hapless Charles finds himself plagued by two spirit-spouses.

It seems strange to many students of the drama that almost all comedy has its basic appeal to the intellect rather than the emotions. However, this is the reason we ask: "Did the audience 'catch on'?" There are several types of comedy, some bringing laughter to the point of tears, some causing inner smiles or chuckles, and others calling up merely a feeling of whimsy.

Humor involves an appeal to the heart, where the audience can gently feel love, tenderness, pity, or compassion. Humor is tied firmly to an emotional empathy, although the laughter itself comes from the thinking process. No one has to tell the actor who has studied people carefully how closely related laughter and tears may be. The proximity of happiness to sorrow, bitterness to sweetness, hopefulness to futility increases comic effect because the leap from one extreme to the other prompts an emotional response.

THE CAUSES OF LAUGHTER

It is very difficult to determine what really makes people laugh. We laugh at very strange things — the exaggerated, the grotesque, even the horrifying. Sometimes we laugh out of embarrassment, sometimes to save ourselves from tears, and sometimes, it seems, for no reason at all. Partly because of this unpredictable quality, truly comic plays are always more difficult to perform successfully than serious plays.

Exaggeration

Exaggeration is probably the first thing we notice when anything is comic. Almost every character, line, or situation must be at least slightly enlarged beyond the normal in order to be funny. One form of exaggeration is the overstatement, sometimes called a hyperbole — the "I can lick you with both hands tied behind my back" or "I always tell the truth" type of statement. Opposite the overstatement is the understatement, which depends upon a negative approach: "She wasn't quite the ugliest girl in the kingdom."

Exaggeration may also be applied to physical characteristics, such as a bulbous nose or buck teeth; mental characteristics, such as the almost-too-brilliant child prodigy, or the incredibly-too-stupid servant; or personality characteristics, such as miserliness, prissiness, or fanciful romanticism.

Another form of exaggeration stems from the "humours" of Shakespeare's time. The humours are personality determiners making people giggly, gay, carefree, happy-go-lucky (air); moody, philosophical, love-sick (earth); impatient, hot-headed, passionate (fire); and dull, lazy, sluggish (water). Each of these personality types is such an exaggeration from the normal that we must respond with laughter or tears.

Incongruity

That which seems out of place, out of time, or out of character is called incongruous. Man has a built-in system of order, and if what is expected does not occur, we laugh. Someone waltzing to a rumba beat, the hulking fullback who quotes Shelley and Keats, and the "harmless little fellow" who is as brave as an army are examples of incongruities audiences find amusing. Grotesqueness is another incongruity. The grotesque can become a subject for pathos or comedy depending upon the point of view: Cyrano de Bergerac's nose speech

June Havoc (right) in The Beaux' Stratagem, *George Farquhar's comedy of manners, in a production at the Phoenix Theatre in New York.*

is humorous because he jests at his own ugliness; however, we are compassionate when we realize how painful his physical features are to him. Missing teeth, an exaggerated limp that becomes a hippety-hop, drooping eyelids may cause us to laugh mainly because we do not wish to cry.

Incongruity is found in action that is unnatural or nonhuman. This is often accomplished by machinelike or puppetlike behavior. Lisa Doolittle is often pictured as a marionette-character whose strings are pulled by Henry Higgins. A person who moves about herky-jerky like a windup toy makes us laugh. We find it amusing to see people behave like animals or animal characters behave like people. Ben Jonson's *Volpone* has human beings with animal personalities — a fox, a fly, a vulture, a crow, and a raven. The cowardly lion of *The Wizard of Oz* seems hilariously like his faint-hearted human counterpart. Long sweeps about the stage, seven-league strides, grandiose gestures, almost-too-flowing movements, or a walk with some part of the body seeming to advance or trail unnaturally have always been good for a laugh.

Unnatural sounds — such a brayish laugh piercing as that of a hyena, severely trilled *r*'s that pound like a jackhammer, or an undulating pitch that soars up and down like a slide trombone — are sure to draw laughter from the audience. We will even discover that certain words are comic, not merely because they seem odd, but because the sound is incongruously funny to our ears — we laugh at "Hackensack," but not at "Schenectady."

The twist or the unexpected provides another form of incongruity, since the logical completion of a pattern is reversed inside out or upside down by a strange turn of events. One kind of twist is based upon what the audience knows the character is really like as opposed to what he pretends to be. Abby and Martha, the sweet old ladies of *Arsenic and Old Lace*, have convinced the community that they are the epitome of kindness and generosity, but the audience discovers they have poisoned twelve old gentlemen, eleven of whom are buried in the cellar.

Reversal is a type of incongruity which enables the audience to enjoy seeing "the tables turned." Reversal often involves the weak overcoming the strong, the servant overpowering the master, the underdog winning out over the favorite, as well as changes from unhappiness to happiness, poverty to prosperity, or lowliness to prestige.

The irrelevant or unimportant is a final form of incongruity, especially when concentrated upon the treatment of a lofty subject. All forms of burlesque humor — the travesty, the mock heroic, and the parody — exaggerate the unimportant. A travesty involves a situation in which a subject of noble nature is treated in a lowly fashion; *Man of La Mancha* features a hero who loses a battle with a windmill and then in his dream world mistakes an inn for a castle.

Anticipation

The key to many laughs is anticipation, or looking forward to a potential laugh. The strength of the laugh is determined by how much the audience is "in the know." We wait for the characters of mistaken identity to meet, the "plotter" to become a victim of his own plot, and booby traps to ensnare innocent victims. After Teddy's initial charge up "San Juan Hill," the audience watching *Arsenic and Old*

Christopher Plummer as
Cyrano de Bergerac in
Rostand's sentimental
drama of that name.

NBC PHOTO

Lace anticipates his next exit upstairs, holds its breath as he stops on the landing to draw his imaginery sword, and convulses in laughter as he roars "CHARGE! Charge the blockhouse!"

The old gag of the banana peel on the sidewalk is an excellent example of anticipation. The observer will start to laugh even before the clown takes that disastrous step.

Many times anticipation is created by the plant — an idea, line, or action emphasized early in the play which is used later for a laugh. It must be remembered that it usually takes at least three exposures to an idea to provoke a laugh: one to plant, a second to establish, and the third to clinch or bring out a response. From then on, the gag should be good for a laugh until it is milked dry.

Incompletion is another laugh-getting form of anticipation. Here man's sense of order is appealed to. A line or bit of action is started but never finished — and the audience completes the thought with laughter. In fact, the ability of the actor to leave a comic line "hanging" is a cue to the audience that something funny has been said and their laughter is required to finish it off.

A third type of anticipation is what is called the anticlimax or letdown. The excitement over something is built up to great proportions and then, like a bursting bubble, there is nothing. The follow-

60

through is never equal to the preparation; an example of this is what is called the "flat line," a line delivered with either a drop in pitch or with little or no expression in the voice.

Ambiguity

Ambiguity or double meaning is the heart of many humorous lines. Puns and word play depend upon the audience's recognizing the possible interpretations and, almost always, selecting the one least likely. Even names like Lydia Languish, Lady Teazle, or Sir Fopling Flutter provide comic clues to personality as well as identification of characters. Mistaken identities, lines meant for one person but "accepted" by another as intended for him, and ruses and disguises are other means of creating double meaning. Shakespeare's audiences must have been delighted when watching a boy play the part of a girl who was, in turn, disguised as a boy acting as a girl while a friend rehearsed a proposal — as a comic strip character would put it: "Confusing, but amusing."

Recognition

Recognition is discovering hidden or obscure meanings. "Solving the puzzle," especially in a line or passage of wit where the audience must "think twice," is the basis of high comedy and satire. We find it humorous when we recognize the inner motivation of a character — motivation which is implied by a subtle act, like the sly wink of the coquette as she hides behind her fan and asks: "Why, Sir, were you addressing me?" We are also amused when we discover what is going to happen just before it does. The "take" — the "mouth agape freeze" of farce — has always brought down the house. The character "sees" or "hears" something which apparently does not sink in; he takes a step or two and then "Pow!" it hits him.

Protection

One of the most important elements of comedy we may call the protection factor. Cruel, violent, grotesque, and abusive actions and events often cause laughter when the audience is under the protection of knowing those things are not really happening. The secret of the cartoon in which a character runs off a cliff is this protection factor; the character falls 100 feet to his "doom," but he appears heavily bandaged in the next frame, and then, within fifteen seconds of the horrible catastrophe, he is completely restored. The old "slapstick" is another example; it made considerable noise, but hurt no one. We are truly amused when we are certain that no one is really being injured and we can accept the illusion as being real, for then we laugh because it is not happening to us!

Relief

Relief of pressure, such as comic relief in a tragedy or in a situation that builds up to a point where the audience feels it can take no more, is humorous when the pent-up emotions are allowed to explode in a laugh. When our emotions suddenly erupt, we often explain: "I couldn't hold it in any longer." Good comedies build up pressures and release them, as we can see in the following example which shows how some of these causes of laughter work together.

Good comedy is like the powder keg (plant) with the lighted fuse (anticipation). When the fuse fizzles (unexpected) at just the moment of expected explosion (anticlimax), the audience may laugh. They will probably snicker when the too-curious buffoon approaches the keg to see why it did not go off; but, as we could have predicted (recognition), the keg then blows up in his face (protection). When he emerges ragged and soot-covered (incongruity), we roar even louder (relief).

TYPES OF COMEDY

The traditional classification of comedies is important, for each type demands a special kind of staging.

Farce

This type involves almost everything done strictly for laughs — clowning, practical jokes, improbable characters and situations. Farce frequently features a considerable amount of assault and battery: ears are pulled, shins are kicked, pies are shoved into faces. Many of these actions come within the term "slapstick," which is derived from an old stage prop consisting of two thin boards hinged together; these made a loud but harmless crack when applied to the backside of a performer.

Every age has found farce flourishing, from the ancient Greeks featuring grotesque masks, through Shakespeare, Molière, and modern vaudeville, motion pictures, and TV specials. Farce brings release from the stress of daily life and an opportunity for us to see ourselves as others see us and to learn to laugh at our own foibles.

Some of our most popular plays of every season are well written and brilliantly paced farces, original in plot, situations, and characters. Famous farces repeated constantly include *The Importance of Being Earnest, You Can't Take It with You, Charley's Aunt, The Comedy of Errors, The Inspector General,* and *My Three Angels.*

Melodrama

A melodrama is a serious play written to arouse intense emotion by bloodcurdling events, terrific suspense, and horrifying details centering around plotted murders, thwarted love and greed, and revenge. Motivation and logical explanations are not so important in melodrama; therefore we do not question why things turn out as they do. Some melodramas you will enjoy are *Arsenic and Old Lace, Night Must Fall, Ten Little Indians, Angel Street (Gaslight), Witness for the Prosecution, Dial M for Murder,* and *The Night of January 16th.*

A mystery play is a melodrama of the "whodunit" class, with the plot centering about the tracking down of a criminal and saving the falsely accused protagonist. Dame Agatha Christie's *The Mousetrap* holds the all-time long-run record for this type. The melodramatic features of the Western, modern horror films, TV shows of violence, and the theater of cruelty are the backbone of their popularity.

High Comedy

This is sometimes called the comedy of manners; it has always been the delight of sophisticated actors and audiences. Built on clever use of language, its wit includes puns, paradoxes, epigrams, and ironies. The dialogue is brilliant conversation between amusing people, often razor-sharp in disparaging the socially accepted standards of the day. The plays are as entertaining to read as to see.

Satire is closely affiliated with high comedy; it holds human frailty up to ridicule and is a humorous attack on accepted conventions of society or only a humorous observation of the foibles and follies of man. Restoration drama, in almost continuous production somewhere these days, represents the masterpieces of high comedy; such plays as Wycherley's *The Country Wife* and Congreve's *The Way of the World* later were followed by Goldsmith's *She Stoops to Conquer* and Sheridan's *The School for Scandal* and *The Rivals.*

Oscar Wilde and George Bernard Shaw will probably remain unsurpassed in the field of satire. Twentieth-century dramatists of expert comedies of this type include Noel Coward, Somerset Maugham,

S. H. Berhman, Rachel Crothers, George S. Kaufman, and Edna Ferber. You will especially enjoy such plays as Clare Boothe's *The Women*, Kaufman and Ferber's *The Royal Family*, satirizing the famous Barrymore theatrical family, and Kaufman and Hart's *Once in a Lifetime*, which keeps alive the humorous tragedy of the days when silent films began to talk!

Sentimental Comedy

Despite its loss of allure at the moment, this type of comedy has an enduring place as one of the most popular forms of drama. Hundreds of plays loved in the past may well come back when the public is bored with the depressing and tasteless trends in many current films and productions. Based on the themes of self-sacrifice, patriotism, lost affection, mother love, and youthful romance, these plays at their best meet the universal need of average men and women to have faith in the finest of human traits and to lose themselves in the lives of simple people like themselves.

You should not overlook the superior dramas of this type, especially when selecting plays for high school production. Among the most appealing are those by James M. Barrie, with his whimsical humor and amazing understanding of women; his *Dear Brutus*, *What Every Woman Knows*, *Quality Street*, and his lightly satirical *The Admirable Crichton* are frequently produced with great success. John Van Druten's *I Remember Mama*, Philip Barry's *Holiday*, Clemence Dane's *A Bill of Divorcement*, Guy Bolton's *Anastasia*, and Rudolf Besier's *The Barretts of Wimpole Street* are only a few of the perennial favorites of this type.

At their worst, the sentimental comedies were the "soap operas" of radio and the "tear jerkers" of stage and screen which continue in TV. At their best, as in the tremendously popular *The Forsyte Saga* based on Galsworthy's trilogy, they meet a deep theatrical need.

Social Drama

Sometimes called the problem play, social drama will always be produced in one form or another as dramatists seek to right the wrongs of society. These plays are frequently comedies in the sense that they offer a solution for the problems they present, but of course many are tragedies because of the loss of the protagonist's life in his battle against evil. The social drama differs from the "plays of protest" in their constructive rather than destructive point of view.

Molière's Le Misanthrope *as performed by the Madeleine Renaud — Jean-Louis Barrault Company. This company's type of presentation is often called "total theater."*

Some of the famous social dramas are Ibsen's *An Enemy of the People*, which shows how a man in a small town stands for civic integrity against all the citizens of his community; Galsworthy's *Justice*, which reveals the tragedy of a crime committed to save someone else; Rice's *Street Scene* and Kingsley's *Dead End*, which depict the effects of living in New York's crowded streets; Kelly's *Craig's Wife*, which shows how a wife's absorption in her belongings means keeping house, not making a home; and Odet's *Waiting for Lefty*, which is a picture of the effects of a strike on workers in New York.

ARSENIC AND OLD LACE
by Joseph Kesselring

MORTIMER *has just discovered that his sweet old aunts have murdered several old gentlemen.*

MORTIMER. TWELVE!

MARTHA. Yes, Abby thinks we ought to count the first one and that makes twelve. (*She goes back to sideboard.*)

MORTIMER (*Placing a chair; then takes* MARTHA's *hand, leads her to chair and sets her in it*). All right — now — who was the first one?

ABBY (*Crossing from above table to* MORTIMER). Mr. Midgely. He was a Baptist.

MARTHA. Of course, I still think we can't claim full credit for him because he just died.

ABBY. Martha means without any help from us. You see, Mr. Midgely came here looking for a room —

Cyril Ritchard as Oberon and Jerry Dodge as Puck in the 1967 production of the fantasy A Midsummer Night's Dream *at The American Shakespeare Festival Theatre in Stratford, Connecticut. Ritchard directed the play.*

MARTHA.   It was right after you moved to New York.

ABBY.   And it didn't seem right for that lovely room to be going to waste when there were so many people who needed it—

MARTHA.   He was such a lonely old man. . . .

ABBY.   All his kith and kin were dead and it left him so forlorn and unhappy —

MARTHA.   We felt so sorry for him.

ABBY.   And then when his heart attack came — and he sat dead in that chair (*Pointing to armchair*) looking so peaceful — remember, Martha — we made up our minds then and there that if we could help other lonely old men to that same peace — we would!

MORTIMER   (*All ears*).   He dropped dead right in that chair! How awful for you!

MARTHA. Oh, no, dear. Why, it was rather like old times. Your grandfather always used to have a cadaver or two around the house. You see, Teddy had been digging in Panama and he thought Mr. Midgely was a yellow fever victim.

ABBY. That meant he had to be buried immediately.

MARTHA. So we all took him down to Panama and put him in the lock. (*She rises, puts her arm around* ABBY.) Now that's why we told you not to worry about it because we know exactly what's to be done.

MORTIMER. And that's how all this started — that man walking in here and dropping dead.

ABBY. Of course, we realized we couldn't depend on that happening again. So —

MARTHA (*Crosses to* MORTIMER). You remember those jars of poison that have been up on the shelves in Grandfather's laboratory all these years —?

ABBY. You know your Aunt Martha's knack for mixing things. You've eaten enough of her piccalilli.

MARTHA. Well, dear, for a gallon of elderberry wine I take one teaspoonful of arsenic, then add a half teaspoonful of strychnine and then just a pinch of cyanide.

MORTIMER (*Appraisingly*). Should have quite a kick.

ABBY. Yes! As a matter of fact one of our gentlemen found time to say "How delicious!"

MARTHA. Well, I'll have to get things started in the kitchen.

ABBY (*To* MORTIMER). I wish you could stay for dinner.

MARTHA. I'm trying out a new recipe.

MORTIMER. I couldn't eat a thing.

BAREFOOT IN THE PARK
by Neil Simon

PAUL *and* CORIE *are newlyweds.* PAUL *has just climbed five flights to the garret apartment* CORIE *has rented.*

CORIE. The furniture will be here by five. They promised.

PAUL (*Dropping affidavits into case, looks at his watch*). Five? . . . It's five-thirty. (*Crosses to bedroom stairs*) What do we do, sleep in Bloomingdale's tonight?

CORIE. They'll be here, Paul. They're probably stuck in traffic.

PAUL (*Crossing up to bedroom*). And what about tonight? I've got a case in court tomorrow. Maybe we should check into a hotel? (*Looks into bedroom*)

In J.B., Archibald MacLeish's contemporary play based on the book of Job, J.B.'s face clearly expresses anguish as he implores God to tell him why he must suffer. This play is an allegory. The actors are Lane Bradbury and Pat Hingle.

CORIE   (*Rises and moves towards* PAUL). We just checked *out* of a hotel. I don't care if the furniture *doesn't* come. I'm sleeping in my apartment *tonight*.

PAUL.   Where? Where? (*Looks into bathroom, closes door, and starts to come back down the steps*) There's only room for one in the bathtub. (*He suddenly turns, goes back up steps and opens door to the bathroom.*) Where's the bathtub?

CORIE   (*Hesitantly*). There is no bathtub.

PAUL.   No bathtub?

CORIE.   There's a shower . . .

PAUL.   How am I going to take a bath?

CORIE.   You won't take a bath. You'll take a shower.

PAUL.   I don't like showers. I like baths. Corie, how am I going to take a bath?

CORIE.   You'll lie down in the shower and hang your feet over the sink. . . . I'm sorry there's no bathtub, Paul.

PAUL   (*Closes door, and crosses down into the room*). Hmmmm. . . Boy, of all the nights . . . (*He suddenly shivers.*) It's freezing in here. (*He rubs his hands.*) Isn't there any heat?

CORIE.   Of course there's heat. We have a radiator.

PAUL   (*Gets up on steps and feels radiator*). The *radiator's* the coldest thing in the room.

CORIE.   It's probably the boiler. It's probably off in the whole building.

PAUL   (*Putting on gloves*). No, it was warm coming up the stairs. (*Goes out door into hall*) See . . . It's nice and warm out here.

CORIE.   Maybe it's because the apartment is empty.

PAUL.   The *hall* is empty too but it's warm out here.

CORIE   (*Moves to the stove*). It'll be all right once I get a fire going.

PAUL   (*Goes to phone*). A fire? You'd have to keep the flame going night and day. . . . I'll call the landlord.

CORIE   (*Putting log into stove*). He's not home.

PAUL.   Where is he?

CORIE.   In Florida! . . . There's a handy man that comes Mondays, Wednesdays, and Fridays.

PAUL.   You mean we freeze on Tuesdays, Thursdays, and Saturdays?

CORIE.   He'll be here in the morning.

PAUL   (*Moving R.*). And what'll we do tonight? I've got a case in court in the morning.

CORIE   (*Moves to* PAUL). Will you stop saying it like you always have a case in court in the morning. This is your first one.

PAUL.   Well, what'll we do?

CORIE.   The furniture will be here. In the meantime I can light the stove and you can sit over the fire with your law books and a shawl like Abraham Lincoln. (*Crosses to the Franklin Stove and gets matches from the top of the stove*)

PAUL.   Is that supposed to be funny? (*Begins to investigate small windows*)

CORIE.   No. It was supposed to be nasty. It just came out funny. (*She strikes match and attempts to light the log in stove.* PAUL *tries the windows.*) What are you doing? (*Gives up attempting to light log*)

PAUL.   I'm checking to see if the windows are closed.

CORIE.   They're closed. I looked.

PAUL.   Then why is it windy in here?

CORIE   (*Moves R. to* PAUL). I don't feel a draft.

PAUL   (*Moves away from windows*). I didn't say draft. I said wind . . . There's a brisk, northeasterly wind blowing in this room.

CORIE.   You don't have to get sarcastic.

PAUL   (*Moving up into the kitchen area*). I'm not getting sarcastic, I'm getting chapped lips. (*Looking up, he glimpses the hole in the skylight.*)

CORIE.   How could there be wind in a closed room?

PAUL.   How's this for an answer? There's a hole in the skylight. (*He points up.*)

CORIE.   (*She looks up, sees it and is obviously embarrassed by it.*) Gee, I didn't see that before. Did you?

PAUL   (*Moves to ladder*). I didn't see the *apartment* before.

CORIE   (*Defensively. Crosses to the railing and gets her coat*). All right, Paul, don't get upset. I'm sure it'll be fixed. We could plug it up with something for tonight.

PAUL   (*Gets up on ladder*). How? How? That's twenty feet high. You'd have to fly over in a plane and *drop* something in.

CORIE   (*Putting on coat*). It's only for one night. And it's not that cold.

PAUL.   In February? Do you know what it's like at three o'clock in the morning? In February? Ice-cold freezing.

CORIE.   It's not going to be freezing. I called the weather bureau. It's going to be cloudy with a light s— (*She catches herself and looks up.*)

PAUL.   What? (CORIE *turns away.*) What? . . . A light what?

CORIE.   Snow!

PAUL   (*Coming down ladder*). Snow?? . . . It's going to snow tonight? . . . In here?

CORIE.   They're wrong as often as they're right.

PAUL.   I'm going to be shoveling snow in my own living room.

CORIE.   It's a little hole.

PAUL.   With that wind it could blow six-foot drifts in the bathroom. Honestly, Corie, I don't see how you can be so calm about all this.

CORIE.   Well, what is it you want me to do?

PAUL.   Go to pieces, like me. It's only natural.

A THOUSAND CLOWNS
by Herb Gardner

MURRAY   (*Picks up phone and speaks immediately into it*). Is this somebody with good news or money? No? Good-bye. (*He hangs up.*) It's always voices like that you hear at eight A.M. Maniacs. (*He pulls up the shade to see what kind of day it is outside. As usual the lighting of the room changes not at all with the shade up; as before, he sees nothing but the blank, grayish wall opposite.*) Crap. (*With a sign of resignation, he picks up the phone, dials, listens.*) Hello, Weather Lady. I am fine, how are you? What is the weather? Uh-huh—uh-huh—uh-huh— very nice. Only a *chance* of showers? Well, what exactly does that—? Aw, there she goes again. (*He hangs up.*) Chance of showers. (*Phone rings. He picks it up, speaks immediately into it.*) United States Weather Bureau forecast for New York City and vicinity: eight A.M. temperature, sixty-five degrees, somewhat cooler in the suburbs, cloudy later today with a chance of — (*Looks incredulously at phone*) He hung up. Fool. Probably the most informative phone call he'll make all day. (*He stands, opens the window, leans out, raising his voice, shouting out the window.*) This is your neighbor speaking! Something must be done about your garbage cans in the alley here. It is definitely second-rate garbage! By next week I want to see a better class of garbage, more empty champagne bottles and caviar cans! So let's *snap* it up and get on the *ball!*

YOU CAN'T TAKE IT WITH YOU
by Moss Hart and George S. Kaufman

MR. HENDERSON *of the Internal Revenue Service calls on* GRANDPA VANDERHOF, *who has never filed an income tax return.*

HENDERSON (*Pulling a sheaf of papers from his pocket*). Now, Mr. Vanderhof, (*A quick look toward hall*) we've written you several letters about this, but have not had any reply.

GRANDPA. Oh, that's what those letters were.

ESSIE (*Sitting on couch R.*). I told you they were from the Government.

HENDERSON. According to our records, Mr. Vanderhof, you have never paid an income tax.

GRANDPA. That's right.

HENDERSON. Why not?

GRANDPA. I don't believe in it.

HENDERSON. Well — you own property, don't you?

GRANDPA. Yes, sir.

HENDERSON. And you receive a yearly income from it?

GRANDPA. I do.

HENDERSON. Of — (*He consults his records.*) — between three and four thousand dollars.

GRANDPA. About that.

HENDERSON. You've been receiving it for years.

GRANDPA. I have. 1901, if you want the exact date.

HENDERSON. Well, the Government is only concerned from 1914 on. That's when the income tax started. (*Pause*)

GRANDPA. Well?

HENDERSON. Well — it seems, Mr. Vanderhof, that you owe the Government twenty-four years' back income tax. Now, Mr. Vanderhof, you know there's quite a penalty for not filing an income tax return.

GRANDPA. Look, Mr. Henderson, let me ask you something.

A scene from Elmer Rice's The Adding Machine, *showing Mr. Zero on the keys of the machine which has taken over his position. The exaggerated size of the machine is an example of expressionism in scenic design.*

HENDERSON. Well?

GRANDPA. Suppose I pay you this money — mind you, I don't say I'm going to pay it — but just for the sake of argument — what's the Government going to do with it?

HENDERSON. How do you mean?

GRANDPA. Well, what do I get for my money? If I go into Macy's and buy something, there it *is* — I see it. What's the Government give me?

HENDERSON. Why, the Government gives you everything. It protects you.

GRANDPA. What from?

HENDERSON. Well — invasion. Foreigners that might come over here and take everything you've got.

GRANDPA. Oh, I don't think they're going to do that.

HENDERSON. If you didn't pay an income tax, they would. How do you think the Government keeps up the Army and Navy? All those battleships. . .

GRANDPA. Last time we used battleships was in the Spanish-American War, and what did we get out of it? Cuba — and we gave that back. I wouldn't mind paying if it were something sensible.

HENDERSON. Sensible? Well, what about Congress, and the Supreme Court, and the President? We've got to pay *them*, don't we?

GRANDPA. Not with my money — no, sir.

HENDERSON (*Furious. Rises, picks up papers*). Now wait a minute! I'm not here to argue with you. (*Crossing L.*) All I know is that you haven't paid an income tax and you've got to pay it!

GRANDPA. They've got to show me.

HENDERSON (*Yelling*). We *don't* have to show you! I just told you! All those buildings down in Washington, and Interstate Commerce, and the Constitution!

GRANDPA. The Constitution was paid for long ago. And Interstate Commerce — what *is* Interstate Commerce, anyhow?

HENDERSON (*Business of a look at* GRANDPA. *With murderous calm, crosses and places his hands on table*). There are forty-eight states — see? And if there weren't Interstate Commerce, nothing could go from one state to another. See?

GRANDPA. Why not? They got fences?

HENDERSON (*To* GRANDPA). No, they haven't got fences. They've got *laws!* (*Crossing up to arch L.*) My God, I never came across anything like *this* before!

GRANDPA. Well, I might pay about seventy-five dollars, but that's all it's worth.

HENDERSON. You'll pay every cent of it, like everybody else! And let me tell you something else! You'll go to jail if you don't pay, do you hear that? That's the law, and if you think you're bigger than the law, you've got another think coming. You're no better than anybody else, and the sooner you get that through your head, the better . . . you'll hear from the United States Government, that's all I can say . . . (*The music has stopped. He is backing out of the room.*)

GRANDPA (*Quietly*). Look out for those snakes.

(HENDERSON, *jumping, exits off L.*)

STYLES

The term "style" refers to the way in which a play is written, acted, and produced. Dramatists adopt the language and action they feel best express their ideas, and directors and scenic artists present the plays in the form most suited to the spirit of the script.

Classification of plays today is complicated by the fact that many modern playwrights are breaking away from the definite styles which have proved popular or of special value in the past, ignoring or combining them to suit themselves. Seeking emotional responses primarily, they disregard conventional structure and standards.

Fortunately for you, plays of all eras and areas are now being made available to you as the number of theaters across the country increases. Therefore, you can become familiar with all styles of drama of the past and present. You can discover those which appeal to you most by appreciating the intrinsic values of all of them.

Classicism

Classicism was the style made popular in France; it was based upon the Greek and Roman conventions. Etienne Jodelle established it in the 1550's, Pierre Corneille perfected it in the seventeenth century, and Eugene Scribe crystallized the tradition of "the well-made play" in the early nineteenth century. Scribe's hundreds of mediocre plays were imitated and greatly improved upon in the Victorian plays popular in England and America. Many of the finest plays of the twentieth century exemplify its best characteristics in plot and character development, worthwhile themes, and perfected dialogue.

Romanticism

In romantic drama, life is shown as people dream it should be: the setting is an ideal spot of great beauty; the language is polished, frequently poetry at its best; the characters belong to the aristocracy and live magnificently; the protagonist is a great soul facing meaningful problems and conflicts in which he may succeed or fail, but always nobly; and the antagonist is worthy in many ways, perhaps possessing courage and intellectual power, but he is evil on a big scale. Comic relief is usually afforded by richly humorous members of the "lower orders." As you read the fascinating biographies of the nineteenth-century romantic actors, you will find them shining in exalted roles in which they face terrific odds.

At its best, romantic drama reaches the heights of Shakespeare, Goethe, Schiller, Rostand, and, among our contemporaries, Maxwell Anderson, Christopher Fry, Ferenc Molnár, Jean Giraudoux, and Robert Bolt. At its poorest, romantic drama becomes overly sentimental, flowery, exaggerated, and theatrical. However, it did produce the "grand" style of acting, with renowned stars playing famous roles, in the brilliant sets and costumes of the days of Booth, Barrett, Irving, Ellen Terry, Bernhardt, and many other famous stars.

Realism

In protest against the artificiality and impossibility of too much romanticism, realism developed in the late nineteenth century. Plays depicted life as it actually is — often sordid, ugly, and unhappy, although not necessarily so. The characters talk and act as people in ordinary life do in whatever social group they belong; the outcome of their problems is what it would logically be in the world today under ordinary conditions. Selective realism — using selected scenes to typify reality — is now the usual style of plays dominating almost all forms of theater, both of stage and of screen.

Henrik Ibsen was the father of realism. He shocked the romantically indoctrinated audiences with his significant dramas, destined to be produced the world over although not accepted in his own country when they were written. You have probably seen some of his great plays — *An Enemy of the People, Ghosts, The Master Builder*, and *A Doll's House.*

George Bernard Shaw introduced Ibsen to the English-speaking world, but the plays had to be produced in a private club because they were barred from the public theaters. Shaw himself followed the realistic style, and introduced philosophical discussion between voluble people so successfully that he became the outstanding dramatist of his era. The brilliant humor and extraordinary situations in which he places his stimulating characters account for his continued popularity. This is exemplified in his *Pygmalion*, so exquisitely revamped in its musical version, *My Fair Lady*. Shaw's *Saint Joan* is considered by many theater lovers to be the greatest play of the twentieth century. In it the heretofore romanticized historical figure becomes a real person of common sense and courage, stubbornness, and idealism, who is capable of spiritual leadership in a time of national crisis.

Naturalism

The style called naturalism grew out of realism but became exaggerated in the early years of this century, culminating in photographic perfection of detail under its exponent, David Belasco. Naturalism is often sordid and shocking. Life as it is with no holds barred is its central topic. The famous director-actor Constantin Stanislavski brought the naturalism of acting to its finest level in the realistic plays of Anton Chekhov, produced in the Moscow Art Theater, where the tradition is still carried on.

Fantasy

Largely a form of romantic drama but frequently introduced into sequences in realistic plays, fantasy deals with unreal characters in dreams and scenes imaginary in time and space. The land of make-believe forms the background — inhabited by spirits with supernatural powers, gods from another world, and the eternal personalities of

Pierrot and Pierrette, Harlequin and Columbine, Punchinello, witches and will-o-the-wisps. Some of the most popular adult productions are Shakespeare's *A Midsummer Night's Dream* and *The Tempest*, and such modern plays as Maxwell Anderson's *High Tor* and *Star-Wagon*, Paul Osborn's *On Borrowed Time*, and J. M. Barrie's *Peter Pan* and *Mary Rose*.

Symbolism

In the symbolic play, the dramatist points his theme by having his characters and props, even sets, actually exemplify his ideas. In Maeterlinck's *The Blue Bird*, Mytyl and Tyltyl are woman and man seeking to find happiness by learning life's secrets; the diamond in Tyltyl's cap is truth, which shows inner realities when turned; and happiness is the blue bird in their home, which they recognize after their dream is presented in ten symbolic scenes.

Many of our finest modern plays have symbolic overtones. In *Death of a Salesman*, Arthur Miller uses his protagonist as the symbol of the ordinary, blundering man caught in the incomprehensible problems of earning a living for his family and meeting the spiritual obligations of fatherhood. Eugene O'Neill uses masks in *The Great God Brown* to show the phases of his protagonist's personality in relation to other people; he shows the personification of jungle fears in *The Emperor Jones*, and in *Anna Christie*, of the "debil sea." Tennessee Williams in *The Night of the Iguana* uses the captive Mexican lizard as a symbol for the people, who are literally "at the end of their rope" but who are freed from their particular obsessions.

Allegory

Closely allied to symbolism, the allegory definitely represents abstract qualities like Truth, Justice, Love or personalities like Death, God, and Man as characters in a play which has as its goal the teaching of moral concepts. It has been a popular form of storytelling throughout the history of mankind.

The greatest allegory of them all is *Everyman*. Everyman is suddenly summoned to meet Death. He must appear before God and seek salvation. In his desperate need, all of his friends fail him — Five Wits, Fellowship, Kindred, Discretion, Beauty, Strength, and Knowledge; only his Good Deeds, enchained and feeble, will go with him. *J.B.* by Archibald MacLeish, the modern version of *The Book of Job*, is a fine contemporary allegory. Thornton Wilder's *Our Town*, which

A scene from Edmond Rostand's Le Chantecler, *which illustrates stylization. Oversized scenery was used so that the "characters" appear in proportion.*

shows how typical human beings in a modern small town are failing to realize the beauty of mankind's daily life, has many characteristics of the allegorical play.

Stylization

A coalescence of script and production is achieved in stylized drama. Stylized productions bear the stamp of the personality and individual point of view of the director-designer. Orson Welles, in his WPA productions, staged a modern-dress version of *Julius Caesar* on a barren stage without scenery, and a most original voodoo *Macbeth*, with an all-Negro cast in a West Indian jungle. In 1968 in the "mod" presentation of *Love's Labour's Lost* at the Stratford, Connecticut, Shakespeare Festival Theatre, King Ferdinand was a bearded guru and his young lords were robed pilgrims; the princess arrived on a motorcycle in a silver sports outfit; and the tempo and feverish type of entertainment was typical of rock and roll. Apparently limitless are the stylized versions of *Hamlet;* more than one makes a welcome or unwelcome appearance every season somewhere.

Other stylized productions have included current presentations of Ben Jonson's *Volpone*, with the characters masked like the animals they resemble in spirit; *R. U. R.*, in which robots take over a factory   **77** from human inventors, and *The Insect Comedy*, in which insects experience events similar to those of human beings (both of these plays are by the Capek brothers of Czechoslovakia); *Dynamo* by Eugene O'Neill, in which the stage is a huge machine. Rostand's *Chantecler* was a most successful play. It is set in a barnyard and in a forest; the trees and props are magnified in keeping with actors dressed like animals, especially fowls and birds.

The constructivistic sets, consisting of platforms and ladders and ramps, which were introduced by Meyerhold in Moscow, have been imitated in various ingenious ways everywhere today. Such sets form the background for many stylized dramas.

Period plays are considered as stylized when they are presented with exactitude in staging and costuming in the same way they were produced and acted in historical eras and geographical areas. The frequent revivals of Sheridan's Restoration comedies are typical period plays, especially those produced by John Gielgud in London and New York.

Some of television's finest productions, like Galsworthy's *The Forsyte Saga*, Chekhov's splendid dramas, and numerous BBC and Granada plays, are highly stylized period productions.

TWENTIETH CENTURY EXPERIMENTAL DRAMA

This century has seen many changes in theatrical trends; these are continuing to manifest themselves every season. How much they will affect the drama of the future cannot be estimated at the present time, but they will undoubtedly afford plenty of excitement for theatergoers.

The abstract theories of dramatic presentation, expressionism and impressionism, came into being in Germany after the first World War and are still exerting a strong influence on the relation between the script and its interpretation by simplified, nonrealistic sets and emotionally effective use of lights. Closely related to symbolism, expressionism and impressionism are affiliated but not synonymous.

Expressionism

In expressionism the dramatist has a theme, usually centered about ideas of justice, social relationships, and the evils of the machine age. The qualities and thoughts of the characters are expressed against highly imaginative symbolic sets.

The first such play to become a hit in the United States was *Beggar on Horseback*, produced in the twenties and revived in 1970. The

Bertold Brecht's Mother Courage *is an example of epic theater. Note the use of a suggestive rather than a realistic setting, a "token of environment" rather than a copy of a real scene.*

hero, a young musician, is on the verge of marrying the daughter of a big businessman; in a dream he experiences the horrors of an industrial career, an unhappy marriage, and in-law troubles in an exaggerated and amusing nightmare; incidents are all accompanied by the jazz rhythms from a nearby orchestra, the last impression he had before going to sleep. Georg Kaiser's *From Morn to Midnight* and O'Neill's *The Hairy Ape* are expressionistic plays.

Impressionism

The impressionistic play gives the audience the inner reactions of characters under great stress. The trial scene from *The Adding Machine*, Elmer Rice's symbolic drama, is definitely impressionistic in that red lights flash over the stage and the witness box revolves, with the audience feeling with Mr. Zero as he did under the shock of being declared guilty. Georg Kaiser's *Gas* and Ernest Toller's *Man and the Masses* were two of the first impressionistic dramas, both written in protest against war and its effect upon men and women.

Constructivism

This style is having stronger and stronger repercussions in current theater. Originated in the first quarter of the century by Vsevolod Meyerhold in Moscow, it was in direct contrast with the far more widely renowned Stanislavski's realism. Instead of presenting productions based on real life on a picture frame stage, Meyerhold constructed backgrounds of mechanical skeletons on various levels connected by arches, ramps, ladders, and platforms; on these, actors dressed in nondescript coveralls were trained to move with precise symbolic movements at various speeds, representing different states of mind and classes of society. He used movement to take the place of language in his desire to bring the audience into direct participation in the action. He developed the space stage idea and eliminated footlights, bringing the actors into the auditorium, thus foreshadowing the thrust and arena stages of today. The "skeleton scenery" you see so often is the current form of constructivism.

To understand this movement completely, you should read the two authoritative and charmingly written books on Russian drama by Norris Houghton, *Moscow Rehearsals* and *Return Engagement: A Postscript to Moscow Rehearsals.*

You have probably seen similar sets in productions like *Oliver Twist, The Threepenny Opera*, and numerous modern plays; but the acting style is far more rare, appearing in episodes rather than in entire plays.

The Epic Theater

This provocative style also originated in Germany between the two world wars; it is strongly influencing the so-called "modern drama." You can see many productions based upon its principles. Bertolt Brecht's plays are frequently produced in the repertory theaters. These include *Mother Courage and Her Children, Man Is Man, The Caucasian Chalk Circle*, and Brecht's popular opera based on Gay's *The Beggar's Opera*, which he produced as *The Threepenny Opera*. Associated with Brecht was Erwin Piscator, who introduced the use of mixed media: such devices as lantern slides, motion pictures, loudspeakers, radio, and new forms of functional lighting, used instead of conventional scenery. He invented all sorts of heavy as well as mobile

In Jo Mielziner's set for Winterset, *the height of the buildings and the hugeness of the bridge support have a symbolic relationship to the overpowering and tragic situation the central character faces.*

stage machinery for experimental effects. There was no realistic setting for illusion-light was used only to illuminate, never to arouse moods, and only functional and necessary pieces of scenery or furniture were employed.

Mordecai Gorelik, the eminent scenic artist-director, first analyzed the epic theater for the American public in his stimulating book *New Theatres for Old*. In it he explains that it is essentially a "learning theater," whose purpose is to cause viewers to think deeply about important social problems in order to rectify them. The Epic Theater is a reaction against emotionalism and naturalism and the "well made play." Brecht's plays do not involve the spectators in the problems and feelings of the characters as most plays do, and entertainment is a secondary goal. The plays objectively set forth events in episodic form, using broad phases of human experience rather than individual relationships. These plays are therefore easily adapted to the thrust stage and nonrealist backgrounds.

81

Mr. Gorelik predicts that, following the lines laid down by Piscator, theaters of the future will have large mobile units which will enable sets to hang in space, revolve, and tilt at angles, thus serving as tokens of environment rather than as copies of real scenes.

The Avant-Garde Theater

The term "avant-garde" has been used loosely to cover all the controversial styles of advanced theatrical techniques in recent decades. Many techniques accepted today as general theater practices were considered avant-garde at their inception — expressionism, the symbolist plays, epic theater, playing in the round, thrust staging. The translation into English of Antonin Artaud's influential book *The Theater and Its Double* in 1958 strongly affected current play styles in Great Britain and the United States. Artaud stressed that all the senses of the spectators must be caught up in the action of a performance in order to impel an emotional response; the use of enveloping light, sound, and movement rather than words thus encourages breaking away from the traditions of the proscenium stage and the literary structure of plays in order to intensify feeling, not thinking.

In the United States, much of the new experimentation originated in off-Broadway and off- off-Broadway small, obscure buildings; to avoid complications of censorship and the problems of conventional play production, some groups established themselves in cafes and coffee houses to try out exceptionally advanced plays by unknown playwrights. Among these, one of the first to become successful and later to grow into a practical auditorium was Cafe La Mama under the sponsorship of Ellen Stewart. It is important to note that many of these avant-garde movements die in their infancy, some linger awhile, and a few become a part of the living, continuing theater.

Theater of the Absurd

The theater of the absurd is no longer considered by the general public as even avant-garde, but it introduced American audiences to a style of "antiplay" which got nowhere from the standpoint of theme, plot, or characterization. *Waiting for Godot* by Samuel Beckett was the first example to reach Broadway; it was played later the world over. Its success was facilitated by featuring Bert Lahr at the height of his popularity. This lured people into marveling at the unique and incomprehensible production, which had amazed Europe after its opening on January 5, 1953, in Paris. From Paris also came

Eugene Ionesco and Jean Genêt with their revolutionary ideas for backgrounds and situations which produce an emotional reaction, not suspense or motivation. The use of gesture and movement instead of expressive dialogue, and characters without a personality to attract or repel, are also a part of their style.

The absurdists seem to fear that language is deteriorating. In a mechanized society there is little need to think, and, consequently, little need to communicate. In *The Bald Soprano* Ionesco uses worn-out phrases and idioms to show language breaking down into nothingness. In *The Lesson* he lashes out at stifling educational systems which tend to kill off what imagination and spark may be left in the children of a society intellectualized by worthless knowledge. He taunts the audience with a lesson in murder that parallels the potential destruction of man's intellectual pursuits because emphasis is placed on superfluous and purposeless knowledge.

One of the major difficulties encountered in a study of the theater of the absurd is its frequent obscurity in meaning. Audiences have often shaken their heads in confusion at what seemed to be "meaningless attacks on the meaningless." Though sometimes difficult to follow, well-written plays such as Carlino's *Objective Case* and Albee's *The Sand Box* provide a challenge to both the actor and the audience which hopefully would accomplish the goal of the absurdists — to make man feel and react before complete absurdity destroys him.

Total Theater

The concept of total theater will undoubtedly prove a lasting theatrical style. It fuses all the performing arts. At its best it combines a strong plot with impassioned characters, well-written dialogue, and first-class acting, These are enhanced by delineative dancing and mime, atmospheric music with inspirational lyrics, and creative costuming and staging. *The Royal Hunt of the Sun* and *Man of La Mancha* are two you must see on stage and screen.

Theater of Involvement

The participation of the members of the audience in the action of the performance is the keynote of this controversial style. *Paradise Now* was one of the first productions staged by the Living Theater, a group of enthusiasts fostered by Judith Molina; it has become well known here and abroad and has been accepted and rejected with equal fervor. Theatergoers have declared themselves bored, annoyed, intrigued, flattered, and disgusted when they found themselves involved with members of the cast in arguments, physical attacks, and invitations actually to take part in the proceedings. Critics wrote cynical and amusing reviews of the episodes of "liberation, mysteries, and rites" which made up the evening's activities.

Numerous productions have appeared with the obvious objective of producing shock values in episodes and ceremonies. Whole auditoriums become the stage, without sets or scenery but completely surrounding the spectators with light and sound, while actors appear from all directions to intermingle with the audience. Many such productions have been presented by inexperienced producers, but there are some sensational and powerful ones by Peter Brook, the brilliant director of the Royal Shakespeare Theatre in Aldwych Theatre in London; by Jerzy Growtowski of the Polish Lab Theater; and by Dean Robert Brustein of Yale and other heads of university theaters.

Cab Calloway and Pearl Bailey in Hello, Dolly!, *the long-running musical hit.*

ZODIAC PHOTOGRAPHERS

ALLIED TRENDS

Plays are appearing every season using these various styles and utilizing revolutionary technical developments in production media. Future theater may be the sum total of these forms and techniques.

The Musical Play

The use of music in the theater is as old as the dramatic impulse itself. Its modern applications vary from background and mood music used in straight dramatic plays, pantomimes, and variety shows to operas, operettas, musical comedies, and musical plays.

When *Oklahoma!* with its original choreography, delightful music, and spontaneous charm, opened in 1943, it became America's distinctive contribution to modern theater. Based on *Green Grow the Lilacs*, the romantic play by Lynn Riggs, it created the modern form of musical drama. Particularly important in the stage of the school, the musical play has become one of the most popular forms of high school drama. The reason for this new emphasis is obvious — a well-produced musical play contains almost all of the elements necessary for audience appeal: a good story, clever dialogue, interesting characters, well-designed choreography, bouncy tunes, and beautiful and meaningful ballads woven into a sparkling package of color and spectacle that provides excellent opportunities for showmanship and talent. Musical plays have replaced many operettas and variety and "talent" shows because of the tightly interwoven unity of the performing arts.

Oklahoma! has since been followed by a continuous succession of hits and failures on both stage and screen. Some have been based on plays, some on novels or short stories, and some on original plots. A few of the outstanding musical plays are *My Fair Lady*, *Brigadoon*, and *Camelot* by Lerner and Loewe; *Oklahoma!*, *The King and I*, *South Pacific*, *Carousel*, and *The Sound of Music* by Rodgers and Hammerstein; *The Music Man* by Meredith Willson; *West Side Story* by Laurents, Sondheim, and Bernstein; *Annie Get Your Gun* by Berlin and Fields; *Guys and Dolls* by Loesser and Runyan; *The Fantasticks* by Jones and Schmidt; *Lil' Abner* by Panama and Frank; *Oliver!* by Lionel Bart; *Fiddler on the Roof* by Bock, Harnick, and Stein; and *Hello, Dolly!* by Stewart and Herman.

The comic opera is closely associated with the great ones written and composed by Gilbert and Sullivan, in which they satirized the British government and other established institutions during the closing decades of the 1800's. William S. Gilbert developed a close relationship between librettist and composer; this originated the precedent for later successful writing teams like Rodgers and Hammerstein, and Lerner and Loewe, whose words and lyrics were not only extremely witty but also had depth of meaning. A good example is Hammerstein's theme, "You've got to be taught to hate and fear," in a song in *South Pacific*.

The famed D'Oyly Carte troupe has been bringing the Gilbert and Sullivan operas from England to America since the nineties and delighting audiences across the country. These operas are frequently performed in high schools, *The Mikado* and *H.M.S. Pinafore* being perennial favorites.

One-Person Shows

At one time the monodrama was a favorite vehicle for personal appearances. The supreme example was *Before Breakfast*, the Eugene O'Neill tragedy in which a nagging wife drives her husband into committing suicide offstage. Today the one-man show has taken its place in the theater, and a number of actors and actresses have become famous with their arrangements of the life stories and literary works of well-known authors. Witness Hal Holbrook's presentations of Mark Twain and Charles Dickens.

Cornelia Otis Skinner's programs — two, in stunning costumes, centering around the wives of Henry the Eighth, and the modern solo drama in which she plays the three women dominating a man's life — are very popular. Max Morath, although primarily a ragtime piano specialist, has brought back the gay nineties, making a huge hit with critics and public alike in New York, after a great success in old-style theaters scattered throughout the Rockies. Barry Morse in *Merely Players* was also popular in his series of great theatrical personalities in their finest roles, like David Garrick, Henry Irving, and other stars; you may catch this on TV. Television comics use this form frequently on all types of shows, and it is a trend of growing importance in both playwriting and performance.

You will be seeing more and more of these one-man shows, and you may want to work some up for yourself; they are a most appealing form of easily produced theater. The structure is loosely woven, but the presentation should have interesting incidents, with natural conversation, depicting events in the life story of a well-known personality.

In Barrie's lightly satirical comedy, The Admirable Crichton, *the roles of the obsequious butler and the haughty Lady Mary are reversed when the high-born family and its servants are shipwrecked. Bill Travers and Virginia McKenna play the parts here.* NBC PHOTO

Dance Drama

Dance drama is increasingly exciting and dramatic and is rapidly becoming exceedingly popular, reaching a large audience across the country as the formal ballet has never done. Since Martha Graham, Ruth St. Denis and Ted Shawn, Isadora Duncan, and many others broke away from the highly formal and traditional dance forms to create modern choreography, dancing, acting, and music have become allies. Agnes de Mille, Jerome Robbins, Gower Champion, and Robert Joffrey have made the choreographer a key person in modern staging.

Theater of Light

The new art form known as Lumia has been generated from the keyed projection instrument, the Clavilux, which Thomas Wilfred played in public performances in 1922; but it was not until the sixties that it became a potential form of drama. Previously, Pythagorus, Isaac Newton, Bertant Cassel, and others had visualized the connection between the vibrations of sound, light, and color, but only recently has the artist known as the Luminist come into importance in creating dramatic compositions. You can already see the Hall of Light in the Museum of Modern Art in New York, and similar halls are being set up across the country. Lumia is being used in dramatic productions as a visual accompaniment to speech and action, and as projected scenery. Artists are being encouraged to produce abstract dramas in a distinctly new theatrical form. The enthusiasm for psychedelic colors in stage lighting, and in static and mobile scenery to reflect them in exciting effects, will possibly grow into a theater in space without actual scenery, experimented with by Gordon Craig in the early part of this century.

Discussion

1. Which theatrical trends of today are interesting you most?
2. What directions do you think the dramatic forms of the future will take?
3. Do you think the traditions of the enduring plays from the past should be ignored, adapted, or followed in contemporary theater?
4. Discuss the various styles of stage, screen, and TV fare you are seeing this season. What general patterns are they following? Which styles do you think may become lasting successes?
5. What dramatists now popular do you think are writing enduring plays?

A scene from Gilbert and Sullivan's The Mikado. *Kenneth Sandford plays Pooh-Bah and John Reed plays Ko-Ko. This operetta is popular with high schools.*

Bibliography

Brustein, Robert: *Seasons of Discontent*, Simon and Schuster, New York, 1967.

Corrigan, Robert: *Theatre in the Twentieth Century*, Grove Press, New York, 1965.

Esslin, Martin: *The Theatre of the Absurd*, Doubleday, Garden City, N. Y., 1961.

Gorelik, Mordecai: *New Theatres for Old*, Dutton, Everyman's Library, New York, 1962.

Jones, Robert Edmond: *The Dramatic Imagination*, Theatre Arts, New York, 1956.

Priestley, John B.: *The Wonderful World of the Theatre*, Doubleday, Garden City, N. Y., 1969.

EVALUATION OF DRAMA

Watching plays has provided universal entertainment since the days of ancient Greece, but never before have so many people watched so many plays of so many varieties. You can see the best contemporary plays in the increasing number of Performing Arts Centers or local theaters converted from motion-picture houses, the famous dramas of the past in the repertory theaters, and the ultra-modern productions in experimental playhouses. The fine films of the past are available on TV in your own home; and satellite TV presentations of actual performances in the best theaters of England and America will probably be coming to you regularly in the near future.

Many television specials produced by large corporations enable you to see stars of the first magnitude in great dramas you can't afford to miss. Current Broadway commercial hits are probably reaching you in roadshows and summer stock. Theater festivals on practically every university campus are available every summer and make delightful goals for holiday tours. In the motion-picture houses, you have the choice of every form of film from the finest of the highest quality to the lowest and most tasteless ever produced. What plays you watch depends entirely upon your own judgment as to how you wish to use your precious leisure hours.

YOU AND THE DRAMA

Perhaps the biggest bonus of the dramatics class is gaining a real appreciation of theatrical values in order to watch plays, not only intelligently, but with aesthetic and emotional delight. As the work of the dramatics class advances, you will gain a deeper satisfaction in watching the technical backgrounds of distinguished actors bear fruit in their perfected interpretations. The study of plays and their production will give you a cumulative enjoyment in seeing them come alive before your eyes. Therefore, you should see every possible professional performance and then discuss it in class.

In addition there are deeper values. In real life you can seldom follow through the ramifications of the intricate life stories crowding around on all sides; in the theater, because of the art of the playwright, you can see exactly what line of conduct leads to what result. Thus your interest in humanity and the problems common to all men can be intensified and clarified. Also, you can widen your horizon and broaden your interests through the unlimited fields of activity now presented on stage and screen.

You have a still wider responsibility. The future of the theater in the United States depends upon the development of a sound public taste. As a student of drama, you play an important role in improving stage and screen fare by supporting the best and refusing to be satisfied with tawdry, sensational, and vulgar entertainment. Worthy dramatic offerings depend upon the people before as well as behind the footlights. Concerning the relation between the playgoer and the plays offered, the following remarks by Colley Cibber, the famous actor-manager of the early 1700's, are amazingly appropriate 200 years later:

> "It is not to the actor . . . but to the vitiated and low taste of the spectator that the corruptions of the stage (of what kindsoever) have been owing. If the publick, by whom they must live, had spirit enough to discountenance and declare against all the trash and fopperies they have been so frequently fond of, both the actors and the authors, to the best of their power, must naturally have served their daily table with sound and wholesome

diet . . . . For as their hearers are, so will actors be; worse or better, as the false and true taste applauds or discommends them. Hence only can our theaters improve, or must degenerate."

You, too, should demand and know sound theatrical fare, not to become hypercritical by going to a play to tear it to pieces, but to enjoy it thoroughly. Usually the most highly trained theatergoers are the most enthusiastic, because they appreciate the art behind the combined labors of the playwright, the producer, and the actor. They find little enjoyment in a poor play badly acted and produced, but deep satisfaction in a good play beautifully produced and acted. When you have enthusiastically studied all phases of the drama and then have lost yourself in a fine production of a fine play, you will experience the same satisfaction that comes to an artist before a superb masterpiece or to a musician at a splendid concert. Also, when you read a drama, your imagination will set the stage for you and breathe living power into the lines of the play. Thus your leisure hours can afford you a joy many people never experience, and your inner life will be broadened and enriched.

GOING TO THE THEATER

No matter what degree of mechanical perfection plus electronic effects television and screen drama may achieve, they can never create that intangible, magnetic quality which passes from actor to audience. They can never become the coalescence of light and color, voice and movement, mass and perspective, imagination and reality which is a play produced by living actors before a living audience.

To appreciate fully any type of drama and judge it fairly, you must consider the play itself, its interpretation by the actors, its staging by the producer, and its reception by the audience. Your judgment is naturally colored by your personal preference, your immediate state of mind, your social background, and your technical theatrical knowledge. Often the company you are in can make or mar the joy of a performance.

Judging the Play

The type of play must color your attitude toward it. A frothy social satire cannot be judged by the same standards as a romantic drama in blank verse, nor a heavy tragedy by those of a farce, nor an avant-garde vehicle by those of a traditional production.

A scene from Barefoot in the Park, *with Tony Roberts and Penny Fuller. This is a good example of a grouping in which elevation gives emphasis to one actor.*

The theme of the play should receive your first consideration if you are a judicious playgoer. It is the theme about which the keen discussion following a "first night" of a new play centers, and it is their themes which hold the attention of the theatrical world on dramatists of the first rank. Determine for yourself what is the playwright's purpose and be prepared to justify your belief with adequate reasons. You might follow Goethe's example and ask: "What did the author try to do? Did he do it? Was it worth doing?"

The plot should hold your intense interest. If the play is any good at all, you will be asking most of the time: "What is going to happen next?" If you don't care, focus on whether the events are plausible and the situations interesting in themselves. Decide whether there is a convincing climax which stirs you emotionally and a logical conclusion which satisfies you intellectually.

The dialogue and characterization should hold your attention more and more as you see many plays. It is through the dialogue that the dramatist's style reveals itself. His style colors all of his plays, no matter how naturally the characters may seem to speak and act. Clever repartee (the swift give and take of sparkling conversation), apt figures of speech which are a natural phase of the characterization and do not call attention to themselves, and the turn of phrase which only the person speaking would use are all aspects of dialogue to be enjoyed.

Characterization is brought out by the dialogue and gives the actors the incentive to interpret their roles correctly. The individual characterizations you see in performances are frequently the result of careful analysis and discussion between the director and the actors. As you view the completed production, closely watch the characters of the play meet and solve their problems.

Part of the fun of going to a play comes during the intermissions, when you can discuss the theme, the plot, the dialogue, and the characters, and listen to the opinions of people about you concerning them. It is then that you can consider the playwright and the skill with which he has given the actors worthwhile things to say and interesting things to do.

Judging the Acting

It is the acting of the play which arouses the keenest response from the onlookers. Just appraisal of the work of the artists is to be expected as the result of theatrical training. After even a short time in a dramatics class, you should appreciate the discipline and skill responsible for a fine piece of acting. If an actor created a living person for you, you should recognize his ability in utilizing all that is best in his own physical and spiritual equipment to assume another individuality. His projection of his role to the farthest seat in the theater is something you have a right to expect. Failure to do this is a weakness of some modern actors, who frequently seem to become so involved with their own reactions to a role that they forget they have an audience.

A good actor creates a role which is convincing all the time; he is always an integral part of the action. He avoids attracting attention to himself and, by speaking and listening in character, he helps to bring out the center of interest at every moment of the play. He builds up a personality in which you can believe by being natural and

Thornton Wilder's play The Matchmaker *was the source for the musical* Hello, Dolly! *This scene is the same in both versions. The actors are Chapman Roberts and Mary Louise, with Dewitt Hemsley below, under the table.*

spontaneous and by identifying himself with the period and spirit of the play. In this way he makes you think of him not as an actor but as a person really involved in the action taking place.

Today the appearance of actors is playing a smaller and smaller part, and therefore typecasting is not as essential in an actor's career. The public is demanding convincing characterization regardless of reputation, nationality, race, and publicity. The repertory system gives you the advantage of seeing actors in many contrasting roles; the old-style stock companies offered this advantage also. Because many successful Broadway and London plays are brought from the stage to the screen, later to be viewed on TV, you have the opportunity to see the best actors of several generations at close range. Their roles and performances should serve you as friendly challenges and inspiration for your own interpretations, in school and later in your amateur or professional acting.

Appreciating the Production

Never before have audiences been as knowledgeable concerning the actual putting on of a play as they are now, largely because so many theatergoers have specialized in drama in high school and college and have had actual experience backstage. Formerly the average theatergoer knew nothing about the problems of designing and staging a play; he only wanted to enjoy the show without analyzing how it was put together. You will have the advantage of understanding the drama in all its phases and of scrutinizing the methods of its presentation with an intelligent appreciation. You will naturally be more interested in some phases than in others, and may even want to take up some of them as a profession.

The director is the most important factor in the ultimate success of a production and is today being recognized as such. In the past he was the last person involved to receive his deserved praise or blame from the public and press. The director is personally responsible for every phase of the production: the selection and adaptation of the play, the casting of the parts, the interpretation of the characters, the effectiveness of the staging, the length of the rehearsal period, and the total effect of the production.

You will get real enjoyment from noting how the director has developed contrast in casting, costuming, and interpretation; how he has worked out interesting stage pictures which emphasize the center of interest at all times; and how he has created the proper atmosphere to bring out the dramatist's meaning through all his tools — actors, lights, setting, and costumes. You will soon know the names of the best directors as well as those of your favorite actors.

The setting determines the atmosphere of the play. The scenic artist works closely with the director in designing the sets, and is in many ways responsible for the play's success. Working with the stage manager and backstage crew, he creates the proper effects with sets and lighting.

The modern tendencies in scenic art are to create the proper atmosphere, establish the right tempo, and keep the balance of the stage pictures in such a manner that the setting itself is an unobtrusive means of carrying out the fundamental purpose of the play. The magic of modern lighting and mechanical and electronic effects plays a vital part in this. Simplicity, naturalness, effectiveness are the principles in back of modern staging. More and more, for many reasons — the expense of labor in handling sets, the kind of stage being used, the available lighting equipment and mechanical devices— elaborate scenery is giving way to bare stages or screen projections or one flexible plastic center of interest easily rearranged. The disappearance of the proscenium arch and its attendant curtain entails the use of stairways, platforms, and even filmstrips to bring out the meaning. Fortunately you can still see many dramas produced in the style of their own eras—with the naturalistic, period, or elaborately artificial sets of the past.

The reaction of the audience may or may not be a fair criterion in judging the ultimate success of a performance. However, a play is written to be presented before spectators, and if it does not hold the attention of playgoers, something must be wrong somewhere. Usually the fault lies in the play or its production, for the average audience is eager to be pleased.

Of course all plays are not suitable for presentation before all audiences. Off- and off- off-Broadway shows are certainly out of place in conservative towns across the country, and often a play that succeeds on Broadway fails on the road—or vice versa. Local conditions may be colored by religious views or political situations. The degree of culture and sophistication of a community strongly influences the reception of a play. Nevertheless, if a drama deals with fundamental human reactions, presents a definite phase of a universal theme, and is produced in an adequate manner, it is certain to hold the interest of the better type of playgoer.

Cinda Siler, Robyn Baker Flatt, Mary Sue Jones in the Dallas Theater Center's production of Chekhov's The Three Sisters. *The grouping is effective.*

Judging the Avant-Garde Theater

In every era the arts have introduced experimental innovations in attempts to express ideas through fresh techniques, and the theater is no exception. Until an innovation is widely accepted, it is often referred to as "avant-garde."

It is difficult to judge avant-garde theater because the novelty often impresses audiences more than the lasting contribution the new approach might be making to the dramatic arts. Man likes to experiment, yet at the same time he tries to hold on to the traditional and familiar. Especially when the innovation seems too extreme, too unnatural, or too "new," the observer demands a return to the kind of theater he is used to. Changes in form away from Scribe's "well-made play"; use of shock treatment in language, theme, or physical behavior; bizarre makeup or costumes; extreme naturalism in photographic portrayal — all have been tried in recent years. These departures from the "old theater" familiar to Broadway have been initiated in the hope of keeping the legitimate theater from dying out at the hands of the motion picture and television, and of a society straining to break away from tradition and convention.

As a student of the drama, you should want to evaluate the merits of experimental theater. A critic must evaluate these experiments from certain "traditional" criteria. First of all, theater is illusion, and illusion, not reality, is one of its major strengths. Shakespeare said the role of theater is "to hold, as 'twere the mirror up to nature; to show virtue her own feature, scorn her own image, and the very age and body of the time its form and pressure." A mirror shows a reflection of life—never life itself. Therefore, if the events presented in a play appear to be a newscast, the audience is not really observing "theater."

Second, whenever you judge a work of literature, all shock, all spectacle, all obscenity in language and action should be stripped away; if what remains has something to say, provides a clever or entertaining situation, or affords insight into interesting characters, the play may stand as "good drama." But if the work has no theme, no plot, no situation, no characterization, no effective use of meaningful language, it must be rejected as a poor work of art and unworthy of the term "theater."

Third, the ability of such a play to survive time, socio-economic changes, people, and nations is very important. Universality is a prime requisite of great works of literature and art.

Theater cannot stand still, for man and his arts cannot stand still, but change in the theater must be judged carefully in order that this, the most forceful of man's artistic expressions, does not become self-destructive. Past experience has shown that when the appeal of theater was to man's weaknesses rather than his strivings upwards and outwards, both the theater and society retrograded.

WATCHING DRAMA ON TELEVISION

Watching television drama can be a memorable experience when a fine play, novel, or story has been intelligently adapted to the medium and produced with a cast of distinguished artists. In the busy life you live these days, it is not always possible to watch quietly at close range the actors interpreting great roles. However, your dramatics teacher may be glad to give you credit for doing so if you report with discrimination. There are, alas, not too many television dramas worthy of your time and effort!

Selecting Your Plays

Check each week's dramatic offerings for those you can't afford to miss and arrange your schedule accordingly. The NET Playhouse and BBC productions and any presented by the Public Broadcast Corporation, frequently via communication satellites, are likely to be first class. You will probably see changes in the terminologies of such programs, and some form of pay TV may come in for the better type. The great corporations, like Hallmark and Xerox, will, however, continue to present outstanding theatrical productions with the most brilliant casts available. The seventies may well bring you actual productions from the great stages of the world beamed by satellites and presented in three-dimensional TV. Video cassettes will encourage the creation of home libraries of play productions and thus allow unlimited choice of audio-visual cartridges.

Rental libraries of drama on tape may soon become available as TV cameras convert the home set into a projector for your own programs. Perhaps some of the splendid plays of the late sixties, like Michael Redgrave's adaptation of *Uncle Vanya*, *Blithe Spirit* with Rosemary Harris, *The Magnificent Yankee* with the Lunts, and *Macbeth* with Maurice Evans and Judith Anderson will be repeated by some means. In addition, comparatively recent fine films and many of the old ones of great value will continue to be presented.

Values of Video

As you watch carefully, you will find that television intensifies every word, gesture, and facial expression. When a director has vision and the ability to inspire his actors and technicians with an appreciation of the peculiar values of video, televised plays can achieve a reality lacking on both the stage and motion-picture screen. Of course, videotape has eliminated live television to a great extent and has permitted far greater accuracy in performance and greater variety in locations and effects, but it has lost the immediacy and vitality of some of the early video plays.

There are interesting comparisons to be made while watching TV and stage plays. Of course, like stage plays, television dramas also involve the play itself, actors interpreting the characters, the staging, and the unseen audience. Although videotape permits a greater variety of locations and effects, it does limit the TV playwright in other ways. With only the average thirty, sixty, or ninety minutes in which to present his story, the TV playwright must establish his characters and their problems rapidly and proceed to solutions without delay. Another important influence is that television audiences vary widely in age and background. This diversity, plus economic pressures demanding that television must be understood by huge numbers of people in many localities, tests the writer's skill in selecting material and writing dialogue. However, the style of TV drama has been strongly affected by the techniques of successful commercials.

Genevieve Bujold and Roddy McDowall in the Hallmark Hall of Fame production of George Bernard Shaw's Saint Joan *on TV. The closeups of television allow appreciation of the subtleties of acting.*

NBC PHOTO

These encourage rapid-fire production of episodes and situations, with striking close-ups and cinematographic effects rather than dialogue. Thus plots are advanced by one scene blending into another contrasted one without loss of continuity.

In viewing televised drama, you are no longer in the class of the first enthusiasts who would sit for hours walleyed and inert, without discriminating among the various types of programs or judging their values. You will make use of the medium to increase your theatrical background and to keep up with current trends which bring you the latest developments in drama interpreted by leading actors.

SHOPPING FOR FILMS

Never before has the need for "shopping" for movies been so great. The "good old days" when going to the movies was the cheapest and easiest way of seeking good theatrical entertainment seem gone forever. The continuous performances of excellent films from eleven in the morning till midnight in the first-run picture palaces, and the cheaper second runs in comfortable neighborhood playhouses, meant that audiences of all ages and interests could go regularly to see first-class shows. It is true that never before have there been finer pictures technically—wide screens, gorgeous color, splendid acting, international realistic settings photographed in every country of the world—but the subject matter is frequently quite questionable, prices for admission are excessively high, and the performances are limited to bookings on a definite schedule. Going to a movie has become a matter of real expenditure of time, money, and patience, frequently without sufficient reward. The really fine films produced at prodigious cost are not always available amid the influx of cheaply made, tawdry pictures, frequently the most obscene, violent, and shocking since movies became the great public form of entertainment.

Guidance

From 1930 to 1966, film fare was controlled by the film industry's own "Code to Govern the Making of Motion Pictures." Various agencies backed the publication of the "Green Sheets," reviews of previews of all new pictures by members of leading national organizations. The *Audio-Visual Guide* edited by Dr. William Lewin was available for high schools as *Photoplay Guides*, with reviews and the historical backgrounds of fine films. Thus a student could know which films he wanted to see, and dramatics classes frequently went in groups after studying the guides. When this voluntary censorship by the producers themselves was abandoned in 1966, no standards were set up to take its place, and a few independent companies began making the cheapest possible pictures with the greatest possible shock appeal; profanity, nudity, and vulgarity became their stock in trade.

The major studios began producing novels, and scripts from plays, and plots dealing with subject matter never before permitted in the United States, while the popularity of films of uncensored material from abroad increased. The soaring costs of productions of superior quality forced up the price of admission, and frequently second-rate productions were included in the block bookings, until going to highly advertised pictures did not ensure an evening's worth in time and money.

To aid spectators in choosing their film fare, the first classified code in the United States was set up by the Motion Picture Association of America in 1968, to be modified in 1970. Headed "Movie Ratings for Parents and Young People," it lists the following: G—All ages admitted; GP—All ages admitted but parental guidance suggested; R—Restricted, persons under 17 must be accompanied by parent or adult guardian; X—No one under 17 admitted, though the age limit may vary in certain areas.

As a dramatics student, you cannot afford to miss the best film fare, which ranks with the finest ever offered, but shopping for it involves planning ahead, plus a high financial outlay. Fortunately, critical reviews in first-class magazines and newspapers are available, and you should take them into consideration regularly, although you may not always agree with them. As your classwork develops, you will be enabled to set your own standards, so you won't waste your time and money on tasteless, dull films, but can spend them on the many high-calibre ones being produced all the time here and abroad.

Judging a Film

How can you judge the film fare available to you? Modern films are a coordination of mechanical skills, artistic genius, and utilization of modern electronic development. The motion picture is a synthesis of all the arts—architecture, drama, music, and scientific ingenuity.

There are two considerations to keep in mind when selecting your film fare — the human values involved in the story and its interpretation, and the peculiar art values of its production.

The human values are the most important because through the skill of camera manipulation, we are brought so close to the characters portrayed that we become identified with them. Frequently we find ourselves accepting their reactions as valid and failing to distinguish between the false standards of life depicted on the screen and the real values of daily living. This is particularly dangerous in pictures where criminals become heroes, where selfish, petty people are made glamorous and attractive, and where immorality, sadism, and perversion are set up as ordinary phases of normal society.

This is particularly true of the erroneous view of American life which has been spread around the world: the distortions of the luxury of average American homes, the seeming instability of married life, and the exaggerated rapidity with which material success comes without effort, not to mention the recent exaggerations of horror, degeneracy, and moral delinquency. Fortunately, the box office success of our best pictures and the general type of award winners year after year prove that the average motion-picture fan still wants the finer type of film.

The art values peculiar to screen drama represent the work of directors, cameramen, artists, and costume and makeup specialists who bring into visual form the work of the playwrights and novelists. Fundamentally, a motion picture is movement in light and color, and dialogue and sound should be subordinated to the ever-changing picture before the onlookers. The effective use of light and shadow which fixes the characters and events in the plot is the ultimate aim of film production. The stage and screen differ primarily in that there is no limit, except in the imagination of the artists and technicians, to the scenic backgrounds of films. Any place, real or imaginary, can be reproduced in film, and any action, possible or impossible, can be presented.

The work of the sound engineers follows closely in importance to that of the cameramen. Trends vary a good deal in the use of background music. It should never obscure the meaning of the action or distract the attention except in musical shows. The diction and voices must be distinct and pleasing, and the atmosphere of the setting must be maintained by distinctive and authentic sounds, especially in foreign backgrounds.

As you assess the acting on the screen, you must realize that a photogenic quality, peculiar to the medium, is an absolute necessity. In addition, the screen actor must use his voice, body, and talent

Cockney dialect is essential to the plot of Shaw's Pygmalion, *upon which* My Fair Lady *is based. Raymond Massey and Gertrude Lawrence as Higgins and Eliza.*

intelligently to create a living person. Screen acting demands complete naturalness, a responsive voice and body, and a deep enthusiasm for truth in interpretation; affectation and superficiality are less easily hidden than on the stage.

The script writer does not have the importance that the playwright has in the legitimate theater, for action and visual impact are far more important than words. More and more film maker-directors are controlling all phases of film production. They are introducing untrained actors into films by incorporating actual events into the action or by combining their professionals with amateurs in largely improvised scenes. The star system is fading, and scripts have been displaced by episodic storytelling through visual and aural impact rather than by dialogue. However, the best audiences still respond to well-constructed plots with roles which allow actors to develop characterizations through expressive dialogue.

Judging the Production

The Academy Awards have made audiences conscious of all the phases of movie production, with over twenty categories being recognized every year.

The work of the director is being appreciated more and more, and you will find yourself going to see films because of the film maker-director rather than because of the stars. It is the director who determines what is to be the message and atmosphere of the picture and how these can best be emphasized. He selects and inspires the cast to their highest endeavors. He builds up the morale of his army of assistants so that all of them, from the "grips" to the stars, understand his aims and work together to create a perfect unity out of a million details.

One of the most important specialists in film making is the film editor. It is he who takes the thousands of feet of film and puts the pieces together to make the unified whole you call a motion picture.

Naturally you must watch the work of the cameraman, of the sound expert, of all the designers of sets and costumes, and of the special-effects people, especially in settings which are unusual or particularly exotic. Today the camera itself, continually improved, is frequently the star performer. By the use of constantly improved equipment — hand-held cameras, superimposed films, mixing consoles, the split screen, freeze frames, video scanners — a new means has been developed of bringing the spectator into the realms of reality

Julie Andrews and Rex Harrison in Alan Jay Lerner and Frederick Loewe's My Fair Lady. *The musical is based on Shaw's play* Pygmalion.

and fantasy and revealing the thoughts, emotions, and personalities of the characters. Advanced theories, first introduced in 1970 by Gene Youngblood in his brilliant book *Expanded Cinema*, are created constantly and are revolutionizing modern art and entertainment. You can keep in touch with these changes through NET featured programs and current magazines.

On the screen the past, the present, and the future can be revealed in sequence, reflection, or retrospect, and with emotional rather than logical coherence. Thus you live with the characters on every plane of their experience and know their intimate dreams and secrets.

A comparison of a stage and a screen production of the same play is a rewarding experience. For example, *A Man for All Seasons* is brilliant in both mediums, but in the screen version the close-ups of the great star Paul Scofield reveal his amazing inner understanding of every nuance of meaning and feeling, and the gorgeous scenes of the city of London and the views of the Thames bring out the spirit of the place and times as the stage cannot do. One misses the Common Man of the stage play with his various roles and pronouncements, but he would have been a confusing element on the screen.

As a good movie fan, you will base your choice of pictures on your own good judgment, on intelligent reviews by recognized critics — such as Arthur Knight, Stefan Kanfer, Vincent Canby, Stanley Penn, Richard Schickel, Hollis Alpert, Marnfield, and Rex Reed — and on the reputation of the director and producers. You will refuse to be lured into wasting your money by false advertising or sensational titles. You will not choose presentations of sentimental drivel, false standards of living, and unethical conduct just because it is the style to revel in violence, horror, or vulgarity. The revolution in Hollywood as the great studios relinquish their power to the independent producers will bring colossal changes in the motion-picture industry and lead you to follow with increasing interest the activities of the best producers, directors, scenarists, and actors, comparing and analyzing their methods. You will support the best pictures by word-of-mouth publicity and thus contribute to their box-office success. By selecting your motion-picture fare wisely, you will increase your appreciation of all the arts of the theater.

DRAMATIC CRITICISM

Dramatic criticism has been an important phase of modern journalism for many years. Some of the leading literary figures of the United States and Great Britain have served as critics on the staffs of famous magazines and newspapers. Browsing through library materials dealing with the world of the theater, you will find many delightful books by these critics, who make their period come alive in their essays on plays, actors and actresses, directors, and scenic artists. Among them are such authors as George Bernard Shaw, William Winters, John Mason Brown, Alexander Woolcott, George Jean Nathan, Brooks Atkinson, and Stark Young.

Most contemporary magazines and important newspapers have editors of drama, television, and motion pictures, whose regular columns you should follow with continuous interest. The current reorganization of publishing companies and personnel makes any listing difficult, but you should be familiar with the comments of such well-known specialists in the Performing Arts as Walter Kerr,

PHOTO BY WINDY DRUM

A scene from Baylor University's dramatization of Thomas Wolfe's novel Of Time and the River. *This production, under the direction of Professor Paul Baker, utilized motion-picture projectors and multiple stages, in front and on both sides of the audience.*

Clive Barnes, John Chapman, Harold Hewes, Richard P. Cooke, John J. O'Connor, Walter T. Terry, Richard Schickel, Michael T. Leech, and Eric Bentley in *Show, Saturday Review, New Yorker, New York Times, Christian Science Monitor, San Francisco Chronicle, Wall Street Journal,* and *Life*; in the London *Observer* and *Times*; and in the Paris *Realities* (English edition).

The television production of Laurence Hausman's play, Victoria Regina, *won Julie Harris an Emmy award. Here she is as the young queen and as the aging widow sixty years later. Helen Hayes played Victoria on Broadway.*

For a number of years there has been a cold war on between the drama critics and the producers and actors; the cause of bitterness is the reviews of the opening nights of plays. The public usually does not buy tickets for a production that gets poor notices, and since box-office returns strongly influence the length of a run in a big city, few producers can hold out long enough for word-of-mouth comments to decide the fate of a show. It is true that professional critics, especially of the drama, have their biases, and regular attendance at opening nights may make them blasé and possibly unfair in their reactions; but most of them are intelligent and remarkably conscientious and appreciative of really first-class entertainment.

There is now a definite decrease in the importance of opening night reviews, since previews of new plays, begun tentatively in the early sixties, have become more frequent. At a reduced price, a play is produced for several weeks as a prolonged dress rehearsal, with the understanding that important changes may be made before the official opening. Many people are therefore enabled to see plays for which they might not be able to afford good seats later. Also, persons especially interested in play production can attend the previews and then go again after the official opening and see how the director has progressed in making the drama come to life. As more previews of more productions are presented, the bloom of opening night is fading, and word-of-mouth publicity by the spectators is offsetting the box-office effect of adverse reviews.

You may some day want to become a professional critic, for this offers a career full of excitement and aesthetic experience, and a means of knowing personally all the greats of the performing arts. Now is the time to begin writing critiques of all the plays and pictures you see on stage and screen. These critiques can be kept in one section of your notebook and will be a source of great interest to you as you watch your developing sense of appreciation. In your scrapbook, also, keep a section for published critiques of current plays. You may some day have the opportunity to see these plays, or movies based on them, and it will be interesting to compare your reactions with those of the best critics. You will also become familiar with the names and achievements of the best actors, playwrights, designers, and directors. Read the plays when they appear in printed form, and whenever possible, compare your imagined sets with photographs of the production.

EVALUATING A PLAY

The real theater enthusiast frees his imagination and emotions while watching a play. At the same time, he uses his intelligence and discrimination to heighten his appreciation of what he is seeing. The following questions may help you to evaluate the plays you attend, the television dramas you watch, and the movies you see.

THEME

1. Is the fundamental idea underlying the play true or false in its concept of life?

2. Is the theme warped by a distorted or limited life experience on the part of the author?

3. Does seeing the play add something positive to your understanding and experience?

4. Is the theme consistent with the setting, plot, and characters presented in the play?

5. Do you agree with the author's philosophy?

6. In your opinion, should the general public be encouraged to see the play? Should it have been produced at all or even written in the first place?

PLOT

1. Does the play have a clear-cut sequence of events?
2. Does it rise to a strong climax?
3. Does the suspense hold until the end?
4. Was the play emotionally stirring?
5. Are you satisfied by the final outcome?
6. If not, what outcome would you consider more satisfactory?
7. Which are most interesting, the events, the people, the style of presentation, or the shock value?

CHARACTERIZATION

1. Are the characters true to life?
2. Do the characters seem to fit into the social and geographical background of the play?
3. Do they definitely arouse such feelings as sympathy, affection, amusement, disgust, admiration, or hatred on the part of the audience?
4. Are their actions in keeping with their motives?
5. Are the situations at the climax and conclusion the result of their inherent natures?

STYLE

1. Is the dialogue brilliant and entertaining in itself?
2. Is the dialogue consistent with the characters and setting?
3. Is the dialogue an end in itself or an adequate means of plot advancement and characterization?
4. Does the dialogue make you think about the playwright or about the characters themselves?
5. After seeing the play, do you remember lines because of their significance or beauty?
6. Would people of the social class represented talk in real life as they do in the play?
7. Is the power of expression worthy of the ideas expressed?
8. Do sound, electronic effects, and staging take the place of words?

COURTESY OF HOFSTRA UNIVERSITY

The Hofstra University Drama Department's Rashomon *was selected as one of the ten best collegiate theater productions for 1968-69, and opened the first National Festival in Washington, D.C., the following spring. Washington critics praised the professional calibre of the production. See also page 90.*

ACTING

1. Is the interpretation of any given role correct from the standpoint of the play itself?

2. Does the actor make his character a living individual?

3. Is he artificial or natural in his technique?

4. Are you conscious of his methods of getting effects?

5. Does he grip you emotionally? Do you weep, laugh, suffer, and exult with him?

6. Is his voice pleasing and his charm magnetic?

7. Is his use of dialect correct in every detail?

8. Does he keep in character every moment?

9. Do you think of him as the character he is depicting or as himself?

10. Does he use the play as a means of self-glorification, or is he an intrinsic part of the action at all times?

11. Does he apparently cooperate with the other actors, the director, and the author in interpreting the play by knowing his lines, helping to focus the attention on the center of interest, and losing himself in his part?

12. Does he become an acceptable part of the style of the production?

STAGING

1. Is the setting in keeping with the play itself?

2. Is it appropriate in its design to the locality and social strata represented?

3. Is it beautiful and artistic in itself?

4. Is it conducive to the proper emotional reaction to the play?

5. Are the costumes and properties in harmony with the background?

6. Does the setting add to or detract from enjoyment of the play?

7. Is the interest centered in the total effect or in the details?

8. Has the expenditure of money on the production been justified by the total value of the effects obtained?

9. Do you enjoy the style of the staging and special effects utilized?

AUDIENCE REACTION

1. Is the audience attentive, involved, or restless during the performance?

2. Is there a definite response of tears, laughter, or applause?

3. Is there an immediate appreciation of clever lines, dramatic situations, and skillful acting?

A scene from a high school production of Little Mary Sunshine, *a "spoof" on the Nelson Eddy-Jeanette McDonald type of musical popular in the twenties.*

4. Is the applause spontaneous and wholehearted, or politely perfunctory?

5. After the performance are people hurrying away, or do they linger to discuss the play? Have any or many people left before the performance ends?

6. Is the audience apathetic or animated, bored or buoyant, serious or scoffing?

7. To what types of people does the play seem to appeal?

Bibliography

Allen, John: *Going to the Theatre*, Phoenix House, London, 1962.

Atkinson, Brooks: *Tuesdays and Fridays*, Random House, New York, 1963.

Blau, Herbert: *Impossible Theatre*, Macmillan, New York, 1964.

Cole, Toby: *Playwrights on Playwriting: The Meaning and Making of Modern Drama*, Hill and Wang, New York, 1960.

Dietrich, R. F.: *Art of Drama*, Holt, New York, 1969.

Kerr, Walter: *Theater in Spite of Itself*, Simon and Schuster, New York, 1963.

Nathan, George Jean: *The Magic Mirror*, Knopf, New York, 1960.

Priestley, John B.: *The Art of the Dramatist*, The Writer, New York, 1955.

Whiting, John: *On Theatre*, Dufour, New York, 1966.

Wright, Edward A., and Lenthiel H. Downs: *A Primer for Playgoers*, Prentice-Hall, Englewood Cliffs, N.J., 1958.

PART 2

Interpreting the Drama

chapter 5

IMPROVISATION

Are you ready to act? The approach that should help you gain confidence "on the boards" is called improvisation — the impromptu portrayal of a character or a scene. You will make up character, lines, and action as you go along without a formal script. You will have a lot of fun at the same time you are learning some of the fundamentals of acting and getting better acquainted with your classmates. Imagination is the key to improvisation. You must learn to "say the most with the least" — that is, you must convey personality and physical traits, conflicts and desires, age and dress with a minimum of aids. Sometimes you may be allowed to use a few props, but character must be conveyed by voice, posture, and bodily movement.

Drama is the link between thought and expression; it depends upon words and action rather than upon words alone. Drama began as pantomimed descriptive action, became stylized dance, and then **118** was ritualized into formal dramas. Words could not convey the full excitement of the great hunt or battle, and so bodily movements were added by the actor-storyteller. The playwright must turn action into words, and the actor must turn those words into action. When improvising, however, you must create both words and action, remembering Shakespeare's advice to the Players: "Suit the action to the word, the word to the action." As a result of your improvising, you should have a better understanding of what goes into a play and should develop a keener appreciation of clever lines, good action, effective blocking, well-developed characters, and strong plots.

Spontaneity and freshness at each performance are the goals of the director of a play, the challenge to the cast, and the pleasure of the audience. However, after weeks of rehearsal or after many performances, the "illusion of the first time" is sometimes difficult to capture and a play becomes stale. Improvisations are enjoyable in their you-never-know-what's-coming-next freshness; they should help you appreciate the sparkle that comes with a first-time performance. You will appreciate the most important factor in the execution of lines or action — timing. Play casts may rehearse for weeks to achieve the kind of fresh, natural timing that may come as you improvise.

FOUNDATION OF INTERPRETATION

Improvisation is the foundation of interpretation just as pantomime is the foundation of acting. It is the first step in learning to laugh and cry at will. At the heart of theater is discipline, especially self-discipline. It demands physical and mental control, adaptability, acceptance of and positive response to criticism. "directability," and cooperation with others.

Although improvising emphasizes the creative — doing rather than telling — the beginning performer often wants to experience the actual emotion rather than to portray it. The student must always bear in mind that a person may go only so far and still be acting. Beyond that point, the actor *is* rather than *is pretending to be.* This is where the discipline enters in: the character, like makeup and costume, must be subject to removal by the actor after the scene is over. The actor should grow as a result of the performance, but he must never allow a characterization to engulf his own identity. When that happens, he is no longer an actor.

What is happening now is the keynote of improvisation. Improvisation focuses your attention on natural actions and reactions and should force you to concentrate on immediate responses. All action

This scene is from the operetta Love Is a Game, *by Pierre Petit.*

should be motivated only by what you already know about the characters and situation and by what is brought forth as you improvise. You do not have the advantage — or disadvantage — of knowing what lines come next in a script. You must play it as it develops. You will learn how a scene may change direction as the result of a single line or action. You may even find it necessary to meet one of the toughest challenges that faces an actor: to "do nothing effectively" — that is, to be on the stage, visible, but not playing an active part in the scene. In such cases, you must get the audience to accept your presence without being distracted; to call attention to your presence would be scene-stealing. You will learn to appreciate the inter-character relationships and how essential it is that each actor play his part as a member of the team.

You will appreciate even more a well-written script, which is the finished product of many improvisations that passed through the author's mind while he was designing the action. In fact, the trial run of most plays is a form of improvisation where the playwright sees "how it plays" and makes necessary changes in the script before the big opening. You will also realize why it is said that a well-written play has no wasted words. Sincere characterization will develop during improvisation to become deeper and more convincing as you proceed toward formal acting. You will begin to feel the role and sense when you are only impersonating the character and when you or a fellow actor is "putting on the cloak but not the soul" of the part.

When your character is described, no matter how simply, you should immediately ask, "Who am I? What kind of person am I? When does this action take place? How should the audience react to me? How am I different from the other characters?" and, finally, "What are the fewest things I can do to convey the most?" You will soon learn that a raised eyebrow, a silent stare, a one-word response, or a groan may convey more than a dozen sentences. Try also to determine the mood of the scene. Ask yourself how your character can contribute to the complication and resolution of the idea to be presented.

In your characterization, do not yield to the common impulse to "play the character down." Shallow characterizations are weak characterizations. Luigi Pirandello said that man plays a "game of masks" in life, putting on a different mask for each person or occasion he faces. Seldom does he want anyone to see what is really behind the mask. The convincing actor lets the audience see the various outer masks of his character, but also allows them to see what is behind, even if only for brief moments. When this is carefully worked out, the audience sees a well-rounded, thoroughly developed personality.

Improvisation provides you with your first opportunities to hold up the masks, but it should also teach you the dangers found in a characterization that is as thin as a single mask. There are certain "masks" that are identifiable in theater. As you read about the commedia dell' arte, the humours, and the stock characters (Chapter 10), you will see how these personality types can give you an insight into character analysis and help you in more complex improvisations.

The improvised approach to acting is being adopted by many directors, and most directors encourage improvising while the actor is feeling his way toward his character. Some directors are using a "completely improvised" approach. This creative experience has certain benefits for the developing actor, but the production usually suffers from want of direction, unity, and coherence. A combination of inner-developed improvisation and outer-lead direction usually brings forth the best in theater.

IMPROVISING SCENES

With the class divided into groups of not more than four persons each, select one incident around which to build your scene, and decide whether it will be the opening event, the climax, or the conclusion of an imagined play. You can get your material from any source you wish. Some suggestions are the pictures in this book, newspaper clippings, cartoon captions, and anecdotes from magazines; events in your own or your parents' and friends' lives; or historical and literary sources. The suggestions at the end of this chapter may be of use.

Decide on the main idea you want to put over and on the general mood. You may do any kind of scene you want — comic or sad, fanciful or realistic — but each character must be a distinct type, totally different from the others. You should avoid such generalized scenes as those involving girls in a dormitory or boys as members of a baseball team. The greater the difference in age, personality, and type among the characters, the more contrast your scene will contain.

Work out your stage setting carefully, knowing just where the real or imaginary entrances will be. You probably will have nothing more than a table and a few chairs to work around. You will not use any doors, windows, or heavy props, but you can explain what they are and where they are located before the action starts. Even better, suggest entrances and major props by your acting. You may carry any small articles you need, since this is improvisation, not panto-mime. You may even use costumes and makeup if the class as a whole decides to do so. In turning the classroom into a street, ballroom, theater dressing room, office, or whatever you choose, you are developing not only your own imagination but also that of the rest of the class. They will see whatever you make clear to them, first by your explanation and then by your performance.

Preparing your part follows the suggestions in Chapter 1 for reading your first scene. Visualize your character in detail and try to feel his emotions. Make up dialogue which you feel will be appropriate to your character and to the situation he is in, though it will not nec-

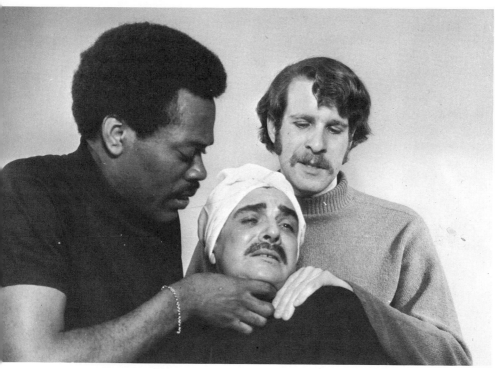

COURTESY OF KARAMU HOUSE

Samuel Watkins, Tedd Burr, Jon Estrin in The Indian Wants the Bronx, *by Israel Horovitz, at the Karamu Arena Theatre in Cleveland.*

essarily be the exact wording to use before the class. Before you enter, take on the physical attitude of your character in accordance with his age, size, and mood. Walk in character as you enter and remember that your audience is out front.

On stage, talk loudly enough to be heard and don't hide behind other people or pieces of furniture. Try not to stand with the others in groups on one side of the stage or in straight lines; instead, keep your stage well balanced. Take plenty of time to speak and move so you can create a definite impression. Most important, keep in character all the time — listen and speak as the character would in the situation, and lose yourself in his actions and reactions.

As you get more practice in improvising scenes, you can begin to learn some of the subtleties of acting. You will find that you can stand still without fidgeting and you can make definite gestures when you feel the need, avoiding the little, aimless ones. When you must move

This scene is from The Hostage. *a play by Brendan Behan, at the Cornell University Theatre in 1969.*

to a chair or toward another person, learn to go straight there without rambling. If you are to pick up an article, actually see it before you touch it. By observation you will learn that the head usually reacts first (sometimes the eyes), then the torso, and then the rest of the body.

INDIVIDUAL IMPROVISATIONS

After working in groups, you can try to develop individual characters in definite situations, reacting to imaginary persons or crowds, or showing particular moods. It is harder to work by yourself than in a group, but you can, by yourself, take more time to create a personality and to feel more deeply.

In these improvisations, keep relaxed and have fun. Don't make the scenes a chore or feel embarassed by the reactions of other students.

COURTESY OF HARRY H. SCHANKER

In a high school production of Blithe Spirit *by Noel Coward, the spirits of Charles'
deceased wives blow into the ears of Madam Arcati, the mystic.*

Remember that they are on the same spot! Don't let classmates who
seem to fall right into a character without apparent effort discourage
you from trying to do the same thing.

If you keep practicing all sorts of characterizations on the spur of
the moment at home, you will find doing so in class much easier. Try
being all sorts of people — Joan of Arc at her trial, a star during a
television interview, an Olympic champion after a big event, and so
on. Get yourself into all sorts of emotional states, laughing out loud
and even crying if you can. With no one around, you will not feel
silly, and the practice will show in your classwork because you will
be more responsive and sensitive to changing moods and situations.
You will find your voice and body becoming more flexible and expressive and your impersonations much better.

REMEMBER: Improvise! Fill the "gaps" made by your own or another performer's actions or lines and make "gaps" for others to fill. Feel free to experiment, using motivation as your impelling force. Imagination will be the key to characterization, so make every look, every line, and every action count! Every now and then, you will realize that you have caught another personality, if just for a moment, and will know what it is to feel like an actor!

Applications

The following suggestions for improvisations provide a step-by-step progression from simple emotional responses to the improvised writing of a play.

EMOTIONAL RESPONSES

1. Express the following emotional feelings through, first, a facial response and, second, a facial response combined with a bodily reaction.

love	jealousy	grief	shock
hope	ecstasy	embarrassment	sympathy
fear	kindness	understanding	patience
bitterness	scorn	irritability	fickleness
skepticism	rebuke	disbelief	mockery
longing	sarcasm	pleading	courage
greed	happiness	mourning	surprise

2. Place the following items in individual paper sacks. Each member of the class must reach into a sack, feel the object which is in it, say "one thousand one" silently, and then convey the sensation he received by a facial expression and a one-sentence reaction.

sandpaper	cold cream	raisins
cooked spaghetti	feathers	knitting yarn
a cotton ball	a flower petal	cracker crumbs
rough tree bark	a piece of lettuce	a marble
a pickle	crumpled cellophane	an ice cube
sawdust	a baby's pacifier	a piece of fur
a sprig of parsley	steel wool	wet paper
an English walnut	a grape peel	a sardine
burlap	whipped cream	a spring

3. React to the following sentences with one gesture or bodily stance.

Your face is red!	Do you always look like that?
I hate you!	I think you're frightened.
You have pretty eyes.	You're standing on my toe.

I love you.
Who do you think will win?
Relax, and count to ten.

How much do you really weigh?
Did you understand what I said?
Does the medicine taste so bad?

PANTOMIME

1. Act like the following:

    a tear drop
    a floating cloud
    a clock
    a delicate snowflake

    a raspy hinge
    an animated doll
    a weather vane
    a spinning top

2. React bodily to the following:

    a sharp slap
    a driving rain
    a biting wind
    sticky tape

    a pin prick
    a piercing siren
    a moonless night
    rain on the roof

    a stubbed toe
    frostbitten fingers
    hay down your back
    scorching pavement

3. React facially to these words:

    red
    here
    friend

    twilight
    encourage
    fool

    butterfly
    perpetual
    Sunday afternoon

    springtime
    tranquility
    loneliness

VOCAL RESPONSES

Make up a list of statements similar to the examples below, exchange your list with that of a classmate, and react to one statement as five different people.

Example of statement: You have just said, "I don't like asparagus!"
Respond as: Your mother, your doctor, your waiter, your hostess, your little daughter

Statement: You have just said, "I've been asked to the prom!"
Respond as: Your best friend, a jealous rival, your ex-boyfriend, the teacher whose class you have interrupted, your father

FAMOUS PEOPLE

1. Make up a list of quotations, real or imaginary. Improvise the situation leading up to the quotation and end with the quotation.

    Examples: "Et tu, Brute?"
    "Give me liberty, or give me death!"
    "Damn the torpedoes, full speed ahead!"
    "Ask not what your country can do for you, but what you can do for your country."
    "You may fire when ready, Gridley."
    "Which way did they go, George?"

2. With a single stance, a single gesture, or a combination of the two, portray the following:

> Leonardo da Vinci painting the "Mona Lisa"
> Ben Franklin flying his kite
> Your favorite star accepting his first Oscar
> Napoleon at Waterloo
> Nero playing his lyre while Rome burned

Now create your own list from contemporary situations and people.

3. Improvise the dialogue and actions of famous people in the historical scenes for which they are remembered.
4. Repeat your improvisation of Exercise 3, but change the ending.
5. Have several famous personalities respond in character to the same imaginary situation.

SCRIPTS

1. From a description of the following situations, characters, or both, develop some scripts.
   a. Two salesgirls are discussing a department manager they dislike; he appears and accuses one of them of having stolen a necklace which has disappeared. Work out your own solution.
   b. A father meets his fifteen-year-old daughter in the hall at midnight on her return from a party which ended at ten-thirty. Show what happens when they meet.
2. The microcosm is "the world on the head of a pin" — people from varied walks of life are thrown together by chance to face the same situation.
   a. An elevator is caught between two floors. Work out your own characters, their reactions, and the conclusion.
   b. Do the same thing with people in a lifeboat together, in a taxi stuck in a traffic jam, and on a subway during a power failure.
   c. Read some works of literature having a microcosmic structure and improvise a similar situation — for example, "The Outcasts of Poker Flats," "The Ambitious Guest."
3. Read about the stock characters in the commedia dell' arte in Chapter 10 and write your own scripts using these characters.

LITERARY SKETCHES

1. Improvise a scene from "The Devil and Daniel Webster" by Stephen Vincent Benét.
2. Improvise a scene from one of Guy de Maupassant's short stories, such as "The Necklace" or "A Piece of String."
3. Improvise a scene from "The Lady or the Tiger" by Frank R. Stockton.
4. Improvise a scene where the Fox and the Cat tell Pinnochio of the wonders of Candyland.

IF YOU WERE . . .

After deciding what roles each person will play in the scene, reenact some event, real or imaginary, such as the following:

1. You are members of the Roman Senate when Julius Caesar has just been stabbed to death. Each of you must recall something Caesar did to you that makes you support or reject the conspirators.
2. At lunch someone rushes in with the news that a spaceship has just landed in City Park. Speculate on ship, occupants, origin, and so forth.
3. Just given an engagement ring, tell the world about it, including your ex-boyfriends and your fiancé's former admirers.
4. The Duke Godiva and his court are together when word is brought in that Lady Godiva has just ridden through the streets.

RUMORS ARE FLYING

Begin with a simple rumor and expand it, each person adding a new detail, character, twist, and so on, and tell the next person about it by improvised action until you have created a working script.

POTPOURRI

Now, after everyone has been in at least two improvisations, dream up new situations, rewrite scripts you have previously used, or make new scripts from news articles or works of literature. Use some of the characters the class has created and let them play out the new situations.

CREATING THE IMPROVISED PLAY

Divide the class into groups of five to eight persons. In a discussion, each group is to work out a script that could be made into a simple, improvised play. Decide on the theme of your play, the characters, the basic conflicts, and the style that you would like to try. After improvising the script several times to establish some blocking, lines, and workable scenes, fill in your outline until you have a skeletal script. Improvise two or three more times and you will be able to set down a written script created by the improvised approach to acting.

Bibliography

Rockwood, Jerome: *The Craftsmen of Dionysus: An Approach to Acting,* Scott, Foresman, Glenview, Ill., 1966.

Spolin, Viola: *Improvisation for the Theater: A Handbook of Teaching and Directing Techniques,* Northwestern University Press, Evanston, Ill., 1963.

chapter **6**

PANTOMIME

Pantomime is the art of expressing dramatic ideas without speech. Because the actor is seen before he is heard or understood, it is the first technical phase of your interpretive training. It was also the first form of acting, or as Webster puts it, "theatrical entertainment in dumb show." Pantomime preceded the drama in ancient times, kept pace with it through the Middle Ages and Renaissance, and threatened to overshadow it in the first quarter of the twentieth century with the silent picture. Throughout the ages pantomime has gone hand in hand with dancing and is now outdistancing the formal ballet in the intensely dramatic modern trends entrancing the public today.

Traditional pantomimes have delighted European and Asiatic audiences for centuries, attaining their highest form in the commedia dell' arte of Italy in the sixteenth century. Emphasizing polished bodily response in formalized scenes, the famous characters of Harlequin, Columbine, Pantaloon, Pierrot, and Pierrette have survived in many popular one-act plays. Traditional pantomimes can still be seen in the renowned Tivoli Gardens of Copenhagen, Denmark. Americans are not familiar with the "pantomimic alphabet" forming the basis of conventional mimes. However, the contemporary master of the individual pantomime, Marcel Marceau, has introduced it here, in his full evening programs on stage and as guest star on television. If you ever have the delight of seeing him in person, watch carefully every expression and movement; these perfectly exemplify the original art.

Current drama is becoming increasingly pantomimic. The outstanding London and New York success *Stop the World — I Want to Get Off*, originally starring Anthony Newley and Anna Quale, was essentially a pantomime in which they acted out scene after scene with technical precision. You may have seen Francisco Reynders and other conventional pantomimists on TV, and of course Charlie Chaplin, Harpo Marx, and Laurel and Hardy films are still in evidence. Popular performers like Danny Kaye, Dick Van Dyke, Carol Burnett, Red Skelton, Julie Andrews, and Martha Raye are only some of the artists whose bodies are instantly responsive and expressive in every role they play.

VALUE OF PANTOMIME

Pantomime is rapidly becoming a part of modern theater. Courses in mime, movement, bodily coordination — under various labels — are a part of the training in fundamentals in all specialized schools of drama and on many university campuses. For example, pantomime is stressed in the highly technical courses required of all members of the American Conservatory Theatre (ACT) of San Francisco. Many of these courses feature excellence in bodily training and are responsible for much of the success of their productions.

You, of course, must remember that technique in acting is never an end in itself but only a valuable means of making your stage movements and facial expressions effective and your voice and speech audible. Acting techniques will help you to communicate more effectively, not only in acting but in daily living. As you meet professional actors everywhere, you will become aware that their mobile features and meaningful gestures are a part of their personal charm. With action taking the place of words in many trends of modern theater, producers are looking for actors physically responsive to direction. The realistic style of acting on the stage exactly as in real life, which was a protest against the ranting and posturing of earlier forms, is giving way to the belief that acting is a performing art responsive to the type of drama being presented.

Your work with pantomime logically follows your experience with improvisation; it will give you the technical means by which gesture and movement may become pictorially effective. In many high schools, improvisation has taken the place of pantomime, but you will find the fundamental principles put into use in daily physical exercises most valuable. Far too many young people today, for fear of becoming artificial and stagey in acting or too conforming to accepted standards of behavior in daily life, are slovenly in appearance and movement. You, as a student of drama, should make every effort to develop a sound technique in the efficient and flexible use of your body. By so doing, you will be able to meet the inner demands of a role under the stress and strain of performance before an audience.

The amateur can never become the artist until he has so mastered the art of acting that he becomes unconscious of his technique, presenting his role naturally while amplifying it sufficiently to form a contact with the person farthest from him in the audience. His innate talent, his intellectual grasp of meaning, his motivation for action, and his emotional involvement with his character are all important; but even they cannot be realized unless the people before him can grasp what he is doing and saying. You can cultivate dramatic skills by study and daily practice until a flexible, graceful body, pleasing, carrying voice, and cultured diction can become a part of your personality.

PURPOSE OF PANTOMIME

A responsive, expressive body is an actor's greatest asset today. For most people, physical coordination and poise are more a matter of training than heredity. The purpose of pantomime is to encourage meaningful movement, significant gesture, and animated facial expression. These can be acquired by systematic exercise to keep your muscles supple, by regular daily practice, and by checking your physical responses throughout the day.

Pantomime demands a flexible and expressive body. Because of the close relationship between physical and emotional attitudes, it is vital that you learn to use your body correctly and effectively by conscious exercise until the right habits are set up and become automatic. All

Children are adept at pantomime. Note what these young actors are expressing as they rehearse a scene for a production of Tom Sawyer. *At the left is Gwen Yarnell, Director of Children's Theatre at Karamu House in Cleveland.*

forms of correct physical exercise are important, especially those which develop muscular coordination and freedom of movement.

The body is to some extent the outer expression of the inner personality; but the inner personality is also partly the result of bodily attitudes. Vigorous health encourages a constructive outlook on life, just as bodily mastery stimulates emotional and mental control. Physical exhaustion after intense emotional acting, illness after a temper tantrum, weeping at moments of great joy or sorrow — all show the close relationship of our internal and external responses.

Since an actor's personal appearance plays a paramount part in his chosen profession, the first work in pantomime deals with normal posture, movement, and gesture. Gracefulness is the happy medium between overrelaxation or flabbiness and overtension or rigidity. Perfect coordination of all parts of the body is a basic requirement of bodily poise and expressive movement.

PHYSICAL TRAINING FOR PANTOMIME

All exercise which coordinates the bodily skills is valuable for you and, of course, today is considered an absolute necessity for health. Fencing and dancing are required courses in most dramatic schools; **133** tennis, golf, swimming, and skiing are urged as hobbies; and jogging, "isometric exercises" which can be practiced at any time, and the deep breathing of yoga are among the many forms of physical exercise advocated on all sides. The insistence upon keeping slim and in good physical condition as well is universal, and regular exercise is considered a necessity today. The good old "daily dozen" and other formal and regular bending, twisting, and stretching of all muscles, as well as deep breathing routines, are still simple means of keeping fit. And whenever possible, do not take a car, elevator, or bus — walk. This is still one of the best exercises.

At all times your body should move or sit as a whole. From the top of your head to the tips of your fingers and toes, the body should be expressive. As a matter of fact, it always is, but not always in the way you might desire. For example, a slovenly walk, a rigid or slouching posture, irritatingly aimless gestures, or a wooden face reveal your personality just as clearly as do purposeful, vigorous movements and a radiant, mobile face. Nine times out of ten, the world will take you at your "face value." You are judged first by your appearance and manner, only much later by what you say and how you say it.

Relaxation

Behind bodily poise and skill in action is relaxation; this is a matter of inner composure and mental awareness as well as physical flexibility. Successful actors, like athletes, must not be tense, emotionally "uptight," or physically stiff; you should learn right away to let go consciously all over, from the top of your head to the sole of your feet, whenever you feel a sense of strain on the stage or in real life. A few deep breaths and loosening muscles all over also help.

Before starting a daily practice of physical exercises, you must get your body relaxed. A complete process for relaxation is given on pages 157 to 160 for your voice work; it is advisable for you to practice this after the following exercises.

1. Raise, lower, and rotate your head without moving your shoulders. Let it roll freely, without the slightest tension.

2. Rotate your shoulders up and down, forward and back, in circles.

3. Move your arms in wide circles, first close to the body and then at shoulder height.

4. Rotate your lower arms from the elbow, toward and away from the body.

5. Rotate your hands from the wrists.

6. Move your arms horizontally and vertically, with wrists leading.

7. Shake your hands vigorously, keeping them completely relaxed.

8. Open and close your fists, stretching the fingers apart and drawing them together.

9. Do the five-finger exercises. Alternate your fingers: little, middle, ring, first, and thumb.

10. Bend your body forward, back, and to the sides.

11. Clasping your hands together, push your arms vigorously above your head. Then rotate your body, keeping your head within your arms.

12. Rotate each leg in circles, kick as high as possible, swing forward and back.

13. Rise on your toes, bend your knees, and sit on your heels.

14. Rotate each foot at the ankle.

15. Pick up marbles with your toes.

Posture

Your posture is fundamental, not only to your health, but to your personal appearance as well. Often good posture offsets a plain face, and certainly in the theater it is of far greater importance. Therefore, the next step in training the body deals with normal posture, movement, and gesture.

To stand properly, hold your body easily erect with chest high, chin up, back flat, and arms and legs straight but not tense. Keep one foot slightly in front of the other, the weight centering on the ball of the forward foot. The following exercise will help you to cultivate good posture. It should be repeated many times.

1. Stand easily erect with your weight on the balls of your feet.

2. Bend forward, perfectly relaxed, with your loosely hanging arms almost touching the floor.

3. Place your right hand on your chest and your left hand at the small of your back.

4. Raise your body, expanding the torso so that you feel your hands being pushed apart.

5. Bring your head to an upright position, with the chin held at right angles to the throat.

6. Drop your arms to the sides. Shift your weight to the ball of one foot and move forward. Keep your chest high, head erect, and the small of your back flat.

Marcel Marceau, contemporary master of the art of individual pantomime.

Walking

In walking, maintain good posture and a sense of exuberant alertness. Face the world squarely with high chest, erect body, and direct glance. "Thinking yourself tall" may help you to carry yourself gracefully. Although the heel strikes the ground a slight fraction of a second before the toes, your movement should spring from the balls of your feet, and it should be easy, poised, and rhythmical.

The length of your step will be modified by many elements such as your height, build, and physical energy. However, avoid striding, mincing, plodding, or tottering. Toeing straight ahead with your weight on the balls of your feet is the natural way to walk, and walking in a straight line keeps the moving silhouette narrow. Except when playing parts which call for it, never place your feet more than two inches apart. Your body should swing easily from the hips, and your arms should swing in easy opposition to your legs. Beware of habitually looking at the ground.

When you turn, rotate on the balls of your feet, shifting your weight from one foot to the other. Never turn on your heels or cross one foot over the other, tripping yourself. Turn your entire body, including your head.

136

Remember to hold yourself easily erect when standing or walking. Avoid the common habits of leaning forward, holding one shoulder higher than the other, looking down as you walk, dragging your feet, walking on your heels, keeping your feet apart as you walk, or tensing any part of your body.

These exercises from daily life are designed to help you to stand and walk in the right way.

Imagine you are standing:
1. At the microphone in your auditorium, ready to give a speech
2. In the doorway of your date's living room, waiting to meet her parents
3. In the garden, watching a sky lark
4. At the curb, waiting to dash across the street when the lights change
5. At the airport, waiting for friends to arrive
Imagine you are walking:
1. On a sandy beach with a fresh wind blowing over the waves
2. On Fifth Avenue in New York City, with the skyscrapers and church spires rising above you
3. In a forest of tall trees on a lovely fall day
4. On a ballroom floor at a formal dance
5. On the stage, trying out for the part of Petruchio or Katharine in *The Taming of the Shrew*

Walking up and down stairs is an excellent exercise. Place one foot in front of the other and lift your weight from the balls of the feet. Think yourself tall and vigorous, keeping a high chest and head. Try not to look at the stairs.

Sitting

Getting to, getting into, and getting out of a chair is often a series of problems. First of all decide where and why you are being seated, and what is the best way to the chair, stool, or bench you will occupy. Normally you walk directly there, but sometimes you have to plan how to get around people and obstacles on the way. When you arrive, you turn and unobtrusively back until the calf of your leg touches the chair and you can drop into it.

In sitting, maintain an erect position. Keep the base of your spine at a 90-degree angle to the seat and lean easily against the back of the chair. Your hands will ordinarily rest in your lap or on the arms of the chair. Crossing your arms on your chest or folding them restricts your breathing and looks tense. Avoid playing with buttons, jewelry, or your hair. Just sit easily erect against the chair. Your feet may be crossed at the ankles, or one foot may be placed slightly in front of the other. Avoid crossing your legs, spreading your feet apart, and resting your hands or elbows on your knees.

In rising, let your chest lead, not your head. Keep your weight balanced on the balls of your feet, placing one foot slightly forward and using the rear one as a lever in pushing yourself up. Never hang on to the arms of the chair or push yourself up from them. Take a deep breath while rising. This relaxes the throat, gives a sense of control, keeps the chest high, and leads into a good standing position.

Crossing and Turning

The center of the stage area is called center, the front is downstage, and the back is upstage. The actor's right is stage right and his left, stage left. To cross means to move from one position to another. On entering the stage, the actor leads with his upstage foot to turn his body toward the audience. Normally all turns are made to the front. In making turns, rotate on the balls of your feet.

Try these exercises in crossing and turning, walking, sitting, and rising.

1. Enter stage right to speak at a microphone downstage center. Cross to center and turn downstage. Stand with your right foot slightly advanced and weight forward. To leave, turn right, shift weight to left foot, and go off right.

2. Enter stage right and cross to center. Remember that you have forgotten something and turn front, rotating on balls of the feet. Go back right.

3. Enter left and walk diagonally upstage to up center where there is an imaginary bookcase. Get a book and go off right.

4. Enter right to wait for someone at a store entrance up center. Turn front and look around. Then turn and pace up and down, looking into the windows on both sides of the entrance. Each time you reach center, turn to look around. Finally give up and go off left.

5. Enter stage right to make a speech. Cross to chair at left center. Without looking at chair, turn front, touching chair with calf of upstage leg. Shift weight to upstage foot and lower body into the chair, keeping head and chest high. Rise, pushing with the upstage leg.

Shift your weight to forward foot and step with back foot. Move to front center. Then turn and bow to chairman. Turn front with weight on forward foot. Return to chair and be seated. Rise to bow for continued applause and sit again. Rise and go off stage right.

6. Enter a living room. Greet the hostess and be seated on a couch. Rise to greet an older person and be seated again. Rise, bow, and leave.

Falling

Some roles will require you to fall onstage. Practicing the following steps will enable you to fall safely and convincingly.

1. Relax, and sway or stagger backwards.
2. Sway forward, dropping the hands and arms.
3. Relax from the ankles and drop on the knees.
4. Bend the knees. Pivot slowly and, as you do so, go closer and closer to the floor. Lower the shoulder which is closest to the floor and slide down.
5. Lower the head to the ground.

Gesture

Gesture is the movement of any part of the body to help express an idea. It may be a lift of the eyebrow, a toss of the head, or a sweeping movement of the arm and hand. A change of attitude is usually expressed first by the eyes, then by the response of the mouth and facial muscles, then by the reaction of the torso, and lastly by the motion of the arm, hand, and finger tips. These movements are so rapid that they seem simultaneous, but in training exercises you must try to follow their natural sequence.

A few practical suggestions regarding the use of the arm and hand may help you to cultivate controlled gestures. However, you should remember that all technical practice must eventually become habitual if your gestures are not to appear artificial and affected.

Use exercises to free your tight muscles and establish habits of graceful coordination. Every movement of the arm should begin at the shoulder, pass through the elbow and wrist, and "slip off" the ends of the fingers. It is most important that every arm gesture finish at the finger tips, for nothing is more ineffective than an arm movement in which the fingers are curled flabbily at the ends. The movement should be from the body, and the wrist should lead in horizontal and vertical gestures. Every gesture must have a definite purpose; if

A responsive and expressive body is an actor's greatest asset. Alfred Lunt and his wife Lynn Fontanne in Durrenmatt's The Visit.

there is no purpose, there should be no gesture. Since the sole purpose of a gesture is to emphasize or clarify a thought or feeling, it is better to do nothing at all than to make meaningless movements. Try to cultivate definite, clear-cut, telling gestures.

In the following exercises use your entire body but focus your attention on the objects mentioned. See the object, touch it, and finally react. Let your eyes, eyebrows, and mouth show your reactions. Lift your arms from the shoulder, letting the movement pass through the elbow and hand and end in the tips of your fingers. Show the shape, weight, and size of any object you pick up. After you have shown that you have picked it up, be sure to hold it, or put it down definitely.

1. You are walking in a garden. Pick flowers from plants, bushes, and vines, and pull weeds. Select fruit from a tree, taste it, and throw it away. Select another piece and eat it.

2. You go into the garage and find a flat tire; fix it.

3. You are in a big railroad station, looking in vain for a porter. You are carrying a suitcase, handbag, umbrella, box of candy, and magazines. You drop your handbag and everything spills out. Put down everything else you are carrying in the process of recovering

the contents of your handbag. Retrieve everything and lift the suit-case last of all.

4. You are wandering around a department store. You feel the fabrics, smell the perfume, and look at costume jewelry without buying anything. You see a hat bar. Try on several hats. Buy one and wear it out, carrying your old one in a bag.

ACTING WITHOUT WORDS

Pantomime is the basis of characterization, which in turn is the basis of acting. People express themselves in their bodily actions before they speak, so it is natural that the first step in acting is to create personalities without the use of words.

The interdependence of bodily response and feeling begins at birth and continues through life. It is the mainspring of psychotherapy and all mind-over-matter theories. For example, if you habitually slump as you walk, draw down your face, and look at the ground, you will soon become physically and mentally lazy and emotionally listless. Note that a phlegmatic person does slump, draw down his face, look at the ground, and drag his feet. If, therefore, you want to impersonate such a character, you can do those things and give a pretty good imitation. However, it would be better dramatically to imagine you are so utterly lazy, bored, and weary with life that your chest will naturally slump, your face droop, and your feet drag.

In other words, try to feel the emotion first and allow it to gain control of your body, but then consciously respond from your head to your feet. You will probably respond awkwardly at first; then apply the technical principles and train yourself to respond not only sincerely but artistically as well.

General Principles

General principles of the techniques of pantomime are based on what human beings do physically in response to emotional stimuli. Your richest source of authentic material for pantomimes is very careful observation of people in daily life, on the stage and screen, and individually or in crowds. Watch facial expressions, mannerisms, gestures, and ways of walking. You may find it profitable to analyze the movements of television, movie, and stage actors. Also note how your own bodily responses reflect your feelings.

There are two phases of your work with pantomime. You have studied the first — exercises to relax your muscles and free your body for quick expression of feeling. The second phase is the creation of impersonations in which feeling prompts a bodily response. Both activities demand concentration of thought and interest in detail. You will find it takes a great deal of time and practice to create the exact effect you desire.

Studying technical principles and applying them mechanically will limber the body and train it to react effectively. If you practice the physical exercises and then work out pantomimes, you will be surprised to realize suddenly that you are carrying yourself better and reacting to your ideas with spontaneous facial expressions and gestures as you have never done before.

Physical Principles

There are a few established principles which affect acting because they are based on what people often do in real life as well as on the best way to communicate a feeling or idea. The following are some of these. Try to apply them as you work out your pantomimes.

1. The chest is the key to all bodily action.

2. Positive emotions such as love, honor, courage, and sympathy expand the body and tend toward a high chest and head, free movement, broad gestures, and animated features.

3. Negative emotions such as hate, greed, fear, and suffering contract the body and tend toward a shrunken chest, tense movement, restricted gestures, and drawn features.

4. Facial expression — the use of the eyes, eyebrows, and mouth — usually precedes action.

5. Whenever possible, make all gestures with the upstage arm, the one away from the audience, and avoid all tendency to cover the face.

6. Some exaggeration of bodily response is essential to being clearly understood.

7. Always keep the audience in mind and direct reactions to them.

8. Keep the arms away from the body in gesturing. Except on specific occasions when it is necessary for communication purposes, do not gesture above the head or below the waistline.

9. Arms and hands should always be moved in curves, never in straight lines, unless you are deliberately trying to give the impression of awkwardness or being ill-at-ease.

10. All action must be definite in concept and execution, and all movement clearly motivated.

Localized Pantomimic Practices

The suggestions below are acceptable pantomimic practices. After you have familiarized yourself with them, choose one that stimulates your imagination and create a character and situation to fit it.

Body as a Whole

1. Feet together, weight on both feet, and body passive represent timidity, indifference, or trained self-control.

2. Weight carried to the front foot with the body leaning slightly forward represents interest, persuasion, sympathy, enthusiasm, and positive emotions.

3. Weight carried to the rear foot represents fear, hesitation, deep thought, amazement, and negative emotions.

4. Shrunken chest and bowed head represent old age, envy, greed, and negative emotions.

Hands and Arms

1. Arms extended, palms up, are appropriate for pleading, presenting ideas, and offering sympathy. Let movement reach fingertips.

2. Arms drawn up or back with palms down are appropriate for negation, refusal, condemnation, fear, horror, and negative ideas.

3. Clenched fists represent anger and effort at control.

4. Pointed finger and extended arm are useful for pointing out, commanding, and directing.

Feet and Legs

1. Feet apart with legs straight denote arrogance or stolidity.

2. Feet apart with legs bent denote lack of bodily control, old age, great fatigue.

3. Tapping the foot depicts irritation, impatience, nervousness.

4. Twisting one foot denotes embarrassment.

5. Feet apart, head high, and arms akimbo represent conceit, scorn, contempt, and self-assertiveness.

Head and Face

1. Head raised, eyebrows lifted, eyes wide, and mouth open represent fear, horror, joy, and surprise.

2. Head raised, eyebrows lifted, and mouth drawn down depict comic bewilderment or a quizzical state.

3. Head down, eyebrows down, and mouth set or twisted by biting lips show worry, meditation, and suffering.

4. Twisted mouth and eyebrows can show petulance, irony, anger, pain, sophisticated attitudes, and various subtle emotions.

5. Raised eyebrows, wide eyes, smiling or open lips may depict innocence, stupidity, or coquetry.

Characterization

Characterization in pantomime involves placing a character in a situation and showing a change in his mood. This entails two mental processes — imitation and imagination. Many professional actors keep notebooks with them at all times. When they see a person of particular interest, especially if they happen to catch him in a moment of excitement, they jot down notes on his exact expression, gestures, and eccentricities of movement. They draw upon these notes when creating parts to be sure they are being true to life. However, this is only the beginning, for they then use their imaginations to place and maintain themselves in the parts they are playing and so create roles.

After you have put on some comfortable clothes which leave your body free for action, run through the relaxing and other practice exercises. Then imagine yourself in such situations as the following:

1. You are alone in your home. Go to the television set and adjust it. You find that you are watching the climax of a horror picture. Suddenly you hear a sound at the window. As you listen, the sound continues. The window slowly opens and a hand appears. You seize a book and hurl it at the hand, which promptly disappears. You tiptoe to the window, lock it, and fall into a chair, exhausted.

2. Practice falling several times (see page 139). Then imagine yourself in the following situations.
   a. You have been wounded in the shoulder. Fall from loss of blood.
   b. You have stubbed your toe on roller skates left on the floor. Fall, get up, and put away the skates, limping from a sprained ankle.
   c. You suddenly feel faint and fall. Then you recover, get up, and stagger to a chair.

3. Relating each to an imagined situation, show fear, agony, appeal, embarrassment, hate, sympathy, indecision, power, weariness, and joy. First employ your face, next your hands, and then your feet. Finally express these emotions with your entire body.

Flip Wilson is a versatile pantomimist, seen regularly on television.

Showing Emotional Responses

Emotion affects our bodies in various ways. In practicing the exercises below, be sure that you feel the emotion first; then let your face and body respond. Apply the physical principles given above.

1. You have quarreled with your girlfriend or boyfriend. You are standing by a window, looking out, frowning, and biting your lip. Your chest is sunken, your body slumped. The phone rings. Your face lights up, with eyes wide and lips smiling. Your chest is up. You wait expectantly to hear your name called. Then you run to the phone and lift the receiver, holding it in your upstage hand. Let your face reflect the conversation. When you hang up, you show by your movements whether the quarrel is over or not.

2. You are a feeble old man or woman, coming out to sit in the sun. You walk with short, uncertain steps; your head is down and your face drawn. You sit down slowly with great effort and gradually relax as the sun warms you. Someone calls you and you express your irritation by frowning and shaking your head. Then you rise, pushing yourself up from the arms of the chair. Hurry away as fast as your stiffness of limbs will allow, expressing worry and agitation.

3. Pantomime individual speeches from selections in this book expressing contrasting emotions.

INDIVIDUAL PANTOMIMES

Now you can begin working out real pantomimes involving careful planning, rehearsing, and presentation before the class. The individual pantomimes may well be divided into life studies, imitations of people you know, and imaginary characterizations.

Preparation

In your imitation of a real person, you should first determine his chief characteristics. Is he friendly? Timid? Boisterous? Suspicious? Glamorous? Physically vigorous? Discontented? Next, note mentally the details of his habitual facial expression, especially his eyes and mouth. Observe how he holds his head, the kinds of hand movements he makes, and the way in which he walks. Decide what makes him different from any other human being. Then place him in a situation. (You need not have actually seen him in such a situation, but you must be able to imagine how he would react to it.) Take plenty of time to think through his exact reactions to your imaginary situation. Visualize them as if you were watching him on a television screen. Finally, imitate what you have imagined he would do.

In your imaginary characterizations, you should follow much the same procedure. You will, however, have to begin by inventing the details which will characterize the person you plan to play. What is his age? What are his physical traits? How does he dress? What makes him a distinctive individual? Only when you can see him as clearly as someone you actually know will you be able to make him live.

Whether your character is imitated or imaginary, you must work out in detail the situation in which you plan to place him. Have your character enter a definite environment in a clear-cut state of mind and body. Invent something that will change his mood. The conclusion of your pantomime should leave no uncertainty in the mind of your audience about the mental state of the character as he leaves the stage.

You will also need to visualize in detail the setting of your pantomime. Be sure you know the exact position of the doors, windows, furniture, and props you will employ. Last of all, assume the physical appearance of your character as nearly as you can. Feel yourself to be his age and of his size. Let his state of mind take possession of you until your face, hands, and feet are reacting as his would in the imagined circumstances.

While working out your individual pantomime, keep the following directions constantly in mind.

1. Set your mental stage in detail, knowing exactly how much space you are to use, the location of the furniture, and the shape, weight, and position of every imaginary prop you will be using. If you move an object, make very clear its shape, weight, and new position. After you have made your audience see your setting and props, you must remember not to break the illusion by shifting an article without clear motivation and action.

2. Visualize the appearance and emotional state of your character in minute detail.

3. Imagine yourself to be dressed in the clothes of your character, making your audience see the weight, shape, and material of each garment and its effect upon you in your particular mood and situation.

4. Remember that in all dramatic work the thought comes first — think, see, and feel before you move. Let your eyes respond first, then your face and head, and finally the rest of your body. This is a "motivated sequence."

5. Keep your action simple and clear-cut.

6. Keep every movement and expression visible at all times to your entire audience.

7. Never make a movement or gesture without a reason. Ask yourself: "Does it make clear who I am, how I feel, or why I feel as I do?" Take time to make every movement clear and definite.

8. Try out and analyze every movement and gesture until you are satisfied that it is the most truthful, effective, and direct means of expressing your idea or feeling.

9. Make only one gesture or movement at a time, but coordinate your entire body with it and focus the attention of the audience upon it.

10. Rehearse until you know that you have created a clear-cut characterization and that the action has begun definitely, remained clear throughout, and come to a conclusion.

11. Plan your introduction very carefully. It may be humorous or serious, but it must arouse interest in your character and the situation in which he is placed. It also must make clear all the details of the setting and preliminary situation.

12. Plan the ending very carefully. You should either leave the stage in character or come back to your own personality and end with a bow or smile.

Suggestions for Individual Pantomimes

If you find it difficult to get started, the following suggestions may help you. At first it is not a bad idea to run through them all in rather rapid succession to get yourself limbered up physically and imaginatively. Then select one and work it out in detail, elaborating on mannerisms and concentrating on details. After creating a single study which satisfies you with its clarity, build up a sequence of events which brings about a change of mood and situation. Finally build up to a definite emotional climax and conclusion. Such a pantomime will require hours of preparation before it will be ready for class presentation.

1. Standing erect, with your feet close together, suggest the following:
   a. A butler
   b. A model waiting to display a gorgeous evening gown
   c. A dowager contemptuously watching the behavior of the younger generation
2. With legs wide apart and a comfortable posture, represent the following:
   a. A genial gentleman in front of his fireplace beaming at his guests
   b. An activist student addressing a mass meeting
   c. A contented farmer smoking a pipe and standing in his doorway studying the weather
3. With alert posture, one foot somewhat ahead of the other and your weight definitely placed on the ball of the forward foot, represent the following:
   a. A high school boy watching a football game
   b. An energetic cheerleader addressing a mass meeting
4. With a similar posture, except that the weight is definitely shifted to the rear foot, impersonate the following:
   a. An old lady afraid to cross the street
   b. A mother disgusted with the caterpillar her son is showing her
   c. A little girl hesitating to ask a favor of her teacher
   d. A hunter terrified at seeing a snake swinging from a tree in front of him
5. Cross the room, suggesting by your posture and walk the following:
   a. A burglar stealing across an unfamiliar, dark room
   b. A vigorous athlete walking across the campus
   c. An Indian looking for enemies in the forest
   d. A murderer stealing up on his victim with uplifted knife
   e. A tired soldier marching in a parade
   f. A weary father returning from a long, hard day at the office
   g. A model displaying evening wraps
   h. A criminal awaiting a last-minute reprieve in the death cell

6. Walk across the room, kneel, and kiss a lady's hand in the manner of:
   a. A knight in armor of the Middle Ages
   b. A cavalier of the court of Charles II, with a long curled wig, a stiff, outstanding coat with ruffled sleeves, and a plumed hat
   c. A modern boy burlesquing a romantic lover
7. Walk across the room and curtsy in the manner of the following characters:
   a. A colonial lady at a formal party in a full-skirted gown and towering headdress
   b. A Civil War beauty of the old South
   c. A timid country girl at the squire's house
   d. A naughty little girl at dancing school
8. Cross the room, sit in a chair, and rise as the following characters:
   a. A criminal leaving the witness box at his trial
   b. A coquettish old lady flirting with a gay young man
   c. A miser counting his money and listening for eavesdroppers
   d. A middle-aged gossip retelling the latest scandal
   e. A mother at the bedside of her sick child
   f. A queen dismissing her court
   g. A sleepy child trying to keep awake
   h. A young man at his first dance
   i. A frightened substitute teacher in her first class
   j. An angry traffic cop
   k. A spoiled child sulking because he is denied something
9. Suggest, by smiling, the following characters:
   a. A seasick traveler trying to appear sociable
   b. A Sunday school superintendent greeting some new students
   c. A tired salesgirl trying to sell a hat to a fussy customer
10. Suggest, by facial expression, the following situations:
    a. A boarder opening a spoiled egg
    b. A small boy taking castor oil
    c. A junior high school girl watching a sentimental movie on television
    d. A butler admitting unwelcome guests
11. Assume the following characters as completely as you can. Sit or walk, as you choose, and include enough action to show them in a real situation:
    a. An egotistical, self-confident businessman
    b. A pompous butler
    c. A swaggering bully
    d. A distinguished society woman
    e. A patient trying to gain courage before his turn in a dentist's chair
    f. An energetic and jovial stenographer
    g. A man bothered by a mosquito while trying to read

GROUP PANTOMIMES

Group pantomimes should follow your individual ones and eventually lead you into the acting of a short play. They will, therefore, demand even more careful planning and rehearsal time than you have devoted to your individual pantomimes. They may be based on plays, novels, stories, or such secondary sources as photographic magazines, newsreels, and films. Feel free, also, to draw upon the daily life about you.

Plan your story as you would a one-act play, centering it around one interesting situation that has a carefully worked out exposition, rising action, climax, and a logical and clear-cut conclusion. Create an interesting setting and five or six strongly contrasted characters. Be sure that each one is a real personality. Motivate all entrances, exits, and side action and be sure that all the characters can be seen at all times. Avoid bunching, huddling behind furniture, or standing in stiff lines. Your stage picture should be well balanced and attractive, and attention should always be focused upon the center of interest. Rehearse together until you have a unified whole in which each character is a living, breathing person. Do not rush your action, for the audience must be able to follow the development of all the roles; take plenty of time to tell your story effectively and pictorially. Remember that you are limited to visual means of presenting your ideas. Try to build your plot around an emotional situation with considerable human interest and avoid trite material. Be original, imaginative, and painstaking.

Suggestions for Group Pantomimes

The suggestions below may be useful to you. Be sure you plan the entrances and exits carefully and keep the action clear and unhurried. See that each character is a distinct personality and that the stage picture is well balanced at all times.

1. A jolly fat woman, a thin disagreeable woman, and a silly young girl are visiting with a motherly old lady when an attractive man joins them.
2. A boy and a girl quarrel and make up.
3. Four models display contrasting types of dresses to a rich lady who is helping her daughter choose a trousseau while the father looks on.
4. Several old soldiers recount their adventures in World War I.
5. A typical "character" actress, a leading man, and a leading woman are awaiting their cues in the greenroom (the room offstage where actors and actresses rest and chat between appearances).

6. Several stenographers apply to a brusque businessman for a position.
7. A babysitter takes charge after the parents have departed.
8. A photographer takes a family picture of four generations.
9. A shy young man pays his first call on a girl who does not know how to put him at ease.

Applications

1. Write on separate pieces of paper twenty suggestions for pantomimes which can be presented by a single person. Four should show just one mood. Four should reveal a transition from one mood to another. Four should require a definite entrance and exit. Four should necessitate sitting and rising. Four should require falling down and getting up again. Bring these suggestions to class and mix them up. Let each class member draw one and present it in class.

2. Give as many individual and group pantomimes as possible before the class. Analyze each performance to see whether it has convincing characterization, clarity, reality, and effectiveness. These questions, among others, should be discussed:

a. Has the pantomime been carefully prepared?

b. Are the characters interesting, lifelike, and vivid? Do you become emotionally involved with them?

c. Do the gestures and movements seem sincere, convincing, clear, and properly motivated?

d. Does all of the action help to delineate the characters and their situation for you?

e. Is the action clear-cut, realistic, prolonged sufficiently, and exaggerated enough to be seen by the whole audience?

f. Can you visualize the setting, the props, and the clothing of the characters?

g. Does the pantomime have a definite beginning and ending?

3. Pantomime scenes from the selections in this book involving deep emotion or light comedy.

Bibliography

Alberti, Eva: *Mme. Alberti's Pantomimes*, French, New York, 1934.
Disher, Maurice: *Clowns and Pantomimes*, Houghton Mifflin, Boston, 1925.
Enters, Angna: *On Mime*, Wesleyan, Middletown, Conn., 1965.
Fast, Julius: *Body Language*, Lippincott, New York, 1970.
Rice, Elmer: *Three Plays Without Words*, French, New York, 1934.

chapter

VOICE AND DICTION

An expressive voice and clear, correct speech are not only indispensable tools for the actor; they are also vital assets in every walk of life. Personnel directors list them among the first considerations for all positions which involve meeting the public and sharing ideas. As Shaw so amusingly points out in *Pygmalion*, a person's social standing and educational background are judged by the way he talks.

The lack of communication between people — individuals and groups — is the cause of much of the confusion of this generation. As you watch on television the confrontations between sectional and racial segments of our own United States, or try to follow trials and panel discussions, you must realize the importance today of clarity in speech and accuracy in choice of words. Since drama is one of the arts of communication, the dramatics class can prove a valuable means of improving your personal speech.

There is more faultfinding from the public and the professional critics concerning the lack of voice clarity and the slovenliness of diction on the part of American actors than of any other phase of acting. Especially in comparison with the British players who appear in the best Broadway and TV plays, this criticism appears justifiable. On the whole, English actors have studied at RADA (The Royal Academy of Dramatic Art) or other specialized schools which stress the use of the speech of Southern England; this tends to become the standard of stage diction. With the popularity of intimate family plays, Westerns, and the rapidfire spots of dialogue on many TV specials, our American speech becomes indistinct in comparison with that of the BBC dramas. In fact, bodily action is being played up and the spoken word overlooked in many stage shows where audience involvement rather than communication is stressed.

You will find, however, that directors in regional and repertory companies, which produce classics and important contemporary dramas of ideas, are expecting young actors to speak clearly and correctly and are not accepting mumbling and provincial pronunciations. As Americans in the superjet age are traveling more and more, they themselves are becoming more conscious of the American nasality of tone and lack of clarity in speech, criticized by foreigners for years, as a very real handicap. Therefore, no matter how your life works out, you will find that current English speech, neither American nor British, will be an asset in whatever lifework you undertake.

The artificial use of "stage diction" is not suitable for average young Americans and becomes an affectation in general communication, but, if you go into the theater professionally, you will pick it up naturally. Familiarity with stage diction will increase your value in many plays, and also your pleasure in understanding the English plays which are now a part of our American theater.

In the drama class, a simple, practical daily routine of exercises and constant attention to your speech are necessary; but it is in the regular speech classes that you should get your detailed information and concentrated drill work. In many schools a course in phonetics and speech in all its phases is a prerequisite for the course in dramatics. If you have not taken such a course, you should certainly try to do so. However, if you understand the fundamental principles explained in this chapter and practice the exercises with regularity, you can definitely improve your vocal and speech habits.

DEVELOPING AN EFFECTIVE VOICE

There is nothing mysterious or complicated about developing an effective voice; it depends primarily upon bodily relaxation and good posture. Few people realize the close relationship between the voice, the emotions, and the body. A person who is ill, tired, worried, angry, nervous, hurried, or tense reflects his feelings in his voice. In spite of himself, his voice becomes high-pitched, monotonous, or colorless. On the other hand, a person who is poised, self-confident, and healthy is likely to have a pleasing voice. Consequently, your first efforts should be directed toward building a vigorous, well-controlled body and a cheerful disposition.

Voice is produced by the air from the lungs passing over the vocal folds, thin curtains of muscles with delicate edges. These folds respond instantly and set up vibrations or waves. The vibrations

BBC PHOTO

Kenneth More as Jo and Nyree Dawn Porter as Irene in the TV serial version of Galsworthy's The Forsyte Saga. *The authentic detail, the beautiful English diction, and the excellent acting won the series high praise.*

become sounds and are amplified when they strike the resonating chambers of the throat, head, nose, and mouth. Exactly what sounds are produced depends upon the shape of the resonating chambers, and this shape is determined by the position of the tongue, soft palate, lips, and lower jaw. For correct speech and voice production, it is necessary for you to have deep central breathing, an open, relaxed throat, flexible tongue and lips, and a relaxed lower jaw.

The human being breathes and makes sounds correctly at birth, using the vocal apparatus in a relaxed, natural way. Unfortunately, as the environment surrounding him, dependent largely upon the attitude of parents and associates, closes about him, tensions set in, tightening the throat muscles and affecting speech habits by the time the baby starts talking. Therefore young people who have reached their teens have frequently established poor vocal habits. These can be eliminated within an amazingly short time by regular exercise and constant vigilance in speaking.

Specialized dramatic schools include required courses in speech and diction, and more and more attention is being paid in public schools to developing clear, correct communication techniques. In your dramatics class homework, you should spend about half an hour a day, when you are feeling fresh and relaxed, in establishing habitual and unaffected speech habits through doing regularly these and the exercises following in this chapter.

Breath Control

Breath control determines the carrying power of your voice and the intelligent reading and speaking of words combined into thought groups. The first exercises should, therefore, deal with central breathing, consciously controlled.

No one can teach you how to breathe, for you have done so successfully since your birth, and you can breathe correctly when you are asleep or perfectly relaxed. There is some difference, however, between regular breathing and breathing for speech. In the former, the inhalation (breathing in) and exhalation (breathing out) periods are of equal length. The latter requires a very brief inhalation period and a slow, controlled exhalation period. This is true because for all practical purposes speech is produced only when the breath is being exhaled. In breathing for speech, therefore, you should inhale through the mouth, since this allows for more rapid intake of breath than does inhalation through the nose. You should work for a prolonged and controlled exhalation so that the outgoing breath will match your needs for sustained vocal tone. Controlled breathing is more important to the actor than deep breathing, for the tone of his voice depends upon it.

The first exercises for you to try in training your voice are those which will focus the breathing process in the center of your body and those which will strengthen and control the breath stream once it has been centered where it belongs.

Practice these exercises every night and morning until central breathing gradually becomes automatic.

1. Place your hands on either side of the lower part of the rib cage and pant rapidly, laugh silently, and sniff in the air in tiny whiffs. Lie down and breathe deeply and regularly. Be sure to keep your hands in the same position.

2. Stand straight with an easy and well-balanced posture. Inhale slowly, making sure from the feeling under your hands that the whole rib cage is expanding. Hold your breath without straining for a count of six. Then exhale slowly and evenly while you mentally count, first to fifteen, then to twenty, twenty-five, and thirty. Be particularly careful to avoid muscular tension.

3. Repeat this exercise, gauging the evenness of your exhalation either by whistling or by making a soft sound as you breathe out (as the sound of *s* or *ah*). If the sound is jerky or irregular or fades at the end, repeat the exercise until you can keep it smooth and regular.

4. Use a favorite poem or prose passage for practice in breath control. Take a deep breath and see how far you can read in the selection before you have to draw a second breath. Do not strain and be sure to relax after each effort. Your breath control will improve. Southey's "Cataract of Ladore" is good practice.

Relaxation

The degree of relaxation determines the beauty of the voice and the carrying power of the vowel sounds, which are made with an open, relaxed throat, relaxed jaw, and flexible lips. Therefore, before any period of voice exercises, you must relax, consciously letting go both mentally and physically. Yawn! Stretch your whole body as an animal does after a nap. (Incidentally, watching a cat relax and move is an excellent exercise in itself for bettering your own reactions.) Feel the big muscles of your back, legs, and arms ease first. Imagine that a warm, relaxing shower is falling over your head. Imagine it passing over your forehead and wiping out the frown lines. Imagine it releasing the tension of the little muscles around your eyes, nose, mouth, and especially your cheeks, so that the lower jaw and lips are loose.

Next roll your head forward and backward and to the sides until both the inner and outer throat muscles are relaxed. Then imagine the shower pouring over your whole body, relaxing your arms and fingertips, your chest, lungs, diaphragm, and even your toes: You should be yawning by this time, and that is one of the best voice exercises there is. With practice you can learn to run through this process imaginatively when you are waiting to make a speech or standing in the wings before an entrance on the stage. You will also find it an excellent cure for stage fright. Also run through the posture exercises on page 135 and then do the breathing exercises on page 156 before you begin vocal work. The importance of an erect, easily relaxed body should not be underestimated.

Vocal practice of the following exercises demands carefully using your vocal apparatus:

For Relaxed Jaw

1. Let your head fall forward on your chest. Lift it up and back, letting the jaw remain loose. Drop it again and slowly roll the head over the right shoulder, back, over the left shoulder, and forward, describing a circle.

2. Drop your head forward again. Place your hands lightly on your cheeks and lift your head with your hands, keeping the jaw relaxed and being careful to avoid using the jaw muscles. When your head is lifted, the jaw should hang open. It helps sometimes to try to make your face as expressionless as possible; looking blank will help to relax the muscles.

3. Babble like a baby, saying *dä-dä-dä-dä lä-lä-lä-lä* brightly, and feeling relaxed and happy, moving only the tip of the tongue. (In these and following exercises, refer to the chart on page 180 for pronunciation of vowel sounds.)

For Open Throat

1. Yawn freely, getting the feeling of an open, relaxed throat.

2. Take in a deep breath, relax your jaw, think of your throat as large, and exhale slowly.

3. Say: "I can talk as if I were going to yawn. Hear me talk as if I were going to yawn."

4. Say *lō-lā-lē-lä-lōo*, gradually increasing the energy for each repetition. Give the vowels fullness and roundness, and relax your jaw. Sing the syllables on one note. Increase your volume by breathing deeply, but do not tighten your throat. Use the tip of your tongue for the *l*'s.

5. Repeat the following expressions, keeping the throat open: *lä-lä-lä-laughs, lä-lä-lä-lose, lä-lä-lä-loaves.*

For Flexible Lips

1. Say *ōo-ō-ô-ŏ-ä*, opening your lips from a small circle to a large one. Then reverse, saying *ä-ŏ-ô-ō-ōo*. These sounds may be sung with the piano, taking them all on one note. Keep the tongue flat in your mouth with the tip at the lower teeth. Keep your throat well open and your jaw relaxed.

2. Say *mē-mō-mē-mō-mē-mō-mē-mō*; then sing these sounds with the piano.

For Flexible Tongue

1. Say rapidly: *fŭd-dŭd-dŭd-dŭd-däh-fŭd-dŭd-dŭd-dŭd-däh-fŭd-dŭd-dŭd-dŭd-däh-frill*. Trill the *r* in *frill*.

2. Keeping your jaw well relaxed, repeat the following sounds, watching with a hand mirror to see that your tongue is slowly arched as you go from one position to the next: *ö-ŭ-ẽr-ă-ĕ-ā-ĭ-ē.*

3. Say *ĭra-ĭra-ĭra-ĭra-ĭra-very*. Trill the *r* in *very*.

For Resonance

Resonance is the vibrant tone produced when sound waves strike the chambers of the throat, head, nose, and mouth. The best practice for resonance is humming with an open, relaxed throat. The nasal passages must be kept open for vibrations to be set up in them, so exhale through the nose using the *m-n-ng* positions. The cavities of the head will vibrate automatically if you hum while throwing the voice forward. If the nasal passages are closed by a cold or raised soft palate, the sound is denasalized. The much-criticized nasal twang of many American voices is due to nervous tension which tightens the throat and raises the soft palate, thus closing the nasal cavities, cutting down resonance, and leaving the voice flat.

1. To locate your larynx and feel the vibration of the vocal cords, place your fingers lightly on your Adam's apple and say *b* and then *p*, *d* and then *t*, *v* and then *f*, *s* and then *z*. Note the vibration on the *b*, *d*, *v*, and *z*. Also note the vibration on the vowel sounds *ā, ē, ī, ō, ū.*

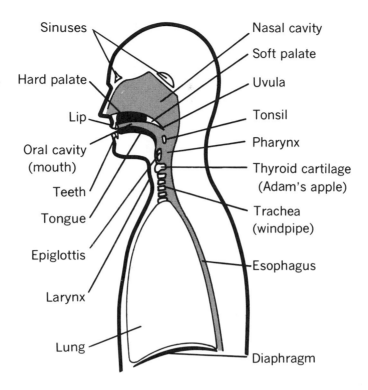

DIAGRAM OF THE VOCAL TRACT

2. To feel the effect of obstructing the resonators, sing the word *"hum"* and repeat while you pinch your nose closed. Say "good morning," opening your mouth and your throat. Say it as if you were on the verge of tears and were swallowing them. Say it holding your nose closed. Say it with your teeth tightly set. Say it while drawing your tongue back in your mouth.

3. Place your fingers gently on your lips and on your nose and hum, feeling the vibration. Place the palm of your hand on the top of your head and hum; try to feel the vibration. Repeat with your fingers at the back of your head. Repeat the exercise using a piano and noting where on the scale the vibration is strongest.

4. Sing the sounds of *m-n-ng*, using a piano. Then combine each of them with the vowel sounds in Exercise 4 of "For Open Throat" and repeat.

5. Say the following words with full resonance: *ring, sing, ding-dong, bells, wind.*

For Speech and Breathing

1. Breathe in, relax your throat and lower jaw; count "one" as you exhale. Repeat and count "one, two"; continue until you can count to twenty on one breath. Be careful not to tighten up. It may take you several weeks before you can reach twenty, but take time so that you can do it without straining. Any tension is bad.

2. Breathe in; relax your throat and lower jaw. Say "Hong-Kong" as you exhale, prolonging the vowel and *ng* sounds.

3. Breathe in; relax your throat and lower jaw. Say "Hear the tolling of the bells — iron bells," prolonging the vowels and the *ng* and *n* sounds.

4. Breathe in; relax your throat and lower jaw. Without straining, try to retain the position of your diaphragm as you exhale, saying, slowly, "Roll on, thou deep and dark blue ocean, roll."

5. Again read the selection used for breath control. This time do not try to see how far you can read on one breath, but read it naturally, inhaling as you have to between the phrases. Form the vowels accurately and sound the *m's*, *n's*, and *ng's* carefully.

VOICE CHARACTERISTICS

There are four characteristics of the voice which must be used correctly if you are to become an effective and expressive speaker. These are quality, pitch, volume, and rate. Their development constitutes voice training.

Quality

Quality is the individual sound of your particular voice. Its beauty and richness can be improved by keeping the resonating chambers of your throat and head open. Your daily speech habits are most important. Never speak with a tight throat, and always try to use a low, clear tone. Relax your throat frequently with a yawn, and breathe through your nose when you are not speaking. Never strain your voice.

The quality of your voice depends, for the most part, upon resonance and the correct formation of vowel sounds by the speech organs.

The vowel sounds, so important in the quality of your tone, are all made with the lower jaw relaxed. The position of the lips and tongue determines the sound. In pronouncing all vowels, you must keep the tip of the tongue at the base of the lower teeth. *Ah* is the most open sound, with the tongue flat and lips loose. By rounding the lips you produce the sounds of ŏ (ŏn), ô (lôrd) ō (ōh), o͝o (lo͝ok) and o͞o (lo͞ose).

Keep the tip of the tongue at the base of the lower teeth, the jaw and lips relaxed, but allow the middle of the tongue to arch up and forward until it almost touches the roof of the mouth to produce the sounds of *ŭ* (*ŭp*), *ẽr* (*makẽr*), *ă* (*ăt*), *ĕ* (*lĕt*), *ā* (*āte*), *ĭ* (*ĭt*), *ē* (*bē*). Practice making these sounds without tightening the throat, concentrating on the tone so that it leaves the mouth and passes beyond the lips and is not muffled or "swallowed." In this way you keep a pure tone in every syllable and word that you utter, and the quality of your voice is at its best.

It is important for the actor to remember that voice quality is definitely affected by emotion. Perhaps you have already realized that your voice responds instantly to your inner feelings. For example, the voice may quiver with fear, sweeten with sympathy, and harden with anger. If you wish to develop a flexible, responsive voice for acting, you must cultivate your imagination to the point where your tone becomes that of your character as he experiences various moods. In addition, the age of your character will affect the quality of the voice appropriate for him. For instance, with old age the vocal apparatus is usually less flexible and the disposition has been obviously affected for better or worse by life's experiences. These things must be made apparent in your characterizations. A good way to help yourself is to listen very carefully as you meet a new person and try to judge his temperament and mood by the tone with which he speaks. Note also voices of your friends and family.

Applications

Practice the following exercises aloud, first feeling the appropriate emotion and then speaking.

1. Repeat an appropriate word — *no, yes, dear, of course, really* — conveying the following emotions: surprise, scorn, irritation, sarcasm, boredom, suspicion, eagerness, love, doubt, weariness, exaltation, determination, horror, pain, despair, and joy.
2. Assume the character of a gay young girl, a cross old man, a dictatorial employer, a discouraged job-seeker, an eloquent minister, a distinguished actor, a plotting criminal, and a hysterical mother. Speak the following sentences as each of these characters would.
   a. Now is the time to make your choice.
   b. Oh, what a beautiful morning!
   c. Whatever will be will be.
   d. Stop! Think it over before you do anything rash!

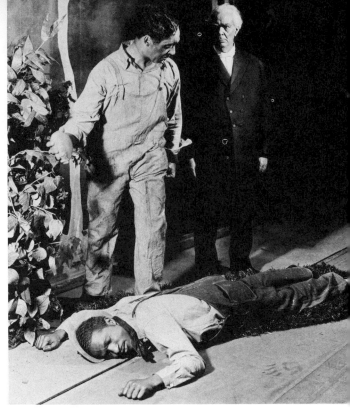

In The Green Pastures *clear diction made a dialect play intelligible to the audience. The play is an exposition of a Sunday School lesson, humorous yet deeply moving. Richard B. Harrison as De Lawd, shown here with Cain and Abel.*

CULVER PICTURES, INC.

3. Say the following words, recalling personal experiences to give them "color," the special tone quality resulting from feeling and imagination: *home, icy, flag, ocean, roar, sunset, welcome, golden, jingle, melancholy, magnificent, dog, star, glamorous, eternal, enemy, splendid, horrible, brilliant, glory, sobbing, autumn, whisper, shot, scream, terrific.*

4. Read the following selections, concentrating mainly on the vowel sounds. Try to make each vowel in an accented syllable as full and rich as possible. Sound these vowels alone many times and then put them back in the words.

(NOTE: In these and in all other excerpts and passages, the student is urged to read the complete work, if possible, in order to understand fully the mood and meaning of the selection.)

a.

[ROMEO:]

> But soft! What light through yonder window breaks?
> It is the east, and Juliet is the sun!
> Arise, fair sun, and kill the envious moon,
> Who is already sick and pale with grief,
> That thou her maid art far more fair than she.

Romeo and Juliet by William Shakespeare

b.

[PROSPERO:]

> Our revels now are ended. These our actors,
> As I foretold you, were all spirits, and
> Are melted into air, into thin air:
> And, like the baseless fabric of this vision,
> The cloud-capp'd towers, the gorgeous palaces,
> The solemn temples, the great globe itself,
> Yea, all which it inherit, shall dissolve
> And, like this insubstantial pageant faded
> Leave not a rack behind.
>
> *The Tempest* by William Shakespeare

c.

[THE GHOST OF HAMLET'S FATHER:]

> I am thy father's spirit;
> Doom'd for a certain term to walk the night,
> And, for the day, confin'd to waste in fires
> Till the foul crimes done in my days of nature
> Are burnt and purg'd away. But that I am forbid
> To tell the secrets of my prison-house,
> I could a tale unfold whose lightest word
> Would harrow up thy soul. . . .
>
> *Hamlet* by William Shakespeare

Pitch

Pitch is the relative highness or lowness of the voice at any given time. Each person's voice has a characteristic pitch level from which it moves up and down. Women's voices are pitched on a higher level than those of men, and children's voices are higher than either. Pitch is determined by the rapidity with which the vocal folds vibrate. This vibration, in turn, is influenced by the length of the vocal folds, their elasticity, the degree of tension in them, their thickness, and the amount of breath pressure applied.

Most persons use only four or five notes in ordinary speaking, but a good speaker can use two octaves or more. Many girls and women pitch their voices, consciously or unconsciously, at too high a level, not realizing that a low voice is far more musical and easily heard. As a rule, therefore, girls should do their vocal exercises on the lower pitch levels.

The pitch of the voice gives meaning to speech. When speakers are excited, interested, and enthusiastic in conversation, they unconsciously lift the pitch on important words to emphasize them and lower the pitch on unimportant words to subordinate them. In repeating conversations, they lower or raise the voice in imitation of various people. Pitch gives life to reading aloud and speaking, and depends largely upon a vital interest in living and in what you are saying and doing. For a colorful and interesting voice, keep your mind alert as you talk, read, and think.

As you speak, you often alter your pitch. There are two primary ways of doing this. In the first, the "step," you shift abruptly from one pitch level to another between words, parts of sentences, or sentences to express a distinct break in thought or feeling. In the second, the "inflection," you gradually raise or lower the pitch level within a word or sentence. A rising inflection shows incompleteness of thought or uncertainty, and is often used in asking a question. A falling inflection indicates completeness and definiteness and is often used in answering a question. The rising-falling inflection is used to convey subtle shades and sharp differences of meaning within words.

Variety in pitch, called "modulation" or "inflection," makes the voice musical. Monotony in pitch, resulting either from speaking continuously on one level or from giving every sentence exactly the same inflection, is a fatal flaw in speaking. Without variety in pitch, a speaker is unable to hold the attention of his audience. Ministers, teachers, and lawyers sometimes fall unconsciously into pitch patterns and monotonous inflections which lessen their influence to a marked degree. Monotony in pitch may be due to two technical deficiencies: a person's inability to hear pitch changes, or a lack of vocal flexibility. The former is probably caused by a defect within the hearing mechanism and should be discussed with a speech correctionist, who may administer a test for "tonal deafness." Lack of flexibility, however, can be overcome by practice and conscious attention. It is due largely to lack of vitality and enthusiasm in thought and feeling or in vocal and bodily response.

As a student of dramatics, you must learn to control the number, length, and direction of pitch changes and the modulation of your voice as you interpret a part. In doing exercises for improving your pitch range and flexibility, a tape recorder is of great value, for it helps to train your ears as well as your voice. Today almost all schools have tape recorders. If you use one, you will be able to hear your voice in scenes and check on your skill in doing interpretative work. In any case, you must learn to go as low and as high as you can without straining. Try to notice your own and other people's changes in pitch in normal conversation and how these changes affect the communication of thoughts and feelings. Notice what anger, exhaustion, irritation, worry, joy, and excitement do to the pitch of people's voices. You will find that the pitch is usually higher when a person is angry, that dominant people use falling inflections for the most part, and timid ones use brief, rising inflections. Sneering and sarcasm are often shown by rising-falling inflections which convey inner, subtle meanings.

The reading aloud of plays or strongly contrasted conversations from stories is extremely helpful in daily practice for pitch variation. In reading aloud, you may find that a complete poem or single passage in prose has a predominant mood. An idea which is lofty and inspiring may need little range in pitch and will be best expressed by long, falling inflections. A passage which is gay, exciting, lyrical, and vital will have a wide range with many short, changing inflections. In all interpretative work, keep asking yourself, "What am I saying?" and then answer the question in the author's words.

Applications

1. Count from one to ten, beginning as low as you can and going as high as you can without strain. Then reverse the count and come down. Be sure that it is pitch and not loudness that makes the difference in each count.
2. Count slowly from one to ten, giving the vowel in each number a long falling inflection. Repeat with a long rising inflection on each. Then alternate the two exercises.
3. Using the alphabet, talk as if you were preaching a sermon, explaining a geometry problem, describing a horrible accident you just saw, putting a little child to sleep, and speaking to someone who is hard of hearing.
4. Take a nursery rhyme and recite it as a father, an old-fashioned elocutionist, a bored small boy, and a frightened little girl.
5. Read these sentences with the widest possible range. Put emphasis on the important words and syllables by raising the pitch, using both the step and inflection shifts. Drop definitely on unimportant words.
   a. What a glorious sunset!
   b. To speak effectively you must raise your voice on the important words.
   c. In direct conversation we change the pitch of the voice constantly.
   d. Did you hear what I said? Then go!

  e. No, I will not go!

  f. Look, that plane is exploding!

  g. I shall never, never, never believe you again!

6. Stand behind a screen or curtain and give the following lines, having someone check on your variations in pitch.

  a. No, never. Well, hardly ever.

  b. To be or not to be, that is the question.

  c. Do unto others as ye would that they should do unto you.

  d. Give me liberty or give me death!

  e. Laugh and the world laughs with you;
     Weep and you weep alone!

7. Analyze the following selections and decide what inflections to use in order to bring out the predominant mood and inner meaning of each. If possible, use a tape recorder and read the lines aloud. Then study the pitch of your voice and try again, concentrating particularly on inflection and modulation.

a.

[PETRUCHIO:]

  Good-morrow, Kate, for that's your name, I hear.

[KATHARINE:]

  Well have you heard, but something hard of hearing:
  They call me Katharine that do talk of me.

[PETRUCHIO:]

  You lie, in faith; for you are called plain Kate,
  And bonny Kate, and sometimes Kate the curst,
  But Kate, the prettiest Kate in Christendom.
          The Taming of the Shrew by William Shakespeare

b.

[THE PIPER:]

  She was my mother. — And she starved and sang;
  And like the wind she wandered and was cold
  Outside your lighted windows, and fled by,
  Storm-hunted, trying to outstrip the snow.
  South, south, and homeless as a broken bird, —
  Limping and hiding! — And she fled, and laughed,
  And kept me warm; and died! To you a Nothing;
  Nothing, forever, oh, you well-housed mothers!
  As always, always for the lighted windows
  Of all the world, the Dark outside is nothing;
  And all that limps and hides there in the dark;
  Famishing, — broken, — lost!
          The Piper by Josephine Preston Peabody

c.

[PAOLO:]

She called me into the hotel. There were other people there, rich people all in grand clothes. Psh, what did I care for that? I'll be the equal of them all soon and more, for I have a fortune in my throat. That's what she said — a fortune in my throat! Maddalena, she's going to send me to Milano — oh, she needn't fear, I'll give her back the money — I'll study there — I don't need much study, it's true — and in a few years you'll see, posted in big head-lines, "Rubini, Paolo Rubini, the greatest tenor in Italy, the greatest in the world."

Poor Maddalena by Louise Saunders

d.

[VIOLA:]

I left no ring with her. What means this lady?
Fortune forbid my outside hath not charm'd her!
She made good view of me; indeed, so much
That sure methought her eyes had lost her tongue,
For she did speak in starts distractedly.
She loves me, sure; the cunning of her passion
Invites me in this churlish messenger.
None of my lord's ring! Why, he sent her none.
I am the man; — if it be so — as 'tis —
Poor lady, she were better love a dream. . . .
How will this fadge? My master loves her dearly,
And I, poor monster, fond as much on him;
And she, mistaken, seems to dote on me.
What will become of this? As I am man,
My state is desperate for my master's love;
As I am woman, now alas the day!
What thriftless sighs shall poor Olivia breathe!
O time, thou must untangle this, not I;
It is too hard a knot for me to untie!

Twelfth Night by William Shakespeare

Volume

Volume is the relative strength, force, or intensity with which sound is made. You must not confuse volume with mere loudness, for you can utter a stage whisper with great intensity or you can call across a room with little intensity. Volume depends upon the pressure with which the air from the lungs strikes the vocal folds, and while a certain amount of tension is required to retain the increased breath pressure, this tension should be minimal. If your throat is as relaxed as possible, you will not become hoarse even when speaking with increased volume and your words will be resonant and forceful.

To speak loudly enough to be heard in the largest auditorium without forcing the words from your throat, you must breathe deeply and centrally. Think that you are talking to the person farthest away from you. Such concentration will cause you to open your mouth wider, speak more slowly, and enunciate more clearly. When you use a microphone, remember that no greater volume is necessary than might be used in ordinary conversation — no matter how large the auditorium may be.

Force is of two types. A sudden, sharp breath pressure creates explosive force which is useful in commands, shouts, loud laughter, and screams. When the breath pressure is held steady and the breath released gradually, the force is said to be expulsive. This type of force is necessary in reading long passages without loss of breath and in building to a dramatic climax.

Like the other voice characteristics, volume is closely related to the expression of ideas and emotions. Fear, excitement, anger, hate, defiance, and other strong emotions are usually accompanied by an explosive intensity. On the other hand, quiet, calm thoughts call for a minimal amount of force. Animated conversation requires an average amount.

Volume is used in combination with other voice characteristics to suggest various feelings. For example, a quiet voice accompanied by a flat quality suggests dullness, indifference, and weariness. A quiet voice with a full tonal quality may express disappointment, shock, despair, bewilderment, and sometimes even great joy.

When you are on the stage, it is important to remember that you must use more energy to convey impressions of all kinds than is necessary off the stage. Thus, if you are merely chatting comfortably at home with a friend, your voice will have relatively little intensity. Put that identical scene on the stage, try to make it equally informal, and you will have to increase your vocal intensity considerably — otherwise the scene will fall flat. Keep the person farthest away from you constantly in mind and talk directly to him, using your jaw, tongue, and lips to enunciate clearly.

Using greater force to emphasize the important words in a sentence is the most common means of clarifying a thought. You can change the meaning of a sentence by shifting the force from one word to another — expressing innocence, surprise, anger, and other emotions.

A scene from the Abbey Players' production of J. M. Synge's In the Shadow of the Glen. *The poetic language shows the lilt and inflections of Irish dialect. The actors are Kathleen Barrington, Michael O'Brioin, and Eddie Golden.*

In acting, the entire thought of a line can be clarified or obscured by emphasizing a word or phrase. Key words brought out forcibly can make a character's personality understandable to the audience.

Applications

1. Pant like a dog. While you do so, feel the movement of your diaphragm with your hands. Then say "ha-ha" as you pant.
2. Repeat "ha-ha" many times, making the syllables by a sharp "kick" of the diaphragm. Gradually work from a light sound to a shout. Be careful not to allow an audible escape of breath on the *h* sound.
3. Take a full breath and call "one" as if you were throwing a ball against a wall at some distance. Exhale, relax, inhale, and call "one, two" in the same manner. Count up to ten in this way, but be careful to relax between each effort. Get your power from a quick "kick" of the rib cage rather than from tightening the vocal bands. In the same way, use the words *no, bell, on, never,* and *yes.*
4. Repeat the letters of the alphabet, increasing your energy whenever you come to a vowel. Then reverse the exercise, beginning with a strong, firm tone and gradually reducing the energy involved. Keep all the sounds on the same pitch.

5. Say the sentence "I am going home" as though you were saying it to the following people:

   a. A friend sitting next to you

   b. A person 10 feet away

   c. Someone across the room

   d. Someone in the back row of your assembly room, when you are on the platform

   Notice that if you are thinking about the person to whom you are speaking, your voice adjusts itself naturally to the distance involved.

6. Change the meaning of the following sentences in as many ways as you can by using force to emphasize different words. Explain your exact meaning.

   a. I didn't say that to her.

   b. You don't think I stole the book, do you?

   c. Why didn't you warn me before it happened?

7. Read these passages aloud, making the mood and meaning clear by the amount of force you use and the words you emphasize. Use volume sufficient for a large auditorium by getting enough breath, keeping an open throat, and sounding the vowels clearly. Stand correctly.

a.

[PORTIA:]

> The quality of mercy is not strained.
> It droppeth as the gentle rain from heaven
> Upon the place beneath. It is twice blest;
> It blesseth him that gives, and him that takes.
> 'Tis mightiest in the mightiest; it becomes
> The throned monarch better than his crown.
> His sceptre shows the force of temporal power,
> The attribute to awe and majesty,
> Wherein doth sit the dread and fear of kings;
> But mercy is above this sceptred sway;
> It is enthroned in the hearts of kings,
> It is an attribute to God himself;
> And earthly power doth then show likest God's
> When mercy seasons justice.

The Merchant of Venice by William Shakespeare

b.

> Boot, saddle, to horse, and away!
> Rescue my castle before the hot day
> Brightens to blue from its silvery gray,
> Boot, saddle, to horse, and away.

"Boot and Saddle" by Robert Browning

c.

The earth is the Lord's and the fullness thereof; the world, and they that dwell therein. For He hath founded it upon the seas, and established it upon the floods.

Psalm 24: 1-2

d.

Swiftly the brazen car comes on . . .
Its eyes are lamps like the eyes of dragons;
It drinks gasoline from big red flagons!

"The Santa Fe Trail" by Vachel Lindsay

e.

OYES! OYES!! OYES!!!

We, the holders of the oldest office in Britain, salute you good people at Hastings by the Sea. Long before Press and Television we cried the King's commands and brought news of the day. Still pursuing our ancient calling, we give you current important tidings, wish you well, and cry with heart and voice:

GOD SAVE THE QUEEN!

Great Britain's Town Criers' Competition
Courtesy of Alfie Howard,
Town Crier of Lambeth

Rate

Rate, in speech, is the speed at which words are spoken. Each person has a characteristic rate of speech, which is usually more rapid in informal conversation than in public speaking or in work in dramatics. Like quality, pitch, and volume, rate is also an important means of suggesting ideas and emotional states. A steadily increasing speed creates a feeling of tension and excitement, while the deliberate delivery of important passages impresses the hearer with their significance. Light, gay, happy, and lyric passages are usually spoken rapidly. Calm, serene, reverent, tragic, and awesome passages are delivered more slowly. Unemotional ideas are conveyed by an average rate of speech.

Practically all of our sentences in both speaking and reading are divided into groups separated by pauses of varying lengths. The breathing pause is a necessity because we must have breath in order to speak. One of the worst faults a beginner can have is gasping for breath because he needs to do so, thus breaking the thought of a sentence. You must train yourself at once to get your breath between

In the comedy Teahouse of the August Moon, *David Wayne as Sakini must use the inflections of an Oriental speaking English.*

NBC PHOTO

thought groups when reading or speaking in front of an audience. You undoubtedly manage it properly in normal conversation, unconsciously putting into groups words which belong together before you catch your breath. You will find it harder to do this on the stage. The number of words in a group necessarily varies with the thought. A single word may be important enough to stand alone or there may be twelve or more in a group; ordinarily there are four or five. Too many breath groups tend to create choppy speech. Punctuation can be of great assistance, for it often clarifies meaning as well as grammatical relationship.

Logical grouping and pausing is a matter of making the thought clear and depends upon your knowing exactly what you are saying. The secret of great interpretative power is the ability to realize an idea — to visualize, emotionalize, and vitalize it for yourself — and then give the audience an opportunity to do the same thing. Logical and dramatic pauses demand thought and feeling on your part or you will not have your audience thinking and feeling with you. Therefore, work out your thought groups very carefully and then remember that pauses are often more effective than words. After the pattern is set, approach each group as if for the first time every time you speak or read aloud. In acting, this is one of the secrets of giving a sense of spontaneity and freshness to every performance through-out a long run.

Go back over the passages you have been reading in the exercises in this chapter and decide where the thought groups divide. Then read the passages aloud again, watching your timing. Hold the important words longer than others and slip rapidly over the unimportant ones. Let the idea speed you up or slow you down and take time to feel the emotions and moods. A skillful use of phrasing and pausing is one of your most valuable tools in putting over ideas and arousing emotion, and the more you practice reading aloud, either from prepared selections or at sight, the more effective you will become.

USING THE VOICE IN INTERPRETATION

Emphasis and subordination are the light and shadow of interpretation in acting. The key words of every passage must be highlighted to be heard by everyone in the audience so that the meaning may be understood. To stress such words, you must first feel their emotional context to give them color. They can be made to stand out in the following ways: by delivering them with greater force, by holding them for a longer period, by lifting or lowering them in pitch, and by giving them a rich resonant quality. They can also be set off by pauses, either before or after, or sometimes both before and after. To subordinate unimportant words or phrases, you can "throw them away" by saying them rapidly at a lower pitch with less volume.

Stress also involves tone placement and projection. There are two rather different but not conflicting ideas regarding the matter of placement of tone. One is that tone should be placed in the mask of the face by forming the sounds of speech with the position of the lips, lower jaw, and tongue, thus producing resonance. The other is that the voice should be thrown as far as the size of the auditorium requires. This is accomplished by breathing deeply, opening the mouth, and forming the sounds accurately, while consciously putting attention on the person farthest away. In both cases the throat is never tightened but kept open. The term "swallowing words" is used when the sound is prevented from reaching the resonating chambers because the throat is closed by tension or carelessness in controlling the breath and the vocal folds cannot vibrate to produce sound.

Climax is another principle of great value in interpretation. A climactic passage must, of course, be well written by the author before it can be effectively spoken by the speaker. In such a passage, the emotional intensity of the lines is increased to a high point of feeling at the end. Naturally, to reach a high point it is necessary to start at a relatively low one. In a strong emotional passage, begin with a relatively slow rate, deliberate utterance, low pitch, and little or medium energy. Gradually increase the energy and speed and change the pitch until you reach the highest point of interest or feeling.

A flexible, responsive voice is the most valuable asset an actor or speaker can have. Speaking is like painting. In both arts, the main purpose is to express an idea. The painter may use dull grays or he may utilize a great variety of colors, exquisitely blended and harmonized. So, too, the speaker or actor may use a lifeless voice — monotonous in tone, energy, and pitch — or he may utilize all the resources of vocal technique. You will achieve the most effective communication if you first think and feel deeply, understanding and visualizing your ideas. Then express these ideas, making full use of voice and body.

In the Applications which follow, try to use all the suggestions made in this chapter, first thinking and feeling, then using the intonation, inflection, and emphasis necessary to express the ideas back of the sounds and words. Be sure to take the time you need and be careful not to tighten your throat.

Applications

1. Tell the story "The Three Bears," stressing the vocal characteristics of Goldilocks and the bears and getting all the contrast possible. Also read Lincoln's Gettysburg Address aloud, doing the same thing.
2. Using the letters of the alphabet instead of words, tell a funny story, a moral tale, a short tragedy, and a ghost story.
3. Say "oh" to suggest keen interest, sudden pain, deep sympathy, utter exhaustion, delight, fear, irritation, anger, sarcasm, hesitation, embarrassment, good-natured banter, polite indifference, horror, and surprise.
4. Address the following sentences first to someone 5 feet away, then to someone 25, 100, 500 feet away. Keep an open throat but control the breath from the diaphragm. Make full use of the vowel sounds.
   a. Run for your life!
   b. Fire! Help!
   c. Are you all right?
   d. Come here at once!
5. Read these passages aloud. First carefully analyze their meanings. Then determine the mood, situation, and emotion portrayed. Finally decide what quality, energy, change of pitch, and rate will best suit your interpretation.

a.

[PIERRETTE:]

Pierrot, don't wait for the moon,
There's a heart-chilling cold in her rays;
And mellow and musical June
Will only last thirty short days.
                    The Maker of Dreams by Oliphant Down

b.

Work!
Thank God for the might of it,
The ardor, the urge, the delight of it —
Work that springs from the heart's desire,
Setting the brain and the soul on fire.
                    "Work" by Angela Morgan

c.

[THE PIPER:]

If I knew all, why should I care to live?
No, No! The game is What-Will-Happen-Next? . . .
It keeps me searching. 'Tis so glad and sad
And strange to find out, What-Will-Happen-Next!
                    The Piper by Josephine Preston Peabody

d.

During the whole of a dull, dark, and soundless day in the autumn
of the year, when clouds hung oppressively low in the heavens, I had
been passing alone, on horseback, through a singularly dreary tract
of country; and at length found myself, as the shades of evening drew
on, within view of the melancholy House of Usher.
                    "The Fall of the House of Usher"
                    by Edgar Allan Poe

e.

[THE PRINCE OF MOROCCO:]

All that glisters is not gold;
Often have you heard that told:
Many a man his life has sold
But my outside to behold:
Gilded tombs do worms infold.
Had you been as wise as bold,
Young in limbs, in judgment old,
Your answer had not been inscroll'd:
Fare you well; your suit is cold.
                    The Merchant of Venice by William Shakespeare

f.

Why so pale and wan, fond lover,
Prithee, why so pale?
Will, when looking well can't move her,
Looking ill prevail?
Prithee, why so pale?

"Song from Aglaura" by Sir John Suckling

g.

[ROMEO:]

Night's candles are burnt out, and jocund day
Stands tiptoe on the misty mountain tops.

Romeo and Juliet by William Shakespeare

h.

[ZARA:]

Heaven has no rage like love to hatred turn'd
Nor hell no fury like a woman scorn'd.

The Mourning Bride by William Congreve

i.

'Tis not too late to seek a newer world,
Push off, and sitting well in order, smite
The sounding furrows; for my purpose holds
To sail beyond the sunset, and the baths
Of all the western stars, until I die.

"Ulysses" by Alfred Lord Tennyson

j.

[MACBETH:]

Ring the alarum bell! Blow, wind, come, wrack!
At least we'll die with harness on our back!

Macbeth by William Shakespeare

6. Study the following passages. Decide what type of person is speaking, exactly what he is saying, what mood he is in, and why he is saying these lines. Read them aloud, trying to convey the exact meaning and mood.

a.

[LADY TEAZLE:]

Sir Peter, Sir Peter, you may bear it or not, as you please; but I ought to have my own way in everything, and what's more, I will too. What! though I was educated in the country, I know very well that women of fashion in London are accountable to nobody after they are married — and am I to blame, Sir Peter, because flowers are dear in cold weather? You should find fault with the climate, not with me. For my part, I'm sure I wish it was spring all the year round, and that roses grew under our feet!

The School for Scandal by Richard Brinsley Sheridan

b.

[MABEL CHILTERN:]

Well, Tommy has proposed to me again. Tommy really does nothing but propose to me. He proposed to me last night in the music room, when I was quite unprotected, as there was an elaborate trio going on. I didn't dare make the smallest repartee, I need hardly tell you. If I had it would have stopped the music at once. Musical people are so absurdly unreasonable. They always want one to be perfectly dumb when one is longing to be absolutely deaf.

An Ideal Husband by Oscar Wilde

c.

[JULIUS CAESAR:]

Cowards die many times before their death,
The valiant never taste of death but once.

Julius Caesar by William Shakespeare

d.

[BEATRICE:]

O that I were a man for his sake! or that I had any friend would be a man for my sake! But manhood is melted into courtesies, valour into compliment, and men are only turned into tongues, and trim ones too: he is now as valiant as Hercules that only tells a lie and swears to it. — I cannot be a man with wishing, therefore, I shall die a woman with grieving.

Much Ado About Nothing by William Shakespeare

e.

Look to this day
For it is life — the very life of life.
In it lie all the verities and realities of existence:
The bliss of growth,
The glory of action,
The wealth of beauty.
For yesterday is but a dream,
And tomorrow is only a vision,
But today well lived
Makes every yesterday a dream of happiness
And every tomorrow a vision of hope,
Look therefore to today!

Sanskrit

IMPROVING YOUR DICTION

There are various definitions of diction, but for all practical purposes it means the selection and pronunciation of words and their combination in speech. Technically, diction involves the correct articulation of sounds, which results in the proper formation of words; careful enunciation of syllables, which results in clear and distinct speech; and the musical rhythm which characterizes cultivated speech.

If your speech is to be an asset rather than a liability, in addition to correct and distinct utterance of sounds, you must also improve your choice of words in your normal daily usage. Your aim should be clear, correct, pleasing speech which carries well. There are some very common habits of slovenly speech you should avoid; they include mumbling, muttering, dropping words at the ends of sentences and letters at the ends of words, and indistinctness due to the lazy use of the vocal apparatus, especially the tongue. There are some less common habits which are likely to creep up on you after a little speech training: speech that is pedantic — too accurate and meticulous and artificial, that is, affected and unnaturally theatrical; and speech that is imitative — expressive of characteristics which you admire in someone else's speech but which do not suit your own personality. Practice reading aloud every day using your own best speech; then relax and speak naturally, and you will find the habitual use of your vocal apparatus improving.

Television offers an opportunity for the study of diction which no other generation has had. In the field of colloquial speech, television is especially useful. In the news reports from all sections of the country and in panels made up of people from all areas, you hear the habitual conversational expressions of people from everywhere. On both sides of the Atlantic there are numerous dialects in the English of daily life; this colloquial or provincial speech is picturesque but confusing in communicating thought, and should be avoided on the stage except when a role demands it. Television has the great advantage of bringing into your home the cultivated speech of the finest actors and most distinguished speakers. You should study their speech to improve your own speech.

The use of speech recorders is another advantage of this generation. You should get someone to set up a recorder when you are unaware of it, in order to get a record of your ordinary diction which you can analyze for its good and its weak points. Also, early in the term you

This scene is from the Bill Cosby Show, *with Henry Fonda, Cosby, and Elsa Lanchester. The scene is a stalled elevator, limiting action, so diction and facial expressions become even more important than usual.*

should record your reading of some of the selections in this book; then remake them at the end and note your improvement.

Records and tapes offer opportunities for studying the diction of professionals. Many excellent records of plays, readings of poetry and prose, examples of the dialects in various sections of the country, and even lessons in speech improvement are available for your entertainment, enlightenment, and instruction.

As suggested earlier, you should take a course in speech as well as in dramatics. Many speech courses include a study of phonetics — the use of symbols rather than letters to represent the sounds — since there is so much confusion in the spelling of words. Such a speech class helps you to distinguish between the styles of speech appropriate for different occasions. In informal conversation, it is natural to use speech patterns that differ somewhat from those you use for formal conversation or platform performance. Speech training helps you to pattern your speech habits on those which are habitual to educated people speaking English that can be understood anywhere in the world.

Ear training is almost as important as speech training. Therefore, you should accustom yourself to the best speech used in your community. As far as possible, associate with people who speak well, for there is nothing more contagious than speech habits.

The exercises which follow are based largely on the standard sounds of vowels and consonants, which can be learned with patience and practice. They will help you to use your vocal apparatus properly and without self-consciousness, making your daily speech correct and clear at all times, and effective when projected from the stage or platform.

Vowel Sounds

The vowel sounds are "unobstructed tones" through the mouth, given characteristic tone by the positions of the lips, tongue, jaw, and soft palate, which necessarily differ for each vowel sound.

The vowel sounds may be classified as front vowels, middle vowels, and back vowels, according to the position of the tongue as each is formed. Look at the diagram of the speech organs and note the parts of the tongue. Remember that the tip of the tongue remains at the base of the lower teeth in all vowels. In the front vowels, the front of the tongue is gradually raised until it almost touches the inner gum ridge, as with $\bar{e}$ in $m\bar{e}$. In the middle vowels, the front of the tongue is midway to the roof of the mouth, as with $\breve{u}$ in $\breve{u}p$. In the back vowels, the back of the tongue is raised, the jaw relaxed, and the lips rounded, as with $\bar{oo}$ in $f\bar{oo}d$. In all the back vowels, the lips are rounded until only a small opening is left. Diphthongs are combinations of two vowel sounds, as in how ($\ddot{a} + \breve{oo}$) or hay ($\bar{a} + \breve{i}$). Prolong the vowel sounds and see how the quality changes from one sound to another.

FRONT	MIDDLE	BACK
$\bar{e}$ as in $\bar{e}ve$	$\breve{u}$ as in $\breve{u}p$	$\ddot{a}$ as in $\ddot{a}h$
$\breve{i}$ as in $h\breve{i}m$	$\dot{a}$ as in $\dot{a}lone$	$\breve{o}$ as in $\breve{o}ccur$
$\breve{e}$ as in $\breve{e}nd$	$\hat{u}$ as in $\hat{u}rn$	$\hat{o}$ as in $l\hat{o}rd$
$\breve{a}$ as in $c\breve{a}t$	$\tilde{e}$ as in $mak\tilde{e}r$	$\bar{o}$ as in $\bar{o}ld$
		$\breve{oo}$ as in $h\breve{oo}d$
		$\bar{oo}$ as in $f\bar{oo}d$

(NOTE: Modern dictionaries use various symbols to represent vowel sounds; these will be shown in the pronunciation key. The system used here is a simplified one.)

Practice to distinguish between the vowel sounds as you read the words in the following lists.

1. feel, fill, fell, fall, fail, file, foil, foul
2. tea, tin, ten, tan, ton, turn, tarn, torn, tune, town
3. eat, it, at, ought, ate
4. peak, pick, peck, pack, puck, perk, park, pock, pork, poke, pike

Consonant Sounds

The consonant sounds are made when the air passage is obstructed at some point by the tongue, soft palate, or lips. If there is no vibration of the vocal folds, the consonant is said to be voiceless; if there is a vibration of the vocal folds, it is voiced. You can tell whether a consonant sound is voiced or voiceless by placing your finger lightly on your throat and feeling whether there is any vibration.

Plosive Consonants

In these sounds the air is stopped and suddenly released.

VOICELESS	VOICED	AIR STOPPED BY
p as in *pop*	*b* as in *bob*	Lip against lip
t as in *tame*	*d* as in *dame*	Tip of tongue against upper gum ridge
c or *k* as in *came*	*g* as in *game*	Back of tongue against soft palate

Fricative Consonants

In these sounds the air passage is narrowed at some point and a slight friction results.

VOICELESS	VOICED	AIR PASSAGE NARROWED BY
f as in *fan*	*v* as in *van*	Upper teeth on lower lip
s as in *bus*	*z* as in *buzz*	Front of tongue against upper and lower teeth which are almost closed
sh as in *sure*	*zh* as in *azure*	Tip of tongue turned toward hard palate, teeth almost closed
th as in *breath*	*th* as in *breathe*	Tip of tongue against upper teeth
wh as in *which*	*w* as in *witch*	Rounded lips and raised tongue

Nasal Consonants

In these sounds the mouth is completely closed at some point and the soft palate is lowered. Thus the air is forced to pass through the nose.

m as in *mammy*	Mouth closed by lip on lip
ng as in *sing*	Mouth closed by back of tongue on soft palate
n as in *ninny*	Mouth closed by tip of tongue on upper gums

Practice to distinguish among the consonant sounds as you read the words in these lists.

1. pen, Ben, ten, den, ken, fen, when, wen
2. have, cat, gap, quack, land, nag, tap, dash, rat, map, pat, bat, fat, vat, thank
3. than, sad, sham, chap, jam, plaid, black, flat, slack, clan, glad, snack, stand
4. smack, span, scan, trap, dram, prank, bran, frank, crab, grab, thrash, shrapnel
5. strap, sprat, scrap, splash, swam, twang, wag, yap
6. hood, could, good, look, nook, put, book, foot, soot, should, brook, crook, wood

There are a number of vowel and consonant sounds which are not formed in the standard way in the colloquial speech of various parts of the United States. The important thing to remember is how they are produced in standard English.

Difficult Consonants

The consonants which give difficulty include the following:

1. The *r* is a consonant sound when it comes before a sounded vowel, whether the vowel is in the same word or is the first letter in the next word. The tip of the tongue should be on the upper gum ridge of the hard palate in such words as *red, grumble, three,* and *breeze,* or in such expressions as *butter and bread, as far as you go,* and *there are three boys.* The *r* is silent before consonant sounds or at the ends of words; the tip of the tongue is held at the base of the lower teeth and is not permitted to turn back to form what we call the "rolled *r.*" When it is retroflex (back in the mouth), the inverted *r* is formed, which gives an incorrect value to the vowel sound which precedes it — *bird* becomes *bŭrrd, mother* becomes *mŭthŭrr,* and *art* becomes *äurrt.* In stage diction the *r* is frequently trilled when it comes between two vowels or when it is doubled in such words as *American, marry, courage, orange.* If you are playing a British role or for some reason wish to use careful stage diction, practice such trilling by saying *ĭra-ĭra-ĭra-ĭra-ĭra-very* with great rapidity.

2. The *l* is formed by pressing the tip of the tongue against the upper gum, with the air passing over the sides of the body of the tongue. Do not turn the tip of the tongue back in the mouth (retroflex), and do not follow it with a *ŭ* in such words as *elm* and *film,* and do not put an *ĕ* before it in such words as *fool.*

3. Such combinations as "Didn't you?" "Wouldn't you?" "Haven't you?" "Shouldn't you?" "Why don't you?" are often run together slightly. Practice them carefully to avoid separating them too much and yet not saying "Didncha?" or "Didn'tchew?"

4. Do not pronounce the *r* at the ends of the following words; keep the tip of the tongue at the base of the lower teeth.

    a. air, bare, care, dare, fare, hair, lair, mare, pare, rare, share, stare, tare, wear

    b. bore, core, door, four, gore, hoar, lore, more, pore, roar, soar, tore, wore, yore

5. Note the distinction between the *w* and *wh* sounds in such words as *wear* and *where, weather* and *whether, wight* and *white.* The *wh* is pronounced like *hw*; if you blow on your finger, you get the correct sound.

Dame Judith Anderson as the Queen and Charlton Heston as Lord Essex in a dramatic moment from Elizabeth the Queen, *the play by Maxwell Anderson.*

Applications

Read the following clearly, pronouncing the consonant sounds carefully.

a.

Dry clashed his harness in the icy caves
And barren chasms, and all to left and right
The bare black cliffs clanged round him, as he based
His feet on juts of slippery crag that rang
Sharp-smitten with the dint of armed heels —
And on a sudden, lo! the level lake
And the long glories of the winter moon.

Idylls of the King by Alfred Lord Tennyson

b.

The chief's eye flashed; but presently
Softened itself, as sheathes
A film the mother-eagle's eye
When her bruised eaglet breathes.

"Incident of the French Camp" by Robert Browning

c.

Over the cobbles he clatters and clangs in the dark inn-yard.
He taps with his whip on the shutters, but all is locked
  and barred.
He whistles a tune to the window, and who should be waiting
  there
But the landlord's black-eyed daughter,
  Bess, the landlord's daughter,
Plaiting a dark red love-knot into her long black hair.

"The Highwayman" by Alfred Noyes

Difficult Vowels

The vowels which give difficulty include the following:

1. à as in *last, ask, after, path, dance, pass* (This sound is often confused with the short ă.)

2. ô as in *audience, lord, daughter, because, water, automobile, thought* (This sound is often confused with the short ŏ.)

3. o͞o as in *root, soon, bloom, roof, soup, rude* (This sound is often confused with the short ŭ or the diphthong iu.)

4. ŏ as in *God, John, stop, was, yacht* (This sound is often confused with äw or äh.)

5. ē as in *sleek, creek, sheep, clique* (Often confused with ĭ.)

6. ă as in *have, man, began, shall, and, than, glad* (This sound is often confused with **à** or **ä** when a student is being particularly careful, or when a ŭ is sounded after it.

7. The vowel sound in *perfect, purple, world, girl, learn, nerve* (This sound is often confused with ŭ or the diphthong *oi.*)

8. The diphthong *iu* as in *assume, Tuesday, student, duty, stupid, avenue* (This sound is often confused with o͞o.)

9. The indeterminate *e* in unstressed syllables is barely sounded.

10. The ĕ sound as in *men, experiment, engineer, sincerity* (This sound is often confused with ĭ.)

Applications

1. Read clearly, pronouncing the vowel sounds carefully.

a.

Water, water, everywhere,
And all the boards did shrink.
Water, water, everywhere,
Nor any drop to drink.
"The Rime of the Ancient Mariner" by Samuel Taylor Coleridge

b.

She left the web, she left the loom,
She made three paces through the room,
She saw the water-lily bloom,
She saw the helmet and the plume,
She looked down to Camelot.
"The Lady of Shalott" by Alfred Lord Tennyson

2. Read these excerpts, making the consonants distinct.

a.

By the margin, willow-veiled,
Slide the heavy barges trail'd
By slow horses; and unhailed
The shallop flitteth silken-sailed
Skimming down to Camelot.
"The Lady of Shalott" by Alfred Lord Tennyson

b.

Great rats, small rats, lean rats, brawny rats,
Brown rats, black rats, gray rats, tawny rats.
"The Pied Piper of Hamelin" by Robert Browning

Pronunciation

Good pronunciation entails the use of correct vowel and consonant sounds in words and the placing of the accent on the stressed syllables.

The following words are only a very few of those in ordinary use which are being constantly mispronounced.

1. Place the accent on the first syllable in the following words:

ex'qui site	pos'i tive ly	in'flu ence
des'pi ca ble	mis'chie vous	the'a ter
lam'en ta ble	ad'mi ra ble	in'ter est ing
ab'so lute ly	req'ui site	hos'pi ta ble

2. Place the accent on the second syllable in the following words.

ho tel'	ro mance'	en tire'
in quir'y	ad dress'	al ly'
a dult'	a dept'	man kind'

3. Drop the silent letters in the following words.

often	corps	heir
toward	subtlety	indictment
debt	forehead	business

Note the consonant and vowel sounds, as well as the accent marks, in the following list of words. Say these words according to the pronunciation spellings which are given within the parentheses following the words themselves. An italicized vowel or a vowel marked with a half-long (ŭ, ŏ) is pronounced rapidly. The first pronunciation is considered preferable, but the others are also in good usage.

hearth (härth)	Feb'ru·ar'y (fĕb'rŏŏ·ĕr'ĭ; fĕb'ŭ·ĕr'ĭ;
na·ive' (nä·ēv')	fĕb'ŏŏ·ĕr'ĭ; fĕb'ŏŏ·ẽr·ĭ)
gen'u·ine (jen'ŭ·ĭn)	vau·de·ville (vô'de·vĭl; vōd'vĭl)
I·tal'ian (ĭ·tăl'yȧn)	ir·rev'o·ca·ble (ĭ·rĕv'ŏ·kȧ·b'l)
come'ly (kŭm'lĭ)	har'ass (hăr'ȧs; hȧ·răs')
with (wĭth; wĭth)	bou·quet' (bŏŏ·kā'; bō·kā')
bade (băd)	ac·cli'mate (ȧ·klī'mĭt; ăk'lĭ·māt)
her'o·ine (hĕr'ŏ·ĭn)	fin'an·cier' (fĭn'ăn·sēr'; fĭ'năn·sēr';
col'umn (kŏl' um)	fĭ·năn'sĭ·ẽr)
ab·surd' (ăb·sûrd')	sin·cer'i·ty (sĭn·sĕr'i·tĭ)
says (sĕz)	am'a·teur' (ăm'ȧ·tûr'; ăm'ȧ·tûr;
been (bĭn; bēn)	ăm'ȧ·tŭr)
a'li·as (ā'lĭ·ăs)	chauf·feur' (shŏ·fûr'; shō'fẽr)
wom'en (wĭm'ĕn; wĭm'ĭn)	ar'chi·tec'ture (är'kĭ·tĕk'tŭr)

Read these sentences aloud very carefully.

1. The speech of the children over the radio was scarcely intelligible and entirely lacking in spirit and enthusiasm.
2. Some sparks from the largest of the rockets burned holes in her scarlet jacket.
3. The President of the United States of America delivered the dedicatory address.
4. His vocabulary is as meager as when he was in the elementary grades, and he is entirely lacking in intellectual curiosity; this is a sad commentary on his secondary education.
5. His thought that remaining in the automobile would allow them to see over the audience placed them in an awkward position.
6. They quarreled as to whether or not to take the spotted dog on the yacht.
7. Aunt Blanche answered his demand by advancing with her passport.
8. We hope next year to hear that he has started his career as an engineer rather than a mere cashier.
9. He was so boorish that he could endure the lonely moor and the obscure rural life.

Read the following as rapidly as you can, keeping the sounds clear.

1. The perfectly purple bird unfurled its curled wings and whirled over the world.
2. Amidst the mists and coldest frosts
    With stoutest wrists and sternest boasts,
   He thrusts his fists against the posts
    And still insists he sees the ghosts.
3. The weary wanderer wondered wistfully whether winsome Winifred would weep.
4. When and where will you go and why?
5. The sea ceaseth and sufficeth us.
6. To sit in solemn silence in a dull, dark dock
   In a pestilential prison with a life-long lock,
   Awaiting the sensation of a short, sharp shock
   From a cheap and chippy chopper on a big black block!
7. The queen was a coquette.
8. They know not whence, nor whither, where, nor why.
9. Judge not that ye be not judged, for with what judgment ye judge ye shall be judged.

10. The clumsy kitchen clock click-clacked.
11. Didn't you enjoy the rich shrimp salad?
12. The very merry Mary crossed the ferry in a furry coat.

Careful diction also involves discrimination in the choice and use of words. A wide and constantly increasing vocabulary, free from an overuse of slang, is a cultural asset you cannot afford to neglect. Standard usage and grammatical structure are taken for granted.

VOICE AND DICTION IN ACTING

A play comes to life by means of the voices and words of the actors; it is their ability to arouse emotion through the playwright's lines that creates the illusion of reality for the audience. Actors must make the meaning of every passage clear to all listeners by the proper projection of the key words. It is their responsibility to avoid spoiling lines by blurring pronunciation, muffling enunciation, or speaking with a nervous rhythm. The inner soul of the characters they are creating must be expressed through clear-cut patterns, which are suitable to the roles but which are varied with every change of mood and situation.

The presentation of a character through voice alone is only possible if you can visualize him accurately and feel with him. As in daily life, each character has his own voice quality, pitch, and tempo. However, these must all be varied in keeping with an immediate situation and mood without the loss of the character's individuality.

Remember that variety is the spice of speech, and that a flexible, responsive voice is an invaluable asset to the speaker and actor. A lifeless voice, monotonous in pitch, lacking in energy, unpleasant in tone, and uniform in rate, is ruinous to an actor. Colloquial, mumbled, or inarticulate diction is equally disastrous on the stage; more actors today are not heard and understood because of poor enunciation than because of lack of vocal power. Think always of the persons in the audience who are farthest from you, emphasize the important words and sounds of letters, and subordinate the unimportant ones, for only in that way can you make your role live for your audience. No matter how sensitive and responsive you are as an actor, if you are not heard and understood, your characterization will fail. Only training and experience can free your abilities; your dramatics classwork can give you a sound foundation if you make use of it by daily practice.

Applications

1. The following play excerpts present strongly contrasted roles, worthy of careful practice. Work with the passages until you have created totally individual characterizations for each of the speakers.

a.

[MARY ROSE:]

Have I been a nice wife to you, Simon? I don't mean always and always. There was that awful time when I threw the butterdish at you. I am so sorry. But have I been a tolerably good wife on the whole, not a wonderful one, but a wife that would pass in a crowd?

Mary Rose by James M. Barrie

b.

[ABE LINCOLN:]

I went through something like this once before! Someone you love — standing helpless — waiting. I sat day by day reading Ma parts of the Bible she liked best. On the sixth day she called me to her bed— talked of many strange things — principalities and powers — and things present — and things to come — urged me and Sairy always to walk in paths of goodness and truth — and told us many things would come t'him that served God — an' th' best way t'serve Him was t'serve His people. (*Pause*) She was amongst the lowliest of mankind. She walked the earth with her poor feet in the dust — her head in the stars — (*Pause*) Pa took me down into the woods t' make her a coffin. Pa was sawin' and I was hammerin' the pegs in. The hammer dropped at my feet; it was like someone was drivin' 'em into my heart. It's — just goin' through all that again — now!

Prologue to Glory by E. P. Conkle

c.

[THE VICAR:]

Every year of my life — of our life — my dear Ann has altered. Only a little of course — a line here, a grey hair there — a point of view every now and then — no one notices these things so quickly as a husband. No one hides his knowledge so closely. Every year of our married life — and they are well over twenty — every year I have started my romance all over again. I shall continue to perform that astonishing miracle until I leave this rather absurd planet altogether; I am inclined to think, if I am lucky, that I shall be allowed, in a future condition, to go on being idiotic about my wife. If harps are to be played, I cannot conceive of anything else but that Ann and myself — however inadequately — will take turns at the same instrument.

The Lilies of the Field by John Hastings Turner

2. Practice reading aloud any selections in this book, applying the technical principles brought out in this chapter. Use a speech recorder as you work with the selections, and check your progress. Many of the selections can be found in records of the plays from which they were chosen; do not imitate the stars in their vocal habits or interpretations but use them in speech as a means of clarifying and expanding your own.

3. Turn to the chapter on pantomime and put words into the mouths of the characters in all the suggested situations. Practice changing your voice completely for each character and coordinating your voice and body as you present each situation.

4. Using the following play excerpts, paint voice pictures of each of the characters by employing as much beauty, variety, and effectiveness of voice and speech as you can.

a.

[GWENDOLINE:]

Ernest, we may never be married. From the expression on mamma's face, I fear we never shall. Few parents nowadays pay any regard to what their children say to them. The old-fashioned respect for the young is rapidly dying out. Whatever influence I ever had over mamma I lost at the age of three. But though she may prevent us from becoming man and wife, and I may marry someone else, and marry often, nothing that she can possibly do can alter my eternal devotion to you.

The Importance of Being Earnest by Oscar Wilde

b.

A very young husband protests a change in diet.
[HE:]

A change?
You thought
I'd like
a change?
What!
From the godliest of vegetables,
my kingly bean,
that soft, soothing
succulent, caressing,
creamy, persuasively serene,
my buttery entity?
You would dethrone it?
You would play renegade?
You'd raise an usurper
in the person of this
elongated, cadaverous,

throat-scratching, greenish
caterpillar —
you'd honor a parochial,
menial pleb,
an accursed legume,
sans even the petty grandeur
of cauliflower,
radish, pea,
onion, asparagus,
potato, tomato —
to the rank of household god?
Is this your marriage?
Is this your creed of love?
Is this your contribution?
Dear, dear,
was there some witch at the altar
who linked your hand with mine in troth
only to have it broken in a bowl?
Ah, dear, dear!

*Lima Beans** by Alfred Kreymborg

c.

[ANTONIO:]

Give me your hand, Bassanio; fare you well,
Grieve not that I am fallen to this for you.

The Merchant of Venice by William Shakespeare

Bibliography

Fischer, Hilda B.: *Improving Voice and Articulation*, Houghton Mifflin, Boston, 1966.

King, R. G., and E. M. DeMichael: *Improving Articulation and Voice*, Macmillan, New York, 1966.

Mayer, Lyle V.: *Fundamentals of Voice and Diction*, Wm. C. Brown Company, Dubuque, Iowa, 1968.

Wise, Claude M.: *Applied Phonetics*, Prentice-Hall, Englewood Cliffs, N.J., 1957.

Woolbert, C. H., and S. E. Nelson: *Art of Interpretive Speech: Principles and Practice*, Appleton-Century-Crofts, New York, 1947.

*Copies of this play, in individual, paper-covered, acting editions, are available from Samuel French, Inc., 25 W. 45th St., New York, N. Y., or 7623 Sunset Blvd., Hollywood, Calif., or in Canada from Samuel French (Canada) Ltd., 26 Grenville St., Toronto, Canada.

ACTING

Acting brings the play to life against a scenic background which creates the proper mood and atmosphere. The play is the culmination of the ideas of the dramatist; the feeling, understanding, and techniques of the director and actors; and the aesthetic standards and practical abilities of the backstage personnel. Without the appeal of creative acting, the drama would not be the power it has been for the generations who have sought inspiration and joy in the theater. It is the acting of roles in your classroom and in public performances that will bring you that inspiration and joy.

In all forms of creative art, teachers and textbooks can only point the way to achievement. Inborn talent backed by ambition and a driving force controlled by self-discipline and perseverance must transform the amateur into the artist. Even in cases of exceptional talent, the tools of the trade must be mastered, the divine spark **192** nourished, and the student inspired.

In your school dramatics work today, you have the advantage of the trained teacher-director to stimulate your highest achievement in both your inspirational and practical development, but your real growth depends upon your personal grasp of the fundamentals of the art. Acting is both intensely individual and intensely social: the actor must develop himself to his highest powers only to lose himself in a characterization which is but a part of a unified whole. Therefore, analyze your own and other persons' reactions while improving your ability to create another personality. The wise director will encourage you to use your own interpretation as long as it is in harmony with the underlying spirit of the production. Learn to check your individual reactions to the internal and external phases of your role, and of the other roles as they relate to the meaning of the scenes and plays of your various assignments. Also check your own improvement and powers of interpretation.

SHAKESPEARE'S ADVICE TO ACTORS

The finest lesson in dramatic art ever expressed in concrete form is Hamlet's advice to the players (Act III, Sc. 2), from the world's greatest actor-director-dramatist. The standards he formulated in it are those of yesterday, today, and forever.

The fundamental principles can be modernized for you to apply.

Speak the lines of the author as he wrote them, distinctly and fluently, with understanding of their meaning.

Do not use elaborate and artificial gestures, but keep a reserve force in order to build to an emotional climax smoothly and effectively.

Do not resort to farfetched action and noise to please unintelligent and unappreciative onlookers.

Do not be apathetic or dull, either, but let your inner understanding of the role guide your movements: suit the action to the word and the word to the action, with this special warning, that you are always natural. Overacting is not true interpretation; the purpose of true interpretation is always to present the real character so as to bring out his virtues and faults truthfully. The purpose of acting is to show life as it is in accordance with the time and custom of the play.

Do not either overact or underact to get a laugh from the audience; anything you do that is not true to life will spoil the play for the intelligent few whose criticism outweighs that of all the rest of the audience.

There are actors, sometimes highly praised, who show no resemblance to the people they are portraying, or even to humanity, when they strut and bellow in their bad imitations on the stage.

Never put in extemporaneous lines, especially in humorous roles, even when these lines are clever enough to make some stupid people in the audience laugh or when the actors themselves laugh at their antics; such methods draw the attention away from the center of interest and ensure the loss of important lines. Such action is inexcusable and shows a most pitiful ambition in the fools who use it.

Modern directors usually say the same sort of thing to beginners in the first few rehearsals: Get your lines; speak clearly; keep your hands still; don't overact; be natural and easy; don't play to the gallery; hold back; be yourself at your best; stick to the script; use your head; act like a human being; don't steal the scene from the main business.

A scene from the Prospect Theatre Company's 1969 Edinburgh Fesitval production of Christopher Marlowe's play Edward II, *later televised on BBC. See also the picture on page 192.* Actors: Ian McKellen, Michael Spice, and Michael Godfrey.

BBC PHOTO

EMOTION AND/OR TECHNIQUE?

There have always been two schools of acting, with ardent supporters upholding each and pointing out exponents from among the world's artists to support their claims.

In the one, the actor lives his part so that he actually weeps, suffers, and triumphs before the audience; he is the part he is playing, as far as possible, and experiences all that his character does. In the other, absolute control based upon perfect technique is the aim. No emotional response is allowed to interfere with the conscious artistry which alone is responsible for the results obtained. The actor does not live his part but he acts it so well that the illusion of living is maintained. In the first case, the emphasis is placed upon the actor's emotional response because of his own inner reactions; in the other, upon an assumed personality based on a conscious technique.

There is much to be said for both points of view, but today the standard is largely that of a middle course. You would do well, then, so to identify yourself with your part that you can interpret it naturally, simply, and spontaneously, utilizing your technical training toward the end of clear-cut, convincing, and consistent characterization. Lose your own individuality in the part you play, but never forget that you are presenting it to be seen, heard, and appreciated by your entire audience.

Today there are a constantly increasing number of books on acting available to you from which you should be collecting your personal library — books which you can mark and refer to as you establish your own theory of acting. Many of them are paperbacks, easy to carry around with you as a source of ideas. Among the most inclusive is *Actors on Acting*, edited by Toby Cole and Helen Krich Chinoy. Its extensive Bibliography can be of great value to you. The book presents, in the actual words of the greatest actors of Europe and America, their theories of acting based on their experiences in the finest roles of their times. The book also has reviews of these roles by the most distinguished dramatic critics. The Table of Contents gives you a means of being introduced to the theatrical authorities from Plato to contemporary ones, and the contents should make clear to you the values of both emotion and technique in acting.

Also obtainable in most readable form are new books clarifying the most discussed theory today, "The Method," formulated by the dominant actor-director of this century, Constantin Stanislavski. His own books — *My Life In Art, An Actor Prepares, Building a*

MCKAGUE

TASS FROM SOVFOTO

Sir Tyrone Guthrie   *Constantin Stanislavski*

Character, and *Creating a Role* — set forth his theories on the art of acting together with practical exercises in the techniques of vocal and bodily expression.

These theories have been interpreted and misinterpreted by earnest theater people, because too much emphasis has been put on the actor's use of self-analysis and his own emotional experiences in creating a role and not enough on Stanislavski's equal insistence on disciplined control of the techniques of vocal and bodily expressiveness. As a result, many so-called Method actors on the stage become so involved with their inner resources that they fail to communicate with the audience because of slovenly speech and action.

Probably Stanislavski's most valuable counsel to help you in creating a characterization is his "magic *if*," which can be called the key to his method. While using the full powers of concentration and imagination, the actor should ask himself what he would do if the events in the play were actually happening to him and he himself were intimately involved in them. The answers to these questions lead to an analysis of both his own and his character's inner natures, the basis for kinship with the part. Only then can the actor use the technical resources of his voice and body to interpret the reactions of the character truthfully and naturally. This analysis also leads to appreciating exactly what the author had in mind and to a correct understanding of the play itself.

Today actors, directors, and teachers who use the Method have advanced their own approaches to it. The Actor's Studio, under the direction of Lee Strasberg, has been the controversial center where many well-known actors have studied and worked. You are probably familiar with many of them — Geraldine Page, Rod Steiger, Anne Bancroft, Marilyn Monroe, Marlon Brando, Paul Newman, Julie Harris, Eli Wallach, David Wayne, Shelley Winters. You should certainly read some of the books about Stanislavski's system in order to familiarize yourself with ideas that will undoubtedly have a lasting influence on acting, especially for actors emphasizing the emotional and analytical approach.

In contrast to Method acting is the theatrical style which emphasizes conscious technique rather than emotional involvement. Its outstanding exponent was the dynamic director, Tyrone Guthrie. Guthrie disapproved of the intensive analysis and frequently inarticulate speech of Method actors, believing that people go to the theater to be thrilled and entertained. His influence has been very strong in this country, where he directed and lectured on many university campuses and produced in a number of repertory and regional theaters.

Most first-class actors today believe in working seriously and imaginatively to create roles through understanding them, and in using their own abilities of interpretation to present them effectively to the audience. There is a growing enthusiasm for active motivation of bodily response. Bringing the play to life and making the author's meaning clear through careful teamwork is the aim of most director-teachers. As a student, you should try to be as flexible and spontaneous as you can, applying your technical training to making your character a living personality for your audience. Thus you will appreciate that the best principle to employ is emotion *and* technique, not *or*.

CREATING A CHARACTER

Characterization is the "be-all and end-all" of acting — a creative process involving inner grasp of the fundamental personality of your role and its projection to your audience so that it becomes a living, convincing human being.

The Background of Characterization

An actor's life experience as well as his inherent dramatic talent determines his ability to live a part. You must broaden not only your own interests along many lines but increase your knowledge of the lives and emotions of theater people in order to understand how they created their roles. You will find that a constant study of human beings in all walks of life and in all types of literature can be an unending source of material and inspiration upon which to draw.

Successful projection of character depends not only upon the skillful use of techniques but also upon the lights and shades that distinguish a fine piece of acting. These lights and shades come naturally only with continued rehearsing and with the acting of many parts in various types of plays. Restrained action, which, however, is still sufficiently exaggerated to be appreciated in the top row; the use of the pause, in which emotion pulsates while the body and voice are still; originality, which colors the work of every distinguished artist; versatility, which surprises and delights — these are some of the means by which a character becomes a unique individual. Look for them and other fine points in acting as you watch the work of first-class actors — not only on the stage, but in motion pictures, and best of all, in the intimate contact of TV.

Studying the Play

To understand a role, you must make a careful study of the whole play. Usually the first rehearsal is the reading of the entire script, either by the director or author, or by the actors assigned to the parts. This reading should bring out the author's purpose in writing the play, the chief problems of the protagonist, the locality and type of speech, and the plot structure, especially the ways it builds up to the climax and holds interest to the conclusion. Pay close attention not only to your own lines, but also to those lines about your character spoken by the other characters. Note closely the shifting of moods throughout the play and how your character is affected by them.

You will want to know what kind of person you are in the play, why you behave as you do, what you want, and what stands in the way of your achieving your aims. Pay careful attention to the lines your character speaks, for he will reveal himself in his speech and his actions. Try to imagine what might have happened to him in his childhood to affect his personality. Note any changes that take place in him during the action of the play.

The Great White Hope, *starring James Earl Jones, was made into a movie following its success on the stage. With Jones are Jane Alexander and Jimmy Pelham.*

If the setting is an unfamiliar one, make a study of the place and period. Learn all you can from books, pictures, and travelers so that you may enter into the atmosphere, wear the costumes naturally, and feel a part of the life depicted by the playwright. Where dialect is involved, try to talk with people from the locality or listen to recordings of their voices and notice their inflections and pronunciation.

You will find it helpful to make an outline of the character traits brought out by your own lines and those spoken to and about your character. Use any main headings which seem appropriate, such as physical, mental, and spiritual characteristics; individual and social behavior; and emotional, environmental, physical, and intellectual motivations. As soon as you can, visualize your character in detail and begin working out specific ways to clarify him for your audience.

It is wise not to see a motion picture or stage production of the play you are working on, for you are likely to find yourself copying another person's mannerisms rather than developing a sound understanding of the play and the role. A better means of getting material **199** for building a characterization is to observe carefully a person in real life who is similar to your conception of the part. This individual is your primary source. You may wish to adopt his posture, movements, vocal inflections, and habit patterns. Ordinarily you will combine characteristics from several primary sources. The books you read are your secondary sources. They are helpful, but the best actor must always refer to life for his materials and his inspiration.

As you get better acquainted with your part, ask yourself questions: How good is the social adjustment of my character? Is he shy or uninhibited? How intelligent is he? Is he suffering from major or minor maladjustments? In what way has he been influenced by his environment? What are his particular problems? Is he meeting or evading his responsibilities? How and why? How does he react to all the other characters in the play? Has he developed a defense mechanism to evade the main issues of his situation? What makes him cynical, talkative, rowdyish, tense, aggressive, shy, charming, friendly, fearful, envious, courageous, idealistic? Altogether, you must understand both the social and personal background of your character.

Naturally the study of the play involves knowing the exact meaning and correct pronunciation of all unfamiliar words, for vocal inflections convey the speaker's inner reactions of the moment. This phase of your acting experience will carry over into all your classes and into your future enjoyment of books, an extra bonus.

Building Up Your Part

There are two phases of building up your part. After study of the play and analysis of the playwright's characters, you work on your own conception of your part. A valuable experience for this phase is actually preparing for acting a part in a play. You do this by working out, memorizing, and presenting one-person scenes showing many contrasted personalities. The second phase is going into rehearsal of the play with the cast under the director's guidance. It is, of course, in rehearsing that your character becomes a living person as you react to others and incorporate the principles of acting before an audience. These two phases make up the main content of your high school courses in dramatics. It is in this second phase that you work with scenes from many plays with members of the class.

After you have determined the general interpretation of your part, you must grow into it physically and spiritually during both phases. Your character's actions and speech are your means of making him real to your audience. If you have an understanding of the character, you will be able to create movements which reveal his inner nature. You may want to develop what is called a master gesture — some distinctive action that can be repeated effectively as a clue to the personality: a peculiar walk, laugh, or turn of the head. The position of your feet while you are standing, walking, or sitting can help to characterize your part truly.

Never drop out of character from the moment you assume it before you make your entrance. Then enter, coming from somewhere for some reason, and when you leave, depart for some place, keeping in character until you are safely in the wings.

Keeping in Character

To keep in character means that every gesture and facial expression must be in keeping with the underlying mood of both person and play. It is easy to stay in character when you are the center of interest, but it is most difficult to listen in character, without attracting attention to yourself, when you are in the background. It is always a temptation, if you are a talented actor, to work out clever bits of byplay when it is really your business to assist the character speaking by focusing your attention on him. At all times every unnecessary movement or gesture must be eliminated in order that you point up important words and feelings with effective gestures timed exactly right to clarify the thought. However, you must never become passive when listening and then come to life on a cue. If you are imaginatively in character every moment, you will soon learn to be alive and spontaneous, with no aimless fidgeting or stealing of scenes.

Working out details comes after setting your character in clear-cut lines by your bodily attitude and a few expressive gestures; then plan how to use the small muscles of the face and body to point essential lines or feelings. However, in your interest in details, never forget that the coordination of the entire body is essential every moment, and that the tone and inflections of your voice, the glance of your eye, the gestures of your hands, and the position of your body must create a single impression at any one instant. Doing one thing at a time and doing it effectively will keep your role clear-cut.

You and Your Role

The image of your role which the audience will accept or reject is determined by your identification with the character. When you

Two high school students in the popular musical Guys and Dolls.

have studied his reactions intellectually, you must bring your powers of imagination to feeling with him in the incidents of the play. Your sensitiveness to his words and actions and his relationship to the other persons in the play will naturally depend upon your own personality and past experiences; it is the creative imagination of an actor that permits him to feel with the character sympathetically. As you work alone with a part, you can so lose yourself in his emotion that you cry or laugh and use your voice and body exactly as he would. These intuitive responses you must fix by marking your script in some personal way so you can repeat the responses in rehearsals and performances without losing control — you want your auditors to laugh and cry, not you yourself.

This ability to arouse your own emotions comes as you work aloud and actively with many roles. That is the value of studying and reading the scenes in this book (and others) as a means of freeing your feelings. Every day you should read passages from fine plays until you find your voice and body reacting quickly to every shift in feeling because your creative imagination is functioning.

Acting is exceedingly personal, and methods of coordinating yourself with a role depend upon your training in techniques and your experience in rehearsing and acting before an audience. An important point to remember is that imagination, concentration, alertness, attention to both general effects and small details are all vital — the mere dependence upon a facile talent and an appealing personality will never lead beyond the exhibitionary stage.

Never try to think of the techniques of movement and speech when you are absorbing the emotions either by yourself or in rehearsals. Follow a daily routine of bodily and vocal exercises and practice improvisational and reading applications of them, ending with interpretative passages from poems and plays. Then forget all about exercises when emotionally developing a role. If you listen to your voice and diction and watch your own movements, you will become stilted and self-conscious and will think of yourself rather than your character. Effective bodily and vocal responses are absolutely essential in acting, but they have to become subconscious when feeling a part. Every detail of characterization must be worked out alone and in rehearsals, and nothing should be left to the inspiration of the presence of an audience.

There are many means of bringing a character to life that involve special techniques. You can find an answer to all your problems if you browse among the theater books in any good library. The following are some elements you should familiarize yourself with.

LEADING AND SUPPORTING ROLES

The leading roles are those through which the playwright brings out his theme. They include the protagonist, who must solve the problem, win, or go down to defeat in the conflict; and the hero and the heroine, who are usually the romantic and ideal parts. Most young actors are disappointed if they aren't cast in leading roles, when in reality the supporting roles are often more interesting to work with and more demanding of ability. The difference lies in function and degree, and the challenge lies in the type of person to be portrayed — no matter how long or short the part may be.

Both leading and supporting roles may be straight or character parts, although most leading roles are straight parts or are called "character leads." Straight parts are usually attractive, normal people of any age. Supporting roles calling for very young people are called "ingenue" for the feminine and "juvenile" for the masculine. The actors chosen for straight parts usually resemble the persons envisioned by the dramatist in appearance and personality; in a sense the actors are playing themselves and are said to be "cast to type." Character parts embody some degree of eccentricity — physical, psychological, mental, or spiritual — and demand a high degree of ability to interpret; such roles seldom resemble their actors in either appearance or personality. Many directors and actors feel that all parts should be considered character parts.

The great appeal of the old stock companies and of the present-day regional and repertory companies is that the audience has the opportunity to watch actors in many contrasting roles. A variety of roles really tests the actors' artistic powers and shows their versatility and flexibility. It is in such variety of roles that actors can receive the finest training; most of the stars in theater history gained their fame through such training.

Character Acting

Character parts include many interesting phases in which you should get some experience while in school. In classwork you will be wise to choose difficult roles, roles entirely different from your own self, so that you can develop as both an actor and an individual. For your own benefit, work out several bodily and vocal reactions, and in your daily practice really have fun with very difficult parts.

Character parts are usually roles dealing with interesting characteristics like age, nationality or section of a country, race, physical divergence, psychological idiosyncrasies, or erratic behavior. They are fascinating to work with. Of course external resources are very important — makeup, hairdo, dress, posture, gestures, facial expression, movement — but inner reactions are far more significant in that you want to avoid artificiality and exaggeration. Young people especially have to work very hard to be convincing in character roles.

Old age offers an intermingling of humor and pathos, tragedy and comedy, serenity and uncertainty which is challenging emotionally and physically. Even in the youth-oriented society of today, when it is fairly difficult to assess the age of older people, the character part must be intensified for the purpose of contrast to other characters. The varying success with which individuals have met the experiences of their lifetimes is reflected in old age in mellowness or irascibility of temperament. Physically there is a slowing down of bodily responses, with a resulting insecurity of movement, a lack of vigor, and a dependence upon others. The voice is higher or lower in pitch, slower in rate, and thinner in quality than in normal speech, and there are many mannerisms and tricks of inflection which have become set with the years. Old people are likely to be either spare, angular, thin-lipped, and reserved or fat, flabby, and garrulous.

Middle age often affords a real problem for high school actors. Here your own physical build is of great importance and you are really lucky to be tall or a bit overweight; makeup and padding can more easily give you the appearance of the father, mother, uncle, aunt, or family friend. These parts are usually straight; professional actors can often be themselves in such parts. Your best bet is to find someone like the role you are playing and imitate some of his mannerisms and facial expressions. In the latter case, the accenting of the slight wrinkles you may already have acquired can be of great help, with a touch of gray added over the temples. Usually poise, sophistication, and self-control are dominant traits in such roles, with slightly sharpened intonations of voice. Otherwise you have to put yourself in the place of the character and imagine what your mature reactions to the situations in the play may be when you are forty or fifty. Watching TV movie films with the older stars in outstanding roles can be of real value. Current pictures with Katharine Hepburn, Cary Grant, Paul Scofield, Emlyn Williams, and other excellent actors are a continuous source of ideas.

Children's parts are frequently of vital value in high school plays. Again you are lucky to be different — very slight of build and spontaneous in your reactions. Teen-agers are likely to overdo the childish voice and movements and thus spoil what could be utterly charming characterizations. Studying children at play, when they are unconscious of being watched, is your main source of inspiration. Children are naturally graceful, unselfconscious, and full of delightful surprises in every way. Usually their responses are exactly right when they are allowed to be themselves. You may have the opportunity of playing Margaret in Barrie's *Dear Brutus*, Prince Arthur in *King John*, and the many contemporary sub-teen roles, like those in Thornton Wilder's *Skin of Our Teeth*.

Minor roles demand as careful attention as supporting roles; the difference lies only in the number of lines and scenes involved. The lasting fame of the Moscow Art Players today rests largely on the perfect performance of every actor, even the extras, at every instant. Such ensemble playing should be the goal in every production. Actors who have only a few lines are called "bit" players, and those who appear briefly with no lines at all are called "walk-on" actors.

Laughing

Laughing is difficult on the stage, for laughter demands a sense of relaxation seldom felt under the strain of a performance. You must become interested in laughs all the time, both in real life and on the stage and TV; listen constantly for unusual ones and form the habit of catching the vowel sounds and inflections employed by people.

There are uproarious guffaws, artificial simperings, musical ripples, hysterical gurgles, and sinister snorts. For stage work, all types of laughter must have a definite vocal sound. Beginners usually manage merely to grimace and gasp without making a sound.

A laugh is produced by a sudden contraction of the abdominal muscles which forces the breath out in sharp gasps. These gasps must be given sound as they pass through the larynx. The first step in learning to laugh is to pant like a dog, tightening your abdominal muscles as you exhale and relaxing them as you breathe in. You will probably only make faces without sound when you first try, because you will undoubtedly try to say "ha" when you are drawing in the breath instead of when you are expelling it in sharp, quick spurts. As you practice, you will literally "laugh until your sides ache"; it is the continuous, rapid movement of the abdominal muscles which causes this perfectly harmless ache.

In order to master the laugh, you must relax first and then let yourself go. Take such vowel combinations heard in laughter as "ha-ha-ha, ho-ho-ho, he-he-he, hoo, hoo, hoo," and say them in rapid succession with sharp contractions of the abdominal area. Do not stop or become self-conscious. Begin at a high pitch and run down the scale. Begin at a low level and go up the scale. Then use a circumflex pitch pattern and go both up and down, prolonging some sounds and shortening others in various combinations. Be sure to spread the laughter throughout a whole sentence or speech in your part; let it die off as you speak, "Ha-ha-ha, you don't say so! Ha-ha-ho-ho, that's the funniest thing, ha-ha-ha-ha, I ever heard, ho-ho-huh-huh."

Applications

1. Practice laughing like the following people: a giggling schoolgirl on the telephone, a fat man at a comic television show, a polite lady at a joke she has heard many times, a villain who has at last captured the hero, a miser gloating over his gold, a boy when his pal trips over a brick,

a minister at a ladies' guild meeting, a farmer at a motorist whose car is stalled, a charming girl much thrilled over her date.

2. Read the following passages from Shakespeare, accompanying the lines with appropriate laughing.

a.

[PORTIA:]

God made him, therefore, let him pass for a man.

The Merchant of Venice

b.

[JAQUES:]

A fool, a fool! — I met a fool i' the forest
A motley fool; — a miserable world!

As You Like It

c.

[CELIA:]

O wonderful, wonderful, and most wonderful, wonderful, and yet again wonderful!

As You Like It

d.

[MARIA:]

Get ye all three into the box-tree: Malvolio is coming down this walk: he has been yonder i' the sun practicing behavior to his own shadow this half-hour: observe him for the love of mockery; for I know this letter will make a contemplative idiot of him. Close, in the name of jesting.

Twelfth Night

e.

[GRATIANO:]

Let me play the fool;
With mirth and laughter let old wrinkles come.

The Merchant of Venice

Crying

Crying is much easier on the stage than laughing, although the technique is much the same. Gasp for breath, using the abdominal muscles in short, sharp movements. Words are spoken on the gasping breath, but you must be very careful to keep the thought clear by not obscuring the key words. In sobbing without words, sound the syllable "oh" through the gasps, intensifying and prolonging the sound to avoid monotony. Occasional indrawn and audible breaths for the "catch in the throat" are effective, and "swallowing tears" is achieved by tightening the throat muscles and really swallowing. In uncontrolled or hysterical weeping, your "oh" will be stronger, and if words are needed they will be greatly intensified. Your entire body should react in crying. Facial expression is most important and can be created by puckering the eyebrows, biting the lips, and twisting the features to obtain the necessary effect.

Applications

1. Practice sobbing like a young child put in the corner for punishment, a wife at the bedside of her sick husband who is asleep, a spoiled child putting on an act, a hysterical woman after a serious automobile accident, an old woman alone on Christmas.
2. Read the following passages, crying through the words and being careful to keep the meaning clear.

a.

A young girl has just heard that her brother is a thief.

[POLLY:]
    I can't believe it. I can't — I can't — He's only a little boy — just a kid.

Pearls by Dan Totheroh

b.

An American tourist in her thirties has had an unfortunate flirtation with a charming Italian.

[LEONA:]
    I'm Leona Samish. I *am* attractive. I'm bright and I'm warm and I'm nice! So *want me!* Want me! — Oh, why couldn't you love me, Renato? Why couldn't you just *say* you loved me?

The Time of the Cuckoo by Arthur Laurents

DIALECT

Dialect presents interesting problems in many roles. National and sectional speech differences show themselves in the pronunciation and selection of words and in the inflections of sentences. You should train your ears to catch the changes in quality, pitch, timing, stress, and rhythm and the occasional substitutions and omissions of sounds. As you travel around our own country and abroad, the lilt of language can give you great pleasure.

When you are beginning work with a role involving a dialectal shift in English, you can find records most valuable; you can play them again and again. TV is also becoming a growing source for the study of dialectical variances in speech. Books presenting patterns of dialects, idioms, and many types of colloquial speech are coming out all the time. Actors with a natural gift for dialects are never without opportunities to act on stage, screen, and TV. However, unusual speech can be very distracting to an audience, as you have probably discovered in some BBC teleplays set in the British provinces. Panelists and famous people from all nations are appearing more and more frequently on television; you can also study their variance in speech.

A few suggestions may help you in interpreting the most commonly used dialects, but nothing can take the place of speaking with people who use the dialects until you catch the inflections, omissions, and elisions of sounds. Having a tape recorder with you on interviews will be of great value for later practice. Dialects can be imitated orally until they become more or less natural to an actor, but the audience must never be forgotten; communication is the first consideration.

British

At its best British speech is the basis for so-called "stage diction." It can be heard in the BBC dramas on TV or on records made by such players as Olivier, Gielgud, Edith Evans, especially in Shakespearean plays. A rerun of *The Forsyte Saga* would be most valuable for you to study.

The *ä* is emphasized in such words as *bäsket, äunt, bänänä, läugh;* in America these are usually *ă*. However, the British do say *ă* in *chăp, făncy, ăn, mădam, hănd;* the *ä* appears in unexpected words like *rahly* for *really,* and in *Derby, Berkeley,* and in the sound at the end of words like *fathäh, neväh, remembäh.*

The short *ĭ* is used in the words *Tuesday, nobody,* and in the *ly* in *certainly* and other adverbs. Long *ēē* is used in *bēēn,* long *ā* in *agāin;* long *ī* in *eīther* and *neīther. Leisure* is *lĕshà.* The *ŏ* is made with the rounded lips and is never *aw* or *äh.*

In words like *dictionary* and *necessary,* the accent is on the first syllable, the *ary* is slurred, and the *y* is *ĭ.*

The *r* between vowels or the doubled *r* is definitely trilled in such words as *very, America, orange, courage, marry,* and *spirit;* the *r* is silent before consonants and is practically an *äh* in words ending in *er*. The authority which actors follow most carefully in British roles is Daniel Jones' *An English Pronouncing Dictionary*.

Cockney

This is British speech at its worst. A record of *My Fair Lady* gives excellent examples in the speech of Eliza and her father. The outstanding vowel changes include the long *ī* for the long *ā*, as in *plīce* for *plāce*; the *äh* for long *ī*, as *räht* for *right*; *ow* for *ō* as in *now* for *knōw*. The sounded *h* at the beginning of words is dropped — *'abit*, *'ome* — and added to words beginning with vowels — *hit* for *it*. A peculiar *l* sound is confusing, and the rhythms and phrasing are very difficult to acquire.

> Thärt's ärl räht. The bĕttäh the plīce the bĕttäh the seat. Hit īnte a featha bed in the howld 'ous at 'ōm, but h'I've sorta lorst the featha bed 'abit lītelĭ.
>
> *Maid of France* by Harold Brighouse

Irish

The Irish dialect is a lilting one, marked by much variety in pitch and inflection. The natural speech of the cultivated Irish and their fine actors is very beautiful; the provincial accents of Southern Ireland are charming and are used in most characterizations on the stage.

Vowel changes include notably *oi* for *ī*, *ĭ* for *ĕ*, *ă* for *ŭ*, *ä* for *ŭ*, and *ā* for *ē*. Thus we have *foine* for *fine*, *whĭn* for *when*, *wăn* for *one*, *äv* for *of*, and *dāle* for *deal*. The pronouns *my* and *you* become *mĭ* and *yĕ*.

Consonant changes are more difficult to explain; the sound of *s* before another consonant is almost a *sh*; thus we have *shlāpe* for *sleep* and *shmile* for *smile*. The final *ing* is usually shorted to *in'* and sometimes a *t* is substituted for *g* and we have *darlint* for *darling*.

American

Dialects vary in practically every state in the United States, but there are a few distinguishing characteristics used in whole areas. Broad colloquial accents are noticeable in news reports on TV, and there are records available of regional speech from many isolated places.

A few general suggestions should be considered in regional roles. The Western accent is very nasal and noticeably rolls the *r*, especially

The grouping of characters, their expressions, and their positions create tension in this scene from Red's My Color, What's Yours? *at the Cleveland Play House. Actors: Richard Halverson, Richard Oberlin, Cleo Holladay, Nick Devlin.*

BEN BLISS

at the ends of words, and replaces the trilled *r* always. The short *ă* always takes the place of the *ä* or *ȧ*. The short *ĭ* frequently takes the place of long *ē*; and *ŏŏ* is practically always used for *ū* and *ōō*. The *ē, ō, ī*, and *ū* are seldom heard.

The Southern accent is unusually pure and pleasing because of relaxation of the vocal apparatus and general lack of nervous tension; this probably is because of the warmer climate. There are numerous dialects in all the Southern states. In general, the vowels are rich and round, but there is a good deal of substitution of one vowel for another in different sections.

Frequently the *ī* becomes *äh*, as in *I, my*, and *like*. The final *er* is practically always *äh* because of the dropping of *r* at the ends of words; thus you might hear "Ah lähk that view oväh yondäh."

Many consonants are dropped because of the lazy use of the tongue, as in *lemme* for *let me*, *fac'* for *fact*; practically all final *g*'s in *ing* words are also dropped. In some places *haid* takes the place of *head*, a *y* is added as in *hyeah* for *hear*, and *ĕ* becomes *ä* as in *yäs* for *yes*.

There is a great deal of vocal inflection and sustained, drawled, slow sounds. Andy Griffith's early monologue records are great fun to imitate if you want the colloquial expressions and inflections of isolated regions. The attractive cultivated speech of the leading roles of Tennessee Williams' plays centering around Southern women can be followed in recordings.

The Eastern and Northern speech has a decided nasal quality, possibly because of the cold climate and consequent tightening of the vocal apparatus. Bostonians speak more nearly like the British than do other Americans, but they frequently add an *r* to words like *idea*; their use of the *ä* is correct for the stage, as is the dropping of the final *r* in words and sentences and before consonants; their vowel sounds are accurate and pleasing.

The Yankee accent is used in many plays: spoken with tight lips and tense muscles, it is nasal and not inflected; final consonants are dropped, the short *ĭ* and long *ē* are interchanged, and the short *ă* is used for the *ä* and *ȧ*.

European

European accents are too difficult to imitate without listening to people who use them habitually. A few suggestions may be helpful.

Italian is exceedingly musical and pleasant to hear, with many attractive inflections. The vowels are open and pure, but the short *ĭ* becomes *ē*; the *ä* is marked and the short *ă* seldom heard. The occasional *ä* sound added to consonant sounds is most pleasing, as in *soft-ä-ting* (soft thing) or *fruit-ä-stand*, and "I gottä" as in T. A. Daly's delightful poem "I gotta love for Angela, I love Carlotta, too." All of Daly's poems offer excellent phrasing and pronunciations; he uses *dä* for *the*, *āy* for *ē*, and adds *ä*'s between words.

The German dialect is definitely gutteral; many of the sounds are made with the back of the tongue: *v* takes the place of *w*; and *t* is used for *d*, *p* for *b*, and *ē* for *ī*.

Swedish is inclined to be high in pitch, with recurring rising inflections and a flat tone which is not nasal. The *ŏŏ* is *ū*, so *good* becomes *gude*; *w* is *v*; and *j* is *y*, as in *yūst* for *jŭst*.

All the European dialects depend upon the original inflections and rhythms of their speech and the position of the parts of the sentence, which frequently differ very much from those of the English language. Authors can give some help in writing passages, but listening to people and recordings is essential to an actor using the dialects.

Applications

1. The following are selections for practice in dialect.

a.

A very old lady in a small town in Wisconsin has been pushed aside by the energetic younger members of her family and talks to herself by the fireplace.

[GRANDMA:]

Dum 'em. They've gone off to do things. And I'm so old, so fool old. Oh, God! Can't you make us hurry? Can't you make us hurry? Get us to the time when we don't have to dry up like a pippin before we're ready to be took off? Our heads an' our hearts an' our legs an' our backs — oh, make 'em last busy, busy, right up to the time the hearse backs up to the door!

Neighbours by Zona Gale

b.

A middle-aged Irish woman quarrels with another woman.

[MRS. FALLON:]

Is that what you are saying, Bridget Tully, and is that what you think? I tell you it's too much talk you have, making yourself out to be such a great one, and to be running down every respectable person!

Spreading the News by Lady Gregory

c.

An old Irish woman muses to herself after her last son has been drowned at sea.

[MAURYA:]

They're all gone now, and there isn't anything more the sea can do to me. I'll have no call to be up crying and praying when the wind breaks from the south, and you can hear the surf is in the east, and the surf is in the west, making a great stir with the two noises, and they hitting one on the other.

Riders to the Sea by John Millington Synge

d.

A young Englishman of twenty tries to propose.

[BRYAN ROPES:]

I say, look here, I'm not a bit mad, you know. There never has been any madness in my family. I mean that might be important, you know. — Look here, I'm awfully sorry but I love you. — I was awake all night about it. It's frightfully short notice, I know.

The Lilies of the Field by John Hastings Turner

e.

Mr. Doolittle, a Cockney dustman, has become a gentleman in London society due to a benefactor's having left him a great deal of money. He objects violently to his new position.

[MR. DOOLITTLE:]

It's making a gentleman of me that I object to. Who asked him to make a gentleman of me? I was happy. I was free. I touched pretty nigh everybody for money when I wanted it, same as I touched you, 'Enry 'Iggins. Now I am worrited; tied neck and heels; and everybody touches me for money. It's a fine thing for you, says my solicitor. Is it? says I. You mean it's a good thing for you, I says. A year ago I hadn't a relative in the world except two or three that wouldn't speak to me. Now I've fifty, and not a decent weeks's wages among the lot of them. — And the next one to touch me will be you, 'Enry 'Iggins. I'll have to learn to speak middle class language from you, instead of speaking proper English. . . .

Pygmalion by George Bernard Shaw

f.

A very dominating Southern woman talks condescendingly to her seventeen-year-old son about his girl, who has just jilted him.

[ELIZA:]

Gene. You know what I'd do if I were you? I'd just show her I was a good sport, that's what! I wouldn't let on to her that it affected me one bit. I'd write her just as big as you please and laugh about the whole thing. — Why, I'd be ashamed to let any girl get my goat like that. When you're older, you'll just look back on this and laugh. You'll see. You'll be going to college next year, and you won't remember a thing about it. . . .

Look Homeward, Angel adapted by Ketti Frings
from the novel by Thomas Wolfe

g.

A kindly, old Italian discusses life and its beauties with his friend, Mr. Carp.

[MR. BONAPARTE:]

You make-a me laugh, Mr. Carp. You say life'sa bad. No, life'sa good. — You say life'sa bad — well, is pleasure for you to say so. No? The streets, winter a' summer — trees, cats — I love-a them all. The gooda boys and girls, they who sing and whistle — very good! The eating and sleeping, drinking wine — very good! I gone around on my wagon and talk to many people — nice! Howa you like the big buildings of the city?

Golden Boy by Clifford Odets

2. Select one of the following plays and work up several speeches in it for further practice in dialect.

Neighbours by Zona Gale
Trifles by Susan Glasspell
The Emperor Jones by Eugene O'Neill
The Glass Menagerie by Tennessee Williams
Welsh Honeymoon by Jeannette Marks
The Corn is Green by Emlyn Williams
Pygmalion by George Bernard Shaw
Spreading the News by Lady Gregory
Anna Christie by Eugene O'Neill
Tovarich by Jacques Deval, translated by Robert E. Sherwood
Night Over Taos by Maxwell Anderson
Lady Precious Stream by S. I. Hsiung
Sunup by Lula Vollmer
The Green Pastures by Marc Connelly

There are more than a dozen actors in this scene from the Gilbert and Sullivan operetta The Pirates of Penzance *as produced by the D'Oyly Carte Opera Company. Note that every one is "in character" and reacting to the situation.*

COMPLIMENTS OF THE SECRETARY, THE D'OYLY CARTE OPERA TRUST LIMITED

EMOTIONAL ACTING

Emotional acting is the recapitulation of all phases of acting so far presented in this discussion of characterization, beginning even with "Reading Scenes Aloud" in Chapter 1, which you should review. With added work on the technique of vocal and bodily responses, you are now ready to approach an impassioned scene with understanding.

If you are seriously considering a theatrical career, now is the time to read one or two of the current books on the Stanislavski system, listed at the end of this chapter. Apply his ideas about recalling some emotional experience of your past life and comparing your reactions to those of the character you are creating in the situation depicted; about thinking out the problems of the scene; about seeing and analyzing the character; about feeling with him in his initial mood and changing as he does; about then using your voice and body to make him real to your audience.

In passages with rising emotional intensity, strike a balance between overacting and underplaying your role. It is best to begin quietly, saving your vocal and physical resources for the most intense moment at the climax of the speech or scene. Go over your lines until you are so caught up in the spirit of the situation that you speak and move as the character would under the circumstance.

When you have satisfied yourself that you have caught the feeling which will result in the right inflections, pauses, movements, and emotional buildup, mark your script to help you retain them. Then go over the lines orally again and again. When at last you have so immersed yourself in the character and situation that it moves you deeply, you can be sure the audience will react the same way.

Applications

In the following excerpts from plays, rise to the appropriate emotional pitch.

1. *A young prince pleads with his jailor, who is threatening to put out his eyes.*

[PRINCE ARTHUR:]
> Alas, what need you be so boisterous-rough?
> I will not struggle, I will stand stone-still.
> For heaven's sake, Hubert, let me not be bound!
> Nay, hear me, Hubert! — Drive these men away,
> And I will sit as quiet as a lamb.
>> *The Life and Death of King John* by William Shakespeare

2. *Cyrano, a seventeenth-century poet, swordsman, and philosopher is charming, witty, and bold. However, his huge nose often makes him the object of ridicule. In this speech, he sadly tells a friend that he knows no woman can ever love him.*

[CYRANO:]

> My old friend — look at me,
> And tell me how much hope remains for me
> With this protuberance! Oh I have no more
> Illusions! Now and then — bah! I may grow
> Tender, walking alone in the blue cool
> Of evening, through some garden fresh with flowers
> After the benediction of the rain;
> My poor big devil of a nose inhales
> April . . . and so I follow with my eyes
> Where some boy, with a girl upon his arm,
> Passes a patch of silver . . . and I feel
> Somehow, I wish I had a woman too,
> Walking with little steps under the moon,
> And holding my arm so, and smiling. Then
> I dream — and I forget. . . . And then I see
> The shadow of my profile on the wall!
> *Cyrano de Bergerac* by Edmond Rostand, translated by Brian Hooker

3. *A middle-aged mother vehemently expresses her views on marriage.*

[MRS. HARDY:]

Well, James, aren't you going to say something? Aren't you a judge? You're not going to uphold these girls in this nonsense about not being happy, are you? What has happiness to do with marriage, I'd like to know? Marriage means discipline and duty and you know it. Any man and woman can get along if they're willing to sacrifice their own desires once in a while. If one won't the other must. Somebody has to yield. Generally it's the woman. — Now, Myra, you think you'd be better off if you had a more practical man to deal with and Estelle thinks she'd like a little more attention. I don't doubt you would, both of you. I don't doubt that many a woman would like to shake her own husband and get another picked to order. But husbands aren't made to order. You took George and Terrill for better or for worse and even if it's worse than you expected, you'll have to make the best of it! I've raised one family. I'm not going to start in now and raise another. I've had my problems to work out and I've stood it. You can! — Do you imagine my life's been a bed of roses? At times I have been dissatisfied, mighty dissatisfied. I'd have liked a husband who took me to parties and brought me roses and carnations and chocolate creams — but I didn't get them. You never sent me a box of flowers in your life! Sometimes when I've spent the day darning your socks and turning your cuffs and hemming flour sacks for dishcloths, and buying round steak when I wanted porterhouse, and I've seen one of my old chums drive past in her new automobile while I was hanging out the wash — I've been so dissatisfied I could have smashed the whole house down. But I didn't do it. I pitched in and beat up some batter cake and scrubbed down the back steps and worked it off. And so can they!

Skidding by Aurania Rouverol

4. *Mercutio dies by the sword of Tybalt.*

[MERCUTIO:]

I am hurt; — 'tis not so deep as a well, nor so wide as a church door; but 'tis enough, 'twill serve; ask for me tomorrow and you shall find me a grave man. I am peppered, I warrant, for this world. A plague o' both your houses! Zounds, a dog, a rat, a mouse, a cat, to scratch a man to death! — Why the devil came you between us? I was hurt under your arm.

Romeo and Juliet by William Shakespeare

5. *Brutus rebukes Cassius for taking bribes.*

[BRUTUS:]

Remember March, the ides of March, remember!
Did not great Julius bleed for justice' sake?
What villain touch'd his body, that did stab,
And not for justice? What, shall one of us,
That struck the foremost man of all this world
But for supporting robbers, shall we now
Contaminate our fingers with base bribes,
And sell the mighty space of our large honors
For so much trash as may be grasped thus? —
I'd rather be a dog and bay the moon
Than such a Roman!

Julius Caesar by William Shakespeare

6. *Fanny, an elderly actress, is answering her granddaughter who has just said, "Acting isn't everything."*

[FANNY:]

It's everything! They'll tell you it isn't — your fancy friends — but it's a lie! And they know it's a lie! They'd give their ears to be in your place! Don't make any mistake about that! . . . You've got to leave, and go down to a stuffy dressing room and smear paint on your face and go out on the stage and speak a lot of fool lines, and you love it! You couldn't live without it! Do you suppose I could have stood these two years, hobbling around with this thing (*brandishing her cane*) if I hadn't known I was going back to it? . . . Every night when I've been sitting here alone I'm really down at the theater! Seven-thirty, and they're going in at the stage door! Good evening to the doorman. Taking down their keys and looking in the mail rack. Eight o'clock! The stage hands are setting up.

Half hour, Miss Cavendish! Grease paint, rouge, mascara! Fifteen minutes, Miss Cavendish! My costume! More rouge! Where's the rabbit's foot? Overture! How's the house tonight? The curtain's up! Props! Cue! Enter! That's all that's kept me alive these two years. If you weren't down there for me, I wouldn't want to live. . . . I couldn't live. You . . . down there . . . for me . . . going on . . . going on . . . going on. (*She goes limp, topples over, and crumples.*)

*The Royal Family** by George S. Kaufman and Edna Ferber

PRESENTING ONE-PERSON SCENES

The presentation of poetic or prose selections with only one person speaking is an excellent first step to acting a part, for it demands the same analysis of character, visualization of situation, and understanding of meaning. In a sense, one-person scenes afford an even greater opportunity for characterization, for the interpreter alone bears the responsibility of revealing the soul of a human being caught at a crucial moment and of presenting it sympathetically to an audience.

Formerly such scenes were called monologues, but the term went into disrepute when many elocutionists presented trite and exaggerated situations purely for entertainment and they became highly artificial and "hammy." Today, however, monologues are coming back; comedians use them, especially on TV and in night clubs, in a far more sophisticated form and usually in a humorous presentation of themselves. When the "Specials" came into television, such scenes and dramatic sketches were featured with marked success; you can learn a great deal from watching the best of them. In fact, you can possibly work up some original monologues, present them yourself, and give real pleasure with them.

A scene from Thornton Wilder's play Our Town, *played without scenery and popular with high schools.*

CULVER PICTURES, INC.

One-man performances for full evening programs are becoming more and more popular. In them an actor, made up in detail and costumed correctly, presents a first-person sketch based on selections from an author's works. He brings out the character of the great man himself as well as the leading incidents in his life. Hal Holbrook as Mark Twain and Emlyn Williams as Dylan Thomas and Charles Dickens are among the most distinguished successes in this field.

In the dramatics class, you may make your choice of a selection from two viewpoints, with the advice of your teacher. Either choose for a public performance a role for which you are well-suited in type; or select one which will develop you as an individual seeking improvement in emotional or mental attitudes, vocal power, or clarity in speech and movement. Since you will spend a great deal of time and effort in perfecting this assignment, your choice is important. There are four steps to take as you work out your character.

Preparation

The first step is to study the selection carefully. Look up the meanings of words and expressions and study any dialects employed. Determine the author's purpose and divide the selection into logical units leading to the climax and an effective conclusion. Plan your general outline of actions, centered upon the person or persons whom you are addressing. Most short selections have only one imaginary
220 individual with whom you are talking, but sometimes people come

and go and you must plan definitely when they enter and where they are placed and when they leave. In many cases, the audience is to be addressed as a person.

The second step is to analyze the character speaking. Who is he? How old is he? What are his predominating physical and spiritual characteristics? How did he get into the situation in which we find him? What is his present state of mind? How is he dressed? How does he move? How does he speak? Does he use polished diction? To give validity to your analysis, use a primary source — a real person who resembles the character you are delineating. Study his speech, gestures, and movements.

The third step is to imagine the stage setting for the character. It is especially important to visualize the person whom you are addressing and talk to him throughout the selection. Imagine him on a diagonal line downstage, so that you may face your audience. The angle or direction of your glance is a vital consideration; it tells the audience where the other characters are and helps to identify them. For example, a child speaking to an adult looks up, a woman speaking to someone in bed looks down, a man talking with friends around a table looks first at one and then another of them. Visualize, too, the imaginary stage setting with the essential furniture, doors, and windows in set places. Once places are established, you may not move the person to whom you are speaking or the furniture without losing the illusion — unless, of course, such action is necessary in the story. If new imaginary characters enter during the scene, they should receive your attention as you turn to address them. It is not an easy matter to make clear-cut turns toward imaginary characters and still keep the entire audience in view.

The fourth step is to memorize and rehearse the selection. Memorizing is the final, not the first, step. You will naturally memorize in any manner you prefer, but the "whole method" is to be recommended. Repeat the entire selection orally over and over again until it is fixed in your mind as a complete unit; then polish it off paragraph by paragraph, stanza by stanza, and at last sentence by sentence and word by word. Combine the memorizing with rehearsing in order to avoid falling into errors of emphasis, phrasing, and pronunciation; these errors are almost impossible to eradicate after they are fixed in your mind.

Rehearse out loud and constantly imagine the person to whom you are speaking, the setting, and the audience. It is usually better to memorize while moving about, for when the body is active, the brain is alert. Fixing the entire selection by several repetitions immediately before going to sleep is also helpful.

Presenting Your Monologue

When you present the selection, step to the front of the stage in your own person; include the entire audience in a friendly and confident glance. Give any introductory remarks in a clear voice, using good articulation and speaking unaffectedly and graciously. Then pause for a moment as you assume the bodily attitude of your character. The opening words should suggest to the audience the age, sex, personality, strength, and mood of the character. During the performance, keep your character consistent in voice, gesture, and movement. Hold the person to whom you are speaking and the properties clearly before the audience by the position of your body and the direction of your glance. Complete the closing sentence in character; then pause and, in your own person, depart.

THE TEAHOUSE OF THE AUGUST MOON
by John Patrick

SAKINI. Tootie Fruitie. (*He takes the gum out of his mouth and, wrapping it carefully in a piece of paper, puts it in a matchbox and restores it to pocket in shirt.*)
Most generous gift of American soldier.
Lovely ladies and gentlemen: Please to introduce myself.
Sakini by name. Interpretor by profession.
Educated by ancient dictionary.
Okinawan by whim of gods. History of Okinawa reveal distinguished record of conquerors. We have honor to be subjugated in fourth century by Chinese pirates. In sixteenth century by English missionaries. In eighteenth century by Japanese war lords. And in twentieth century by American Marines. Okinawa very fortunate. Culture brought to us. . . . Not have to leave for it. Learn many things. Most important that rest of world not like Okinawa. World filled with delightful variation. Illustration. In Okinawa. . . . no lock on doors. Bad manners not to trust neighbors. In America. . . . lock and key big industry. Conclusion? Bad manners good business. In Okinawa. . . . wash self in public bath with nude lady quite proper. Picture of nude lady in private home quite improper. In America — statue of nude lady in park win

prize. But lady in flesh in park win penalty. Conclusion? Pornography question of geography. But Okinawans most eager to be educated by conquerors. Deep desire to improve friction. Not easy to learn. Sometimes painful. But pain makes man think. Thought makes man wise. Wisdom makes life endurable.

JOAN OF LORRAINE
by Maxwell Anderson

(*In her cell,* JOAN *is kneeling in prayer.*)

JOAN. King of Heaven, the night is over. My jailors have worn themselves out with tormenting me, and have gone to sleep. And I should sleep — I could sleep safely now — but the bishop's questions come back to me over and over. What if I were wrong? How do I know my visions were good? I stare wide awake at the dawn in the window and I cannot find an answer.

So many things they said were true. It is true the king we crowned at Rheims is not wise nor just nor honest. It is true that his realm is not well governed. It is true that I am alone, that my friends have forgotten me, both the king and the nobles who fought beside me. There is no word from them, no offer of ransom.

And I am doubly alone, for I have denied my visions, and they will come to me no more. I believe my visions to be good, but I do not know how to defend them. When I am brought into a court, and must prove what I believe, how can I prove that they are good and not evil?

Yes, and I ask myself whether I have been honest always, for when I went among men, I acted my part. It was not only that I wore boy's clothes — I stood as my brother stood and spoke heartily as he spoke, and put challenges in the words he would have spoken. When I spoke with my own voice, nobody listened, nobody heard me, yet was it honest to assume ways that were not my own? I know there's to be no answer.

I can expect no answer now, after I have betrayed and denied my saints. They will not burn me now because I admitted that I could not prove my Voices good — and I submitted to the church. And now, when I am to live, when I have done what they say is right, I am more unhappy than when they said I was wrong and must die.

CYRANO DE BERGERAC
by Edmond Rostand

A boorish young man has attempted to insult CYRANO *by stating,* "*Your nose is rather large.*" CYRANO *responds by suggesting all the imaginative descriptions a more perceptive person might have used.*

CYRANO.   Ah, no, young sir!
You are too simple. Why, you might have said —
Oh, a great many things! Mon dieu, why waste
Your opportunity? For example, thus: —
AGGRESSIVE: I, sir, if that nose were mine,
I'd have it amputated — on the spot!
FRIENDLY: How do you drink with such a nose?
You ought to have a cup made specially.
DESCRIPTIVE: 'Tis a rock — a crag — a cape —
A cape? say rather, a peninsula!
INQUISITIVE: What is that receptacle —
A razor-case or a portfolio?
KINDLY: Ah, do you love the little birds
So much that when they come and sing to you,
You give them this to perch on?   INSOLENT:
Sir, when you smoke, the neighbors must suppose
Your chimney is on fire. CAUTIOUS: Take care —
A weight like that might make you topheavy.
THOUGHTFUL: Somebody fetch my parasol —
Those delicate colors fade so in the sun!
PEDANTIC: Does not Aristophanes
Mention a mythologic monster called
Hippocampelephantocamelos?
Surely we have here the original!
FAMILIAR: Well, old torchlight! Hang your hat
Over that chandelier — it hurts my eyes.
ELOQUENT: When it blows, the typhoon howls,
And the clouds darken. DRAMATIC: When it bleeds —
The Red Sea! ENTERPRISING: What a sign
For some perfumer! LYRIC: Hark — the horn
Of Roland calls to summon Charlemagne! —
SIMPLE: When do they unveil the monument?
RESPECTFUL: Sir, I recognize in you
A man of parts, a man of prominence —
RUSTIC: Hey? What? Call that a nose? Na na —
I be no fool like what you think I be —
That there's a blue cucumber! MILITARY:

Point against cavalry! PRACTICAL: Why not
A lottery with this for the grand prize?
Or — parodying Faustus in the play —
"Was this the nose that launched a thousand ships
And burned the topless towers of Ilium?"
These, my dear sir, are things you might have said
Had you some tinge of letters, or of wit
To color your discourse. But wit, — not so,
You never had an atom — and of letters,
You need but three to write you down — an Ass.

A THOUSAND CLOWNS
by Herb Gardner

MURRAY.   Oh, Arnie, you don't understand any more. You got that wide stare that people stick in their eyes so nobody'll know their head's asleep. You got to be a shuffler, a moaner. You want me to come sit and eat fruit with you and watch the clock run out. You start to drag and stumble with the rotten weight of all the people who should have been told off, all the things you should have said, all the specifications that aren't yours. The only thing you got left to reject is your food in a restaurant if they do it wrong and you can send it back and make a big fuss with the waiter. (MURRAY *turns away from* ARNOLD, *goes to window seat, sits down.*) Arnold, five months ago I forgot what *day* it was. I'm on the subway on my way to work and I didn't know what day it was and it scared the hell out of me. (*Quietly*) I was sitting in the express looking out the window same as every morning watching the local stops go by in the dark with an empty head and my arms folded, not feeling great and not feeling rotten, just not feeling, and for a minute I couldn't remember, I didn't know, unless I really concentrated, whether it was a Tuesday or a Thursday — or a — for a minute it could have been *any* day, Arnie — sitting in the train going through any day — in the dark through any year — Arnie, it scared the hell out of me. (*Stands up*) You got to know what day it is. You got to know what's the name of the game and what the rules are with nobody else telling you. You have to own your days and name them, each one of them, every one of them, or else the years go right by and none of them belong to you.

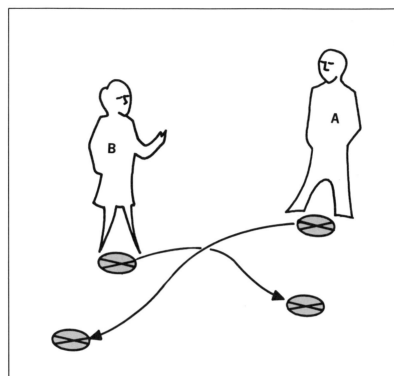

Diagram of a countercross. When character A crosses from his UL position, to DR, character B will move from UC to LC to balance the stage, to offset the movement of A, and to avoid being blocked by A's new position.

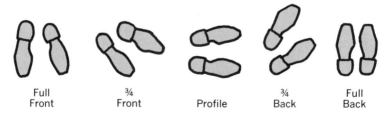

| Full
Front | ¾
Front | Profile | ¾
Back | Full
Back |

Decreasing emphasis

THE ACTOR'S POSITIONS

INTERPRETING MEMORIZED SCENES

Interpreting scenes has become the most vital part of high school dramatic work, serving two purposes. First, it gives you a chance to create a number of brief but contrasting roles in varying moods. Second, it brings you in contact with sections of plays in different classifications and of historical interest, and lets you become acquainted with the styles of many dramatists. Interpreting scenes is the most important step in acting. In class, the presenting of scenes is an excellent means of interesting students not taking dramatics. You may invite other classes to watch organized groups of scenes from appropriate plays.

Selecting Scenes

The selection of scenes to be memorized and produced as classwork involves both the teacher and student. Psychologically it is often wise to find roles for members which tend to bring out latent abilities or which give experience in needed emotional and physical responses rather than to cast to type. However, playing a part you really know you can do beautifully is not only a joy you must experience but, if you are appearing before an audience, is a requirement.

Depending upon the teacher's wishes, you and the members of the group should select a scene which you are enthusiastic about and which will give each of you a real opportunity to create a good part. Small casts are preferable, for they give greater opportunities for characterization in depth. Duet-scenes are especially valuable, since close interaction of interpretation is more easily worked out in them.

Producing memorized scenes will give you a greater sense of accomplishment than either reading or improvising them. You will be able to create a role and give an accurate interpretation of what a distinguished playwright has written. If you take time to produce a scene carefully, you have the satisfied feeling of having presented a finished performance. In rehearsing such scenes throughout the course, you will put into use the fundamentals of acting; this will help you greatly when you take part in public performances.

The scenes presented in all the chapters of this book have been chosen with care to give you special insights into theater experience. In addition you will find other scenes in the plays you read and see during the course which you will enjoy working on by yourself or with groups. If possible, you should read the entire play from which the scene to be produced has been selected.

Rehearsing

You are now ready to put into practice what you have learned in creating a role and responding to the other characters. Read the scene with the rest of the cast conversationally, and discuss what is the emotional high point of the scene and how best to work up to it. Then make plans for rehearsing outside of class as well as in it, when probably all students will be working in groups. Rehearsing in class is excellent training for complete concentration on everyone's part; but, if you do the play really well, you will need to work outside also. At this time, decide what period the scene is in and what style of acting is appropriate and what essential pieces of furniture you will need. Plan an effective stage arrangement which can function easily and simply.

Rehearsing scenes demands a sacrifice of time and effort, but you will acquire working knowledge of the following essentials of acting.

Memorization of lines should be letter-perfect. You cannot create a part if your mind is thinking, "What do I say next?" Apply the "whole method" to the entire scene so you are fixing ideas and not words, not only in your own lines but in all of them. Do not begin memorizing until you have worked out the movements and stage business, with the group holding scripts in hands. Mark the directions and then memorize your lines, beginning with paragraphs and polishing off with sentences and words. Be sure of your pronunciation, phrasing, and emphasis so that false inflections do not become fixed.

Picking up of cues rapidly determines the timing of the scene. Most amateurs slow up the action of plays by pausing slightly between speeches. The cue is the last phrase of the line before you speak, so be prepared to come in right on its final word without a break.

Listening in character without moving allows your facial reaction to follow the meaning of the words you are hearing and permits you to hold a vital, not an apathetic, position. Then when your cue is coming up, your face, body, and voice will respond on time together, and you won't begin to act only when you hear your cue, thus causing the scene to drag.

Keep the stage picture constantly in mind in order to permit all action to be clear to the entire audience all the time. In other words, don't cover other actors, don't huddle in tight groups, and don't stand in straight lines.

Emphasize the center of interest at all times — whether it is the person speaking, an object, or a sound offstage — by giving it your alert attention. The attention of the audience should always be focused where it should be.

Make no movement or gesture without a definite reason inherent in the script or action of the scene. This means to keep still without being rigid or disinterested and to be intelligently alert and in character without distracting the attention of the audience. Avoid aimless little gestures or fidgeting in position. When you move, walk in an S or curved pattern but go directly to the chair, person, or entrance without ambling about uncertainly. Stage crosses should always have a purpose.

Keep the action in view of the audience without appearing to do so. This is not easy. The person speaking for any length of time should be upstage center so that other characters are looking at him and so that his voice can more easily reach the audience. Usually gestures should be made with the upstage arm and turns made toward the front. Move forward on the upstage foot and kneel on the downstage knee. Do not, when speaking, cover your face with your hands or with an object like a fan or a telephone. A duet-scene has to be carefully worked out to avoid actors covering each other, or holding the same positions too long, or using similar gestures (like folded arms or clasped hands in lap) at the same time; find reasons for not doing so.

Your eyes are your most expressive feature. The speed and direction of a single glance can tell volumes. Always know exactly where you are focusing your attention, but do not make the mistake of keeping your eyes glued to the eyes of the person to whom you are speaking. Remember to include the entire audience in your conversation and avoid looking at the ground or at objects which will throw your voice to the floor.

After establishing your character in clear-cut lines by your bodily attitude and a few striking gestures, use your small muscles in delicate movements to point essential lines but never fidget, wave your arms, or make faces! Coordination of the entire body is essential every moment, and the tone and inflections of your voice, the expression and direction of your eyes, the gestures of your hands, and the position of your body must always create a single impression.

Doing one thing at a time and doing it effectively will help you keep your role clear-cut. Never anticipate what the next line or move is to be by either an uncertain inflection of the voice or the slightest gesture.

It pays to wear clothes that relate to your character in their general impression. Avoid ultra-modern styles entirely out of keeping with your character and extreme hair styles and arrangement. Wear colors your character might select; they help to put you in the mood of the scene. Your shoes are very important and should not have extremely high heels unless the character would be wearing them, or be particularly casual except for the same reason; your movements are greatly affected by footwear. Boys should wear coats in order to have pockets to use in showing feeling and mannerisms. Girls should avoid showy costume jewelry; especially long necklaces are likely to lead to fidgeting with them. Skirts should always be long enough to suggest the age of feminine roles without being so out of style as to be conspicuous.

If all of you work together, you will achieve the joy of the rapid give-and-take of real conversation as you toss the lines back and forth. You will feel the different personalities reacting to each other and realize that acting is a cooperative experience. Discovering how personality plays upon personality in a scene is what makes rehearsing so exciting. It is in rehearsals that you will sense phases of your character you had not fully realized when practicing alone. You will note his prejudices as he reacts to other people, and you will recognize his ideals as they are clarified by his reaction to some remark by another character. In response to a cue, you will suddenly find yourself saying a line exactly as you know it should be said. When this happens, mark the exact inflection and phrasing, for you may forget them. After an especially inspired rehearsal, go home and restudy your lines at once while you are under the spell.

Giving a Program of Scenes

Arranging a program of scenes can be a fascinating class or club project. In arranging such a program you should always have a unifying idea back of your choices. For example, you may select scenes showing different countries or periods, scenes from different plays by the same author, or a group of contrasting quarrels, farewells, or love scenes.

There should be a stage manager for the whole program. He will be responsible for changing the furniture, props, and lights for each scene. He should be given a résumé of the plot; a list of the furniture, props, and effects wanted; and all cues for the curtain and lights.

Your teacher will decide whether or not to have student directors for your scenes, since problems of class procedure must be considered. Someone outside the cast should be the announcer, giving the names of the plays, the writers, and the student actors; he should also give a brief summary of the action leading up to each scene presented.

At the end of the program, if it is presented in class, there should be an evaluation of each scene, either oral or written. The strong and weak points in each characterization and the general effect of the scene as a whole should be analyzed. Suggestions should be constructive, with the aim of improving the acting ability of the performers.

ACTING IN PLAYS

Acting a part is the culmination of your work in dramatics. There are two distinct phases of dramatic activity in high school: the work done in the classroom and the public performance. Acting a part gives you the opportunity to assess your achievements in characterization through an understanding of the dramatist's goals and the development of your communication techniques. Therefore, in both phases, the acting experience is the same; logically, public appearances should be preceded by classroom performances. The differences lie in production methods, which include detailed direction by an experienced teacher-director, on practically a professional stage with full equipment, before a large and critical audience of all ages, and, most important, far longer rehearsals in depth. Today the standards of high school theater are very high, and finished public performances of first-class plays are expected.

Classroom one-act plays will give you excellent experience in creating roles in relation to a full cast. You will have the advice and the overall direction of the teacher, but the group is largely on its own. You may have a director, preferably one who has been in another class play, or work as a group. Your staging will be simple, but should be as complete as the facilities of the classroom permit. In large, new buildings, such facilities are almost like a little theater, but equally high-grade class performances can be given without such facilities if creative imagination and real effort are put to use by everyone involved. In fact, ingenuity and skill utilized with very limited equipment often encourage far higher accomplishment in acting.

In classroom acting, you are afforded an opportunity for character development. The emphasis is on personal growth, not personal exploitation. With a number of groups putting on different plays, the casts become cooperative teams. In the friendly atmosphere of a classroom, without the strain of public acclaim to worry them, students gain a proper perspective on acting. They develop good sportsmanship, dependability in gathering props, punctuality in attending rehearsals, and ingenuity in working out productions with limited equipment. Many young people discover they can do well as actors, scenic artists, technicians, and directors. In every case, the student's life becomes richer and fuller in experience and artistic achievements, and he gains an added assurance which carries over into all his school activities. The more talented members may be inspired to stage plays in their church and community groups. Many little theaters draw their most capable recruits from school classes in dramatics. In this way, a link is made between the school and the community, and the young people themselves find their leisure time filled with work which is exciting and constructive.

A word of warning might not be amiss here. Too often those brilliant students who are at first the most satisfactory members of the class are later completely spoiled by their success and consider themselves finished artists when they are only beginners. As Touchstone says in *As You Like It*, "The fool doth think he is wise, but the wise man knoweth himself to be a fool." One of the advantages of approaching the theater through the school is that young actors gain a solid foundation while they have the wholesome comradeship of the class and the guidance of the teachers. This lessens the danger of the selfish egotism sometimes encouraged by success behind the footlights.

Several distinct types of people are attracted to participation in theatrical activities. There is the sincere actor who devotes himself wholeheartedly to the creative experience of conveying the spirit of the play to the audience. He helps lift people into the rich world of the imagination. This type of person may later become a professional of value, or a theatergoer who supports the finest of theatrical activities, as patron or amateur actor, in sincere voluntary support of community dramatic groups.

On the other hand, there is the exhibitionist who is the bane of the theater — amateur or professional. He is the clever person, often with good appearance and facile talent, who uses a role as a medium for exhibiting his ability and charm. He cares very little for the meaning of the play or the elements that make up an entire performance. He never learns the great joy of acting, for he is always self-conscious and self-centered. He is likely to be oversensitive to criticism because he is sure his judgment is best. He belittles the work of the other actors and makes them feel awkward as they struggle for a particular effect. Sometimes he even refuses to learn lines accurately, knowing he can improvise readily and easily pass his own mistakes on to other people. His wisecracking and sarcasm will often kill the inspiration of a fine rehearsal and the enthusiasm of the cast. He frequently misses rehearsals or comes late, confident that he can be a hit when before an audience. One advantage of getting your first theatrical experience on the classroom stage is to recognize the exhibitionist complex and curb it in yourself or others.

Another type, which the general public often associates with stage people, is the "arty" individual. Inclined to be artificial in speech and movement, he is conspicuous in dress and appearance, sophisticated and overcritical in his comments on plays and acting, and definitely snobbish in his attitude toward average people and their theatrical tastes. He often becomes the "hanger-on" around the professional stage and seldom makes any important contribution in any phase of the theater.

ACTING TERMINOLOGY

There are a number of expressions with which you must be familiar if you are to work on the stage. Those most frequently used in connection with acting are listed here. Technical terms applying to staging and lighting will be found in the sections dealing with those aspects of the theater.

ad-lib: To extemporize stage business or conversation.

back or *backstage:* The area behind the part of the stage visible to the audience.

blocking yourself: Getting behind furniture or actors so that you cannot be seen by the audience.

building a scene: Using such dramatic devices as increased tempo, volume, or emphasis to achieve a climax.

business: Any action performed on the stage.

C: The symbol used to designate the center of the stage.

countercross: A shifting of position by one or more actors to balance the stage picture.

cover: To obstruct the view of the audience.

cross: The movement by an actor from one location to another onstage.

cue: The last words or action of any one actor which immediately precedes any lines or business of another actor.

curtain: The curtain or drapery which shuts off the stage from the audience; used in a script to indicate that the curtain is lowered.

cut: To stop action or to omit.

cut in: To break into the speech of another character.

down or *downstage:* The part of the stage toward the footlights.

dressing the stage: Keeping the stage picture balanced during the action.

exit or *exeunt:* To leave the stage.

feeding: Giving lines and action in such a way that another actor can make a point or get a laugh.

getting up in a part: Memorizing lines or becoming letter-perfect.

hand props: Personal properties, such as notebooks, letters, or luggage, carried onstage by the individual player.

hit: To emphasize a word or line with extra force.

holding for laughs: Waiting for the audience to quiet down after a funny line or scene.

holding it: Keeping perfectly still.

left and *right:* Terms used to refer to the stage from the actor's point of view, not that of the audience.

left center and *right center:* The areas to the left and right of the center stage, again with reference to the actor and not the audience.

off or *offstage:* Off the visible stage.

on or *onstage:* On the visible stage.

overlap: To speak when someone else does.

pace: The movement or sweep of the play as it progresses.

places: The positions of the actors at the opening of an act or scene.

plot: To plan stage business, as to "plot" the action, or to plan a speech by working out the phrasing, emphasis, and inflections.

pointing lines: Emphasizing an idea.

properties or *props:* All of the stage furnishings, including furniture.

ring up: To raise the curtain.

set: The scenery for an act or scene.

set props: Properties placed onstage for the use of the actor.

showmanship: A sense of theater and feeling for effects.

sides: Half-sheets of typewritten manuscript containing the lines, cues, and business for one character.

stealing a scene: Attracting attention away from the person to whom the center of interest legitimately belongs.

tag line: The last speech in an act or play.

taking the stage: Holding the center of interest; moving over the entire stage area.

tempo: The speed with which speech and action move a play along.

timing: The execution of a line or piece of business at a specific moment to achieve the most telling effect.

top: To build to a climax by speaking at a higher pitch, at a faster rate, or with more force than in the preceding speeches.

up or *upstage:* The area of the stage away from the footlights, toward the rear of the stage.

upstaging: Improperly taking attention away from an actor when he is the focus of interest.

warn: To notify of an upcoming action or cue.

STAGE TECHNIQUES

There are some technical suggestions relating to acting on a stage which should be put to use in your class plays; they should become subconscious in order that you will use them easily before you undertake a public performance, when the director will not have time to train you.

Movement and Grouping

Movement and grouping are important because the audience sees the actors before they speak and thus catches the spirit of the situation upon their appearance.

Entrances set the key to your role, so you must get into character long before you come onstage. Plan exactly how you wish to appear, especially in regard to your posture, which will be affected by your character's age, mood, and attitude toward the people on the stage. Be sure that every detail of your makeup, costume, and hand props is exactly right so you will not be worrying about them onstage. As you wait for your entrance, be careful not to cast a shadow onstage by getting in front of a backstage light; also do not block the exit.

You must always plan your entrance so that you have time to come onstage and speak exactly on cue. If the set has steps for you to come down in making your appearance, negotiate them, deliberately or rapidly, in a direct or curved line, depending upon the mood you are trying to establish. Do not look down at the steps, and suit your rate of motion to your character. If you enter through a door, open it with the hand nearest the hinges and close it with the other as you step in.

A pause in the doorway is effective if the action of the play permits it or if you have a line to say.

In every entrance you should keep the audience in mind without appearing to do so. Enter on the upstage foot, so that your body is turned downstage. If several characters enter together, one of them speaking, the speaker should come last so that he need not turn his head to address the others who can more easily adapt themselves to him than he to them.

Adjust yourself at all times to the stage space, keeping the stage picture in mind. Plan your turns and moves on definite cues which point the lines. If you find yourself blocked, get yourself to the right position as inconspicuously as possible — unless you are the center of interest; then don't hesitate to take the stage and let the other actors adjust to you.

Grouping characters depends upon maintaining the center of interest. Using a triangular arrangement with the important character of the moment at the apex works out well, as does placing him on a higher level for an important speech. When the interest changes, crossing to new positions becomes necessary. Such crossing and countercrossing is an important part of rehearsing and must be worked out to be meaningful and well motivated. It is best not to move on vital lines, either of your own or of another character, because movement distracts from the words themselves. Try to cross between speeches on a definite piece of business, and manage to countercross, when giving way to someone else, easily and naturally. In public performances, the director plans such action carefully, but in your class plays, it is good experience to work it out for yourselves. Be careful to keep all action clear-cut and uncrowded unless the scene demands unusual rapidity and intensity.

Sitting and rising must be a part of strictly motivated action. Practice crossing to a chair or sofa in character and sitting down until it becomes natural for you to do so easily. Be seated as your character would — never cross your knees unless your character would, or spread your feet apart with your knees together; cross your feet at the ankles if the character would do so, but not otherwise. When rising, have one foot slightly in front of the other and push yourself up with the back foot, letting the chest lead. Unless in character, do not grasp the arms of a chair to push yourself up.

In conversations avoid staring steadily at each other by standing at angles to the footlights so that your faces can be seen. Glance occasionally directly at each other to give the illusion of real conversation.

A scene from a high school production of The Fantasticks, *by Tom Jones and Harvey Schmidt. See also the picture on the opening page of Chapter 1.*

Exits are as important as entrances. Plan ahead for them and leave in a definite state of mind, with a definite purpose, to a definite place, keeping in character until you are completely out of sight. If you go through a door, use the hand nearest the hinges to open it. If you are lucky enough to have a good exit line or a reason to look back, turn on the balls of your feet, still holding the doorknob, and deliver the line or glance pointedly. Otherwise, go right off, closing the door with the hand farthest from the hinges.

Speaking Lines

Speaking lines conveys the playwright's meaning and style as well as revealing the characters and their emotions in each situation. Of course, lines are closely involved with action and must not be blurred or lost by movements. Significant words must be heard by each person in the audience no matter where he is seated; you should mark them plainly on your script as soon as you have studied every situation carefully. Recheck them after the first rehearsals, in which movements are determined. Review the techniques of using the voice in interpretation and apply them in both memorizing and rehearsing. Be very careful to avoid fixing imperfect inflections until action is set, for when they become automatic, you can seldom change them.

A rapid picking up of cues must be established as early in rehearsals as possible. Therefore, cues should be memorized along with the lines. Many amateurs wait until their cue has been given before they show any facial or bodily reaction. Let your face respond during the other person's lines and then you will be ready to speak on cue. One secret is to take a breath during the cue; then speak on the last word of the cue. Failure to pick up cues swiftly causes many amateur performances to drag in spite of painstaking rehearsals, for this loss of a fraction of a second before each speech slows the action.

"Ad-libbing" is used in emergencies to avoid a dead silence, and such lines should be spoken as though they were part of the script, without any cutting down in volume and inflection. When one actor forgets his lines or gets into a speech ahead of the appropriate point in the action and skips important information, the other actors have to ad-lib the missing facts while carrying on the conversation naturally. Whole conversations are ad-libbed in crowd or social scenes, but they must be subdued to avoid drowning out the lines of the speaker carrying the scene. Frequently reciting the alphabet with appropriate inflections can be used in background groupings to simulate conversation.

"Pointing" lines means placing the emphasis on exactly the right word, and timing the rate and pauses to enable the audience to get the emotional impact. Stage conversation must be kept fluent, with the give and take of ideal normal conversation. The difference lies in sharing it with the silent partners in the audience, who should become so engrossed that their reactions of laughter or tears are involuntary. Pointing lines is essential in comedy, for getting laughs in the right places makes or breaks a scene. Actors must work together to build up to the laugh line, so feeding cues properly becomes vital; unless the preceding line or word leads to the point of the joke, it will fall flat. On television you can watch people in comic sketches getting laughs by leading into them. Note how they combine pausing in the right place and using their faces to help get laughs without stealing the scene from the actor who should have it. In a play on the stage, it is inexcusable for the actor feeding the line or the one making the point to laugh; this is often done on TV.

"Holding for laughs" is difficult without dropping the scene. The actors must wait to say the next line, keeping the sparkle and action intact without slowing the tempo. After the laughter or applause has begun to die down, the actor can give the first words of his next line at a slower tempo, speeding up when the sound of his voice has silenced the noise. Amateurs seldom can adapt their words and action to the response of the audience with ease. Thus the presentation of rapid fire comedies by amateurs is far more difficult than the playing of serious drama.

Sentences broken in the middle for some reason can also slow a scene, for they leave no sensible cue for a new sentence. In order to avoid abrupt breaks, have a complete thought worded for every sentence which is to be interrupted and go right on speaking until you are stopped by the other person. Be sure to use as full a voice for these extended lines as you do for those which are a part of the script. In a telephone conversation, write out what the other person is supposed to be saying. Count how many beats it would take him to say it and listen with a responsive face while you count.

Playing Comedy

Playing comedy has special techniques depending largely upon pointing both lines and action to bring out the humor. Much of the success of comedy rests in the comic mood established by the cast. A cast should always appear to enjoy what it is doing, particularly in maintaining the fast pace necessary for comedy. Actors need to keep in mind a few techniques for playing comedy: lift the end of the punch line and leave it hanging, or play it "flat" or deadpan in order to say "laugh now"; clinch the line with a facial or body reaction; develop an air of innocence — comic characters are often quite un-knowledgeable; learn to "feed" a line to a fellow performer so that he can catch it in midair and clinch the laugh on his line. Laugh lines are usually short — the length determined by sounds rather than words. A line too long or too short will kill a laugh. This is one reason why actors are admonished to deliver comic lines exactly as written. Even adding or omitting one word may affect the line as far as laughs are concerned.

"Topping" also becomes an important factor. As in any scene which is building to a climax, the actors top one another by increased volume, higher pitch, faster tempo, or greater emphasis. However, when the comedian breaks a topping sequence, he may get a laugh by a sudden change of pitch, by saying his line in almost expression-less manner, or by a look or gesture which seems incongruous to the character or situation. REMEMBER: Timing must be perfectly executed or the laugh may easily be killed. Comedians even learn how to

A silent stare, a raised eyebrow, a gesture may convey more than a dozen sentences. This scene is from Oscar Wilde's comedy The Importance of Being Earnest.

PHOTO BY VANDAMM. THEATRE COLLECTION, THE NEW YORK PUBLIC LIBRARY; ASTOR, LENOX AND TILDEN FOUNDATIONS

"milk" audiences for laughs by adding some exaggerated bit of business to their punch line.

The comic actor needs to play to the audience, using them as his barometer. The saying that "no two audiences are alike" is attributed principally to comedy — one night the response to a line or action may be a trickle of barely discernable chuckles; the next night a roar of laughter may shake the walls. Some audiences will laugh at almost anything, some in outbursts of guffaws, and some never stop laughing from the opening curtain to the end.

One thing the beginning actor often fails to do is "hold for laughs." After weeks of rehearsal to "pick up cues," the performers often rush on from line to line without giving the audience an opportunity to react through laughter. An audience will always silence itself in order to hear lines. Therefore, the actor must have some idea where the audience can be expected to laugh and be prepared to freeze until the laughter begins to die. He must listen to the "laugh curve" which begins with the laughs of the members of the audience who catch on quickly; this swells rapidly as others join in — for laughter is contagious — until a peak is reached.

Just after the peak the laughter will start to fade and then will seem to quaver; it is at this instant that the actor having the "cut in" line must kill the laugh. Usually the line is not essential to the play, its function being to silence the audience. It is very important that an audience is not allowed to "laugh itself out," because they would then sit back relaxed and satisfied, willing to wait awhile before getting so aroused again.

The following passage from the opening scene of a famous comedy is excellent for practice in pointing lines for humor while putting over important facts of the preliminary situation. It must move rapidly, naturally, and clearly. In addition, you can have fun attempting cultivated English speech after you have polished the rate, emphasis, phrasing, pitch, and clarity of speech. Get another member of the class to work with you, for giving cues and picking them up rapidly are vital.

THE IMPORTANCE OF BEING EARNEST
by Oscar Wilde

ALGERNON.   My dear fellow, Gwendoline is my first cousin; and before I allow you to marry her, you will have to clear up the whole question of Cecily.

JACK.   Cecily! What on earth do you mean? What do you mean, Algy, by Cecily! I don't know anyone by the name of Cecily.

ALGERNON (*To butler*).   Bring me that cigarette case Mr. Worthing left in the smoking-room the last time he dined here.

JACK.   Do you mean to say you have had my cigarette case all this time? I wish to goodness you had let me know. I have been writing frantic letters to Scotland Yard about it. I was very nearly offering a large reward.

ALGERNON.   Well, I wish you would offer one. I happen to be more than usually hard up.

JACK.   There is no good offering a large reward now that the thing is found.

ALGERNON (*Taking case from butler*).   I think it rather mean of you, Ernest, I must say. However, it makes no matter, for now that I look at the inscription inside, I find that the thing isn't yours after all.

JACK.   Of course it is mine. You have seen me with it a hundred times, and you have no right whatsoever to read what is written inside. It is a very ungentlemanly thing to read a private cigarette case.

ALGERNON.   Yes, but this is not your cigarette case. This cigarette case is a present from someone of the name of Cecily, and you said you didn't know anyone of that name.

JACK.   Well, if you want to know, Cecily happens to be my aunt.

ALGERNON.   Your aunt!

JACK.   Yes. Charming old lady she is, too. Lives at Tunbridge Wells. Just give it back to me, Algy.

ALGERNON.   But why does she call herself little Cecily if she is your aunt and lives at Tunbridge Wells? "From *little* Cecily with her fondest love."

JACK.   My dear fellow, what on earth is there in *that*? Some aunts are tall, some aunts are not tall. That is a matter that surely an aunt may be allowed to decide for herself. *You* seem to think that every aunt should be exactly like your aunt! That is absurd! For Heaven's sake give me back my cigarette case.

ALGERNON.   Yes. But why does your aunt call you her uncle? "From little Cecily, with her fondest love to her dear Uncle Jack." There is no objection, I admit, to an aunt being a small aunt, but why an aunt, no matter what her size may be, should call her own nephew her uncle, I can't quite make out. Besides, your name isn't Jack at all; it is Ernest.

JACK.   It isn't Ernest; it's Jack.

ALGERNON.   You have always told me it was Ernest. I have introduced you to everyone as Ernest. You answer to the name of Ernest. You look as if your name was Ernest. You are the most earnest-looking person I ever saw in my life. It is perfectly absurd your saying that your name isn't Ernest. It's on your cards. Here is one of them. "Mr. Ernest Worthing, B.4, The Albany." I'll keep this as a proof that your name is Ernest if ever you attempt to deny it to me, or to Gwendoline or to anyone else.

JACK.   Well, my name is Ernest in town and Jack in the country, and the cigarette case was given me in the country.

ALGERNON.   Yes, but that does not account for the fact that your small Aunt Cecily, who lives in Tunbridge Wells, calls you her dear uncle. Come, old boy, you had much better have the thing out at once.

JACK.   My dear Algy, you talk exactly as if you were a dentist. It is very vulgar to talk like a dentist when one isn't a dentist. It produces a false impression.

ALGERNON.   Well, that is exactly what dentists always do. Now, go on! Tell me the whole thing.

JACK.   — Well, old Mr. Thomas Cardew, who adopted me when I was a little boy, made me, in his will, guardian to his grand-daughter, Miss Cecily Cardew. Cecily, who addresses me as her uncle, from motives of respect that you could not possibly appreciate, lives at my place in the country, under the charge of her admirable governess, Miss Prism.

ALGERNON.   Where is that place in the country, by the way?

JACK.   That is nothing to you, dear boy. You are not going to be invited. I may tell you candidly that the place is not in Shropshire.

ALGERNON.   I suspected that, my dear fellow. — Now go on. Why are you Ernest in town and Jack in the country?

JACK.   My dear Algy, when one is placed in the position of guardian, one has to adopt a very high moral tone on all subjects. It's one's duty to do so. And as a high moral tone can hardly be said to conduce very much to either one's health or happiness, in order to get up to town I have always pretended to have a younger brother of the name of Ernest, who lives at the Albany, and gets into the most dreadful scrapes. There, my dear Algy, is the whole truth, pure and simple.

ALGERNON.   The truth is rarely pure and never simple.

Climax is another form of pointing lines in which emotion in a scene rises rapidly. In a one-act play all the scenes rise to the climax of the play, each topping the last one. Climax is a matter of accurate pacing and increasing tempo working up to a high emotional pitch.

The following scene is adapted from a scene near the climatic end of a one-act play. It can be cut for two characters with The Toff speaking Bill's lines. The Toff is a cultivated gentleman and Sniggers is a Cockney, if you want to practice English dialect. Sniggers must start at a low enough emotional level to build to a height of terror. He can try out several different methods of saying the words "*what I didn't like.*" They can be screamed, whispered, spoken amid hysterical tears or in frantic haste; but they must come at the height of his terrific horror.

A NIGHT AT AN INN
by Lord Dunsany

The scene is a deserted cottage on the moors of England in the early 1900's. THE TOFF, BILL, *and* SNIGGERS *have stolen a precious jewel from a mysterious idol in India and are now hiding from avenging worshippers of the idol. In this scene, they begin to realize that a supernatural power, perhaps the idol himself, has followed them and that there is no escape.*

THE TOFF.   Hullo, here's Jacob Smith, Esquire, J.P., alias Sniggers back again.

SNIGGERS.   Toffy, I've been thinking about my share in that ruby. I don't want it. Toffy; I don't want it.

THE TOFF.   Nonsense, Sniggers. Nonsense.

SNIGGERS.   You shall have it, Toffy, you shall have it yourself, only say Sniggers has no share in this 'ere ruby. Say it, Toffy, say it!

BILL.   Want to turn informer, Sniggers?

SNIGGERS.   No, no. Only I don't want the ruby, Toffy —

THE TOFF.   No more nonsense, Sniggers. We're all in together in this. If one hangs, we all hang; but they won't outwit me. Besides, it's not a hanging affair, they had their knives.

SNIGGERS.   Toffy, Toffy, I always treated you fair, Toffy. I was always one to say, "Give Toffy a chance." Take back my share, Toffy.

THE TOFF.   What's the matter? What are you driving at?

SNIGGERS.   Take it back, Toffy.

THE TOFF.   Answer me, what are you up to?

SNIGGERS.   I don't want my share any more.

BILL.   Have you seen the police? —

SNIGGERS.   There's no police.

THE TOFF.   Well, then, what's the matter?

BILL.   Out with it.

SNIGGERS.   I swear to God — I swear I saw something *what I didn't like.*

THE TOFF.   What you didn't like?

SNIGGERS.   O Toffy, take it back. Take my share. Say you take it.

THE TOFF.   What has he seen?

Daily Practice

Stage techniques must become automatic and subconscious during rehearsals and performances. A daily practice schedule the rest of your lives will establish these techniques and keep your body and voice at their best. You will probably be reading the latest ideas

In Harold Pinter's The Homecoming *at the Tyrone Guthrie Theatre in Minneapolis, Lee Richardson plays Max and Robin Gammell is his con-man.*

about such exercises and hearing lessons on TV, but the following outline is a good plan to follow; it is based on Chapters 6 and 7.

Daily Practice Schedule

Deep Breathing — at least twenty full breaths
Setting-up Exercises — stretching, bending, twisting
Pantomime Exercises

> Shaking hands vigorously
> Opening and closing fists
> Moving fingers as in five-finger exercises
> Turning hands from wrists in circles
> Moving entire arms in circles
> Moving arms from elbows in circles
> Moving hands from wrists in circles, making formal
> > gestures of giving, refusing, pointing
> Using body and arms, with gestures flowing from shoul-
> > der to finger tips, representing such emotions as
> > beseeching, fear, commanding

245

Vocal Exercises

    Relaxation of entire body — yawning to relax throat

    Posture exercise

    Jaw exercises

    Lip exercises

    Babbling

    Humming

    Breathing and counting

    Tongue twisters

    Chanting lines and stanzas of poetry

    Reading poems

J. B.

by Archibald MacLeish

NICKLES (*Hurt*).   If you would rather someone else. . . .

MR. ZUSS.   Did what?

NICKLES.   Played Job.

MR. ZUSS.   What's Job to do with it?

NICKLES.   Job was honest. He saw God —

    Saw him by that icy moonlight,

    By that cold disclosing eye

    That stares the color out and strews

    Our lives . . . with light . . . for nothing.

MR. ZUSS.   Job!

    I never thought of you for Job.

NICKLES.   You never thought of me for Job!

    What did you think of?

MR. ZUSS.   Oh, there's always

    Someone playing Job.

NICKLES.   There must be

    Thousands! What's that got to do with it?

    Thousands — not with camels either:

    Millions and millions of mankind

    Burned, crushed, broken, mutilated,

    Slaughtered, and for what? For thinking!

    For walking round the world in the wrong

    Skin, the wrong-shaped noses, eyelids:

    Sleeping the wrong night wrong city —

    London, Dresden, Hiroshima.

    There never could have been so many

Suffered more for less. But where do
I come in?
    (MR. ZUSS *shuffles uncomfortably.*)
Play the dung heap?

MR. ZUSS.   All we have to do is start.
Job will join us. Job will be there.

NICKLES.   I know. I know. I know. I've seen him.
Job is everywhere we go,
His children dead, his work for nothing,
Counting his losses, scraping his boils,
Discussing himself with his friends and physicians,
Questioning everything — the times, the stars,
His own soul, God's providence.
What do *I* do?

MR. ZUSS.   What do *you* do?

NICKLES.   What do I do? You play God.

MR. ZUSS.   I play God. I think I mentioned it.

NICKLES.   You play God and I play . . .
    (*He lets himself down heavily on the rung of the ladder.*)
Ah!

MR. ZUSS (*Embarrassed*).   I had assumed you knew.
    (NICKLES *looks up at him, looks away.*)

MR. ZUSS.   You see,
I think of you and me as . . . opposites.

NICKLES.   Nice of you.

MR. ZUSS.   I didn't mean to be nasty.

NICKLES.   Your opposite! A demanding role!

MR. ZUSS.   I know.

NICKLES.   But worthy of me? Worthy of me!

THE KING AND I

by Richard Rodgers and Oscar Hammerstein II

ANNA.   Who is it?

LADY THIANG.   Mrs. Anna, it is I, Lady Thiang.

ANNA.   At this hour of the night! (*Opening door*) Come in, Lady
Thiang.

LADY THIANG.   Mrs. Anna, will you go to King?

ANNA.   Now? Has he sent for me?

LADY THIANG.   No. But he would be glad to see you. He is deeply
wounded man. No one has ever spoken to him as you did
today in schoolroom.

ANNA.   Lady Thiang, no one has ever behaved to *me* as His Majesty did today in the schoolroom.

LADY THIANG.   And there is more distressing thing. Our agents in Singapore have found letters to British Government from people whose greedy eyes are on Siam. They describe King as a barbarian, and suggest making Siam a protectorate.

ANNA.   That is outrageous! He is many things I do not like, but he is not a barbarian.

LADY THIANG.   Then you will help him?

ANNA.   You mean — advise him?

LADY THIANG.   It must not sound like advice. King cannot take advice. And if you go to him, he will not bring up subject. You must bring it up.

ANNA.   I cannot go to him. It's against all my principles. Certainly not without his having *asked* for me.

LADY THIANG.   He wish to be new-blood King with Western ideas. But it is hard for him, Mrs. Anna. And there is something else — Princess Tuptim. I do not tell him — for his sake. I deal with this my own way. But for these other things, he need help, Mrs. Anna.

ANNA.   He has *you*.

LADY THIANG.   I am not equal to his special needs. He could be great man. But he need special help. He need *you*.

THE CRUCIBLE
by Arthur Miller

HATHORNE.   You say you never saw no spirits, Mary, were never threatened or afflicted by any manifest of the Devil or the Devil's agents?

MARY (*Very faintly*).   No, sir.

HATHORNE.   And yet, when people accused of witchery confronted you in court you would faint, saying their spirits came out of their bodies and choked you. . . .

MARY.   That were pretense, sir.

DANFORTH.   I cannot hear you.

MARY.   Pretense, sir.

PARRIS.   But you did turn cold, did you not? I myself picked you up many times, and your skin were icy. Mister Danforth, you . . .

DANFORTH.   I saw that many times.

PROCTOR.   She only pretended to faint, your Excellency — They're all marvelous pretenders.

HATHORNE.   Then can she pretend to faint now?

PROCTOR.   Now?

PARRIS.   Why not? Now there are no spirits attacking her, for none in this room is accused of witchcraft. So let her turn herself cold now, let her pretend she is attacked now, let her faint. Faint! (*Turns to* MARY)

MARY.   Faint?

PARRIS.   Aye, faint! Prove to us how you pretended in the court so many times.

MARY (*Looks to* PROCTOR).   I . . . cannot faint now, sir.

PROCTOR (*Alarmed. Quietly*).   Can you not pretend it?

MARY.   I . . . I have no *sense* of it now, I . . .

DANFORTH.   Why? What is lacking now?

MARY.   I . . . cannot tell, sir, I . . .

DANFORTH.   Might it be that here we have no afflicting spirit loose, but in the court there were some?

MARY (*Desperately*).   I never saw no spirits.

PARRIS.   Then see no spirits *now*, and prove to us that you can faint by your own will, as you claim.

MARY (*Takes deep breath, stares searching for the emotion of it, and then shakes head*).   I . . . cannot do it.

PARRIS.   Then you will confess, will you not? Attacking spirits *made* you to faint!

MARY.   No, sir, I . . .

PARRIS.   Your Excellency, this is a trick to blind the court.

MARY.   It's not a trick! I . . . I used to faint because . . . I . . . I *thought* I saw spirits.

DANFORTH.   *Thought* you saw them!

MARY.   But I did *not*, your Honor.

HATHORNE.   How could you *think* you saw them *unless* you saw them?

MARY.   I . . . I cannot tell how, but I did. I . . . I heard the other girls screaming, and *you*, your Honor, you seemed to *believe* them and I . . . It were only *sport* in the beginning, sir, but then the whole world cried spirits, spirits, and I . . . I promise you, Mister Danforth, I only thought I saw them but I did not.

PARRIS.   Surely your Excellency is not taken by this simple lie.

DANFORTH (*A threat*).   Abigail Williams! (*She holds her chin up.*) I bid you now search your heart, and tell me this — and beware of it, child, to God every soul is precious and His vengeance is terrible on them that take life without cause. Is it possible, child, that the spirits you have seen are illusion only, some *deception* that may cross your mind when . . .

ABIGAIL (*Indignant*). Why, this . . . this . . . is a base question, sir.

DANFORTH. Child, I would have you consider it —

ABIGAIL (*A step to him. Unafraid*). I have been hurt, Mister Danforth; I have seen my blood runnin' out! I have been near to murdered every day because I done my duty pointing out the Devil's people — and this is my reward? To be mistrusted, denied, questioned like a . . .

DANFORTH. (*He weakens.*) Child, I do not mistrust you . . .

ABIGAIL. (*NOW it pours. She does not wait for his speech.*) Let *you* beware, Mister Danforth — think you to be so mighty that the power of Hell may not turn your wits? — beware of it! (*She shivers and looks at* MARY, *then folds her arms around her.*) — there is . . .

DANFORTH (*Apprehensively*). What is it, child?

ABIGAIL (*Backing away to bench R. and sits. Clasping her arms about her as though cold*). I . . . I know not. A wind, a cold wind has come. (*Her eyes fall on* MARY.)

MARY (*Terrified, pleading*). Abby!

MERCY. Your Honor, I freeze!

PROCTOR. They're pretending!

HATHORNE (*Touching* ABIGAIL'S *hand*). She is cold, your Honor, touch her!

MERCY (*Rises. A threat*). Mary, do you send this shadow on me? (*Sits slowly*)

MARY. Lord save me! (SUSANNA *rises looking at* MARY, *then slowly sits.*)

ABIGAIL (*She is shivering visibly*). I freeze — I freeze. (MERCY *hugs her and they shiver.*)

MARY (*With great fear*). Abby, don't do that! (PROCTOR *crosses to her, grabs her.*)

DANFORTH (*Himself engaged and entered by* ABIGAIL). Mary Warren, do you witch her? I say to you, do you send your spirit out!

MARY (*Almost collapsing. Putting her in seat*). Let me go, Mister Proctor, I cannot, I cannot . . .

ABIGAIL (*Shouting*). "Oh, Heavenly Father, take away this shadow."

ELIZABETH THE QUEEN
by Maxwell Anderson

ESSEX. There's no way out. I've thought of it
    Every way. Speak frankly. Could you forgive me
    And keep your throne?

ELIZABETH. No.

ESSEX.   Are you ready to give
Your crown up to me?

ELIZABETH.   No. It's all I have. (*She rises.*)
Why, who am I
To stand here paltering with a rebel noble!
I am Elizabeth, daughter of a king,
The queen of England, and you are my subject!
What does this mean, you standing here eye to eye
With me, you liege? You whom I made, and gave
All that you have, you, an upstart, defying
Me to grant pardon, lest you should sweep me from power
And take my place from me? I tell you if Christ his blood
Ran streaming from the heavens for a sign
That I should hold my hand you'd die for this,
You pretender to a throne upon which you have
No claim, you pretender to a heart, who have been
Hollow and heartless and faithless to the end!

ESSEX.   If we'd met some other how we might have been happy . . .
But there's an empire between us! I am to die . . .
Let us say that . . . let us begin with that . . .
For then I can tell you that if there'd been no empire
We could have been great lovers. If even now
You were not queen and I were not pretender,
That god who searches heaven and earth and hell
For two who are perfect lovers, could end his search
With you and me. Remember . . . I am to die . . .
And so I can tell you truly, out of all the earth
That I'm to leave, there's nothing I'm very loath
To leave save you. Yet if I live I'll be
Your death or you'll be mine.

ELIZABETH.   Give me the ring.

ESSEX.   No.

ELIZABETH.   Give me the ring. I'd rather you killed me
Than I killed you.

ESSEX.   It's better for me as it is
Than that I should live and batten my fame and fortune
On the woman I love. I've thought of it all. It's better
To die young and unblemished than to live long and rule,
And rule not well.

ELIZABETH.   Aye, I should know that.

ESSEX.   Is it not?

ELIZABETH.   Yes.

ESSEX.   Good-bye, then.

ELIZABETH. Oh, then I'm old, I'm old!
      I could be young with you, but now I'm old.
      I know now how it will be without you. The sun
      Will be empty and circle round an empty earth . . .
      And I will be queen of emptiness and death . . .
      Why could you not have loved me enough to give me
      Your love and let me keep as I was?
ESSEX. I know not.
      I only know I could not. I must go.
ELIZABETH (*Frozen*). Yes. (*He goes to the door.*)
      Lord Essex! (*He turns.*)
      Take my kingdom. It is yours!
      (ESSEX, *as if not hearing, bows and goes on.*)

ANGEL STREET
by Patrick Hamilton

MRS. MANNINGHAM. Jack! Jack! What have they done to you? What have they done?

MR. MANNINGHAM (*Struggling at his bonds, half whispering*). It's all right, Bella. You're clever, my darling. Terribly clever. Now get something to cut this. I can get out through the dressing-room window and make a jump for it. Can you fetch something?

MRS. MANNINGHAM (*Hesitating. Crossing to him*). Yes — yes. I can get somethlng. What can I get?

MR. MANNINGHAM. I've just remembered — There's a razor in my dressing-room. Quick! Can you get it, Bella?

MRS. MANNINGHAM (*Feverishly*). Razor — yes — I'll get it for you.

MR. MANNINGHAM. Hurry — yes — In my dresser — Hurry — Quick and get it.

(*She goes into room up right, talking and mumbling and comes back with the razor and crosses to desk. As she takes the razor from case, a scrap of paper falls to the floor. She stoops to pick it up, almost unconsciously tidy. She glances at it and a happy smile illuminates her face.*)

MRS. MANNINGHAM (*Joyously*). Jack! Here's the grocery bill! (*She comes to him, the grocery bill in one hand, the razor in the other. She is half weeping, half laughing.*) You see, dear, I didn't lose it. I told you I didn't!

MR. MANNINGHAM (*Uncomfortably*). Cut me loose, Bella.

MRS. MANNINGHAM. (*She stares at him for a moment, then at the grocery bill, then back at him.*) Jack — how did this get in here? You said that I — (*Her voice trails off, a wild look comes into her eyes.*)

MR. MANNINGHAM (*Trying to placate her with charm*).   I must have been mistaken about the bill. Now — Quickly, dear, use the razor! Quick!

(*She stares at him for a moment, then moves a step closer. His look falls upon the razor. He glances up at her and a momentary hint of terror comes into his face. He draws back in the chair.*)

MRS. MANNINGHAM.   Razor? What razor? (*She holds it up, under his face.*) You are not suggesting that this is a razor I hold in my hand? Have you gone mad, my husband?

MR. MANNINGHAM.   Bella, what are you up to?

MRS. MANNINGHAM (*With deadly rage that is close to insanity*).   Or is it I who am mad? (*She throws the razor from her.*) Yes. That's it. It's I. Of course, it was a razor. Dear God — I have lost it, haven't I? I am always losing things. And I can never find them. I don't know where I put them.

MR. MANNINGHAM (*Desperately*).   Bella.

MRS. MANNINGHAM.   I must look for it, mustn't I? Yes — if I don't find it you will lock me in my room — you will lock me in the mad-house for my mischief. (*Her voice is compressed with bitterness and hatred.*) Where could it be now? (*Turns and looks around to right*) Could it be behind the picture? Yes, it must be there! (*She goes to the picture swiftly and takes it down.*) No, it's not there — how strange! I must put the picture back. I have taken it down, and I must put it back. There. (*She puts it back askew.*) Where now shall I look? (*She is raging like a hunted animal. Turns and sees the desk*) Where shall I look? The desk. Perhaps I put it in the desk. (*Goes to the desk*) No — it is not there — how strange! But here is a letter. Here is a watch. And a bill — See I've found them at last. (*Going to him*) You see! But they don't help you, do they? And I am trying to help you, aren't I? — to help you escape — But how can a mad woman help her husband to escape? What a pity — (*Getting louder and louder*) If I were not mad I could have helped you — if I were not mad, whatever you had done, I could have pitied and protected you! But because I am mad I have hated you, and because I am mad I am rejoicing in my heart — without a shred of pity — without a shred of regret — watching you go with glory in my heart!

MR. MANNINGHAM (*Desperately*).   Bella!

MRS. MANNINGHAM.   Inspector! Inspector! (*Up to door — pounds on door, then flings it open*) Come and take this man away! Come and take this man away!

MARY OF SCOTLAND
by Maxwell Anderson

MARY.   And if I will not sign
       This abdication?
ELIZABETH.   You've tasted prison. Try
       A diet of it.
MARY.   And so I will. . . . I wait for Bothwell —
       And wait for him here.
ELIZABETH.   Where you will wait, bear in mind,
       Is for me to say. Give up Bothwell, give up your throne
       If you'd have a life worth living.
MARY.   I will not.
ELIZABETH.   I can wait.
MARY.   And will not because you play to lose. This trespass
       Against God's right will be known. The nations will know it.
       Mine and yours. They will see you as I see you
       And pull you down.
ELIZABETH.   Child, child, I've studied this gambit
       Before I play it. I will send each year
       This paper to you. Not signing, you will step
       From one cell to another, step lower, always,
       Till you reach the last, forgotten, forgotten of men,
       Forgotten among causes, a wraith that cries
       To fallen gods in another generation
       That's lost your name. Wait then for Bothwell's rescue.
       It will never come.
MARY.   I may never see him?
ELIZABETH.   Never.
       It would not be wise.
MARY   (*Sitting R. of table*). Oh! Oh! —
       And suppose indeed you won
       Within our life-time, still looking down from the heavens
       And up from men around us, God's spies that watch
       The fall of the great and little, they will find you out —
       I will wait for that, wait longer than a life,
       Till men and the times unscroll you, study the tricks
       You play, and laugh, as I shall laugh, being known
       Your better, haunted by your demon, driven
       To death, or exile by you, unjustly, Why,
       When all's done, it's my name I care for, my name and heart,
       To keep them clean.
       (*Rising*)

Win now, take your triumph now,
For I'll win men's hearts in the end — though the sifting
  takes
This hundred years — or a thousand.

ELIZABETH. Child, child,
And are you gulled
By what men write in histories, this or that,
And never true? I am careful of my name
As you are, for this day and longer. It's not what happens
That matters, no, not even what happens that's true,
But what men believe to have happened. . . .
What will be said about us in after-years
By men to come, I control that, being who I am.
It will be said of me that I governed well,
And wisely, but of you, cousin, that your life,
Shot through with ill-loves, battened on lechery, made you
An ensign of evil, that men tore down and trampled.
Shall I call for the lord's parchment? . . .

MARY. And still I win. . . .
This crooked track
You've drawn me on, cover it, let it not be believed
That a woman was a fiend. Yes, cover it deep,
And heap my infamy over it, lest men peer
And catch sight of you as you were and are. In myself
I know you to be an eater of dust. Leave me here
And set me lower this year by year, as you promise,
Till the last is an oubliette, and my name inscribed
On the four winds. Still, STILL I win! I have been
A woman, and I have loved as a woman loves,
Lost as a woman loses. I have borne a son,
And he will rule Scotland — and England. You have no heir!
A devil has no children.

ELIZABETH. By God, you shall suffer
For this, but slowly.

MARY. And that I can do. A woman
Can do that. Come turn the key. I have a hell
For you in my mind, where you will burn and feel it,
Live where you like, and softly.

ELIZABETH. Once more I ask you.
And patiently. Give up your throne.

MARY. No, devil.
My pride is stronger than yours, and my heart beats blood

Such as yours has never known. And in this dungeon, I win
here, alone.

ELIZABETH (*Turning*).   Good night, then.

MARY.   Aye, good night.

SHE STOOPS TO CONQUER
by Oliver Goldsmith

MARLOW, *shy and bumbling under normal conditions, becomes quite
roguish when he encounters* MISS HARDCASTLE, *who is pretending to be
a servant.*

MARLOW.   What a bawling in every part of the house. I have scarce
a moment's repose. If I go to the best room, there I find my
host and his story. If I fly to the gallery, there we have my
hostess with her curtsey down to the ground. I have at last
got a moment to myself, and now for recollection. (*Walks
and muses*)

MISS HARDCASTLE.   Did you call, Sir? Did your honour call?

MARLOW (*Musing*).   As for Miss Hardcastle, she's too grave and
sentimental for me.

MISS HARDCASTLE.   Did your honour call?
(*She still places herself before him, he turning away.*)

MARLOW.   No, child. (*Musing*) Besides, from the glimpse I had of
her, I think she squints.

MISS HARDCASTLE.   I'm sure, Sir, I heard the bell ring.

MARLOW.   No, no. (*Musing*) I have pleased my father, however, by
coming down, and I'll to-morrow please myself by returning.
(*Taking out his tablets, and perusing*)

MISS HARDCASTLE.   Perhaps the other gentleman called, Sir?

MARLOW.   I tell you, no.

MISS HARDCASTLE.   I should be glad to know, Sir. We have such a
parcel of servants.

MARLOW.   No, no, I tell you. (*Looks full in her face*) Yes, child, I
think I did call. I wanted — I wanted — I vow, child, you
are vastly handsome.

MISS HARDCASTLE.   O la, Sir, you'll make one asham'd.

MARLOW.   Never saw a more sprightly malicious eye. Yes, yes, my
dear, I did call. Have you got any of your — a — what d'ye
call it, in the house?

MISS HARDCASTLE.   No, Sir, we have been out of that these ten days.

MARLOW.   One may call in this house, I find, to very little purpose.
Suppose I should call for a taste, just by way of trial, of the

nectar of your lips; perhaps, I might be disappointed in that too.

MISS HARDCASTLE.   Nectar! Nectar! That's a liquor there's no call for in these parts. French, I suppose. We keep no French wines here, Sir.

MARLOW.   Of true English growth, I assure you.

MISS HARDCASTLE.   Then it's odd I should not know it. We brew all sorts of wines in this house, and I have lived here these eighteen years.

MARLOW.   Eighteen years! Why, one would think, child, you kept the bar before you was born. How old are you?

MISS HARDCASTLE.   O! Sir, I must not tell my age. They say women and music should never be dated.

MARLOW.   To guess at this distance you can't be much above forty. (*Approaching*) Yet nearer I don't think so much. (*Approaching*) By coming close to some women, they look younger still; but when we come very close indeed — (*Attempting to kiss her*)

MISS HARDCASTLE.   Pray, Sir, keep your distance. One would think you wanted to know one's age as they do horses, by mark of mouth.

MARLOW.   I protest, child, you use me extremely ill. If you keep me at this distance, how is it possible you and I can ever be acquainted?

MISS HARDCASTLE.   And who wants to be acquainted with you? I want no such acquaintance, not I. I'm sure you did not treat Miss Hardcastle that was here awhile ago in this obstropalous manner. I'll warrant me, before her you look'd dash'd and kept bowing to the ground, and talk'd for all the world, as if you was before a Justice of Peace.

MARLOW (*Aside*).   Egad! She has hit it, sure enough. (*To her*) In awe of her, child? Ha! ha! ha! A mere awkward squinting thing, no, no. I find you don't know me. I laughed and rallied her a little; but I was unwilling to be too severe. No, I could not be too severe, curse me!

MISS HARDCASTLE.   O! then, Sir, you are a favourite, I find, among the ladies?

MARLOW.   Yes, my dear, a great favourite. And yet, hang me, I don't see what they find in me to follow. At the Ladies' Club in town I'm called their agreeable Rattle. Rattle, child, is not my real name, but one I'm known by. My name is Solomons, Mr. Solomons, my dear, at your service. (*Offering to salute her*)

MISS HARDCASTLE. Hold, Sir, you are introducing me to your Club, not to yourself. And you're so great a favourite there, you say?

MARLOW. Yes, my dear. There's Mrs. Mantrap, Lady Betty Blackleg, the Countess of Sligo, Mrs. Longhorns, old Miss Biddy Buckskin, and your humble servant, keep up the spirit of the place.

MISS HARDCASTLE. Then it is a very merry place, I suppose?

MARLOW. Yes, as merry as cards, supper, wine, and old women can make us.

MISS HARDCASTLE. And their agreeable Rattle, ha! ha! ha!

MARLOW (*Aside*). Egad! I don't quite like this chit. She seems knowing, methinks. You laugh, child?

MISS HARDCASTLE. I can't laugh to think what time they all have for minding their work or their family.

MARLOW (*Aside*). All's well; she don't laugh at me. (*To her*) Do you ever work, child?

MISS HARDCASTLE. Ay, sure. There's not a screen or a quilt in the whole house but what can bear witness to that.

MARLOW. Odso! then you must show me your embroidery. I embroider and draw patterns myself a little. If you want a judge of your work you must apply to me. (*Seizing her hand*) (*Enter* HARDCASTLE, *who stands in surprise.*)

MISS HARDCASTLE. Ay, but the colours do not look well by candlelight. You shall see all in the morning. (*Struggling*)

MARLOW. And why not now, my angel? Such beauty fires beyond the power of resistance. — Pshaw! the father here! My old luck: I never nick'd seven that I did not throw ames ace three times following.

Rehearsing a One-Act Play

Rehearsing a one-act play, especially as classwork, does not demand the intensive effort of a long play for public production, although the techniques are the same. Since the relation between an experienced adult director and a student cast are taken up in Chapter 12 in connection with play production, they need not be gone into here; the following suggestions can be adapted to your immediate needs.

A one-act play allows you to produce a complete dramatic experience, demanding a sustained and consistent characterization, without the strain a long play places on the memory and ability of all performers. In a class period, both the actors and audience can appreciate the type of play and the author's style sufficiently to discuss it intelligently and to write a dramatic criticism about it. In it you can prove technical efficiency and talent adequately.

Rehearsing is like football practice: it determines the success or failure of performance before an audience. Each rehearsal should show a decided improvement over the former one, especially in the emotional and technical development of the roles. Work out the stage business as soon as possible, keeping it simple and clear-cut, with good stage pictures all the time and as little distracting movement as possible. All of you must write down on your scripts what the action is, where the pauses come, and where the emphasis should be placed on words of importance.

Apply the technical phases of everything you have studied concerning the interpretation of your lines. The quality, rate, emphasis, and pitch suitable for meaning and characterization must be checked all the time. Dropping the voice at the end of sentences regardless of the importance of words is a fatal error. Keep asking yourself "What am I saying?" until you get an intelligent interpretation of the meaning.

The structure of the play must be considered at all times. Be sure the preliminary situation is made perfectly clear and the initial incident pointed to arouse interest in what is happening. Each situation builds up the emotion to the climax; lines should top each other with rising pitch, speeding up, and greater emphasis, but they should never rise above the one climax of the play. Tempos of contrasted situations must be watched for variety, but in a one-act play the shortness of the action does not permit distracting changes. The conclusion is usually brief, and there is a danger of anticipating it and dropping the intensity before the very end.

The structure of your acting area is equally important. In a classroom, you may not have a stage curtain, so you must plan how to get your characters on the stage at the beginning and off at the end as a part of the action. Be careful to put as much importance on this as on the rest of the play. If you do have a small stage, a schedule must be worked out by the class as a whole and each group given an equal chance to use the stage.

Because this is the opportunity for each of you in the class to play a part before an audience, this one-act play should be an exciting and delightful experience. Avoid getting tense and nervous as details pile up — putting on any production is hard, demanding work, but it is fun!

Producing Plays in Class

Procedure in producing class plays can follow this order so that all concerned will gain the major values from the total experience.

1. Divide the class into groups, and make each group responsible for the production of a one-act play. The teacher should select and cast the plays, so that each member of the class has a part that suits his individual needs. The entire series of plays should include the various types discussed in Chapter 3. A definite production schedule should be posted. If a member of the cast is absent on the day of performance, someone should read the part from a script.

2. Each group should select a student director (preferably an advanced student who is not a member of the cast) to be responsible for calling outside rehearsals, checking on props and costumes, and generally managing the show.

3. Permission to perform in public any play held under copyright must be obtained from the copyright holder before any definite production plans are made. The copyright holder or play publisher will either provide you with copies of the scripts or tell you how to obtain them. Copying parts and cues from plays in your library is expressly forbidden by copyright laws.

4. Rehearsing is not merely going over lines; it is continually planning how to make the most of the allotted time. Every moment of class time must be used to advantage, with the teacher passing from group to group and directing the action and answering questions. Every group should be allowed sufficient use of the stage or platform to plan the action and setting. It is best to take up the action each day from where it was dropped the day before, rather than to begin at the opening every day. Separate scenes between different characters can be rehearsed at the same time, so that no one has to sit around with nothing to do. Several intensive rehearsals at the homes of the cast members provide an opportunity to go through the entire play without interruption. These meetings foster the friendliness which constitutes one of the greatest joys of amateur work in dramatics. All rehearsals should be handled in a businesslike manner, without waste of time and with every effort made toward a satisfactory result. A prompter should keep a record of directions.

5. The setting cannot be elaborate but it should be in keeping with the mood, atmosphere, and period of the play. Simple lighting effects, costumes, makeup, and all the necessary props should make the action

live for the audience. Originality and ingenuity in working out the background should be considered in evaluating the final production.

6. The presentation should be as finished as possible, with lines and cues memorized and the action and tempo developed to create definite emotional reactions. The prompter should be on the job every moment.

7. After each presentation, the group responsible must move all props and leave the stage clear for the next group to take over. Anything brought from home should be returned at once and scripts should be collected and filed for use by other classes in the future.

8. Invite guests to see the plays but make it clear to them that the productions are regular classwork and educational in purpose. At the close of each performance, ask the audience to discuss the play and its interpretation in detail, offering constructive criticism of the acting and pointing out the strong and weak points of the production. A skillful teacher can direct this discussion and bring out the structural phases of the play and the methods of judging it.

9. If some of the plays are sufficiently well produced and likely to appeal to a large audience, they can be repeated in the school auditorium at assembly periods, or for the PTA or community groups. A public production, however, should never be the goal of the classwork, for then the matters of individual development and educational value may be lost in the effort to put the best students into an exhibition of dramatic art. The dramatics club should be the group to present public productions, not the class in dramatics.

10. When the entire series has been presented, a careful discussion should be held, stressing the best characterizations, settings, and emotional appeals. Reasons for any poor productions should be discussed without too much emphasis upon the shortcomings of individual members of the class. Private conferences between the teacher and students concerning their success or failure and their overall dramatic ability can be very valuable after so important a class activity.

Short Plays for Production and Study

A Night at an Inn by Lord Dunsany
Aria da Capo by Edna St. Vincent Millay
At the Hawk's Well by William Butler Yeats
Early Frost by Douglas Parkhirst
Hello, Out There by William Saroyan
Ile by Eugene O'Neill

Impromptu by Tad Mosel
Mr. Flannery's Ocean by Louis John Carlino
Neighbours by Zona Gale
Objective Case by Louis John Carlino
Pearls by Dan Totheroh
Poor Maddalena by Louise Saunders
Riders to the Sea by J. M. Synge
Rosalind by James M. Barrie
Sorry, Wrong Number by Lucille Fletcher
Spreading the News by Lady Gregory
St. Simeon Stylites by F. Sladen-Smith
The Bald Soprano by Eugene Ionesco
The Devil and Daniel Webster by Stephen V. Benét
The Happy Journey to Camden and Trenton by Thornton Wilder
The Lottery adapted by Brainerd Duffield from Shirley Jackson
The Maker of Dreams by Oliphant Down
The Old Lady Shows Her Medals by James M. Barrie
The Rising of the Moon by Lady Gregory
The Sandbox by Edward Albee
The Twelve-Pound Look by James M. Barrie
The Ugly Duckling by A. A. Milne
The Valiant by Holworthy Hall and Robert Middlemass
Trifles by Susan Glaspell

Acting in the Round

Acting in the round is now becoming a necessary part of dramatic training; the arena and thrust stages are being built into modern theaters and auditoriums, and platforms are set up in large rooms and out-of-doors. The open stage, completely or partially surrounded by seats, is somewhat similar to the theaters of the Greeks and Elizabethans and creates a close contact between the actors and spectators. You can use it in your classroom, if you do not have a stage, by placing chairs around an open space and leaving one or two aisles for entrances.

Staging plays in the round demands careful planning and rehearsing. The director cannot depend on a set for effects, and the audience is so close that every detail of costumes, furniture, and lighting must be right. The acting area must be lighted by spots which do not hit any of the audience in the eyes. Acts can be ended by blacking out the lights or by incorporating exits into the play's action. Either will take the place of the usual stage curtain. The furniture must not block the action from any side, and scenes must be arranged so that they can be seen from all angles. The director also must plan to keep his actors moving and speaking as they cross and countercross rather than have them seated for too long a time. Keeping the actors in motion allows their faces and voices to carry the meaning of the play to everyone. If possible, the director must plan his action to be seen from all sides at once.

The demands on the actors are much greater in round staging than on an orthodox stage. Each actor must be conscious all the time of being surrounded by spectators who must see and hear him. He must speak very clearly, projecting his voice so that he can be heard even when he turns away from part of the audience. Very accurate pointing of lines and accenting of key words must be combined with a few clear-cut gestures which are effective from every angle. With the audience so close, any artificiality or exaggeration becomes so apparent that all sense of reality is lost. Also, fidgeting and aimless gestures are far more irritating at close range.

Plays must be selected rather carefully for an arena production. Entrances must permit effective approaches for actors before they speak, and exits must allow for convenient departures. Actions and lines must be suitable for the close attention of the audience. Sofas, benches, and low-backed chairs must be appropriate as a background for the actors, since there is no setting. When done well in the round, a suitable play can move the spectators deeply; if it is poorly selected or acted, every fault is enlarged and a production which may be good enough for a regular stage is spoiled.

Bibliography

Albright, H. D.: *Working Up a Part*, Houghton Mifflin, Boston, 1959.

Blunt, Jerry: *The Composite Art of Acting*, Macmillan, New York, 1966.

Chilver, Peter: *Staging a School Play*, Harper & Row, New York, 1968.

Cole, Toby, and Helen Krich: *Actors on Acting*, Crown, New York, 1949.

Dolman, John, Jr.: *The Art of Acting*, Harper & Row, New York, 1949.

McGaw, Charles: *Acting Is Believing*, Holt, New York, 1966.

Mackenzie, Frances: *The Amateur Actor*, Theatre Arts, New York, 1966.

Munk, Erika: *Stanislavski and America*, Fawcett, Greenwich, Conn., 1967.

Stanislavski, Constantin: *My Life in Art*, Theatre Arts, New York, 1924.

————: *Building a Character*, Theatre Arts, New York, 1949.

————: *Creating a Role*, Theatre Arts, New York, 1961.

PLATFORM READING OF PLAYS

The Readers Theater is a most popular, and the most recent, phase in the public interpretation of plays. Although Charles Laughton deservedly is credited with introducing this successful professional theatrical form in the early fifties, the group reading of plays has been a favorite means for many years of making drama come alive for audiences. Especially on university campuses and in high school dramatics clubs, the presentation of plays from scripts has formed the basis of programming. Today it is an accepted form of theatrical entertainment which you can enjoy either as a participant or a listener on all levels — stage, television, school.

For example, you may have seen the brilliant professional production of *The Hollow Crown* brought from London, with the original cast, to New York, and shown across the country and later on TV. In it, a distinguished group of British stars read passages from great literature showing the tragedy and humor in the lives of the kings and queens of England.

Actual plays, very difficult to produce scenically, are being constantly presented in this way, as well as plays of special significance in current affairs and trends. Charles Rann Kennedy and his wife Edyth Wynn Mathison introduced his fine religious dramas, *The Terrible Meek* and *The Servant in the House,* in churches many years ago, and authors today are writing forms of literature easily adapted to this growing theatrical mode.

In the amateur field, the group reading of plays is growing with the expanding number of suburban communities at a distance from theatrical centers. It is a favorite pastime of many people who want to keep up-to-date on the best plays or to enjoy the classics together in their homes and clubs. It is one form of theater you can enjoy for the rest of your life, regardless of how undramatic your career may be!

PRESENTING PLATFORM READINGS

A most valuable step in your personal theater experience is taking part in platform presentations of plays both in and out of school. Playreading is not strictly acting, for in it you are presenting yourself as a medium of bringing the drama and its characters before an audience. It is a means of creating an imaginary stage peopled with interesting persons. Therefore, the idea of the play and the style of the playwright are most important, and an exaggerated assumption of roles becomes a distraction. Whether individually or with a group, it is with your voice and facial expression you bring out the contrasted personalities clearly, assisted by an occasional telling gesture and physical stance.

There are several considerations to keep in mind in relation to platform presentation of plays. In the first place, you must be sure of the copyright status of any play given outside the classroom or home in a public performance; always write the accredited publisher or author for permission, whether an admission is charged or not. In the second place, consider carefully the background for the presentation. Neutral curtains, screens, and walls are excellent; against them spotlights or other individual lighting units can be used effectively. Lecterns for individual readers are usually helpful. For groups, use a long table with straight chairs, or individual stools or chairs carefully arranged in relation to the persons reading the longest passages. Simplified stage sets and costumes can be used if actors move about. In the third place, in group readings, the casting should be done on the basis of aural effectiveness and facial flexibility rather than of appearance, although stage empathy always demands physical compatibility.

INDIVIDUAL PLAY READINGS

Individual plays for readings, or the dramatic adaptation of any form of literature, must be selected with great care, especially in relation to the audience which will hear it. The amount of time and energy a first-rate presentation involves should be spent on something that suits you well and that you thoroughly enjoy. Your enthusiasm will be contagious and you can inspire the members of your audience not only to enjoy a play with you, but to read it themselves, as well as other works by the same author or of the same period or style.

Platform readings of a play by one person may take either of two forms: a play review or a dramatic reading. In the first, the play is presented in selected scenes in conjunction with a well-prepared discussion of the author and the literary values of the play. In the second, the play is read or recited — usually in condensed form — without comments of any kind.

Play Reviews

The purpose of a play review is to help your audience enjoy the play by showing them the author's reason for writing it. A satisfactory play review might include four categories. One is a discussion of the author — his life, his central idea in the particular play in relation to his philosophy of life, and his literary style. Another is a condensation of the plot into a two- or three-minute synopsis. Still other categories are an interpretative reading of the finest passages and the reviewer's personal reaction to the play, characters, and theme.

As in all forms of public speaking, consider the people in your audience and their particular interests. Make a unified and logical outline of the entire review. Watch your allotted time or you may devote too much attention to one phase and neglect others. Do not talk over the heads of your audience. In organizing your material, refer to Chapters 2 and 3, which deal with play analysis. Also look up the reviews by dramatic critics listed in the *Readers' Guide to Periodical Literature* or The *New York Times Index*. If possible, get pictures of the author, the actors who have appeared in the play,

Cornelia Otis Skinner as Anne of Cleves and as Jane Howard in her one-woman show, The Wives of Henry VIII.

and the sets which have been designed for it. If it is a period play, pictures of the costumes and furnishings of the time, and a brief discussion of the historical background might add interest; this is possible only if you have been allotted an unusually long time for your review. Use of an opaque or slide projector is the best method of making visual aids available to the entire class.

It is wise to clarify the theme of the play in your own mind by writing it out in one sentence. Base your presentation on this central idea, showing how the dramatist developed it. Strive to arouse in your audience a desire to discuss the theme with you at the end of your review.

Because the first impression is so important in arousing interest in the play, plan your opening sentence carefully. Write it down and, if necessary, memorize it. Then discuss more or less briefly the author's life and place in literature, illustrating his style with several typical passages from the play.

Many people waste time and bore their audiences by a lengthy and pointless telling of the whole story. Condensing the plot into two or three sentences requires intelligent concentration upon the big issues of the play and is perhaps the most difficult part of the review. However, such effort is very important if you wish to make an effective presentation.

Before you read the scenes from the play, briefly describe the main characters. If possible, quote lines which characterize them; use either their own speeches or those by other characters. In choosing passages for reading, remember that the scenes you select must be interesting in themselves. They should be good examples of the author's style, and they should bring out the personalities of the characters. Of course, they should lend themselves to effective reading. Occasionally it is wise to read one act in its entirety, but usually cuttings from a number of scenes are more interesting.

Your personal reaction to the play will be obvious throughout the discussion and will color your interpretation. Remember that you must appreciate, understand, and enjoy the play yourself if you are to share it with others.

The manner in which you close your review is important. A fine reading of a brilliant passage with emotional content is the most dramatic kind of conclusion. If you can leave your listeners genuinely moved, you will deserve the applause you receive.

Dramatic Readings of Plays

If your review takes the form of a presentation of the play without comments, it becomes a dramatic reading, a more formal type of platform interpretation than the play review.

The arrangement and cutting of a play for such a reading is of paramount importance. Reduce all descriptive material to a minimum, leaving only gripping situations which work up to a dramatic climax. The play selected should have a strong emotional appeal, preferably with an intermingling of humor and pathos against an interesting background. The characters should be strongly contrasted in type so that they will be easily identified after their first introduction. When several persons are presented at the same time, place each one clearly, first in your own mind and then for the audience. Always keep their respective positions clear. When they are supposed to speak, turn enough each time to suggest their locations. Be careful to assume the general bodily set of a character as well as a voice suited to his personality. However, remember that you are reading to the audience — there is no illusion of a fourth wall.

Necessary stage directions and descriptions of the set must be given clearly. Although subordinated to the dialogue, they should never be presented so casually that they seem to have no importance.

Because both the play review and the play reading are forms of interpretation, they involve many of the principles discussed in previous chapters. First, of course, you must understand the main idea of the entire play or selection in order to present the atmosphere. Then be sure you understand every character and passage and the relationship of each to the play as a whole. Interpreting a play demands visualizing every situation and character. You must see, feel, and imagine with the playwright and then re-create for the audience what you see and feel. This means that you must re-create the actions and emotions of the characters at the time you present them to your audience. Full control of the techniques of acting, pantomime, and voice is demanded to make the interpretation a living, breathing creation. Again, "The play's the thing." You have the privilege of being the channel through which the play may become a thing of beauty, bringing joy to those with whom you share it.

Producing Individual Play Readings

I. Preliminary preparation
   A. Play reviews
      1. Select a play which you are eager to share with others.
      2. Go to the library and get all the material you can concerning the author and various productions of the play.
      3. Outline this material for presentation to your audience.
      4. Write a brief description of all of the characters you will be interpreting. Analyze their personalities and visualize their appearance and clothing.
      5. Write a brief description of the setting.
      6. Select the passages that you feel you must read aloud to bring out the theme, characterize the people, and show the author's style.
      7. Write a brief synopsis of the essential action of the plot.
      8. Plan your review in its entirety, read it aloud to time it, then cut and rearrange the material and scenes to fit the time allotment. Ask yourself these questions:
         a. What is the central idea of the review?
         b. What is the predominant mood?
         c. How can I best establish this mood for my audience?

Hal Holbrook prepares for his one-man show, Mark Twain Tonight. *Makeup art transforms young Holbrook into Mark Twain at seventy.*

B. Dramatic readings
1. Select a play which is suited to your particular talents and personality. It should have comparatively few, well-contrasted characters and an entertaining plot.
2. Cut it to about forty-five minutes. First select the essential scenes and read them aloud so that you will know how long they are. Then choose minor scenes of special value to meet the time requirement.
3. Write out your introductory remarks if you feel they are necessary to make the setting and characters clear to your audience.
4. Go through your whole reading just as you will present it and check carefully on the time. Remember that it is better to stop ten minutes before your audience wants you to than one minute after they have become tired and bored.
5. If you memorize it, first fix the entire play in your mind, next the important scenes, and then work on individual scenes, speeches, and sentences.

II. Rehearsing for reviews or readings

    A. Study your material. Analyze and visualize the setting and characters. Determine the general mood and the delicate shades of feeling in separate passages. Look up all unfamiliar words, checking their pronunciation and meaning. Divide the thoughts into phrases. Mark the pauses and important words.

    B. If you are reading the scenes from a book, practice with the book in your left hand, turning the pages at the upper right-hand corner with your right hand. Train your eye to grasp a full line ahead so that you may look directly at your entire audience or in the direction of the character to whom you are speaking. Hold your book at shoulder height.

    C. Rehearse out loud. Let yourself be emotionally stirred so that you actually laugh and cry over the lines. Don't feel embarrassed or you may spoil your effectiveness. Of course, in performance you must never lose control of your voice or emotions.

    D. Practice your voice and diction exercises but forget them when you are working on the reading itself.

    E. Plan your stage setting for each scene so that you can visualize clearly where every character stands in relation to the others. Then you can turn slightly and clarify the positions of the different characters. Also visualize the costumes the characters are wearing and suggest them by your posture.

    F. Have the lights and stage decorations properly arranged and rehearse with them at least once. Use the reading stand. Have someone check to be sure that you can be heard in the back of the auditorium.

    G. Plan what you will wear. Boys can usually wear a dark suit and an inconspicuous tie. Girls must decide on either an afternoon or evening dress, appropriate hairdo, and makeup.

    H. Remember that you are presenting the play, not yourself. Subordinate your appearance and delivery to the reading.

III. Presenting your review or reading

    A. Get to the auditorium in ample time to check on all stage details, especially the lighting and acoustics. No externals should upset you during your presentation.

    B. Name the author and give any introductory remarks in your own person. Use your best diction and talk directly to your entire audience — simply, naturally, and, above all, distinctly.

C. When presenting a dramatic reading or scenes from the play in a review, assume the personality of your opening character, making a marked distinction between his personality and your own. As you present each new character, make a definite change in order to fix his voice upon the audience so that you will not need to repeat his name before or after his speeches.

D. After your closing speech, reassume your own personality, bow and smile slightly, and leave the stage. Or, if you have it definitely arranged and rehearsed, keep in character and have the curtains drawn on the final line.

GROUP PLAY READINGS

A play read by a carefully chosen cast avoids certain involved production details, but it does demand rehearsals and planning. Parts mumbled at sight can ruin a play. When a group reading is well cast and well presented, it is a very popular form of dramatic entertainment.

The first difficulty is securing scripts for the entire cast. Technically, a public reading and the copying of an entire play are prohibited for any copyrighted piece of literature. The proper procedure is to write to the publisher of the play and explain the exact purpose of the reading and the conditions under which it will be given. Since a good play reading is one of the best possible forms of advertising, you will have a good talking point if the play or film is coming to town.

Usually, the play must then be cut to make an interesting evening's entertainment. Keep the main thread of the plot clear by cutting detailed subplots and lengthy speeches. Be sure to include the passages containing the best acting scenes and those essential to the theme. Any introductory or descriptive material should be written out for a narrator to read. When important parts are omitted, they should be summarized if there is any danger of the audience's losing the thread of the plot.

A group reading can be done in several ways. You can place the performers around a table or in a row and have them read in turn, picking up their cues, characterizing their roles, and building the tempo and climax. Plan an attractive background. For example, if you have black or very dark drapes, all the men and women can wear formal black clothes and then be lighted by spots so that only their faces stand out. In planning the lighting, be sure the pages of the readers' scripts are illuminated so they can read without strain.

A more exciting method of presentation is to have the cast move about a stage equipped with the essential furniture. Stage business should be quite simple in order not to detract from the lines. Limited costumes in keeping with the characters and period can bring further reality to the roles. Both settings and costumes should help to create an illusion, but they should not be made too striking or realistic.

Producing Group Play Readings

I. Planning
    A. The director must make all arrangements: royalty rights, scripts or books for each reader, and stage setting. He must also decide on the method of presentation before the first rehearsal. Then his explanations will be clear and definite, and the cast can go right to work. He should also cut the play.
    B. The first rehearsal should be the long, careful one in which the meaning of the play and of individual passages is made clear, pronunciations are set, characters are clarified, and all plans are laid, including costumes.
II. Presenting
    A. Succeeding rehearsals should build up moods, climax, contrast, and tempos. The lines for the narrator must be carefully written and inserted into the reading as an integral part of the presentation.
    B. The actual performance should be a finished whole in which the play comes to life. Every character should be clear-cut, and scripts should be handled unobtrusively.

READERS THEATER

Readers Theater is glorified group playreading. Professional presentations have proved that it can hold its own as theatrical entertainment because members of the audience enjoy using their imaginations to visualize characters and backgrounds while they center their attention on the author's ideas rather than on the realism of stage productions. It is literally what the term states: the interpreters are readers, not actors, and the communication of the meaning of the selection and the author's style is the goal. The appeal lies in the vocal and facial expression of the interpreters, and the action is

Helen Hayes and Maurice Evans in their program Shakespeare Revisited, *produced in evening dress at The American Shakespeare Festival Theatre, Stratford, Connecticut, in 1962.*

mental, not physical. The subject matter can be any form of literature — poems, novels, short stories, as well as plays — but it must be presented vividly, in order that the audience may become involved emotionally in the ideas generated by the author.

Presenting Readers and Scripts

Great variety and ingenuity are employed in working out interesting ways of presenting the readers and scripts and, as yet, no rules and restrictions have been set up. A copy of *Readers Theatre Handbook* should be made available; written by Leslie Irene Coger and Melvin R. White, it is an artistic paperback. It covers the field in detail, presenting motivation, methods of staging, photographs of varied productions, and practical suggestions for seating arrangements, lighting, and costuming.

One point this book stresses is a unified focus of attention when the readers are not actually looking at the script; for example, placing the focus in the center of the auditorium right above the heads of the audience enables the voices to be carried front and prevents distracting head movements. Another consideration is pointing exits and entrances. One suggestion for this pointing is to seat the readers in a semicircle or straight line, and to have those in a scene in which they read rise together and be seated when finished. Another suggestion is to have the readers each illuminated with a spotlight when appearing in a scene, which is cut off when they exit. Costuming must also be unified and inconspicuous but in harmony with the spirit and period of the play. All elements except the voice and facial expression should be kept impersonal, for the subject matter, not the individuals, is the center of interest.

Vocally all members of the cast must be excellent readers who can employ all the techniques of speech training to advantage and can use creative imagination to feel and express every shade of meaning. Personally they should be alert, animated, expressive people who understand and thoroughly enjoy sharing that particular piece of literature, and who are capable of thinking, visualizing, and feeling with the author at all times.

The two key people of the Readers Theater are the director and narrator.

The Director

The director has need of great originality and ingenuity in selecting, preparing, and presenting the subject matter. In the first place, the script must be dramatic — this is why plays are so effective — with strongly contrasted, exciting people in situations which arouse emotion and stimulate intense interest; the language must read well; that is, the sound and use of words must be appealing and thought-provoking, stirring images in the minds of the listeners.

The director must then analyze the script in depth in order to appreciate its meaning and values, cutting and arranging the material so it will be truly effective, with no extraneous ideas intruding on the dominant one. This includes the use of the author's or his own wording for the narrator, and inserting comments whenever the narrator's explanations are needed to clarify the production.

And last, the director must plan the stage background, the methods of seating the readers, and — very important — the lighting, which must always enable the cast to see and at the same time must point the action and create the proper atmosphere for the play. Possible movement on the part of the actors is the most delicate consideration, for it must never attract attention or be used unless necessary. The use of projected figures or scenery on the backdrop, music, special lighting and sound effects, and unusual grouping of characters is also the director's prerogative.

The Narrator

The narrator must be selected with great care, for he can affect the entire presentation more than any other one person. His voice must be especially clear and pleasing, but not theatrical or striking. The narrator must have a strong sense of timing and climax; he often is responsible for the growing intensity of the action of the plot but must not interfere with the effectiveness of the reading itself. He is usually placed slightly outside the cast, either on a platform or behind a lectern, and is frequently in a spotlight only when he is reading.

Rehearsals

Rehearsing is as important as in a play, but with greater emphasis on vocal techniques, tempo, rhythms, and climax. No shade of meaning must be lost by bad inflections, and the phrasing of thought groups between breaths must be worked out most carefully. Breathiness, monotony, falling inflections at the end of all sentences, lack of clarity of speech, improper emphasis — these are only some of the pitfalls which imperil a production.

The Readers Theater is the only form where one person can take two or more parts without the help of makeup and costuming. Frequently groups of four to six persons work together to present a series of productions, taking several parts in each one. This demands flexibility and vocal variety and very careful rehearsing.

In rehearsals the director must work for clarity, unity, variety in tempo, and contrast in characterization. By his enthusiasm and encouragement, he must keep alive the spontaneity, motivation, and sparkle that make this intimate form of theater a continuous means of imaginative communication with the audience.

Performances

The performance itself must be a delight to readers and listeners alike. There should be a sense of combined imaginative experience in which emotion and understanding are shared and the true meaning which the author desired to convey is fully appreciated. You should take every opportunity to be a participant or listener in this vital form of theater. It is a growing means of keeping the public in touch with current trends, and you can keep your present enjoyment of drama a part of your leisure-time activity by organizing and working with it for years to come.

IMPROMPTU
by Tad Mosel

The scene is a nondescript room, the walls of which are not very high. They are set at peculiar angles to one another. There is a distorted doorway rear center. The furniture consists of a sofa, a chair, and perhaps a small table. Beyond the entrance and surrounding the room there is nothing but blackness.

The stage is dark. Nothing is visible but the glow of Winifred's cigarette. There is a pause, and then the actors speak out of the darkness.

WINIFRED.   Well, we're here. Somebody say something.

TONY.   Is the curtain up?

WINIFRED.   Yes.

TONY.   But we can't see anything. It's like the end instead of the beginning. What's wrong?

ERNEST.   That fool stage manager has forgotten to bring up the lights.

WINIFRED.   Oh, no, Ernest, he didn't forget. There's something deliberate about this. I don't trust him.

LORA.   You've got him wrong, Winifred. He was very nice. He wouldn't play tricks on us. Not him.

ERNEST.   Just leave everything to me. I'll go out and talk to him.

TONY.   But you can't!

ERNEST.   Why not?

TONY.   Don't you remember what he said? We're not to leave the stage until we have acted out the play.

ERNEST.   He was just trying to be impressive. I've met his kind before. It's time he learned that actors are more important than stage managers.

TONY.   He said it as if it were a law.

ERNEST.   Well, I won't stand here in the dark. (*Shouting*) Lights! Hey, you, out there — lights! (*There is a pause.*)

LORA.   Maybe we're not as important as you think, Ernest. Let's just be quiet and wait.

TONY.   Is there an audience out there?

WINIFRED. Yes, I can hear them soughing.

ERNEST. You can hear them what?

WINIFRED. Soughing, dear. Breathing heavily, as in sleep.

TONY. I feel as if I'm asleep, too.

WINIFRED. If everybody's going to feel things, we won't get anywhere at all. (*Pause*)

TONY. Yes. Asleep and dreaming. I'm a child again. I can see myself being led into a room full of people. They laugh and tell me to dance. I don't know what to do. I can't dance. So I hop up and down on one foot. Up and down, up and down. Now they're applauding. I'm a great success. Why do I want to cry? (*There is a pause. The lights come on.*)

ERNEST. That's more like it!

LORA. I knew he'd take care of us! I knew it!

WINIFRED. The stage manager said, "Let there be light," and there was light.

TONY. But the lights won't stand still. They seem to be changing! It's worse than it was before.

WINIFRED. Why don't you go off in a corner and have that cry? (TONY *looks at her.*)

ERNEST. And look, Winifred, you were right. There is an audience!

WINIFRED. So there is!

LORA. Isn't it wonderful? Do you see them, Tony?

TONY. Yes, I see them.

ERNEST. They're waiting for us to begin.

TONY. Do they know what we're going to do? Has it been explained to them?

WINIFRED. I defy you to explain anything that is happening on this stage.

TONY. I was just asking a question.

LORA. Don't ask questions, Tony. You'll only make yourself unhappy. Ernest says they're waiting for us to begin. Well, let's begin!

ERNEST. Wait a minute, Lora. Tony may have a point there. I wonder if they do know what we're doing.

TONY. Maybe we ought to tell them.

WINIFRED. All right, then, tell them!

TONY. Me?

WINIFRED. Certainly. It's your bright idea.

ERNEST. I'm sure I could explain everything very lucidly.

WINIFRED. You probably could, Ernest. That's why I want him to do it.

TONY. I wouldn't know what to say.

WINIFRED.   I know you wouldn't.

TONY   (*Naively, inquiringly*). Are you making fun of me, Winifred?

WINIFRED.   Whatever gave you that idea? (*She laughs lightly.* TONY *looks at her a moment, then he steps down to the edge of the stage and addresses the audience.*)

TONY.   Ladies and gentlemen, we are here to — they say every actor has a dream — a recurring dream — and he's on a stage and there's an audience, and — he doesn't know what the play is or what his lines are. That's the way it is with us. This afternoon. Maybe we are dreaming — maybe we're not really here — I don't know —

WINIFRED.   You can stop right there! I know that I'm here, thank you. Irrevocably, unwillingly, disgustingly here.

ERNEST   (*With great tolerance*). You'd better let me do it, Tony. (*To the audience*) Ladies and gentlemen, an hour ago each of us received a message to report to this theater; there were jobs waiting for us. When we arrived, the stage manager told us we were to go on stage immediately, before an audience,

Carol Channing recording Ludwig Bemelman's Madeline *for Caedmon Records. Notice that, though she has no audience, Miss Channing reacts to the reading with her whole body.*

COURTESY OF CAEDMON RECORDS

and improvise a play — which we are about to do. (*To* TONY)
You see how easy it is?

TONY. Yes, it's easy to say what happened. You didn't say what
it means. Who are we? Why are we here? That's the important
thing.

WINIFRED. That young man has rocks in his head.

LORA. Would it help if we told them our names, Tony?

ERNEST. An excellent suggestion, Lora. I was about to think of it
myself. (*He turns to the audience.*)

WINIFRED. Here we go!

ERNEST (*To the audience*). You have no programs, so you know nothing about us. My name is Ernest. I am returning to the stage
after several successful seasons on the West Coast, where I
scored personal successes in more than two-score films. Born
of a theatrical family, I was reared in stage dressing rooms.
At the age of five, I scored a personal success in —

TONY. Ernest, you're not explaining anything!

ERNEST. I'm telling them who I am!

TONY. But it's more than that!

LORA. Be quiet, Tony. This is very interesting. I love hearing about
other people.

TONY. All right. I'll be quiet.

LORA. Go on, Ernest.

(ERNEST *begins to speak.*)

WINIFRED (*Quickly*). Why don't you be quiet, too, Ernest?

ERNEST. I haven't finished.

WINIFRED. Surely they know all about you — an actor of your standing. You don't want to bore them by telling them things they
know, do you?

ERNEST. Well — no.

WINIFRED. Then sit down. (*He does so.*)

LORA. It's your turn, Winifred.

WINIFRED (*Shrugs her shoulders, moves down to the edge of the stage,
and addresses the audience*). I'm Winifred. I have had rather
a cloudy career as an actress. You may have seen me, but
you won't remember. I usually play the leading lady's best
friend. I don't like the theater because you can't trust it.
This is an example of what I mean. Next. (*Indicating* LORA)

LORA (*After thinking a moment*). My name used to be Loralee, but
somebody said a long stage name is bad luck, so I shortened
it to Lora. It hasn't helped me much, but I don't really
mind. Perhaps I wasn't meant to be an actress. I think that's
all. (*She steps back.*)

WINIFRED.   Hold tight, everybody. (*With mock seriousness*) Your turn, Tony.

TONY.   I have nothing to say.

LORA.   But, Tony, you've got to tell them something about yourself.

TONY.   Why? None of you did. It's all so unreal. (*To the audience*) Who are you? Why are you here? Did you come for escape, for enlightenment, for curiosity? Or were you, too, commanded?

ERNEST.   We weren't any of us commanded!

TONY.   Then what are we doing here? It's the only explanation! You're a celebrity — surely this is beneath you. Lora wasn't meant to be an actress. Winifred hates the stage.

WINIFRED   (*Cuttingly*). And you're afraid, aren't you?

TONY.   Yes, I'm afraid! There — I've told them something about myself!

WINIFRED.   If that's all you've got to say, sit down. You were amusing for a while, but no longer. Soul-searching is the lowest form of entertainment.

ERNEST.   I don't see why you're afraid, Tony. You ask what we're doing here, and the answer is simple. We are here to please the audience, and they are here to be pleased.

WINIFRED.   Why can't you be like Ernest, Tony? He knows everything.

LORA.   The stage manager's not going to like it if we don't do something soon.

ERNEST.   Of course, Lora. (*To the audience*) I hope you will be patient with outbursts of this sort, ladies and gentlemen. Naturally, some of us are a little confused. But don't worry, we're going to begin our play as soon as we've made a few preparations. You see, the stage manager gave us instructions —

WINIFRED.   He wrote upon the table the words of the Covenant —

ERNEST.   Shut up, Winifred. (*To the audience*) And I think it only fair to let you know what they are. First of all, our play will not end until he is completely satisfied with our performance.

WINIFRED.   That's a cheerful thing to tell them. (*To the audience*) He's one of those sour little men who never like anything.

LORA.   You'd better stop talking that way about him, Winifred. He's right over there behind that wall; he can hear you. You might offend him.

WINIFRED.   That's nothing compared to what he's done to me.

LORA.   But he's so important, and — good. I think he's been very kind to me. I have great faith in him.

ERNEST.   I thought you wanted to begin, Lora.

LORA.   Oh — I'm sorry, Ernest.

ERNEST   (*To the audience*). Secondly, we are not permitted to leave the
    stage until the play has ended. And last of all, our play is to
    be an imitation of life.

TONY.   No, that's wrong! (ERNEST *looks at him annoyed.*) Well, it is.
    He didn't say that.

LORA.   Are you sure, Tony?

TONY.   I listened very carefully. He didn't say it was to be an imita-
    tion of life. It's supposed to *be* life.

SPOON RIVER ANTHOLOGY
adapted by Charles Aidman from Edgar Lee Masters

WILLIAM AND EMILY

BOTH.   There is something about death.

EMILY.   Like love itself!

WILLIAM.   If with someone with whom you have known passion,

EMILY.   And the glow of youthful love,

WILLIAM.   You also

EMILY.   After years of life together

WILLIAM.   Feel the sinking of the fire,

EMILY.   And thus fade away together . . . gradually —

WILLIAM.   Faintly —

EMILY.   Delicately —

WILLIAM.   As it were in each other's arms.

EMILY.   Passing from the familar room

BOTH.   That is a power of unison
    Between souls
    Like love itself.

LUCINDA MATLOCK.   I went to the dances at Chandlerville,
    And played snap-out at Winchester.
    One time we changed partners,
    Driving home in the moonlight of middle June,
    And then I found Davis.
    We were married and lived together for seventy years,
    Enjoying, working, raising the twelve children,
    Eight of whom we lost
    Ere I had reached the age of sixty.
    I spun, I wove, I kept the house, I nursed the sick.
    I made the garden, and for holiday
    Rambled over the fields where sang the larks,
    And by Spoon River gathering many a shell,
    And many a flower and medicinal weed —
    Shouting to the wooded hills, winging to the green valleys.

At ninety-six I had lived enough, that is all,
And passed to a sweet repose.
What is this I hear of sorrow and weariness,
Anger, discontent and drooping hopes?
Degenerate sons and daughters,
Life is too strong for you —
It takes life to love life.

PETIT, THE POET. Seeds in a dry pod, tick, tick, tick,
Tick, tick, tick, like mites in a quarrel —
Faint iambics that the full breeze wakens —
But the pine tree makes a symphony thereof.
Triolets, villanelles, rondels, rondeaus,
Ballades by the score with the same old thought:
The snows and the roses of yesterday are vanished;
And what is love but a rose that fades?
Life all around me here in the village:
Tragedy, comedy, valor and truth,
Courage, constancy, heroism, failure —
All in the loom, and oh what patterns!
Woodlands, meadows, streams and rivers —
Blind to all of it all my life long.
Triolets, villanelles, rondels, rondeaus,
Seeds in a dry pod, tick, tick, tick,
Tick, tick, tick, what little iambics,
While Homer and Whitman roared in the pines?

FIDDLER JONES. The earth keeps some vibration going.
There in your heart, and that is you.
And if the people find you can fiddle,
Why fiddle you must, for all your life.
How could I till my forty acres
Not to speak of getting more,
With a medley of horns, bassoons, and piccolos
Stirred in my brain by crows and robins
And the creak of a wind-mill — only these?
And I never started to plow in my life
That someone did not stop in the road
And take me away to a dance or picnic.
I ended up with forty acres;
I ended up with a broken fiddle —
And a broken laugh and a thousand memories,
And not a single regret.

SCHOFIELD HUXLEY

ACTOR ONE.   God . . .

ALL.   Ask us not to record your wonders, we admit
      The stars and the suns and the countless
      Worlds.

ACTOR THREE.   But we have measured their distances and weighed
      Them and discovered their substances.

ACTOR ONE.   We have devised wings for the air

ACTOR THREE.   And keels for water

ACTOR ONE.   And horses of iron for the earth.

ACTRESS TWO.   We have lengthened the vision You gave us a
      Million times,

ACTRESS FOUR.   And the hearing You gave us a million times.

ACTOR ONE.   We have leaped over space with speech

ACTOR THREE.   And taken fire for light out of the air.

ACTOR ONE.   We have built great cities and bored through
      The hills and bridged majestic waters.

ACTOR THREE.   We have written the *Iliad* and *Hamlet*,

ACTRESS TWO.   And we have explored Your mysteries and searched
      For You without ceasing.

ACTRESS FOUR.   And found You again after losing You in hours
      Of weariness,

ALL.   And we ask You
      How would You like to create a sun
      And the next day
      Have the worms
      Slipping in and out
      Between Your fingers?

DIPPOLD THE OPTICIAN

ACTOR or

ACTRESS:

ONE.   Try this lens . . . what do you see now?

TWO.   Globes of red, yellow, purple —

ONE.   Just a moment. And now?

TWO.   My father and mother and sisters.

ONE.   Yes. And now?

TWO.   Knights at arms, beautiful women, kind faces —

ONE.   Try this.

THREE.   A field of grain — a city.

ONE.   Very good! And now?

THREE.   A young woman with angels bending over her.

ONE.   A heavier lens. And now?

THREE.   Many women with bright eyes and open lips.

On a TV show, Orson Welles reads a scary Halloween script so well that it lures a monster (Alan Sues) out of the woodwork.

ONE. Try this.

FOUR. Just a goblet on a table.

ONE. Oh, I see. Try this lens.

FOUR. Just an open space — I see nothing in
Particular.

ONE. Well . . . and now?

FOUR. Pine trees, a lake, a summer sky.

ONE. That's better. And now?

FOUR. A book.

ONE. Read a page for me.

FOUR. I can't. My eyes are carried beyond the page.

ONE. Try this lens.

ALL. Ooohh, depths of air.

ONE. Excellent! And now?

ALL. Light, just light, making everything below it
A toy world.

ONE. Very well, we'll make the glasses accordingly.

285

J. B.

by Archibald MacLeish

SARAH   (*Confused, holding out the small green branch like a child*).
Look, Job.
The first few leaves . . .
Not leaves though —
Petals. I found it in the ashes growing
Green as though it did not know . . .
All that's left there now is ashes. . . .
Mountains of ashes, shattered glass,
Glittering cliffs of glass all shattered
Steeper than a cat could climb
If there were cats still. . . .

J. B.   Why?

SARAH.   I broke the
Branch to strip the leaves off.
Petals
        (*Fastens branch to pole at R. C., under porch*)
Again!
But they so clung to it!

J. B.   Curse
God and die! You said that to me.

SARAH.   Yes. You wanted justice, didn't you?

J. B.   Cry for justice and the stars
Will stare until your eyes sting! Weep,
Enormous winds will thrash the water!

SARAH.   Cry in sleep for your lost children,
Snow will fall . . .
                        snow will fall.

J. B.   You left me, Sarah.

SARAH.   Yes, I left you.
I thought there was a way away.
Out of the world. Out of the world.
Water under bridges opens
Closing and the companion stars
Still float there afterwards. I thought the door
Opened into closing water.

J. B.   Sarah!

SARAH.   Oh, I never could.
I never could. Even this —
Even the green leaf on the branch — could stop me.

J. B.   Why have you come back again?

SARAH.   (*Kneels C. She has found a stub of candle in her pocket.*)
      Because I love you.

J. B.   Because you love me!
      The one thing certain in this hurtful world
      Is love's inevitable heartbreak.
      What's the future but the past to come
      Over and over, love and loss,
      What's loved most lost most.
         (SARAH *has moved into the rubble of the ring. She kneels,*
      setting things to rights. Her mind is on her task, not on J. B.'s
      words.)

SARAH.   I know that, Job.

J. B.   Nothing is certain but the loss of love.
      And yet . . . you say you love me!

SARAH.   Yes.

J. B.   The stones in those dead streets would crack
      With terrible indecent laughter
      Hearing *you* and *me* say love!

SARAH.   I have no light to light the candle.

J. B.   (*Violently*). You have our love to light it with!
      Blow on the coal of the heart, poor Sarah.

SARAH.   Blow on the coal of the heart . . . ?

J. B.   The candles in churches are out.
      The lights have gone out in the sky!

SARAH.   The candles in churches are out.
      The lights have gone out in the sky.
      Blow on the coal of the heart
      And we'll see by and by . . .
                              we'll see where we are.
      We'll know. We'll know.

J. B.   (*Slowly, with difficulty, the hard words said at last*).
      We can never *know*.
      He answered me like the stillness of a star
      That silences us asking.
      No, Sarah, no:
         (*Kneels beside her*)
      We *are* and that is all our answer.
      We are and what we are can suffer.
      But . . .
                what suffers loves.
      And love
      Will live its suffering again,
      Risk its own defeat again,

Endure the loss of everything again
And yet again and yet again
In doubt, in dread, in ignorance, unanswered,
Over and over with the dark before,
The dark behind it . . . and still live . . . still love.
(J. B. *strikes match, touches* SARAH's *cheek with his hand.*)

THE HOLLOW CROWN

The Epilogue from Morte D'Arthur, *Devised by John Barton**

NARRATOR.   And thus they fought all the long day until it was near night, and by that time was there an hundred thousand lay dead upon the down. Then the noble King Arthur, being wounded unto death, looked about him and said:

KING ARTHUR.   Jesu mercy! Where are all my noble knights become? Alas that I should ever see this doleful day, for now I am come to mine end.

NARRATOR.   Then the King fell in a swoon to the earth, and Sir Bedivere, the last of all his knights, led him weakly and with great mourning, to a little chapel not far from the sea-side.

KING ARTHUR.   Now leave this mourning and weeping, gentle knight,

NARRATOR.   Said the King,

KING ARTHUR.   For all this will not avail me. For my time passeth on fast. Therefore, take thou here Excalibur, my good sword, and go with it to yonder water's side, and when thou comest there, I charge thee throw my sword in that water, and come again and tell me what thou seest there.

NARRATOR.   So Sir Bedivere departed. And by the way he beheld that noble sword, that the pommel and haft was all precious stones. And then he said to himself:

Emlyn Williams as the novelist Charles Dickens in his one-man performance based on extracts from the works of this famous Victorian author. See also Page 264.

HUROK CONCERTS, INC.

SIR BEDIVERE. If I throw this rich sword in the water, thereof shall never come good, but harm and loss.

NARRATOR. So he hid Excalibur under a tree, and came again unto the King, and said he had been at the water and had thrown the sword into the water.

KING ARTHUR. What saw thou there?

NARRATOR. Said the King.

SIR BEDIVERE. Sir,

NARRATOR. He said,

SIR BEDIVERE. I saw nothing but waves and winds.

KING ARTHUR. That is untruly said of thee,

NARRATOR. Said the King.

KING ARTHUR. And therefore go thou lightly again, and do my commandment.

NARRATOR. Then Sir Bedivere returned again, and yet him thought sin and shame to throw away that noble sword. And so he hid the sword, and returned again, and told the King that he had been at the water and done his commandment.

KING ARTHUR. What sawest thou there?

NARRATOR. Said the King.

SIR BEDIVERE. Sir,

NARRATOR. He said,

SIR BEDIVERE. I saw nothing but the waters wappe and wave wanne.

KING ARTHUR. Ah, traitor unto me and untrue!

NARRATOR. Said King Arthur.

KING ARTHUR. Now has thou betrayed me twice! Thou art named a noble knight, and would betray me for the riches of this sword. But now go again lightly, for thy long tarrying putteth me in great jeopardy of my life, for I have taken cold.

NARRATOR. Then Sir Bedivere departed, and went to the sword, and lightly took it up, and went unto the water's side. And there he threw the sword as far into the water as he might. And there came an arm and an hand above the water and met it, and caught it, and so shook it thrice and brandished, and then vanished away with the sword into the water. So Sir Bedivere came again to the King, and told him what he saw.

KING ARTHUR. Alas,

NARRATOR. Said the King,

KING ARTHUR. Help me hence, for I dread me I have tarried over long.

NARRATOR. Then Sir Bedivere took the King upon his back, and so went with him to the water's side. And by the bank hoved a little barge with many fair ladies in it, and all they had black hoods.

KING ARTHUR. Now put me into that barge.

NARRATOR. Said the King. And so he did softly; and there received him three ladies with great mourning. And in one of their laps King Arthur laid his head. And anon they rowed from the land, and when Sir Bedivere beheld all those ladies go from him, he cried:

SIR BEDIVERE: Ah, my lord Arthur, my King, what shall become of me, now ye go from me?

KING ARTHUR: Comfort thyself,

NARRATOR. Said the King.

KING ARTHUR. And do as well as thou mayest, for in me is no trust for to trust in. For I will into the vale of Avilion to heal me of my grievous wound. And if thou hear never-more of me, pray for my soul.

NARRATOR. And as soon as Sir Bedivere had lost sight of the barge, he wept and wailed, and so took to the forest; and so he went all that night.

Thus of Arthur I find no more written; neither more of the very certainty of his death heard I never read. Yet some men say in many parts of England that King Arthur is not dead, but had by the will of our Lord Jesu into another place; and men say that he shall come again. I will not say that it shall be so, but rather I would say, here in this world, he changed his life. But many men say that there is written upon his tomb this verse:

HIC JACET ARTHURUS REX, QUONDAM REX QUE FUTURUS . . .
The Once and Future King.

Plays Suitable for Readers Theater

Thornton Wilder: *Skin of our Teeth, Our Town, Happy Journey to Camden and Trenton*

T. Sladen Smith: *St. Simeon Stylites*

G. B. Shaw: *Back to Methuselah, Man and Superman, Dark Lady of the Sonnets*

Christopher Fry: *The Lady's Not for Burning*

J. M. Barrie: *Shall We Join the Ladies?, What Every Woman Knows, The Admirable Crichton, Dear Brutus*

Tom Stoppard: *Rosencrantz and Guildenstern Are Dead*

J. L. Balderston: *Berkeley Square*

Sutton Vane: *Outward Bound*

Robert Bolt: *A Man for All Seasons*

Eugene O'Neill: *Beyond the Horizon, Strange Interlude, The Great God Brown, Lazarus Laughed*

Eugene Ionesco: *The Bald Soprano, The Chairs, The Lesson*

Jean Giraudoux: *Tiger at the Gates*

Jean Anouilh: *Antigone, Becket*

Robert Sherwood: *There Shall Be No Night*

Rudolph Besier: *The Barretts of Wimpole Street*

Stephen Benét: *John Brown's Body*

Bibliography

Coger, Leslie Irene, and Melvin R. White: *Readers Theater Handbook: A Dramatic Approach to Literature*, Scott, Foresman, Glenview, Ill. 1967.

PART **3**

Appreciating the Drama

🎨🔟

HISTORY OF
THE DRAMA

The history of the drama is closely related to the history of mankind. When the first hunters recounted their adventures by means of vivid pantomime, when the first storytellers told their tales in rhythmic chants, and when the first organized groups of people found expression in the pantomimic intricacies of hunting, war, and love dances, the dramatic impulse was manifesting itself. Later the primitive actor hid himself behind a mask, to become a god or animal to his peers. The key to man's dramatic action seems to be his desire to imitate. As civilization developed, drama took definite form in the worship of heavenly gods and the glorification of earthly rulers. The mighty *Book of Job* and allegorical *Song of Songs* (Solomon) of the Old Testament are written in dramatic form. Then tales were told of noble men engaged in mighty conflicts and lesser men bumbling along through their comic paces; and at last the tales produced dramatic presentations, ultimately to be written and acted in concrete form.

THE ORIGINS OF WESTERN DRAMA

The earliest record of a theatrical performance comes from Egypt, the birthplace of much of the world's art. Carved on a stone tablet some 4,000 years ago, this account tells how I-Kher-Wofret of Abydos arranged and played the leading role in a three-day pageant made up of actual battles, boat processions, and elaborate ceremonies which told the story of the murder, dismemberment, and resurrection of the great god Osiris. Also, carvings and murals on the walls of ancient temples and tombs show highly theatrical pictures of dancing girls and triumphal processions. The Hymns to the Sun-god Aton, written and sung by Ikhnaton, the spiritual-minded Pharaoh, rank even today among the finest examples of dramatic religious poetry.

Greek Drama

Drama as we know it came into being in Greece in the sixth century B.C. as part of the worship of Dionysus, god of wine and fertility. To commemorate the god's death, a group of chanters, called the chorus, danced around an altar upon which a goat was sacrified. This chorus was called the "goat-singers," and their ritualistic chant was called the "tragos," or goat-song; from this term the word "tragedy" came. These ceremonies in honor of Dionysus evolved into dramatic contests, the first of which was won by Thespis. In 534 B.C., he stepped from the chorus and engaged in a dialogue between the chorus and himself. Thus he became the first actor, and the term "thespian" has been given to actors ever since. This actor-playwright is also credited with introducing masks into the Greek plays. These dramatic contests were part of a festival which lasted five or six days.

The most famous of these festivals was the City Dionysia. The first day was devoted to a grand procession, games, and general celebration. The second, and possibly third, day was reserved for dithyrambic poetry contests. On each of the last three days a different playwright would present four plays. The first three plays were tragedies, often a trilogy — three plays related in theme, myth, or characters. The fourth play was called a satyr play — what we might call a tragicomedy. It was considered a great honor to win the ivy wreath of victory in the play contests.

Production in the Greek Theater was a highly complex art which made use of clever mechanical devices. The theater existed originally for men, both as performers and audience, and women were not permitted to attend performances until the fourth century B.C. The performances were at first held in the open hillsides surrounding a circular area called the "orchestra" where the dancing of the chorus took place. Wooden and then stone seats were added to form the theater; at the same time the dancing circle was paved with stone. In the front row facing the orchestra were special seats for the priests of Dionysus. The altar of Dionysus, located in the center of the orchestra, was sometimes used as a stage prop.

Originally, at the rear of the acting area was a small hut called the "skene" where the actors changed masks and costumes. After a time, the skene was enlarged into a stone building; a second story and wings (parascenia) were added and scenery was painted on the front. On the roof was the god-walk, from which the gods delivered their monologues. Also, at a later date, periaktoi, three-sided revolving pieces of scenery, were placed on both sides of the stage. Violence was not permitted on the Greek stage, but a movable platform called the eccyclema could be rolled out to reveal a tableau of the results of violent acts.

The Theatre of Dionysus as it appears today after approximately four centuries of use. Productions of the Greek classics are given here each summer.

D. A. HARISSIADIS, ATHENS

Another device used in Greek plays was the machina, a cranelike hoist which permitted actors to appear above the stage as if flying and to be lowered from the roof of the skene to the orchestra. The machina was heavy enough to carry a chariot and horses or several persons. Most frequently the character lowered represented a god from Mount Olympus who came to earth to settle the affairs of men — and the problems of a playwright who could not resolve his conflict satisfactorily. From the use of this contrivance came the term "deus ex machina" (god from the machine), which is still used today to indicate some device an author introduces late in a play to resolve plot difficulties — the unknown relative who leaves a legacy, a long-lost letter, the discovery of a kinsman given up for dead. Usually such a plot resolution weakens the play and works out acceptably only in farce, melodrama, or fantasy.

In ancient Greece actors were held in high repute and were organized into powerful guilds. They were classified into three groups on the basis of their vocal flexibility and clarity, and emotional appeal; all of them played several roles — both masculine and feminine — in every production. The important companies were centered in the cities, but traveling troupes toured in repertoires of the most popular plays. The expensive productions were supported by organizations or wealthy citizens who provided magnificent masks and costumes.

The Greek tragic actors wore masks with a built-in megaphone, padded costumes, and boots with thick soles called "cothurni," or in Latin, buskins. The mask was enlarged and heightened by a crown or onkus. The comic actors wore rather grotesque masks, usually padded in a humorously deformed way, and wore a type of sandal called a sock. You are probably familiar with the "masks of comedy and tragedy," and some of you may even belong to a drama club named "Sock and Buskin" after the shoes of comedy and tragedy.

The actors and members of the chorus moved in stylized dances before huge audiences — it is believed that some theaters could seat over 17,000 patrons. There were fifty dancers in the early chorus, but that number was eventually decreased to twelve or fifteen. Gradually the responsibilities of the chorus diminished as actors took over the emphatic roles.

The chorus, however, was an integral part of the early Greek theater; it served to explain the situation, to bring the audience up-to-date, to make a commentary on the action from the point of view of establisled ideas or the group it represented, and to engage in dialogue with the actors. Vestiges of the Greek chorus are found in theater even today: the Stage Manager in *Our Town* and El Gallo in *The Fantasticks* are two well-known examples of a modern chorus embodied in one character.

Greek Tragedy

The main conflicts of the Greek tragedies evolved from the clash between the will of the gods and the ambitions and desires of men, and showed how futile were the efforts of man to circumvent the decrees of fate. The greatest writers of Greek tragedy were Aeschylus (525–456 B.C.), Sophocles (497–405 B.C.), and Euripides (485–406 B.C.). Aeschylus was a warrior-playwright who held firmly to the Greek religion of his day. He added the second actor, reduced the chorus to twelve, and is noted for his elevation and majesty of language, which has never been surpassed. Many critics refer to him as the "father of tragedy." Of his seventy to ninety plays, only seven remain.

Prometheus Bound is the tragedy of the mythological "Firebearer" who felt compassion for his creation, man. Zeus, infuriated by Prometheus' defiance, had him chained to a rock at the edge of the world. Aeschylus also left us the only extant trilogy, the *Oresteia*. The first play, *Agamemnon*, is the story of the return of Agamemnon from Troy and his murder at the hands of his wife, Clytemnestra, and her lover, Aegisthus. The second play, *The Libation Bearers* (*Choephori*) tells of the revenge Orestes and Electra take upon their mother Clytemnestra and Aegisthus. The third play, *The Eumenides*, tells of Orestes' torment by the Furies, his trial, and his acquittal. The *Oresteia* was brought to life in the sixties by Sir Tyrone Guthrie in his now famous *House of Atreus*, adapted by John Lewin, and in the United States first performed at the Tyrone Guthrie Theatre in Minneapolis and later in New York.

The greatest of the Greek tragedians, ranked with Shakespeare as one of the greatest playwrights of all time, was Sophocles. This craftsman of perfection added the third actor, and introduced dramatic action leading to a definite plot structure of unity and beauty. He achieved an amazing balance between the power of the gods and the importance of man, believing man has a little of the divinity in him that elevates his struggle against fate. Questioning yet reverent, Sophocles allowed his characters to ask "Why?" within the framework of acceptance of the will of the gods and the web of destiny.

As a result, his characters are among the strongest ever to walk upon the stage. He wrote at least 110 plays, of which only seven have survived. However we do know that Sophocles won the first prize eighteen times.

Sophocles' *Oedipus Rex* stands as one of the world's most powerful plays of dramatic irony. Aristotle describes it as the most ideal tragedy he had ever seen. It is the tragic story of a man in search of Truth whose fate had been preordained by the gods: he unwittingly kills his own father and marries his mother. It is not until he gouges out his own eyes that Oedipus perceives the Truth his human eyesight was blind to.

Sophocles' *Antigone* is also ranked among the great tragedies. Antigone is Oedipus' daughter. Her two brothers, Eteocles and Polyneices, are left to rule jointly, but civil war breaks out when Eteocles refuses to step down when his term on the throne comes to an end. The two brothers meet on the battlefield and slay each other. Their uncle, Creon, takes over the throne and decrees that Polyneices' body must remain unburied. The Greeks believed that desecration of the dead was offensive to the gods and that the soul of a body not given proper burial was doomed to wander eternally, never finding rest. Antigone defies Creon's mandate in order to fulfill her higher loyalties to family and gods. She attempts to bury Polyneices, is caught, and placed alive in a cave to die. It is not until his own world crumbles about him that Creon realizes that the laws of man cannot supplant the laws of the gods. A widely produced modern version of *Antigone* by Jean Anouilh is extremely popular now, especially in colleges and high schools.

Euripides was a playwright who seriously questioned life and became more concerned with the human interest element than with the religious views of his day. He emphasized man-to-man relationships and became a master of pathos. He wrote over ninety plays, but only four won first place. *The Trojan Women* is one of literature's strongest indictments against war. As the atrocities of murder, pillage, and slavery unfold outside the walls of burning Troy, the audience is deeply moved by the cruel pathos of women and war. *Medea* is the tragedy of a woman who seeks revenge upon her husband, Jason. In her desire to make Jason pay the highest price for his infidelity, Medea sacrifices that which is dearest to her also — their two sons. These two plays still rank among the most poignant portrayals of women in dramatic literature.

The elevation of man as a noble being, the elevation of language, and the elevation of man's conflicts lifted Greek tragedy to heights attained since only by Shakespeare.

Greek Comedy

The outstanding author of Greek comedy was Aristophanes (450–380 B.C.) who contributed forty plays, eleven of which still remain. Aristophanes was a skilled satirist and a keen observer of mankind. He considered nothing sacred to his barbed wit and mocked the leaders of Athens and the gods themselves in a rollicking, bawdy fashion. Three of his best known plays are *The Frogs*, a writer's contest between Aeschylus and Euripides in Hades judged by Dionysus himself; *The Clouds*, a travesty on Socrates and Greek education; and *Lysistrata*, a scathing attack on war.

Aristophanes was the chief writer of "Old Comedy." Many of the Roman and Renaissance writers were influenced by the "New Comedy," whose best-known author was Menander (342–291 B.C.). Only one complete script, *The Curmudgeon*, is known, and only three fragments remain of his other plays. Menander's comedies seem to be gentle compared to those of Aristophanes. Satire gave way to sentimental comedy based upon a love story. By this time the chorus had disappeared and stock characters had made their appearance upon the stage.

The Greek comedies are less comprehensible and interesting to modern audiences because they were often topical in subject matter, usually satirizing political leaders and prominent persons. There have been a number of adaptations of several of the comedies of Aristophanes. *Lysistrata* has proved especially popular and has been performed by professionals and in universities with great success. The chief charm of *The Frogs* and *The Birds* lies in the opportunity to devise fantastic costumes and grotesque masks; their clever lines and biting satire are also most appropriate for current adaptations.

Roman Theater

Roman drama was a decadent imitation of the Greek, deteriorating at last into sensual interpretive dances called pantomimes, vulgar farces called mimes, and colossal gladiatorial contests in which the slaughter of human beings and beasts became the emotional delight of the audience. The Roman theater at first resembled the Greek, with heightened skene decorated elaborately with arches and statues

Masks similar to those used in ancient Greek drama were worn in the production of
Oedipus Rex *at the Stratford Festival Theatre in Stratford, Ontario, Canada.*

of varying sizes; gradually the theater was extended into a circular
arena surrounded by towering tiers of seats. Strangely enough, when
Rome had no theaters, only two writers of comedy stood out —
Plautus and Terence. Two hundred years later when Rome had
constructed huge amphitheaters, only Seneca, a writer of bombastic
tragedies, attempted anything like a play. Seneca's plays are usually
referred to as "closet dramas" — plays meant to be read rather than
acted. Although these three playwrights offered little compared to
their Greek predecessors, their plays did influence later writers,
including Shakespeare.

It is easy to see that a playwright could not compete with the real
conflicts of life and death in the arena, the thrills of the chariot races
in the Circus Maximus, or real naval battles in artificial seas. The
only type of performance people wished to see was that permeated
with vulgarity. The worship of Dionysus had deteriorated into Bac-
chanalian orgies. The cruelty of the great spectacles and the coarse-
ness of the dramatic entertainment was representative of the moral
decay of Rome, which brought about the hostility of the rising
Christian Church. During the Dark Ages following the decline of
Rome, only wandering players called histriones and minstrels called
jongleurs kept the drama alive with their dancing, singing, juggling,   **301**

acrobatics, and marionette shows. Sad as it seems, from 400 B.C. to the Elizabethan Age of England nearly two thousand years later, not a single great play was written.

Medieval Drama

The drama owed its revival, like its origin, to religion. During the period extending roughly from the fifth to the fifteenth centuries, drama developed along slightly different lines in the various European nations. In each case, however, its rebirth came about through the Christian Church, a strange coincidence considering that the church associated the worship rites of Dionysus and Bacchus with those of Baal. Nevertheless, the priests gradually introduced tropes, liturgical chants added to the mass, in order that the many people who could neither read nor write might learn of the great events in Biblical history.

From mere tableaux at the altar and the stations of the cross, these church plays evolved into elaborate productions which drew increasingly larger crowds and necessitated out-of-doors presentations. Latin was used, as in the masses, and the performers were nuns, priests, and talented choirboys.

Gradually, church drama expanded to present more and more Bible stories; plays were translated into the vernacular; and little by little, lay members of the parishes took part in the performances. The Miracle and Mystery plays were based on the lives of the saints and stories in the Bible. The *Passion Play*, which is concerned with the last week in the life of Christ, is an example of these medieval church dramas. It still is given in Europe at Oberammergau, Germany, by the citizens of the charming Bavarian village where it was first performed in 1634. It has been produced every ten years since 1760 on the opening of each decade and has never been commercialized. The 1970 performance in the perfectly equipped theater seating 5,200, with glassed-over stage, drew 600,000 spectators. In the United States, the Black Hills Passion Play group at Spearfish, South Dakota, performs all summer, and in Florida during the winter.

The early Miracle and Mystery plays were performed with what were called mansions, a series of acting stations placed in a line. The mansions, or houses, were Biblical localities like Heaven, Limbo, Pilate's House, Jerusalem, The Temple, and Hell's Mouth. The plays often portrayed the many temptations and challenges facing man between Heaven and Hell. Hell's Mouth seemed to be of keen interest to the medieval audiences. It breathed fire and smoke, its jaws opened and closed, and as the wicked were pushed in by the Devil's tribe, the pitiful cries of the eternally damned would be heard. Lee Simonson's *The Stage Is Set* gives a delightful account of the elaborate effects and quaint stage directions for Hell's Mouth.

By the twelfth century, the medieval trade unions, or guilds, had taken over the presentation of most of the plays during the festival of Corpus Christi. Each guild presented one part in the story according to the craft of its members; the bakers presented *The Last Supper*; the goldsmiths, *The Three Wise Men*; the shipwrights, *The Construction of the Ark*; and the cooks, *The Harrowing of Hell*.

Each guild had its own pageant wagon, or stage on wheels. The pageant wagon was divided into two levels. The upper level was a platform stage and the lower level, curtained off, served as a dressing room. The wagons would travel from town to town in a sequential procession. The audience could remain in one spot while the pageant wagons moved through town one by one. The entire sequence of plays was called a cycle. The guilds vied with one another to see which could stage the most elaborate production.

The cycles were highly developed in England, and manuscripts are still preserved from Chester, York, Coventry, and Wakefield. However, the release of control by the Church allowed an increasingly greater amount of secular material to creep into performances, especially humorous incidents. For example, in the Chester *Noah's Flood*, the water is rising rapidly but Noah's wife refuses to get on the ark without her gossipy friends. *The Second Shepherd's Play* is ninety percent secular burlesque focused upon a clever rogue named Mak, who steals a sheep, hides it in a crib, and passes it off as his son. His deception is discovered and just before a brief nativity tableau, Mak is punished for his theft with a blanket-tossing. Hell's Mouth became a catch-all for non-Biblical, farcical, and often obscene characters who were pitched with anything but churchly dignity into the inferno by blackhaired devils.

The Play of Daniel, a thirteenth century liturgical drama, based on a manuscript dating from 1230, was given a magnificent revival in Westminster Abbey in 1959. Since then it has continued to be presented in Great Britain and in cathedrals in the United States.

The Morality play followed the Biblically inspired plays, but was primarily ethical in purpose, dealing with the principles of right and wrong. The plays usually took the form of allegories dramatized by

The back of the stage in the Teatro Olimpico, in which the illusion of depth was created by placing perspective paintings of streets behind the entrances.

symbolic characters who represented abstract qualities. The most important survival of the Morality plays is *Everyman*, described in Chapter 3.

Gradually groups of strolling players began presenting the Miracle and Mystery plays; they drew criticism from the church fathers, and the number of performances declined. These wandering troupes, without sanction of either the Church or State, were, however, the originators of the first acting companies, which later were taken under the patronage of the nobility and restored to favor.

Other transitional dramatic forms developed in the fifteenth century. They included interludes, short humorous sketches performed between serious plays; chronicle plays, based on historical events; and masques, highly artistic spectacles written and performed for the glorification of the nobility. The backgrounds for the masques were designed by renowned artists like Leonardo da Vinci, with elaborate mechanical effects on which these artists wasted their genius.

THE RENAISSANCE AND DRAMA

The historical period known as the Renaissance (meaning rebirth) began in Italy in the early fourteenth century. Painting, sculpture, and architecture flourished, but dramatic literature did not.

The Renaissance in Italy

Italy did develop theater architecture and stage equipment, introducing sets with perspective and colored light. Among Italy's architectural contributions to theater were the Teatre Farnese at Parma and the famous Teatro Olimpico still preserved at Vicenza. The Olimpico was the theater of the Olympian Academy and is sometimes known as the Palladian, after the architect Andrea Palladio, who made the initial designs. In 1585 Palladio's pupil Vincenzo Scamozzi completed it.

The early offerings of Italian playwrights, however, were only weak imitations of classical plays, paltry obscenities, or poorly constructed scripts.

The "commedia dell' arte" afforded much of the new interest in the theater. The commedia was professional improvised comedy. The term "comedy of art" meant just that — these troupes had mastered the art of playing out their comic scenarios — plot outlines posted backstage before each performance. There were no fully composed play scripts as we know them; instead, the scenarios were quite detailed plot outlines which included "lazzi" and certain memorized lines. The lazzi were special humorous bits of stage business usually set apart from the main action. A well-known lazzi was one in which the stage action continued while a comic actor laboriously caught a fly. Set speeches, such as the expressions of love, jealousy, hate, and madness, were memorized and used for designated scenes. Also committed to memory were comments on extraneous matters that could be inserted wherever convenient, and stock jokes, proverbs, songs, and exit speeches.

Each troupe was led by a manager who usually was the author in the company. The plots were almost always comic intrigue involving fathers putting obstacles in the way of their offspring's romances. Servants were very important figures in the plot, often proving instrumental in successfully completing the matchmaking. All the characters of the commedia were stock types identified by their costumes and masks. There were usually two young male lovers, called innamorati, and their female counterparts, the innamorate. All four were beautifully dressed and spoke in refined language, but their parts did not require masks. The love matches were hampered by the fathers; and the young man often found himself competing against his own father as a suitor.

The only other character to perform unmasked was the "fontesca," a serving maid. She appears in many plays as Columbina, a clever and gay flirt. The fontesca was the forerunner of the witty soubrette of the musical comedy.

The "zanne" were the male servants, excellent at ad-libbing and acrobatics. Most zanne belong to the same character-type as Mak — the rogue or clever rascal. It is difficult to categorize them by name, but there were basically two kinds of zanne, the clever prankster, agile in mind and body, and the dullard, blundering in thought and action. Of the first type Arlecchino was probably the most popular. He is more commonly known to us by his French name, Harlequin. Little pantomimes and playlets based on the style of the commedia are often called Harlequinades. However, the diamond-patterned costume we associate with Harlequin came late in the history of the commedia.

Opposite Arlecchino was Brighella, slow, dishonest, cruel, and vulgar. Another name used for a servant was Pulchinello. This malicious character with his hooked nose and high-peaked hat was the ancestor of Punch of the Punch and Judy shows. Still another of the male servants was Pedrolino, who later became known as Pierrot, the moonstruck eternal lover — melancholy and gentle, but always too romantic and too sad. Later, a sincerely devoted sweetheart, Pierrette, was paired with him. One other variation of the zanne must be mentioned — Pagliacci, the man who must make others laugh while his own heart breaks.

Pantalone was an old man — the father competing romantically against his own son, the husband deceived by a young wife, or an overly protective father zealously guarding his young daughter from suitors. His costume consisted of a black coat with flowing sleeves, a red vest, and the breeches from which we have taken the words "pantaloon" and "pants." His mask was brown, with a large hooked nose and a long gray beard. The Pantalone is a common character in later drama. We see him as Polonius in *Hamlet* and as Aragon in *The Miser*. Another old man, Dottore, was the man of law or science impressed with his own knowledge. Garbed in his doctor's hat and robe, the Dottore inserted many Latin phrases into his pretentious boasting. Professor Willard in *Our Town* is a modern example of Dottore.

The last character important to recognize was the Capitano, a mustached, boastful, but cowardly Spaniard who quaked at his own shadow. He is often considered the ancestor of the villain of the Victorian melodramas. The great "save-your-own-skin" death speech of Falstaff is typical of the "brave" Capitano.

The Renaissance Elsewhere on the Continent

Written drama evolved in Spain, where Cervantes (1547–1616), Lope de Vega (1562–1635), and Calderón (1600–1681) contributed to the mounting interest in theater. *Man of La Mancha*, the modern musical adaptation by Dale Wasserman of Cervantes' famed *Don Quixote* promises to survive as a classic in its own right.

France developed the professional theater under the patronage of the state with such great plays as the *Cid* by Corneille (1606–1684), *The Miser, The Misanthrope*, and *The Imaginary Invalid* by Molière (1622–1673), and *Phaedra* by Racine (1639–1699).

So many of Molière's sparkling comedy-dramas are being presented today in the regional theaters across the country that they are becoming more familiar to American audiences than many contemporary plays. The famous company of Jean-Louis Barrault has given periodic productions here of the plays of Molière and of the other great French playwrights in the grand manner in which they were written originally. Racine's *Phaedra*, adapted by Robert Lowell, is also being given a number of excellent productions almost every season. Racine's tragic dramas attained their greatest fame when the challenging roles were being variously interpreted by such great actresses as Sarah Bernhardt, pictured on page 292.

Strolling players kept the drama alive during this period, appearing before the public in village squares and before the nobility in their castles. They created melodramatic history plays, rowdy comedies, and romantic love stories which were the germs of the great dramas of later generations.

The Renaissance in England

The climax of the dramatic renaissance came during the Elizabethan Age in England, a period in which the drama was the expression of the soul of a nation, and the theater became a vital force in the life of the people.

The first English comedy was *Ralph Roister Doister* produced in 1553, which the author Nicholas Udall modeled on Plautus. It was followed by *Gammer Gurton's Needle*, authorship uncertain, which became famous after its first production at Cambridge. The first true English tragedy was *Gorboduc*, which was performed in 1561. Among the many writers in this period were John Lyly (*Endymion*), George Peele (*The Old Wives' Tale* and *King Edward the First*), Robert Greene (*Friar Bacon and Friar Bungay*), John Webster (*The Duchess of Malfi*), Thomas Dekker (*A Shoemaker's Holiday*), Thomas Heywood (*A Woman Killed with Kindness*), Philip Massinger (*A New Way to Pay Old Debts*), Thomas Kyd (*The Spanish Tragedy*), and Francis Beaumont and John Fletcher (*The Knight of the Burning Pestle* and *The Maid's Tragedy*).

Three Monumental Elizabethan Dramatists

Towering above all the other brilliant actor-playwrights responsible for the glory of the period, three men produced plays which have never lost their popular appeal — Marlowe, Jonson, and Shakespeare.

Christopher Marlowe (1564–1593) introduced the first important use of blank verse, the "mighty line" of English poetic drama. Combining extraordinary use of language and the excitement of melodramatic plots, he wrote *Tamburlaine the Great*, *The Jew of Malta*, and *Edward II*. These plays present the glory and the horror of the age and suited the physical and theatrical power of the actor Edward Alleyn, for whom they were written. However, it is *Doctor Faustus*, the story of a man who sells his soul for twenty-four hours of damning knowledge, that brilliantly bridges the gap between the medieval and the renaissance man.

Ben Jonson (1573–1637) was the first master of English comedy; he wrote *Volpone*, *The Alchemist*, and *Every Man in His Humour*.

To the Elizabethan, the word "humour," as used in the phrase "He's in a good humour," did not refer to an attitude of amusement. In addition to the arts, the Renaissance was also a period of anatomical study. Physicians were amazed by the amount of fluids (humours) found in the human body. Scholars believed that all matter was made up of four elements — air, earth, fire, and water. It was also assumed that the human body was composed of these same four elements, each having its own effect on the personality. Air was identified with blood and caused the sanguine humour — light-hearted, airy, gay. Fire was associated with bile and brought about the choleric humour — angry, hot-tempered, impetuous. Water was identified with phlegm and caused the phlegmatic humour — dull, listless, lethargic.

The humour of most interest in Elizabethan plays is that of black bile, Earth, which resulted in the melancholy humour. The melancholy character fell into three main types: the lover, the malcontent, and the intellectual. Hamlet is an excellent example of the intellectual melancholy humour. Although most stage figures have a predominating humour, a balanced personality was the most desirable; this is evidenced by Antony's tribute to Brutus in *Julius Caesar:* ". . . the elements [were] so mixed in him that Nature might stand up and say to all the world, this was a man."

Jonson widened the scope of the humours to include any strong personality trait, especially a weakness, foible, or folly that could make a character a cause for laughter.

A scene from the Passion Play, *given every ten years at Oberammergau in Germany. The last production of the* Passion Play *was in 1970.*

COURTESY OF THE GERMAN INFORMATION CENTER

William Shakespeare (1564–1616) was the greatest Elizabethan dramatist as well as the greatest dramatist of all time. For more than four centuries the public has acclaimed him the most popular playwright; the foremost actors have interpreted his roles; readers have read and reread his plays with increasing delight; and the greatest minds of modern civilization have bowed before his genius. He followed his dramatic career as playwright, actor, and manager for only twenty years. In that time he wrote thirty-six plays and made a fortune sufficient to permit him to retire. Not only is Shakespeare the towering literary figure of all the ages, but his characterizations, beautiful poetry, and never-to-be-forgotten lines echo a majesty best expressed by the "Bard's" friendly rival, Ben Jonson, when he said that Shakespeare "was not of an age but for all time."

The Shakespearean Playhouse

The first English public playhouse, the Theatre, was built across the Thames River from London in 1576 by James Burbage. He was the manager of the company later housed in the famous Globe Theatre, with which Shakespeare was associated as actor-playwright. The theaters were modeled after the medieval innyards where the wandering acting companies had played for years. The inns had open courtyards where the audience could stand around a platform stage or sit in the galleries surrounding the courtyard. The animal pits may also have served as models for the theater. Located in the same neighborhood as the theaters, the animal pits were constructed primarily for bear-baiting and bull-baiting. These leftovers from the Roman arenas provided entertainment in the form of animal torment. At times stages were placed in these circular arenas for the presentation of plays.

The playhouses were round or octagonal in shape and had three tiers of galleries. The stage has been called an "unlocalized platform stage" because this 5- to 6-foot high acting area used little scenery to indicate locale; a sign or an actor's line was usually enough to inform the audience of geographical locations. The area surrounding the stage was called the pit, and the motley playgoers who paid a modest fee to stand there were called groundlings. The groundlings were, for the most part, tradesmen, apprentices, soldiers, sailors, and country folk who had come to the great city of London. In some of his plays, Shakespeare commented sharply on the lack of discernment in this fickle mob that reeked of garlic and body odor, ate and drank during the performances, and reacted vociferously to what they liked or disliked. Wandering through this crowd were the "cut-purses," or what we might call Elizabethan pickpockets. The more refined audience occupied the gallery seats, for which an additional fee was charged, but the most expensive seats were on the stage itself.

Over the stage was the Heavens, a roof suported by two 3-story columns. The underneath side of the Heavens was painted blue, with a golden sun in the center surrounded by stars and the signs of the zodiac. When the actor spoke of the heavens and the earth, he had only to point to the roof over his head and the stage floor beneath his feet to create the illusion of a microcosmic universe. The "back wall" of the stage looked like the outside of a multi-storied building.

The area backstage was called the tiring house. In the center rear was a curtained recess called the inner below or study. This area could be used for "reveal" scenes such as a bedroom or the tent of Antony. There were second floor acting areas also: a central area consisting of the shallow balcony; the tarras, separated by a curtain, the arras, from a recess called the chamber; on either side of the chamber were the window boxes, probably used for such settings as the balcony scene of *Romeo and Juliet*. A third level could be used for acting when necessary, but seems to have served primarily as the musician's gallery. In all these acting levels there were trapdoors, some mechanically operated. They were used in scenes like that of the gravediggers in *Hamlet*.

Over the third level was what appeared to be a small house, which was appropriately called the scenery hut. This structure housed stage machinery and a cannon. From the peak of the roof a flag was flown to inform the residents of London when a play was to be given. Since there was no artificial lighting, plays were presented in the afternoon, which accounts for the description of the Globe as a "wooden O" — a circular building open to the sky.

All female roles were played by specially trained boys. Costumes were often very beautiful, since they were provided by the wealthy patrons who sponsored the acting companies and who competed with one another for the success of their troupes. Of course this meant little attempt was made to costume the actors with historical accuracy. Roman citizens in *Julius Caesar* appeared in the gorgeous satins, velvets, and plumes of the sixteenth century. The audiences loved color, sound, and pageantry. A march of armies garbed in the royal colors, the ringing of the alarum bell, and the firing of the cannon heightened the action on the stage.

Never in the history of the world has the theater found so congenial an environment as during the Elizabethan Age. Actors and playwrights were often liberally rewarded by their noble patrons. Many of the actors and dramatists were a gay, swashbuckling, reckless lot, who squandered their youth in riotous living and often died, rapier in hand, before their genius had a chance to flower.

The nobility eagerly sponsored new plays, hoping to gain an approving glance from Queen Elizabeth, the brilliant figure so theatrical in her own person about whom the glorious age gravitated. You should familiarize yourself with the many enthralling as well as authentic books about the period which have been published since 1950, frequently because of the four hundredth anniversary in 1964 of Shakespeare's birth. Recent research has revealed details of the lives of the Elizabethan playwrights, never before published, which make the biographies read like novels and make the age a reality to the reader. Modern revivals of Renaissance drama, which more and more are taking the form of adaptations, are appearing every season on Broadway and in the regional and university theaters.

A model of the Fortune Theatre of Shakespeare's day, constructed by Father Henry Revers when he was a student in the Oberlin, Ohio, High School.

GLEN M. PRINCEHORN

DRAMA IN ENGLAND

Naturally the American stage has always reflected its British origins, but with the current interchange of actors, producers, and famous companies, we are gradually thinking of an English-speaking theater rather than a British or American one. Hence you should know a great deal about the history of drama in Great Britain to understand better the present and future trends in the United States.

Restoration Drama

The glory of the Elizabethan drama was abruptly dimmed by the Puritan rebellion in 1642, when an edict was issued for the suppression of all stage plays. Even during the height of the enthusiasm for the drama, theaters had been condemned as breeders of the plague, and actors were looked upon as instruments of the devil by many of the citizens of London as well as by the Puritans. When the Puritans took over under Cromwell, the Stuarts fled to the protection of the French court. In 1600 Charles II was "restored" to the English throne. He and his followers brought back with them a delight in sophisticated comedies featuring sparkling, risqué dialogue and improperly humorous situations.

Important innovations were made during the Restoration. Women were allowed to appear as players by the English Royal Patent of 1662, which said that "all women's parts should be performed by women" and provided that plays and acting might be esteemed "not only harmless delights but useful and instructive representations of human life." Elaborate scenery and mechanical equipment, earlier introduced from Europe by Inigo Jones for court masques, came into general use. The licensing of theaters still continued, though only two playhouses were officially sanctioned, the famed Drury Lane Theater and the Covent Garden. From these patent theaters came the term "legitimate theater," which we use now simply to refer to professional stage plays.

Sir William Davenant was a distinguished producer at Drury Lane, where Thomas Betterton was not only the first actor to appear with the very popular leading ladies, but was also commissioned by Charles II to go to the continent and bring back the latest theatrical equipment and trends.

Among the Restoration dramatists are a few whose plays have survived until today. William Wycherley (1640–1716) in *The Country*

Wife and *The Plain Dealer* started the fashionable trend in comedies, largely because of his education in France. William Congreve (1670–1729) ranks as one of the great masters of comedy; the brilliant art and pace of *Love for Love* and *The Way of the World* have consistently amused sophisticated audiences and set a standard for later comedies of manners. George Farquhar (1678–1707), in his *The Beaux' Stratagem*, brought a refreshing breath of the country into the dissolute city life depicted on the stage; this play strongly influenced later playwrights. John Gay (1685–1732) was primarily a poet, but his biting satire, *The Beggar's Opera*, was revamped in 1928 by Bertolt Brecht as *The Threepenny Opera*, with the bewitching music of Kurt Weill. Both forms are frequently revived today.

Later English Drama

The eighteenth century produced only two outstanding playwrights. Richard Brinsley Sheridan (1751–1816) wrote two scintillating social comedies which are seen in frequent revivals today. *The School for Scandal* has been the vehicle for both masculine and feminine stars for generations; John Gielgud revived this play as producer and as actor in the hypocritical role of Sir Joseph Surface. *The Rivals* features the immortal Mrs. Malaprop, the world's greatest misuser of words.

Oliver Goldsmith (1728–1774) is one of England's notable literary figures, whose *She Stoops to Conquer* is revived season after season; every character is a "fat part," from Tony Lumpkin to Kate Hardcastle, who pretends to be a servant to win a bashful suitor. The play is especially suited for high school production and is excellent training in the grand manner of eighteenth-century acting typified in such famous personalities as Sarah Kemble Siddons and Edmund Kean. The great David Garrick (1717–1779) for thirty-five years was the shining light of the English stage in this age of brilliant acting. He played all the famous Restoration roles and also adapted Shakespeare, giving renowned interpretations of the comic and tragic roles for thirty-five years.

The London stage of the nineteenth century established the trends which have given it the prestige it holds today. T. W. Robertson (1829–1871) was the originator of the typical English social satire in his *Caste*; Gilbert and Sullivan created their clever comic operas, imitated but never surpassed; and Henry Arthur Jones wrote his comedies with serious undertones.

The Victorian Era brought a reaction to the comedies of manners. Arthur Wing Pinero shocked the public with *The Second Mrs. Tanqueray* but delighted it with his *Trelawny of the "Wells."* Oscar Wilde with his genius for epigrams and brilliant dialogue wrote his enduring plays, among which *The Importance of Being Earnest* has achieved undying popularity in both amateur and professional productions.

George Bernard Shaw (1856–1950), the indefatigable Irishman distinguished as critic and dramatist, ranks as the greatest playwright of his long period of eminence, and has been acclaimed next to Shakespeare among English dramatists of imperishable fame. Although he is primarily a philosopher frankly declaiming his theories, the pungency of his humor and the fascination of his characters will keep alive, as long as spoken drama exists, such plays as *Saint Joan*, *Candida*, *Man and Superman*, *Caesar and Cleopatra*, *Pygmalion*, *Androcles and the Lion*, and *Arms and the Man*. Every season sees Shaw's plays acted by the world's finest actors.

The nineteenth century fostered literally hundreds of great actors and actresses. Henry Irving and Ellen Terry enchanted the Victorians for twenty years at the famed Lyceum Theater in elaborate productions of Shakespeare and of classic drama. Irving was knighted in 1895, the first actor to receive that honor, and Ellen Terry became Dame in 1925. Her son Gordon Craig, as a world-famous scenic artist, and her nephew John Gielgud, as noted actor-producer, have carried on her fame in the theatrical world.

The early twentieth century began the close affiliation between the English and American theaters. John Drinkwater, an Englishman, was the first playwright to eulogize Abraham Lincoln; Noel Coward began his rise to fame and fortune in New York through his friendship for the Lunts; James M. Barrie found the perfect actress for his charming feminine roles in the American star, Maude Adams; and such fine dramas as John Galsworthy's *Justice* and Emlyn Williams' *Night Must Fall* and *How Green Was My Valley* are only a few of the British plays whose success developed then.

Drama in England Today

England is the mecca of theater lovers today. They are drawn to London by the assurance that they will find a large number of productions of all types to choose from, where versatile and superlative acting is assured at reasonable prices. In practically every town of any size, they can find excellent repertory companies doing first-class

Jonathan Bolt plays an incorrigible libertine in William Wycherley's bawdy Restoration comedy The Country Wife, *as presented at the Cleveland Play House.*

contemporary plays as well as classics. Among the best known companies are those in Birmingham, Coventry, Chichester, and Leatherhead. This fine drama is largely due to the influence of the Arts Council of Great Britain, incorporated under Royal Charter in 1946, which subsidizes worthy companies and productions. Its great achievment is the establishment of The National Theatre under the direction of Laurence Olivier, the first actor to be made a peer. An elegant theater complex is being erected which will supersede the famous Old Vic, from which the National Theatre has developed.

English summer theater festivals are flourishing. Of these the Royal Shakespeare Memorial Theatre at Stratford-on-Avon, the Edinburgh International Festival, and the Malvern Festival offer the most varied and exciting fare.

The World Theatre season at the Aldwych in London brings an annual series of distinguished offerings from every continent.

Drama students should be familiar with the plays of John Osborne, who introduced the "angry young men," and of J. B. Priestly, T. S. Eliot, Harold Pinter, Robert Bolt, and Tom Stoppard.

DRAMA IN IRELAND

Drama in southern Ireland has had a brief but brilliant history, starting with the plays of William Butler Yeats and Lady Gregory at the turn of the century. First known as the Irish Literary Theatre,

316

their company became famous after the Abbey Theatre was reconstructed from an old Dublin building and opened in 1904.

The Irish playwrights were a distinguished group. Yeats was dedicated to poetic drama, retelling the ancient tales of Ireland; *At the Hawk's Well* beautifully combined myth, dance, and poetry. Lady Gregory excelled in one-act plays based on peasant life in the villages. Her *The Rising of the Moon* has been produced constantly by professional and amateur groups. John Millington Synge is considered by many to be the finest of the Irish dramatists, but his countrymen objected to his portrayal of them in several plays. His *The Playboy of the Western World* and *Riders to the Sea* are frequently produced today.

Sean O'Casey with *Juno and the Paycock*, *Within the Gates*, and *The Plough and the Stars* was the prominent midcentury voice of the Irish theater. As far as America is concerned, it was the Irish actors who are loved, especially Barry Fitzgerald and Sara Algood, who were lured to Hollywood during a cross-country tour in the thirties. The reputation of the players for simple, natural acting of humble Irish roles has not died. Dubliners have always been noted for speaking the most beautiful English in the world; and the lilt and clarity of the voices of the Abbey Players has endeared them particularly. A new Abbey Theatre has recently been dedicated.

DRAMA ON THE CONTINENT

Drama has flourished throughout Europe for three centuries. The chief contributions of the European dramatists has been in initiating trends which have been followed in all countries. Many of them have already been discussed in Chapter 3, "Varieties of Drama." No longer can we divide any discussion into the drama of the various countries, because they are interrelated today. Still, there are great names of national importance with which you should be familiar.

Notable Dramatists

In France, Molière, Voltaire, Victor Hugo, and Alexandre Dumas broke away from classical traditions and produced exciting drama. They were followed by Sardou. All of their plays became the popular vehicles for the great stars Talma, Rachel, Bernhardt, and Réjane. Edmond Rostand created the immortal character of Cyrano de Bergerac, the poet-warrior with the huge nose, whose romance has become world famous. The role was originally written for the great

A scene from Jean Anouilh's The Lark, *translated from the French by Christopher Fry. The play is about the life of Joan of Arc and her trial as a heretic.*

actor Coquelin. Jean Giraudoux (*Tiger at the Gates, The Madwoman of Chaillot*) and Jean Anouilh (*The Lark, Antigone, A Time Remembered*) have also been popular here; their plays have been translated by such dramatists as Christopher Fry and Lillian Hellman. Jean-Paul Sartre's *No Exit* and *The Flies* reflect his existentialist viewpoint.

In Germany, the colossal figure of Goethe towers above all others with his *Faust*, upon which he worked from 1774 to 1832. His poetic drama, telling the tragedy of the man who sold himself to the Devil to get all worldly desires in a new-lived youth, was written in glorious verse and has inspired three grand operas as well as literary works in other languages. Schiller in his *Wilhelm Tell* and *Mary Stuart* also achieved greatness, and Lessing in his *Nathan the Wise* wrote a magnificent drama upholding religious tolerance.

Gerhart Hauptmann in the nineties began the new era of realism in the German theater, and his work culminated in *The Weavers*, one of the great dramas setting forth a social issue built around a "group protagonist." Bertolt Brecht has been mentioned several times in relation to his epic theater, discussed in Chapter 3. *Mother Courage*, *The Caucasian Chalk Circle*, and *The Good Woman of Setzuan* are among his plays most often produced in the United States.

In Czechoslovakia the Capek brothers achieved fame working together and separately in expressionistic plays of social impact like *R.U.R.*, on the theme of machines taking over mankind, and *The Insect Comedy*, showing modern man's similarity to insects in the way he lives. From Belgium Maurice Maeterlinck became famous for his fanciful and allegorical *The Bluebird*.

In Spain, after the great early period, José Echegaray was the only dramatist to be acted abroad until Jacinto Benavente won the Nobel Prize for Literature for *The Passion Flower*. Symbolist playwright Federico García Lorca's *Blood Wedding* is frequently seen in university theaters.

From Italy two playwrights became world famous for very different reasons. Gabriele d'Annunzio was flamboyant and violent in his life and plays, which include *The Daughter of Jorio*, *The Dead City*, and *Gioconda*. Luigi Pirandello's conviction that people are not what they appear to be is described in his "naked masks" theory. His plays are exceedingly complicated and difficult on the whole, but *Six Characters in Search of an Author* and *Henry IV* are frequently produced.

European Drama and the United States

Our drama in this country has been strongly affected by Europe as well as England, both in the influence of playwrights upon our dramatists and in theatrical movements, policies, and trends.

Henrik Ibsen of Norway (1828–1906), sometimes called "the father of modern drama," introduced realism in conversation and presentation. His chief theme — that the individual rights of each person must be protected and developed — naturally had a very special appeal for Americans. His characters — human beings involved in problems affecting other human beings — are far different from the poetic heroes of the great romantic dramas. Ibsen wrote two magnificent poetic dramas, *Peer Gynt* and *Brand*, but it was his *A Doll's*

House, Ghosts, Hedda Gabler, An Enemy of the People, and *The Master Builder* which account for his world influence.

Constantin Stanislavski (1863–1938) of Russia was the other European whose influence in this country cannot be estimated. His "Method," discussed earlier, has established the acting theory centered on the inner understanding of a role plus perfection of physical response in presenting it to an audience. The Moscow Art Theatre, founded and directed by him, became the finest in the world from the viewpoint of ensemble acting and realistic production. To name only a few Russian dramatists, there are Gogol with *The Inspector General*; Turgenev, *A Month in the Country*; Tolstoy, *The Power of Darkness*; Andreyev, *He Who Gets Slapped.* The greatest of all the Russian dramatists was the early realist Anton Chekhov (1860–1904), who wrote *The Sea Gull, The Three Sisters, Uncle Vanya,* and *The Cherry Orchard.*

The French with the "Theater of the Absurd" playwrights, especially Ionesco, Beckett, and Genêt, have strongly influenced the contemporary American theater, together with the earlier Artaud, originator of the "theater of shock and involvement," whose book *The Theater and Its Double* revolutionized modern drama.

DRAMA IN ASIA

To the Westerner, the appeal of the drama in the Far East lies largely in the gorgeous costumes which are complemented by masks or elaborate makeup, in the brilliant color, and in the grotesque and expressive pantomime. Everywhere the drama is presented in a highly traditional manner inherited from the distant past, and the subject matter deals with historical and religious legends not easily understood by a foreigner. The length of the performances, the high-pitched voices, and the discordant music are often very wearing, but there is an exotic charm in every program.

The most dramatic spot on earth is the little island of Bali, south of Java, where theatrical productions are staged day and night, year in and year out. Every village has its own gamelan (an orchestra of beautifully made instruments featuring chimes, gongs, and drums) and a wardrobe of magnificent costumes. The villagers themselves appear as actors and dancers in colorful, entertaining, and delightful productions of the Hindu legends.

The Chinese theater, using the same symbolism and techniques as it has for centuries, can still be seen in Hong Kong and occasionally in Honolulu. Historical plays featuring the actions of generals, long journeys by characters, and many battle scenes predominate.

All forms of the drama of Japan have been brought to the United States in the last few years and shown on stage and television, but, to appreciate their full charm and impact, they should be seen, of course, in their own environments. There are three forms of drama distinctly Japanese: The Nō (Noh), the Bunraku or Doll Theater, and the Kabuki.

The Nō theater is the oldest form of drama to be preserved in its exact form, with words, dance, and music rhythmically coordinated as it was produced 600 years ago. The traditional forms have been handed down by generations of actors strictly trained from childhood in what is practically isolation. The special theater is like a temple, with the 18-foot square stage extending into the audience and supported by four wooden pillars which form a part of the action. The characters — all of whom are played by men — include an old man, an old woman, a young man, a child, a monster, a formidable

The picturesque scene for Momiji-gari, *a popular Kabuki play.*

god, a gentle god, and an animal. The essence of Nō lies in creating beauty of motion and speech, and the plots are short and very simple. The language is intricate, and the spectators follow the libretto closely, as if savoring every syllable. Therefore, the drama holds an appeal only for the highly cultivated audience.

The Bunraku features utterly fascinating marionettes about 4 feet tall, carved in wood and gorgeously gowned; they are so realistic that they move their fingers, mouths, eyes, and eyebrows with life-like expressiveness. Each doll is manipulated by three attendants who are dressed in black and wear gauze masks to symbolize their invisibility; amazingly they soon seem to disappear. The dialogue is read in turn by five narrators in elaborate costumes. This remarkable form of theater was brought from Korea to Japan in the sixth century. The traditional movements and play forms of the Kabuki drama originated in the Doll Theater.

The Kabuki came into being in the sixteenth century and was originally an imitation of both the Doll Theater and the Noh drama. Women first produced and acted the plays, but today only men are the players. The actors spend their lives in the theater. They begin as children and continue to act in historical and domestic plays and dance-dramas until they are in their seventies. The infinitely detailed pantomime and the superlative acting, enhanced by elaborate costuming and makeup painted with brushes, are true theater.

Of course, today modern Western drama is popular in Japanese cities, where current Western trends are imitated with enthusiasm. The first contemporary drama after the war was written by Teruaki Miyati in 1947, *The Defeated*, translated into English by Dr. Earle Ernst of the University of Hawaii. For many decades, amateur groups have produced adaptations of Shakespeare, O'Neill, and Ibsen plays, and other Western classics.

DRAMA IN THE UNITED STATES

The theater in America, because of its British origin, has naturally been strongly influenced by the dramatists and actors of England from Colonial days to the present.

Early American Drama

The first theater in America was built in Williamsburg, Virginia, in 1716, but all traces of it had disappeared by the time the entire city was restored in the 1920's. The Dock Street Theater of Charleston, South Carolina, was erected in 1736; though twice rebuilt, it is still in use. The Southwark was built in Philadelphia in 1766 and is acclaimed as the first permanent theater in the country. In New York the first important theater was erected in 1767 on John Street by David Douglass, who had also built the Southwark in Philadelphia.

The first American dramas were produced by the American Company, managed by Douglass. The first play was *The Prince of Parthia* by Thomas Godfrey, given on April 24, 1767, at the Southwark. It was strictly an imitation of British blank-verse tragedies and had only one performance. *The Contrast* by Royall Tyler opened at the John Street Theater on April 16, 1787, and was an instant success. It was a comedy, and introduced for the first time Jonathan, the original typical Yankee — shrewd, wholesome, and humorous — who has appeared in many guises ever since. However, *Fashion* by Anna Cora Mowatt, produced in 1845, is considered our first native comedy on the same theme — poking fun at social pretenders — and it is frequently revived. *Uncle Tom's Cabin*, dramatized by George Aiken from Harriet Beecher Stowe's crucial novel of 1852, holds the record as our most widely produced melodrama.

The first actors were English professional troupes who presented popular London plays. The most important company was that of the Hallam family, who came to America in 1752. The second and now legendary family, which links the early American stage with the modern, was the Barrymores, featured in the sparkling comedy *The Royal Family* by Edna Ferber and George S. Kaufman. John Drew was an Irish actor who came to America in 1846; he married Louise Lane, our first distinguished actress-manager. She had three children: John Drew, who became leading man of the famous Augustine Daly's Company; Sidney, who played comedy roles of importance in early films; and Georgiana, who married Maurice Barrymore, a dashing Irish actor. The Barrymores were the parents of Lionel, Ethel, and John Barrymore, for years America's leading actors.

Edwin Booth (1833–1893) was the greatest romantic actor America has produced. His illustrious career nearly suffered an eclipse when he retired after his brother, John Wilkes Booth, also a well-known actor, assassinated Abraham Lincoln. Edwin Booth later returned to the stage, but never appeared again in Washington.

Steele MacKaye (1842–1894) was one of the most fascinating characters in our theater. He was a playwright and actor, being the first American to appear as Hamlet in London. His inventions, which

Donald Wolfit as the hero in Tyrone Guthrie's production of Christopher Marlowe's Tamburlaine the Great *at the Old Vic in London in 1951. This was the play's first professional production for three hundred years.*

foreshadowed the mechanics of the modern stage, included elevator stages, overhead lighting, and folding theater chairs. He also started America's first dramatic school, the American Academy of Dramatic Art.

Modern Theater

The twenties and thirties brought the United States into the mainstream of world drama. The theater flourished on Broadway because enthusiastic audiences were attracted by many fine plays of varied types, by the painstaking production of the directors and scenic artists staging them, and by a growing number of excellent actors and actresses interpreting them with skill and inspiration. Amateurs across the country established successful groups producing first-class plays artistically, and the educational theater came into being with students in universities and high schools, for the first time, studying plays from the standpoint of acting and producing, not just reading them as a form of literature.

324

The Commercial Theater

The term "commercial theater" denotes every form of dramatic entertainment designed primarily to make money. Professional playwrights, producers, and actors make and lose fortunes in a gamble with the public. "Give the public what it wants" is their battle cry, and colossal or titilating or shocking advertising schemes often intrigue the public into wanting what it gets and then overpaying for it, too.

Vaudeville was for many years tremendously popular, and playing the Palace on Broadway was the supreme desire of every entertainer. The Dover reprint *American Vaudeville* by Douglas Gilbert covers this uproarious history. Great artists appeared in one-act plays to attract the highbrows. Sarah Bernhardt herself, though old and crippled, made several "final" appearances, as did Alla Nazimova, Ethel Barrymore, and Bert Lytel. Specialized artists like Eddie Cantor, Fred and Adele Astaire, George M. Cohan, Danny Kaye, Fanny Brice, Irene and Vernon Castle are only a few of the greats in the days of vaudeville.

Stock companies in almost all cities, with their weekly change of play, were the finest possible training ground for actors and a delight for an adoring public watching with avid interest their favorites appearing in contrasting roles. Founded in Denver, Colorado, in 1891, the Elitch's Garden Theater housed the oldest continuing summer stock company in America until 1965, when it turned to presenting visiting Broadway casts in the current season's productions. Established companies, managed on a subscription basis, have played a vital and distinguished role in Broadway's history. The Theater Guild was founded in 1919; it was destined to become the most illustrious producing company America has known. George Bernard Shaw owed his popularity in this country to its splendid presentations of his great plays. Eugene O'Neill (1888–1953), acclaimed as one of America's leading dramatists, had many of his finest dramas first produced in the Theater Guild's beautiful theater. *Strange Interlude*, *Mourning Becomes Electra*, *Dynamo*, *Ah, Wilderness!*, *The Iceman Cometh*, *Anna Christie*, *The Emperor Jones*, and *The Hairy Ape* are but a few of his great plays. Previously, another established company, the Provincetown Wharf Theater, had presented O'Neill to the world in his sea plays. He was awarded the Nobel Prize for Literature and four Pulitzer prizes, the last one granted posthumously for *Long Day's Journey into Night*. The Theater Guild also presented Alfred Lunt and his wife Lynn Fontanne in a long series of "couple" plays.

The Group Theater was founded in 1931 by Harold Clurman, Lee Strasberg, Cheryl Crawford, and a number of dedicated actors, directors, and scenic artists interested in applying the Stanislavski Method in American productions. A long succession of strong problem plays was presented, including those by Clifford Odets and William Saroyan, with creative sets by Mordecai Gorelik and direction by Elia Kazan. Odets' *Waiting for Lefty* and Saroyan's *The Time of Your Life* achieved lasting recognition. Economic pressures caused the group to disband in 1941. Six years later, Lee Strasberg and Miss Crawford established the Actors' Studio, which has exerted a strong influence on the American stage. Among the well-known actors and actresses to study there have been Marlon Brando, Geraldine Page, Paul Newman, Joanne Woodward, Marilyn Monroe, Julie Harris, and Ben Gazzara.

THE CHANGING SCENE

The commercial theater has been facing problems which are affecting it seriously. In fact, difficulties started at the turn of the century and have been increasing steadily ever since. One difficulty was due to the stranglehold that strong theatrical syndicates had gained across the country when road companies, usually headed by stars from Broadway, were appearing in all the big cities. Bookings and prices of tickets were controlled, and actors were underpaid and overworked and exploited.

In 1913, actors formed a union in self-defense, calling it Actors' Equity; it has become a power today. The actors' strike of 1919 established Equity's control over minimum salaries, length of paid rehearsal periods, and other stipulations. During the strike, leading stars and producers refused to work in controlled theaters and appeared in whatever buildings they could rent, forcing syndicates to meet their terms.

Stage unions have become exceedingly powerful in recent years, driving up production costs in commercial theaters and making it difficult to put on plays of high quality that might have limited drawing power. Exorbitant prices for tickets are keeping theater lovers from supporting many plays that should succeed.

Scarcity of theaters on Broadway is another production problem. This is due to overwhelming real estate costs, which have led to the tearing down of many blocks in the entertainment area to make room for towering skyscrapers in place of traditional theaters. It is

Paxton Whitehead and Astrid Wilsrud in an off-Broadway production of Ibsen's realistic drama A Doll's House. *The plot concerns woman's place in the world.*

becoming more and more difficult for producers to house their shows and increasingly important for them to select only those plays with popular appeal. Serious dramatists, therefore, have less opportunity for seeing their plays on stage. David Merrick may be the last of the giant producers with continuing success at the box office — which is, after all, the controlling force in the entertainment field. Broadway as the Great White Way is losing its glory!

Off-Broadway plays became in the fifties the new source of inspiration for the American theater, with creative producers, actors, and backstage artists bringing fresh talent to reviving our great plays and encouraging new ones to be written. Greenwich Village has been the center for progressive artists since the early twenties, so it was naturally the first area where less expensive, more original, and exceedingly interesting presentations found a congenial environment. By the sixties, off-Broadway theaters had opened all over New York in any type of available building — cafes, churches, lecture halls, lofts — with plays "fragmenting" in style from good to bad to worst.

The Lincoln Center for the Performing Arts is in the process of becoming the cultural hub of New York. Its Vivian Beaumont Theater was planned as its official repertory theater, but difficulties have faced the opening seasons, causing changes in directors and policies. Its Lincoln Center Forum Theater is the experimental unit in the basement, where some interesting new plays have been produced.

You should keep abreast of theatrical happenings away from Times Square if you wish to be up-to-date. Fortunately television offers numerous programs of plays and of interviews with people associated with them; these will help greatly to keep you informed.

Governmental Participation

The U. S. Government and drama have not been closely associated until recently, but in 1965 an important change took place. The National Foundation on the Arts and Humanities was established by President Johnson and signed into law on September 29, 1965. Its purpose is to encourage professional actors, along with all artists unable to realize their creative potentialities because of the necessity of making a living. Roger L. Stevens, the first president, had been important in the theater world for many years. He stated the three-fold purpose: to assist the creative artist; to develop wider audiences, and to stimulate appreciation of the artist and his work.

State foundations on culture and the arts have been set up by governors across the country, under which hundreds of city and community councils are now established. Large grants have been made to regional theaters in the hope that they will be a permanent means of bringing drama to every community. Whether a national theater will grow out of this movement, as it has in England, remains to be seen. The theater over the world has been supported financially by patrons and governments since the early beginnings, and the United States is beginning to follow suit.

The American National Theater and Academy (ANTA) is the forerunner of the National Foundation. It was granted a Federal Charter on July 5, 1935, the only organization to have been so honored. It receives no subsidy from the government and is supported by voluntary subscription, memberships, and donations. It is designed to serve all facets of the American theater and acts as coordinator, consultant, and guide through its National Theater Service, which provides an information center and advisory service and contributes ideas for all types of theater projects.

The International Theater Institute, U.S., was founded in 1948 to promote communication between all the theaters of the world. It is the official theater representative of UNESCO. When the Twelfth Congress was held in New York in 1967, representatives from forty-eight countries around the globe were in attendance.

The Federal Theater (WPA) was a vital experiment in American drama and the first step toward a national theater. Established on August 29, 1935, as an economic relief measure for professional theater workers, it was discontinued June 30, 1939. At its peak it employed 12,700 people, operated in forty cities in twenty-two states, and played before an audience of 25,000,000. One of its most stimulating contributions was "The Living Newspaper," productions based on actual events appearing in newspapers.

The John F. Kennedy Center for the Performing Arts in Washington, D. C., was created in 1958, by an Act of Congress signed by

John and Ethel Barrymore in 1912 in a play called A Slice of Life. *It is obvious that styles in acting have changed appreciably since that time.*

CULVER PICTURES, INC.

President Eisenhower, as the National Cultural Center; and government land on the Potomac was granted as a site. In January, 1964, President Johnson signed the John F. Kennedy Center Act, renaming the cultural center and designating it as the official memorial to President Kennedy. It was formally opened in September, 1971.

Ten units housed under one roof at the Center include the Opera in the central hall, the Concert Hall, the Eisenhower Theater for drama and film production, and the Studio Playhouse on the roof above the theater to be used as an experimental, film, and children's theater and for poetry and drama reading.

Regional and Repertory Theaters

The hope of the American theater lies in the growth of the regional movement, which is rapidly bringing drama of all types to all areas. In a sense this movement is an outgrowth of the amateur movement, for it gives professionally inclined members of existing community groups an opening they have never had, and it also gains an audience from supporters of the same organizations.

The idea was first conceived by ANTA in its unrealized plan to establish theaters in forty cities which would annually stage plays to be shown ultimately in all of them in an exchange series. This plan did not materialize, but the regional theater did.

You are probably wondering about the two terms, regional and repertory. To state the difference briefly, the regional theaters present any type of play for as long as they wish, and can repeat a play when and if they think it wise. The repertory companies set up a definite number of productions, which they repeat at regular intervals or at any time in the future, and they have a seasonal repertoire of plays repeated in rotation as advertised at the beginning of each season. Both are known as resident theaters when guest stars are not used, and they specialize in ensemble acting. They both usually have subscription memberships; individual admissions, at higher cost per performance than the memberships, may or may not be sold.

The importance of the movement has been accepted by the general public, with an unusually enthusiastic attendance on both the subscription and individual admission basis in most of the communities served by the theaters.

Established by Milton Lyon in 1964, a new department of Actors' Equity is playing a most important role in the regional theater—the Foundation for the Extension and Development of the American

Mr. and Mrs. Hardcastle in the Bristol Old Vic's production of She Stoops to Conquer.

Professional Theater. It operates for the benefit of Equity members, who are entering upon a far broader field of activity than ever before. Its four chief aims are to encourage the founding of new theaters; to develop areas other than those in the traditional theater environment in which actors can use their artistic talent; to aid already existing professional theater operations to maintain and extend their employment; and to become involved in the myriad of organizations that directly or indirectly pertain to the professional theater.

The American Playwrights Theater is an imposing link between the amateur and commercial theaters. It was organized to give established playwrights an opportunity to have their plays produced in community and university theaters away from the pressures of Broadway. This would counteract the gambling on a play's success on Broadway. The playwright has security because of the arrangements made on royalty charges by fifty amateur groups who contract to produce the play. Each group pays $200 royalty for a new play. Several leading American dramatists have shown interest, and the plan could revolutionize the quality of plays in this country. Many fine plays which have flopped on Broadway would certainly have succeeded in less sophisticated and more typical communities.

The first regional theater to be built was the dream of the Minnesota Theatre Company, organized to give Tyrone Guthrie opportunity to start a theater in a typical American city far from Broadway. It was named the Tyrone Guthrie Theatre. In 1963 the first season presented an international group of fine plays from contrasting epochs— *Hamlet, The Miser, The Three Sisters,* and *Death of a Salesman;* the theater has maintained the high standard then established. The building resembles the one Guthrie had already designed for the Stratford Festival Theatre, now officially titled the Stratford National Theatre of Canada, at Stratford, Ontario. The trust stage and other features have proved of durable value, according to Peter Zeisler, original director-producer, who was also one of the founders of the theater.

A carefully organized plan for bringing students from surrounding schools to see the plays enables thousands of young people to acquire an enthusiasm for fine drama. Material about the plays is distributed and discussed before the students see them, and interesting evaluations are made afterwards. Drama teachers in the high schools assist the public relations personnel to give the finest possible service in this phase of the theater's community relationship.

The standards of the Tyrone Guthrie Theatre have been based on the classics because, as Guthrie said in his first program, "They are what the best minds in previous generations have united to admire. Only through the classics can intelligent standards of criticism be established."

Practically all of the regional and repertory theaters have received hundreds of thousands of dollars, even millions in some cases, in grants from the great foundations like Ford and Rockefeller and many others, for use in erecting and supporting the theaters and encouraging new playwrights. The Associated Councils of the Arts, established in 1945, is an important supporter of the movement.

It is impossible to list all the theaters that show promise of surviving as permanent institutions, but you should know where you can see some excellent productions in outstanding theaters not mentioned in other sections of this book.

The Arena Stage in Washington, D. C., the Dallas Theater Center, the Alley Theater of Houston, and the Seattle Repertory Theater are among the earliest to achieve success and are all continuing to offer seasons of exciting plays. The Negro Ensemble Company of New York has established itself as a first-class repertory theater and training group under the direction of Douglas Turner Ward. It is presenting plays expressing the real lives and spirit of the black people of America while developing new playwrights and actors. The American Conservatory Theater under the stimulating direction of William Ball is presenting splendidly paced, articulate productions in two theaters in San Francisco and in tours across the country.

Performing Arts Centers are being established in many cities since the origin for the idea of building the Lincoln Arts Center away from Broadway developed into a reality. They all include a number of handsome buildings in a central location to house the phases of the arts which are of interest to the people of the community. Usually these are an opera house; a theater with two auditoriums — one large enough for repertory seasons, with storage and wardrobe room for many classical and period plays, and the other smaller, for experimental and contemporary drama; a concert hall, an art academy; and any additional schools, museums, and art galleries desired.

The Los Angeles Music Center was the second one to be completed and put to use. In it the theater is the Mark Taper Forum, a perfectly equipped auditorium with a large thrust stage; and the smaller one where the New Theater for Now provides a laboratory for new forms and concepts and a place where ultra modern voices for the American theater can be heard.

The Inner City Cultural Center in Los Angeles is another which has a Repertory Theater, also on a smaller, more intimate scale, where plays of racial and international interest can be featured as well as classical plays.

You will undoubtedly hear fine music and see great plays and operas in these centers for the rest of your life. More and more centers are already in the planning stage and others are actually being built.

The Amateur Theater

Amateur means "one who loves"; in America the number of amateurs who give hours and hours of their leisure time to putting on plays is a national fact of importance. If you really want to enjoy acting in, directing, or staging plays, you will become involved in the amateur field.

The Little Theaters were a part of the life of almost every city and town in the twenties and thirties. They were usually formed by groups of congenial people who loved the theater and enjoyed bringing the best Broadway plays to their communities. The one-act play came

All details are realistic in this scene from the Abbey Players' production of John Millington Synge's Playboy of the Western World. *The actors in this scene are Eamon Kelly, Aideen O'Kelly, and Vincent Dowling.*

into prominence in the twenties, largely because tournaments were held in many states where only one-act plays could be entered.

Community Theaters gradually superseded the Little Theaters. They are more democratic, drawing players from all sections of cities and catering to larger and more varied audiences. In many places where no professional theaters are located, community theaters present current plays during their Broadway runs.

University Theater

The finest theater buildings in the world are being constructed today on the campuses of American universities, and their departments of drama are covering every field of theater. Thousands of teachers of dramatics are graduating every year to enter both the high school and elementary fields. Professional aspirants are having practical experience in every type of play — period, classical, contemporary, children's theater. It is interesting to note that at Harvard in 1905 the first dramatic-theory class for playwrights, called the 47 Workshop, was organized by Dr. George Pierce Baker. Here student-writers had the experience of producing their own plays and receiving constructive criticism. Later, when Dr. Baker moved to Yale, he continued his course there. Under his influence, Yale built one of the first really adequate university theaters.

Guest stars are becoming resident instructors and actors under special arrangements made through the Extension Department of Equity. The dramatics majors get first-hand instruction and information from the guest stars, and they in turn get revived inspiration and encouragement from the students.

Repertory theaters of fine quality have become a part of many of the adjoining communities with subscription audiences. The Loretto-Hilton Center Repertory Theater of Webster College in St. Louis has one of the latest of Guthrie's theaters. The University of Washington in Seattle has for years had three working theaters: The Penthouse, where Glen Hughes first introduced the Theater-in-the-Round; the Showboat; and the Playhouse. The Carnegie-Mellon University in Pittsburgh, Pennsylvania, continues the noteworthy dramatic training of the former Carnegie Institute of Technology. The University of Denver maintains its reputation of years with a series of fine plays each season and the introduction of a professionally oriented program.

The Juilliard School, located in Lincoln Center, has recently opened a Drama Department under John Houseman after years of fame as one of the great schools of music.

The first American College Theater Festival was held in the spring of 1969, backed by ANTA and the American Educational Theater Association (AETA) and sponsored by the Smithsonian Institute, the Friends of the Kennedy Center, and American Airlines. There were ten plays selected for the Washington, D. C., Festival from about twenty campuses. It is a continuing impetus toward a high standard of production as well as fresh creativity.

Schools of Acting

Specialized schools of acting and all the performing arts exist in every city of any size, and of course New York City has many. The oldest in this country is the American Academy of Dramatic Art, still offering a solid foundation in techniques and experience in acting. The Neighborhood Playhouse School of the Theater, now located at 340 East Fifty-fourth, settled there after leaving the lower East Side. It has an excellent small theater where the students present plays of all types. The courses center on acting, speech, and movement, with performances which include scenes from plays, demonstrations, and one-act and full-length plays produced under expert direction and presented before selected audiences of managers, agents, and producers.

In San Francisco, the training at the American Conservatory Theater, 450 Geary, is definitely geared toward repertory acting, which demands a variety of techniques for differing periods and styles. The training is therefore most detailed. The instructors are all finished artists of the theater.

Many schools, especially in New York, are established on the Stanislavski Method as taught originally at the Actor's Studio under Lee Strasberg. A number of the repertory companies have started academies in connection with their theaters, selecting students by auditions. The field is thriving and expanding at a phenomenal rate.

The Children's Theater

Another hope of the future lies in the growing value of the hundreds of Theaters of Youth in active production today, with adults bringing well-done plays of first-class stories into the schools, the casts augmented by children in appropriate parts.

The Junior League was the pioneer in the Children's Theater, presenting plays upon which they had expended hours of intense effort. Many community theaters have for about ten years developed departments for producing elaborate and finished plays suitable for children, or actually by children after definite classwork in creative drama. Dozens of universities have courses on the subject, and high school dramatics classes undertake similar projects, going into the elementary schools with appropriate plays. You would thoroughly enjoy doing this with your class or club. You will learn a tremendous amount about audience reaction, and the need for clear, natural speaking and active, effective movement.

Associations

The AETA was founded in 1936 to inspire higher standards of production in our secondary schools, to help solve royalty problems,

Madame Ranevskaya (Carol Gustafson) and her daughters, Anya (left, Pamela Dunlap) and Varya (Gloria Maddox) gaze fondly at a tree in The Cherry Orchard, *the modern classic by Chekhov, at the Arena Stage, Washington, D. C.*

to assist young teachers, and to help unify teaching methods. Starting with a few hundred members, it now has over five thousand members, largely high school and university teachers of dramatics. In 1971 it was reorganized as the American Theatre Association (ATA), made up of the associations of the community, children's, college and university, secondary school, and university-resident theaters. ATA thus covers the various phases of educational drama everywhere in the country and its superior publications keep the members informed on all forms of theater.

The International Thespian Society is an honorary organization which recognizes high school students participating actively in the dramatic arts program of their school. Over three thousand high schools now have International Thespian troupes. Students are eligible for membership once they receive a required number of points earned through roles in plays, backstage and committee work, and other activities associated with their drama departments. *Dramatics*, the fine educational theater magazine published by the International Thespian Society, contains pictures of high school productions, news briefs on the activities of Thespian troupes around the country, and excellent articles on many phases of theater — history, trends, "how-it-was-done," and production techniques. Also available to members are reprints of articles which appeared in past issues on such topics as history of costumes, musical theater, children's theater, and so on. The encouragement the International Thespian Society offers high school students interested in good theater is exemplified by the Thespian motto: "Act well your part; there all the honor lies."

THEATER OF THE FUTURE

Out of our current transitional drama, certain trends will survive. Probably improvisation and involvement will bring an immediacy affecting both playwriting and production. The increasingly popular dance drama may well develop a theater of its own. Electronic effects will give emotional backgrounds in production in which lumia will play an important part. Audiences are tiring of the shock values of the performances of the late sixties, and are showing a definite interest in the best plays of past decades.

What form the productions of the future will take will depend upon the taste of the public. That the commercial theater in all great cities is losing its hold and that nonprofit theater of some sort will have to take over is almost certain. With the increasing spread of the regional theaters all over free Europe, England, and America, and the interchange of plays in festivals and conferences growing more frequent every season there is justifiable hope that drama of the world will hold the best of the past, will safely survive the shock of the present, and will create ever-expanding means of expressing the dreams of humanity.

Never has the theater been in such a state of change in standards of production, methods of acting, content of plays, and ideals of conduct. It is impossible to determine the future. Never have young people had more need for a firm foundation of knowledge upon which to base their judgment of what they choose to see in the theater. They also must not be deprived of the joy of reading and seeing the great dramas of the past. You are fortunate in being introduced to the wonderful world of the theater in a dramatics class where you can become familiar with the great dramas and learn to distinguish between the best and the worst today.

Discussion

1. What are some of the most recent developments in American theater? What do you think some future ones will be?
2. Are there any modern American plays or movements which you think will strongly affect those of the future?
3. Do you think the contemporary American stage exerts as great an influence on today's daily life as the theater did in ancient Greece and Elizabethan England?
4. Which do you enjoy the most, the drama of the stage, screen, or TV? Why?
5. If you could choose any one period in the history of the theater in which to be an actor, which would be your choice? Why?
6. How do you think modern methods of communication and transportation will affect international dramatic trends?

Bibliography

Cheney, Sheldon; *The Theatre: Three Thousand Years of Drama, Acting, and Stagecraft*, McKay, New York, 1959.

Gassner, John: *Masters of the Drama*, Dover, New York, 1953.

Gorelik, Mordecai: *New Theatres for Old*, Dutton, New York, 1962.

Hewitt, Barnard: *Theatre U. S. A., 1668 to 1957*, McGraw-Hill, New York, 1959.

Nicoll, Allardyce: *Development of the Theatre*, Harcourt, Brace, New York, 1958.

General References

Artaud, Antonin: *The Theater and Its Double*, translated by Mary Caroline Richards, Grove Press, Inc., New York, 1958.

Cleaver, James: *Theater Through the Ages*, Hart, New York, 1967.

Freedley, George, and John Reeves: *A History of the Theatre*, Crown, New York, 1968.

Mitchell, William: *Black Drama: The Story of the American Negro in the Theatre*, Hawthorn, New York, 1967.

Priestley, J. B.: *The Story of the Theatre*, Rathbone Books, London, 1959.

SHAKESPEAREAN DRAMA

Shakespeare's popularity is at a new high today throughout the world. In the seventies he maintains his position as leading dramatist, especially in England and the United States, because of his unceasing ability to communicate — which is the fundamental philosophy back of contemporary theater. Today Shakespeare's characters, major and minor alike, are as universally true to life; his ideas as vital; and his plays as inspiring, amusing, and stimulating as they have ever been. They can be adapted endlessly to creative and original methods of production and still convey their meaning clearly and effectively.

The decade opened, for example, with three strongly contrasted productions by famous companies. The National Theatre of Great Britain presented *The Merchant of Venice* as a mid-Victorian comic-melodrama. The production featured highly unique interpretations of all the characters, but especially those of Shylock and Portia by

Laurence Olivier and his wife Joan Plowright. In strong contrast, at the Shakespeare Festival Theatre in Connecticut, a distinctly traditional production of *Othello* found Moses Gunn, an outstanding actor from the excellent Negro Ensemble Company of New York, winning acclaim for his dynamic presentation of the difficult lead. The Royal Shakespeare Company of England, under the direction of Trevor Nunn, its newly appointed head, brought the Stratford Company to its London Aldwych Theatre in a notewothy production of *The Winter's Tale*, played against beautiful, largely white, scenic designs symbolic of the mood and title of the drama.

For a number of years modern dress productions have been featured, set in many localities. Recently avant-garde adaptations are being presented every season — the "mod" *Henry V* and *Love's Labour's Lost*; *West Side Story* and other adaptations of *Romeo and Juliet*; *Your Own Thing*, the prize-winning opera based on *Twelfth Night*; *Kiss Me, Kate*, based on *The Taming of the Shrew*; *The Boys from Syracuse*, based on *The Comedy of Errors*; and a number of far-out *Hamlets*.

Zeffirelli brought youth to *Romeo and Juliet* in the late sixties in his sensitively created film, which you may have seen. About the same time appeared *The Taming of the Shrew* with Elizabeth Taylor and Richard Burton. It is a boisterously conceived motion picture, with an originality which would have delighted Shakespeare.

You should make a point of seeing the reruns of former fine films like the brilliant *Julius Caesar* with an all-star cast; Orson Welles' *Macbeth*; and Maurice Evans' television versions of *Twelfth Night*, *The Taming of the Shrew*, *Macbeth*, and *Richard II*. Old films of Shakespeare's plays are often seen on television. For example, Max Reinhardt's *A Midsummer Night's Dream*, the Leslie Howard-Norma Shearer *Romeo and Juliet*, and Elizabeth Bergner's *As You Like It* have all been shown. Long-playing recordings have been made of scenes and entire plays by such actors as Laurence Olivier, John Gielgud, Claire Bloom, Alec Guinness, Maurice Evans, and Judith Anderson.

However, it is in the splendidly organized and carefully produced festivals rapidly spreading not only across America but around the world every year that you can find the most exciting and varied performances — in Stratford-on-Avon and in Regent's Park in London; in Stratford, Ontario, Canada; and in Stratford, Connecticut. In Central Park in New York City, a professional company has been

As the ghost of Hamlet's father reveals his murder, Hamlet's face and body reflect horror and bewilderment. In a production at the Stratford Festival Theatre in Stratford, Ontario, Christopher Plummer plays Hamlet; Max Helpmann, the ghost; Mervyn Blake, Marcellus; and Lloyd Blochner, Horatio.

presenting "free Shakespeare" during the summers. Season after season there are productions of Shakespeare on Broadway and off Broadway. Every year university and community theaters all over the country give excellent and original productions. The Antioch Area Shakespeare Festival in Ohio has presented all of the plays in a five-year cycle, and annual productions are held on the campuses of the universities of Colorado, Illinois, Oregon, and Utah — to mention only a few. For many years the Old Globe Theatre in San Diego, California, has drawn crowds to see its streamlined versions of the plays. Cycles like *The Wars of the Roses*, arranged from the history plays, are proving especially popular.

SHAKESPEARE, THE PLAYWRIGHT

As you begin your study of Shakespeare, there are a few things you should remember. The ideal way to become acquainted with Shakespeare is to see his plays, not merely to read them or read about them. The plays were written by a practical man of the theater who wrote them to be seen — not read — by a loud, boisterous audience accustomed to shouting its approval or hissing its displeasure. A play had to be exciting, moving, and violent, filled with fury, humor, and truth, in order to keep such an audience interested. The characters Shakespeare wrote of were moved by emotions that are as universal today as they were 400 years ago — love, jealousy, ambition, joy, and grief. It follows that Shakespeare can be vital to you.

Although you may apply to the plays of Shakespeare many of the standards that you use to analyze contemporary plays, you must remember that Shakespeare lived in another age. You will need to accustom yourself to the archaic speech, exaggerated situations, and flowery language of the sixteenth century. Shakespeare was an Elizabethan, and his plays are full of the slang, colloquialisms, and allusions of those times. The wonder is that plays so distinctly Elizabethan in tone and language have appealed to people of the eighteenth and nineteenth centuries alike and are more than holding their own in the twentieth century.

In the school, Shakespeare is useful in three ways. Of all dramatic literature, his plays offer the richest reward for intensive study and his roles afford the finest opportunity for interpretation. His texts furnish the most varied material for practice of vocal and pantomimic technique.

THE PLAYS THEMSELVES

Thoughtful study of Shakespeare's plays (first collected and published seven years after his death by his actor friends, Heminge and Condell) reveals his great humanity and artistic power. The scholar Edward Dowden has said of Shakespeare's plays that they were composed in the workshop, in the world, and in both the depths and on the heights of feeling. In other words, Shakespeare was a skilled craftsman who worked from his experiences and his emotions.

Structure

Shakespeare did not divide his plays into acts and scenes; his characters came and went, explaining in their conversation where they were as well as who they were. In the Elizabethan theater, there was no curtain to be drawn, so there were no dramatic curtain lines — each scene blended into the next. However, Shakespeare often used a rhymed couplet to show when a scene was over, and this is one clue that producers and editors have used in dividing the plays into acts and scenes.

His plays are famous for their openings in which the master dramatist did so much to set the characters, the preliminary situation, and the mood of the play as a whole. The exposition usually takes several scenes because the action is invariably complicated.

The rising action begins in the first act and reveals the main problem of the play, the opposing forces, and the conflict, which may be between two characters or groups of people or within the soul of the leading character himself. The climax usually comes in the third act, when the eventual outcome of the play is definitely foreshadowed and the main groups of characters are brought together in a single dramatic situation.

The action is built, often by the use of minor plots, so as to maintain interest through the fourth and fifth acts. The play concludes with the resolution, and the ending is usually as effective as the beginning. Note how the closing scene helps to make a complete unit of the play.

Characters

It is, of course, in his unsurpassed power of characterization that Shakespeare's genius most brilliantly expresses itself. His stories were seldom original, but when the magic of his hand touched plots and characters, they were transformed into masterpieces which eclipsed the sources from which they sprang. In turn, his masterpieces inspired works of art by the world's greatest composers, painters, and poets.

The characters form the center of the interest of Shakespeare's plays. Note exactly how each is introduced and how well defined his personality becomes immediately. Pick out all the crucial remarks in which he reveals his own individuality and note what the other characters say about him. Shakespeare used the soliloquy and accurate descriptions by other actors to delineate his characters; there were no programs to make any printed explanations. Look for lines in which the actions of the leading characters are motivated and see if the final result is not inevitable. Notice how clear-cut the minor characters are, defining themselves in their few lines as vividly as do the main characters in their thousands of lines. Often Shakespeare used two characters or two sets of characters in direct contrast or comparison, each making the other more interesting as the result.

Among the hundreds of immortal personages waiting to greet you in Shakespearean plays are mirthful Gratiano, dashing Mercutio, mischievous Maria, jovial Sir Toby, imbecilic Sir Andrew, outspoken

PETER SMITH

Douglas Campbell is shown as Falstaff in a scene from The Merry Wives of Windsor *at the Stratford, Ontario, Festival Theatre. The other actors (standing) are Helen Burns, Pauline Jameson, and Robin Gammell.*

Emilia, generous Antonio, engaging Touchstone, and devoted Adam. You will learn much of the tragedy and horror of life from Lady Macbeth, Richard III, Othello, Shylock, and Cardinal Wolsey. You will laugh with Falstaff, the merry wives, and all the fools. You will weep with Prince Arthur, Hermione, and Cordelia. In the world of fantasy Ariel, Puck, Caliban, Oberon, and Titania will enchant you, and in the world of romance you will meet the immortal lovers — Romeo and Juliet, Beatrice and Benedick, Katharine and Petruchio, Portia and Bassanio, Rosalind and Orlando, Miranda and Ferdinand, Perdita and Florizel, and Antony and Cleopatra. You will come to know and appreciate these and many others. And you will find, in spite of blank verse soliloquies and theatrical posturing, that these characters are very human in their strength and weakness, their tragedy and sorrow. It is through his characters that Shakespeare expresses his philosophy of life.

In this scene from Henry V *at the Stratford, Ontario, Festival Theatre, the scene is "turned in" by the arrangement of the actors. Douglas Rain plays Henry.*

Theme

The theme, or underlying idea of the play, may be found by analyzing the leading characters, their motivation and goals, and the manner in which they solve, or fail to solve, their main problem. Usually it is expressed in one important line, but often it is repeated in varied forms for emphasis; frequently it is condensed into the title of the drama.

In every play there are scores of brilliantly worded ideas about which whole dramas could be built — Shakespeare is "full of quotations" — but there is always one dominant thought about which the action centers. In fact, the fascination of working out these key ideas of the great dramas — especially *Hamlet*, considered by many authorities to be the finest play ever written — has caused whole volumes to be published by famous critics and actors.

As Shakespeare himself says, "The Devil can cite Scripture for his purpose." For generations men and women have cited Shakespeare when expressing their thinking on hundreds of subjects as well as on the themes of his plays.

346

Language

As you read a Shakespearean play, its language will strike you with its power and beauty if you do not worry too much about its form. Most school editions of the plays have excellent notes which will help you over the difficulties of Elizabethan speech. You will be amazed, however, to find how modern in spirit the language is. In a recent production of *The Taming of the Shrew* in modern dress, the word *lute* was changed to *uke* for *ukelele* and *thee* and *thou* to *you*, but these were the only changes made. The members of the cast found that they could present the play in exactly the same tempo and manner as contemporary plays. You will, of course, pick out the figurative language in a play and see how greatly it adds to the beauty and force of Shakespeare's ideas. You will also listen to the music of the language and note how the pronunciation and emphasis of words form a definite rhythm. See how the movement of the lines and the choice of words express the spirit of a scene and suggest the manner in which it must be played.

The rhythmic beauty of Shakespeare's poetry and the power of his prose held the noisy Elizabethan audiences enthralled just as they do the politer audiences of today. One of the pleasures of witnessing or reading his plays is to find famous quotations in their original context. Another is to come upon a perfectly expressed idea which you have felt but were never able to put into words. Many passages are amazingly appropriate today. For example:

"What a piece of work is man! How noble in reason! How infinite in faculties! in form and moving how express and admirable! in action how like an angel! in apprehension, how like a god!"

"Lord, what fools these mortals be!"

"God made him, therefore, let him pass for a man."

"I had rather have a fool to make me merry than experience to make me sad."

"A hasty marriage seldom proveth well."

"Maids want nothing but husbands and when they have them they want everything!"

"There's a divinity that shapes our ends, rough-hew them how we will."

"I would there were no age between ten and three-and-twenty, or that youth would sleep out the rest . . ." (There follows a list relevant today of juvenile delinquency!)

*Kenneth Welsh as Hamlet,
with Leo Ciceri (Claudius)
and Angela Wood
(Gertrude) at the Stratford
Festival Theatre in
Stratford, Ontario, in the
summer of 1969.*

DOUGLAS SPILLANE

"We are such stuff as dreams are made on, and our little life is rounded with a sleep."

"How bitter a thing it is to look into happiness through another man's eyes."

"Men have died from time to time, and worms have eaten them, but not for love."

"Cans't thou not minister to a mind diseased, pluck from the memory a rooted sorrow, raze out the written troubles of the brain?"

"The time is out of joint; O cursed spite that ever I was born to set it right."

"Cowards die many times before their deaths; the valiant never taste of death but once."

"There are more things in heaven and earth, Horatio, than are dreamt of in your philosophy."

Among the phrases Shakespeare coined are "primrose path," "flaming youth," "fool's paradise," "heart of gold," "strange bed fellows," "crack of doom," "towering passion," "cares of state," "cold comfort," "for goodness sake," "at one fell swoop," "the tranquil mind," and "single blessedness." These are frequently used today, **348** and few people realize that Shakespeare originated them.

Chronology of the Plays

Since the exact dates for the composition of Shakespeare's plays are not known, an approximate chronology has been devised by scholars from available evidence. In the following list, the plays appear in the order generally agreed upon. (The starred titles are those most suitable for use in class reading.)

1590 — *Love's Labour's Lost*
1591 — *The Comedy of Errors*
     Henry VI
1592 — *Two Gentlemen of Verona*
     Richard III
     *Romeo and Juliet**
1593 — King John
     Richard II
     Titus Andronicus
1594 — *A Midsummer Night's*
     *Dream**
1595 — *All's Well That Ends Well*
     *The Taming of the Shrew**
1596 — *Henry IV*
1597 — *The Merry Wives of*
     Windsor
     *The Merchant of Venice**
1598 — *Much Ado About Nothing*
     Henry V

1599 — *As You Like It**
1600 — *Twelfth Night**
1601 — *Julius Caesar**
1602 — *Hamlet**
1603 — *Troilus and Cressida*
1604 — *Measure for Measure*
     Othello
1605 — *Macbeth**
1606 — *King Lear*
1607 — *Timon of Athens*
1608 — *Pericles*
     Antony and Cleopatra
1609 — *Coriolanus*
1610 — *Cymbeline*
1611 — *The Winter's Tale*
     *The Tempest**
1616 — *Henry VIII*

Reading the plays in chronological order reveals that Shakespeare developed his artistic powers through his own life experiences. You should learn about his life from some of the many biographies available, and about its probable effect on the plays from the commentaries of Shakespearean scholars.

You should own a volume of Shakespeare's complete plays; it will grow in value to you as you develop as a person, and you will find deepening inspiration in the plays as your life unfolds.

You can increase your interpretive powers by reading aloud contrasting passages and by studying the multitude of varied roles. As you see productions of the plays on stage, screen, and TV, make notes of differing interpretations by the actors, and keep a list of the best actors appearing in the important roles.

Laurence Olivier as Hotspur in Shakespeare's play Henry IV (Part One) *jests tenderly with his wife* (Margaret Leighton) *before the battle in which he is killed.*

Stagecraft

Shakespeare's stagecraft is, of course, sound because he took an active part in the production and acting of plays. His craftsmanship is displayed in the clever manner in which he clears his stage at the end of each scene, his apt use of prose and verse, and his painting of a scene so clearly in words that the need for scenery is eliminated. Practically all the stage directions necessary for producing one of his plays are incorporated into the dialogue, and yet there is room for much interpolated action. The devoted theatergoer enjoys comparing different productions of Shakespearean plays, noting the essential action that is similar in them all and the varied methods by which different companies achieve distinctive effects.

Because of the variety and originality of modern staging, seeing the plays on the stage and screen is, of course, the best way to enjoy and appreciate them. You should see every performance you possibly can. Productions of the nineteenth century used spectacular sets which had been developed by such actor-managers as Henry Irving (1838-1905), Richard Mansfield (1854-1907), and Edwin Booth (1833-1893). They depicted palaces, moonlit gardens, the canals and bridges of Venice, battlefields, tombs, and cathedrals against which the elaborate Elizabethan costumes glittered and glowed. Fortunately the library shelves in public and university libraries are filled with volumes describing past productions in detail. Many autobiographies of famous actors include their own analyses of Shakespearean roles and their own techniques of acting them; from these you can learn a great deal about acting.

Contemporary productions have largely returned to open stages resembling Shakespeare's own, and show far greater interest in a stylization symbolic of abstract ideas. The magic of modern lighting and electronic sound are creating effects never used before, as in Svoboda's *Hamlet* in Prague with his "Laterna Magica" and the use of mirrors and sliding stairs and platforms.

One of the latest books (1969) is Margaret Webster's *The Same Only Different*, in which this most distinguished woman director of current Shakespearean productions compares modern interpretations and theories with those in which her famous theatrical family took part. Her *Shakespeare Without Tears* has introduced many people to the famous plays.

The Value of Acting the Plays

By a continuous interpretation of characters, passages, and scenes, and particularly by presenting them in public and acting in the complete plays, you can develop your dramatic talent as you can in no other way. That is why specialized schools spend so much time with Shakespearean plays; most auditions include one memorized passage from Shakespeare as a means of testing emotional power, clarity and beauty of speech, bodily responsiveness, and general effectiveness as a performer.

Read aloud contrasting roles for practice: Launcelot Gobbo and Hamlet; Lady Macbeth and Audrey; Katharine and Juliet; Arthur and Adam; Caliban and Ariel; Beatrice and Cordelia; Mercutio and Richard II.

THE SHAKESPEARE QUATERCENTENARY: 1564-1964

The entire world honored the four hundredth anniversary of Shakespeare's birth. Festivals were held everywhere with professional, university, and amateur groups; magnificent productions of individual plays were presented by stars in famous theaters of the great cities of all nations. Millions saw the plays which were featured on film and television.

Stratford-on-Avon

The center of the celebration was, of course, Shakespeare's birthplace. On his birthday, a procession with representatives of 113 nations was held, and Prince Philip opened the tremendous Exhibition and Panorama erected across the Avon from the Royal Shakespeare Theatre.

The Festival plays presented the cycle of history plays in complete sequence from Richard II through Richard III and was presented under the joint direction of Peter Hall and James Barton with Hugh Griffith, Eric Porter, Dave Warner, Ian Holm, and Peggy Ashcroft

In this scene from The Tempest *at the Stratford, Ontario, Festival Theatre in 1962 Norman Welsh plays Stephano; Hugh Webster, Trinculo; John Colicos, Caliban.*

PETER SMITH

in the leading roles. They were played against a dark metallic but flexible set on an open stage, creating a somber background for the War of the Roses.

The Shakespeare Exhibition was a fantastic avant-garde maze created at great expense to depict the life of Shakespeare. Painted panoramas showed what he saw enroute from Stratford to London and the chief events of his life. There was also a unique symbolic representation of each play in modern ceramics, wire sculptures, huge papier-mâché figures, and paintings. The panorama ended in a replica of the Globe Theater where the voices of all the most distinguished living actors were heard playing the famous scenes.

There were two highly significant special exhibits. The first was the collection of the books Shakespeare might have studied in school and read during his life to inspire his writing. The books were opened at the pages where passages were most significant. The other was a collection of portraits of famous personages who affected Shakespeare's life.

Shakespearean films were featured throughout the festival and included Olivier's *Hamlet, Richard III,* and *Henry V;* splendid Russian productions of *Twelfth Night, Othello,* and *Romeo and Juliet;* and the Japanese *Throne of Blood* version of *Macbeth.*

Other British Events

The Royal Shakespeare Theatre produced the cleverly adapted drama, *The War of the Roses,* at the Aldwych, and organized a tour in Europe and America of Paul Scofield in *King Lear,* considered by many to be the finest interpretation of Lear ever created; it was later filmed in Finland. At the National Theatre, Olivier first presented his controversial *Othello,* seen later on the screen, in which he portrayed Othello as an African Negro torn by almost primitive emotions. You perhaps have seen this film, with Maggie Smith playing Desdemona. The Festival in London featured a performance of *Twelfth Night* by the New Shakespeare Company, directed by Colin Graham, in the Hall of the Middle Temple, presented as it had been presented to Queen Elizabeth by Shakespeare. In all, there were forty-four festivals in the British Isles.

In America

There were twenty-two excellent festivals in America, including those at the Stratford, Ontario, the Stratford, Connecticut, and Ashland, Oregon, theaters; the Globe Theater at San Diego; and

In 1968 The American Shakespeare Festival Theatre in Stratford, Connecticut, put on a "turned on" version of Love's Labour's Lost. *The King of Navarre was shown as a Guru, and in many ways the play was geared toward a modern society. The actors are Rex Everhart, Ken Parker, Stefan Gierasch.*

practically every university campus. Probably the most advertised and exciting production in the United States was the Broadway version of *Hamlet* directed by John Gielgud and starring Richard Burton. It was their gift to the four hundredth birthday celebration. They planned it to show a rehearsal just before the dress rehearsals begin, and the actors chose to wear whatever clothes and carry whatever temporary props they needed.

Excitement was caused across the country when one of the regular performances was filmed by Electronovision under the stage lighting and the film later shown in limited two-day engagements in selected cities. It was purposely an unfinished performance, lacking polish and

careful detail in presenting lines and movements, but having spontaneity and an interesting casual quality.

The Tyrone Guthrie Theatre in Minneapolis opened its second
season in 1964 with *Henry V* under the direction of Tyrone Guthrie,
who felt it is the most popular of Shakespeare's plays because it
combines pageantry and comedy and has strongly contrasted scenes.

Officially the United States centered the celebration at Stratford,
Connecticut, where the Secretariat of the United Nations was invited
to see *Much Ado About Nothing* and *Hamlet*.

On Television

There were almost continuous programs of the plays, readings,
and operas, as well as discussion by panels of experts, on TV around
the world. The outstanding world event was the BBC production, in
association with Danish Television, of *Hamlet* starring Christopher
Plummer and produced at Elsinore Castle. All traffic was silenced
in the surrounding area for days, and the battlements, banquet hall,
towers, and staircases of the castle were utilized for the scenes, thus
creating an authentic setting.

Hamlets Today

Nicol Williamson has created a tremendous stir in his *Hamlet*
on both stage and screen. Williamson is a direct, intelligent young
man of Hamlet's age, with a Scots accent and shifting moods. David
Warner of the Royal Shakespeare Theatre is long, lanky, homely,
temperamental, but fascinating. Richard Chamberlain was the first
American to play Hamlet in England since John Barrymore's tremendous hit in 1929; for his *Hamlet* the setting was put in Russia
before the revolution.

The famous Stratford Festival Theatre in Ontario brought Kenneth
Welsh as a youthful Hamlet, frustrated as young men are today, and
the whole production, directed by John Hirsch, gave a sense of happening now among young people, though it was not done in modern
dress.

Hamlet Revisited, produced for ETV and hopefully to be repeated
frequently, brought Gielgud to TV for the first time as Hamlet
reading three famous passages. Gielgud also introduced a series of
new Hamlets including Chamberlain, Tom Courtenay, and Williamson,
as well as Laurence Olivier in his famous films. He included clips from
foreign productions: Maximilian Schell from Germany, and others

In Shakespeare's Much Ado About Nothing, *Alfred Drake plays the bachelor Benedick and Katharine Hepburn takes the part of the gay and independent Beatrice.*

from Ghana and Russia, and Mme. Asta Neilson in a Danish film portraying Hamlet as a princess masquerading as a man. Older clips brought famous speeches by John Barrymore, Forbes-Robertson, Sarah Bernhardt, Eva La Gallienne, and others.

THE CONTINUED SUCCESS OF SHAKESPEARE'S PLAYS

The reason for the success of Shakespeare's plays is their adaptability to all types of production because of their universal appeal. That appeal is based on the fact that Shakespeare was an actor as well as a playwright and knew his theater as no other man ever has. His practical business sense and stability of character prevented his becoming involved in the reckless excesses of the other actor-dramatists of his time, who failed to reach their full potentialities. He wrote many passages about the stage and its relation to people. among them these:

> All the world's a stage
> And all the men and women merely players.

> I hold the world but as the world, Gratiano,
> A stage where every man must play a part.

> Life's but a walking shadow, a poor player
> That struts and frets his hour upon the stage
> And then is heard no more.

How greatly has the world profited by the fact that Shakespeare's genius lay in both acting and writing plays of infinite variety. Otherwise, he, too, might only have strutted and fretted his hour upon the stage and then been heard no more!

Discussion

1. Why do you think Shakespeare's plays continue to be successful on stage, screen, and television? Which ones that you have seen have you enjoyed most? Why?
2. Compare productions seen by members of the class in conventional Elizabethan style and in modern modes. Have you seen any using electronic effects in sight and sound? Have you seen any adaptations recently in musical comedy, opera, motion pictures, or on TV?
3. Who are some of the best-known English and American actors and actresses of Shakespeare today? Discuss anything you can find about their interpretations.
4. Discuss the Elizabethan theaters; daily life in Elizabethan England; a comparison between Elizabethan England and the United States today.
5. Listen to some of the fine Shakespearean recordings available today and discuss the interpretations.

Bibliography

Quennell, Peter: *Shakespeare, a Biography*, World Publishing, Cleveland, 1963.

Rowse, A. L.: *William Shakespeare, a Biography*, Harper & Row, New York, 1963.

Shakespeare, William: *The Complete Works*, World Publishing, Cleveland, 1965.

Webster, Margaret; *Shakespeare Without Tears*, Fawcett, New York, 1955.
———: *The Same Only Different*, Knopf, New York, 1969.

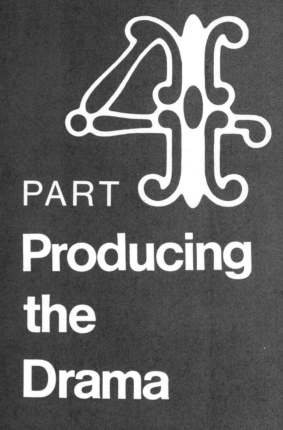

PART 4

Producing
the
Drama

chapter

FUNDAMENTALS OF PLAY PRODUCTION

Play production offers many opportunities which you may well find more stimulating and exciting than acting. All the activities involved in the design and construction of sets and costumes, the handling of lighting equipment, and the managing of affairs backstage and in the front of the house are of absorbing interest when a play once gets under way.

At present your interest centers in the plays given by your own school. School stages may range from simple ones in classrooms to theaters having a fully equipped switchboard, recording and sound equipment, fine dressing rooms, and ample work and storage space. If your school does not have all these facilities, do not be dismayed. A small stage, crowded backstage area, and the minimum of stage lights are limitations which may challenge your imagination and ingenuity.

As a result, your productions may well be superior to those presented more easily with first-class physical equipment. Whatever the size and equipment of your theater, having a share in a big public production is a stimulating experience.

In this chapter your attention is directed to the guiding principles of play production, especially as they pertain to school dramatic groups. Detailed analysis of these principles can be found in the books listed in the Bibliography. In them you will find fascinating ideas which will enable you to work with greater efficiency and which may even inspire you to study some special phase of production in detail. Initially, though, you will want to familiarize yourself with all phases of stage work in order to find the field you enjoy most.

Putting on a public production of a long play means at least six weeks of intensive work by a large group of people. Before that period much preliminary planning and preparation must be done. In order to get the fullest possible experience, follow all the activities from the beginning, carrying out your own special duties with enthusiasm and responsibility.

In school dramatics, the director usually plans the production in accordance with the schedule for school events. He often works with a student executive committee in the selection of individual production staff members and their assistants. The director and this executive committee also set up special committees to assist in all, or some, of the following production procedures: play reading and selection, casting, costuming, publicity, business management, and backstage work. All of the people chosen should be dependable and enthusiastic, since a great deal of the authority in production rests with them.

THE PRODUCTION STAFF

The number of people on the production staff will be determined by the size of the production, the availability of capable people, and the needs of the individual school or class. In the school theater, various departmental activities often center about public production. The class in dramatics may furnish the cast and the direction. The art department may design and/or paint the set. The shops may make and handle the scenery and provide stage carpenters. The home economics classes may make the costumes or do alterations. The music department may provide the incidental music. In the case of an operetta or musical, the music department usually furnishes singers, instrumentalists, and musical direction.

A brief discussion of the tasks of each position to be filled will give you an idea of the work involved in producing a play.

The Director

The director of your public productions in high school is usually your dramatics teacher. No longer are outsiders brought in to "put on a show," and you are indeed lucky to be in a country where almost every high school has a trained, and frequently professionally experienced, teacher-director.

In the modern theater, the director is receiving the appreciation he deserves on both the stage and screen. Actors also seek out the fine directors under whom to work, taking minor parts frequently for the privilege of sharing the experience of creating a perfected performance of a play — the ideal of every dedicated person involved in theater.

The ideal director inspires his actors with confidence in their abilities and intelligence in building their roles, molding all phases of production into a unified whole. Ardent, concentrated attention to every detail maintains an enthusiasm and dedication on the part of every individual involved in each situation and eliminates distracting and nerve-racking crises. The director is responsible for on-stage empathies and backstage morale. The director's primary objective at all times must be to produce the playwright's intentions as faithfully as he can by discovering the values and meanings which are the outgrowth of creative rehearsals. The director's word is law! Only he has visualized the production as it should appear on the night of the performance.

In the school production, the students have a much larger share in every phase, and the director is the teacher. Therefore, putting on a play is far more a cooperative, delightful experience of a team working together in an exciting game. You are fortunate to be having the companionship and joy of school dramatics as your introduction to theater.

The Assistant Director

In the school theater, the position of assistant director is held by a capable student. He must be a person whom the director finds dependable and whom the students respect. He will serve as a liaison officer between the director, cast, and crew, taking charge of rehearsals in the absence of the director. This is a position you must aspire to if you are interested in all phases of the theater.

Captain Hook and Michael in a high school production of Peter Pan.

MAXWELL STUDIO

The Prompter

This position should also be held by a dependable student who will attend every rehearsal. During rehearsals, under the supervision of the director, the prompter, or holder of the book, may hold the director's promptbook and make some of the penciled notes on moves and business, light and sound cues, and warning signals.

The numbering system is recommended for marking the blocking — the movements, positions, and crosses. Under this system, each movement on each page is given a number for easy reference by actors and director. Sound and light cues and other special effects are numbered in different colors. By using sketches in the promptbook, the prompter can clarify any questions concerning stage groupings, crosses, and changes.

The prompter marks special gestures and hurried directions at exciting moments so that such details will not be lost. He must mark every pause so he will not give an unnecessary prompt. During the performance the prompter can often save the show if emergencies arise. He can give the correct cues and lines; and, if the cast starts to skip passages, he can feed the vital lines to keep the meaning clear for the audience. If he fails at these crucial times, the entire production can be ruined. Audiences will often remember and laugh about one moment of confusion after they have forgotten all the fine points of a production.

Some directors do not use the prompter during the performance, preferring to have the actors know they are on their own. Others feel that a skilled prompter is essential. If your school does use a prompter, this is a position from which you may learn a great deal. It is a job that requires both reliability and intelligence.

The Scenic Artist and the Technical Director

The scenic artist, or the designer, usually designs the settings, the costumes and the makeup, and plans the lighting. Though his designs may be simple or complex, they must always give the play visual dimensions in harmony with the aims of the director.

The work of the technical director is also vitally important. It is he who executes the designs of the scenic artist, with the assistance of a crew, for building sets, painting drops, creating costumes, and hanging lights. In some cases, the scenic artist and the technical director are the same person. Though their functions are different, they both aim at serving the director's intentions as effectively, simply, and beautifully as possible to achieve a unified production.

The Stage Manager

Aided by his stage crew, the stage manager takes complete charge backstage during rehearsals and performances. In some cases he and his crew act both as the stage carpenters who build the set and as the "grips" who change the scenery. The stage manager also keeps a promptbook containing all cues and effects. He makes up cue sheets or charts containing the cues for lights, sound, and curtain. For the stage crew, he makes up a chart of set and prop changes to guide them through the play. During the performance the stage manager must handle any and all emergencies that may arise. A good stage manager is essential to a smooth production.

The Backstage Assistants

The property-man and his assistants procure the furniture and props, in accordance with the designer's plans, store them backstage, arrange them, and give the hand props to the actors backstage just before entrances. These hand props should be kept on tables on the appropriate side of the stage. They must be carefully replaced and never touched except when in use. The wardrobe mistress, makeup people, and callboys serve under the stage manager, whose job it is to see that all backstage activities go smoothly, quietly, and rapidly in final rehearsals and all performances. The efficiency, ingenuity, and dependability of these assistants during long hours of hard labor are determining factors in a successful production. Without them, the play cannot go on.

The Business Manager

The business manager is responsible for the financial arrangements of the production. In accordance with school policy, he may be in charge of all funds, pay all bills, and handle the printing and selling of tickets. He and the director should gauge probable receipts and achieve a reasonable profit by watching production and publicity expenses.

In the school theater, the business manager has the difficult task of issuing tickets to many salesmen and checking on sales. He should give out all passes to the show, with the permission of the director. He is also responsible for the "stage-door slips" which are issued to those working backstage. It is most important that people who do not have specific duties in the dressing rooms or backstage area not be admitted during performances. (If stage-door slips are not used, a program listing members of the staff may be substituted. A responsible person may use it to check entrances and exits at the stage door.)

The business manager also has charge of printing the programs, which should be designed by the scenic artist in harmony with the production. The cast is usually listed in the order of appearance. The business manager should be accurate in listing names of cast members, production staff, committee chairmen, and backstage crew. He should also see that acknowledgments are made for favors and assistance. Selling advertising to pay for the program is usually a matter determined by school authorities; if advertising is used, the business manager supervises this.

MASTER PRODUCTION SCHEDULE CHECKLIST

1. Production budget established
2. Play reading committee selected
3. Committee reports
4. Final selection of play
5. Staff organized
6. Research
7. Production rights obtained
8. Scripts ordered
9. Meeting of director and technical director and stage manager
10. Promptbook prepared
11. Floor plan designed
12. Basic design presented — scenery, lights, costumes
13. Tryouts
14. Cast selected
15. Stage and costume crews recruited
16. First publicity release
17. Costume measurements taken
18. Light plot prepared
19. Floor plan laid out on rehearsal floor
20. Blocking rehearsals begun
21. Tickets ordered
22. Publicity committee organized
23. Scenery begun
24. Program prepared for printing
25. Working rehearsals
26. First costume fittings
27. Arrangements made for publicity photos
28. Props secured
29. Second publicity release
30. Tickets placed on sale
31. Construction of scenery completed
32. Special effects (recordings, etc.) secured
33. Lighting, cue sheets, and prop plots completed
34. Tickets distributed and/or racked
35. Rental or purchase of costumes and accessories arranged
36. Second costume fitting
37. First lighting check
38. Polish rehearsal and rehearsal timed
39. Rehearsal with props
40. Set completed
41. Major press releases
42. Technical rehearsals begin
43. Costume parade
44. Final set touches
45. Dress rehearsals
46. Performances
47. Costume and prop check-in
48. Bills paid, tickets audited
49. a. Scenery struck and stored
    b. Props put away
    c. Borrowed furniture, etc., returned
    d. Rented costumes packed and returned
    e. Own costumes cleaned and stored
    f. Dressing rooms cleaned
    g. Thank you letters sent
50. Final financial statement drawn

The Advertising Man

The advertising man must promote the show in the school and in the community. Good publicity is vital to the financial success of the play. The public press, newspapers published at other schools, local radio stations, and church publications will give space and time to notices about public school productions if they are properly approached. In these days of broadcasting systems, tape recordings, and other devices in many high schools, there are almost limitless possibilities for promoting a play.

The advertising man and his assistants have a real opportunity to make original and artistic contributions to the success of a production. In their planning, the advertising staff would do well to consult the art department of the school. With serious dramas, advertising in keeping with the spirit of the play may include well-designed individual notices (wood cuts and black-and-white sketches) sent to all drama enthusiasts in the community. For comedies, cartoons of the cast and humorous items about the funniest situations can be featured, possibly with lively quotations from the play. The title of the play itself, the author, the skill or prominence of the performers, the past achievements of the director, and striking scenic effects can also furnish material for publicity.

If there is a good possibility of filling the house more than once, plans should be made for several consecutive performances before any advertising goes out. The repetition of a play several days or weeks after a single highly successful performance is seldom satisfactory, because both cast and public lose interest rapidly. Also, the expense of renting costumes and furniture again takes what little money has been made. It is always better to have one packed house than several half-empty ones.

The House Manager

The house manager is responsible for the seating and comfort of the audience, the competence and charm of the ushers, and the distribution of the programs. Uniformed ushers or girls in evening dress or appropriate costumes can add much to the pleasure of the audience.

Other Personnel

School productions frequently involve still more people. Firemen and policemen are on hand if they are notified when a production is scheduled. Sometimes members of the faculty are required to be in attendance in the dressing rooms and backstage areas, and they often take or sell tickets out front.

The school orchestra or recordings may furnish music for the overture or intermissions. If so, the program should be selected far in advance and properly rehearsed. Music should also be in keeping with the production and subordinate to it, not added as a special feature. Announcements or stunts between acts should be avoided.

Discussion

1. In your school, what are some of the special problems connected with putting on a play? Are they being solved? Is the entire student body interested in them? Are the people in the community interested?
2. Discuss the school plays you have attended or assisted with and note the part the backstage people had in their success or failure.
3. For what purpose are the proceeds of your dramatic productions used? Are they used exclusively for improving the stage and its equipment, as a means of raising money for other school activities, or for charity? How do you think they ought to be used?
4. Discuss possible difficulties which might arise during a performance. Show how the prompter and/or the stage manager might circumvent or overcome them.

PRE-REHEARSAL ACTIVITIES

After the director and the executive committee have set up the special committees and after individual production staff members have been selected, the next step is to choose a play. This is usually done by the reading committee and the director.

Choosing a Play

Choosing a play is a crucial problem. Before a choice can be made, many plays must be read. A poor choice can ruin the reputation of the producing group; a good one can establish it. The producing group must know the purpose of the proposed production. Is it primarily a school project, recognized as an important artistic group activity? Or is it to raise funds for a specific purpose or organization? A play must be found which will fulfill its designated purpose, appeal to its particular audience, and be adaptable to the ability of the actors, the size and equipment of the stage, and the limits of the budget.

In the desire to reduce the royalty charge and to entertain the public, inexperienced groups sometimes choose silly farces which do

The setting for a high school production of Seven Keys *to Baldpate, with the cast all on stage.*

not warrant an expenditure of time and energy. Rather than compromise on the quality of the script, it is better to present classics (most of which require no royalty) or cut production expenses sufficiently to pay the royalty on a contemporary play by a first-class writer. Remember that there are many classics which the other students and the parents will thoroughly enjoy. There are also many plays of the last century, now released from royalty charges, that are really delightful. Try to avoid plays which a large portion of your audience may have seen recently and try to provide variety in the annual programs of your school.

The size of the cast requires attention in the choice of a play. When the cast is large, more students receive the benefits of training and experience. However, large casts make for difficult rehearsals and staging. Ability to create the necessary stage settings and the possibility of adequate interpretation by available actors must be considered.

Securing Production Rights

Before a play is finally selected, the director or some authorized person should write to the author or company controlling the acting rights of the play. He should state the time and number of performances planned and request authorization to present the play. There **369** are many regulations restricting the presentation of plays by amateurs, especially in the larger cities where stock and road companies appear. Therefore, full permission should be obtained for a public performance before preparations start.

Planning the Production

Planning the production, though largely in the hands of the director, gives the executive committee the privilege of sharing in the fundamental thinking upon which it is based. You have been introduced already to the importance of empathy in such planning.

This principle was first introduced into educational dramatics by John Dolman, Jr., in his first edition of *The Art of Play Production*, as the dominant psychological influence in the universal appeal of the theater. It enters into every phase of production: the selection of the play, the casting, the rehearsing, the staging, and the performance. It includes the imitative response of human beings to other human beings, because the average individual goes to the theater to experience vicariously — that is, to lose himself in the actions of other people in situations which he will probably never meet in his own life. "Detrimental empathies" are caused by such details as needless fidgeting, forgotten lines, poor makeup, badly arranged sets, inharmonious color schemes, and acting which is overdone or underdone. It is the purpose of planning to create only "pleasant empathies" throughout the production, and every person involved from the beginning must work toward that goal. The director, among his many functions, serves as the audience, and his reactions can determine the ultimate success or failure of a play, because he will be alert to his own responses to lines, grouping, and staging.

The director must first study the play from every angle to determine the style and atmosphere he wishes carried out in the sets and costumes. He must understand the theme and decide how best to express it. He must decide how to emphasize the conflict, suspense, and climax of the plot. Most important of all, he must analyze the characters and their relationships to each other. For a period play, he must study the historical background, social conditions, and attitudes of the people represented, as well as the costumes, furnishings, etiquette, and manner of speech and movement.

Early in his work on a play, he must make out a tentative budget. He must estimate the probable size of the audience and take into account sets and props which may be obtained without expense.

After studying the play, the director makes his floor plan. This is his diagram of the physical set and the action which will take place on it. During this early period, the director should have frequent conferences with his scenic artist and stage manager concerning many aspects of the production. Problems of handling the show backstage must be discussed. The director must also carefully adapt his plans for action to the stage design.

The entrances and exits must be practical and logical. The location and size of the furniture should be planned to create helpful, meaningful units for definite bits of action and to form attractive and balanced stage pictures. The light sources must be considered and marked on the floor plan. Windows provide daytime light; lamps, fireplaces, and perhaps chandeliers give light at night. Sufficient backing for windows and doors must be considered in planning the action and the director must make his needs clear to his scenic artist. The backstage storage areas for furniture, props, and sets must be diagrammed. After the director, the scenic artist, and the stage manager have made overall plans, the director will visualize important scenes carefully and plan for effective grouping. Unimportant characters can be momentarily emphasized by being placed upstage or apart from the others.

Making the Promptbook

The promptbook, started by the director during the planning period and containing the entire play script, is the backbone of a production. Into this book go the director's plans as well as the telephone numbers and addresses of all the people involved in the production. The easiest way to make a promptbook is to paste the pages of the play in a large loose-leaf notebook. This system requires two copies of the play. If there is only one copy available for this purpose, page-size windows can be cut in the sheets of the notebook and each page of the script can be fastened with cellophane tape or glue into these windows.

Large margins around the script are essential for the sketches, cues, and notes, first made by the director in his preliminary planning and then added to and changed during rehearsals. The marginal notes show script cuttings, stage directions, and markings of difficult passages for pauses, phrasing, and emphasis. The sketches or diagrams of floor plans and sets show positions of furniture and actors in every scene. Stage groupings of actors can be drawn with the initials of the

GWENDOLEN (*Catching sight of him*). Ernest! My own Ernest!

[margin note: Jack X from D L toward U L past arch]

JACK. Gwendolen! Darling! (*He offers to kiss her.*)

[margin note: 2 tries to be very proper]

GWENDOLEN (*Drawing back*). A moment! May I ask if you are engaged to be married to this young lady? (*She points to* CECILY.)

JACK (*Laughing*). To dear little Cecily! Of course not! What could have put such an idea into your pretty little head?

GWENDOLEN. Thank you. You may. (*She offers her cheek.*)

[margin note: J kisses 2 on cheek - keeps arm around her waist]

CECILY (*Very sweetly*). I knew there must be some misunderstanding, Miss Fairfax. The gentleman whose arm is at present around your waist is my guardian, Mr. John Worthing.

GWENDOLEN. I beg your pardon?

[margin note: Jack runs fingers nervously around inside of collar]

CECILY. This is Uncle Jack.

[margin note: 2 moves DR away from J]

GWENDOLEN. (*Receding*). Jack! Oh!

[margin note: Shock and dismay flutters fan]

CECILY. Here is Ernest. *[margin note: algernon enters R visible to all but Cecily]* (ALGERNON *goes straight over to* CECILY *without noticing anyone else.*) *[margin note: A crosses with both arms outstretched]*

ALGERNON. My own love! (*He offers to kiss her.*)

CECILY (*Drawing back*). A moment, Ernest! May I ask you are you engaged to be married to this young lady? *[margin note: Points to 2]*

ALGERNON (*Looking around*). To what young lady?

[margin note: Take] Good heavens! Gwendolen! *[margin note: Hold]*

CECILY. Yes, to — Good heavens, Gwendolen — I mean to Gwendolen. *[margin notes: Hold / as one turn]*

ALGERNON (*Laughing*). Of course not; what could have put such an idea into your pretty little head?

CECILY. Thank you. (*Presenting her cheek to be kissed*) You may. (ALGERNON *kisses her.*)

GWENDOLEN. I felt there was some slight error, Miss Cardes. The gentleman who is embracing you is my cousin, Mr. Algernon Moncrieff. *[margin note: Pointing with folded fan]*

Sample page from prompt book for **The Importance of Being Earnest** characters' names marked in little circles. Most directors like to sketch important crosses and countercrosses in the promptbook and mark actors' movements with symbols. For example, "XR from C" means that the actor moves to his right from a position in stage center. "Enter UL, exit DR" means that the actor comes in from the farthest upstage entrance on his left and crosses the stage diagonally, going out nearest the audience on his right.

Cues marked in the margin are for lights, curtains, and other effects both on and off the stage. As rehearsals progress, individual cue sheets are made from the book by the stage manager. These sheets are given to the electrician, the wardrobe people, the prop committee, the sound technician, and others whose tasks require written directions. In marking the promptbook, pencil rather than pen should be used so that changes may be made when necessary. It is advisable to use different colors for particular types of cues and warning signals, such as red for lights, blue for curtain, and green for entrances and exits.

When a play is finished, the promptbook should be completed with a copy of the program and photographs of the production. Frequently a school play is repeated in five or six years without much duplication in the audience. Although every production has a new promptbook, the original can be most useful for reference purposes.

CASTING THE PLAY

Few phases of production are more important to the ultimate success or failure of a play than the choice of the cast. No school activity demands greater tact, sincerity, fairness, and judgment than casting. It is usually helpful to have a student casting committee assist the director in conducting tryouts by taking names and addresses and recording the applicants' past experience. Final decisions on casting are made by the director, based on his estimates of which candidates can best capture the spirit of the play. A successful production demands that actors be equipped physically, mentally, and temperamentally to give convincing interpretations of the roles assigned to them. Personality development belongs in classroom dramatic work.

Tryouts

In some public schools, tryouts are limited to drama or speech students. In others, they are open to all students. This is a matter to be decided by the director or by the individual school. Perhaps the director will want to use a point system of stage experience and service to help determine eligibility for an important role. In some schools, scholastic standing in other departments and good citizenship are considered before an applicant is allowed to try out. In any case, eligible applicants must be made to understand that casting is usually probationary until the director has been able to determine the actor's ability to take direction, his willingness to work, and his understanding of his task.

Every possible means of publicizing the roles to be filled should be used prior to the tryouts. Posters, articles in the school paper, and posted mimeographed descriptions of the characters are all good ways of circulating the information. If possible, the director will place a copy of the play on reserve in the school library for all applicants to read or make the play available in some other way.

The tryout arrangements must be determined by the number of people who wish to read for the play, the length of time which can be devoted to casting, and the kind of play to be presented. It is always preferable to hold tryouts in the auditorium or theater in which the play is to be performed. Sometimes, however, this is not possible.

When the applicants have assembled, the director can explain all details of the tryouts, discuss the play briefly, and describe the characters. Applicants should be asked to fill out cards giving name, address, phone number, height, weight, past experience in school plays, and any previous commitments which might interfere with attendance at rehearsals. The casting committee can take charge of getting this information.

Careful organization is essential to keep the tryouts moving rapidly and effectively. Here again the casting committee can assist the director.

Methods of conducting tryouts vary with directors. Some use scenes from the play to be produced, carefully selected to find students best suited to the parts, feeling, and type of production. Others select scenes from other plays in order to avoid having students fix incorrect interpretations and inflections for scenes they may later play. Some work out suggestions for improvisations presenting the spirit and characters of situations in the play to test the flexibility, imagination, and response of the candidates. Others use both reading and improvised scenes, because some students read easily and effectively and then are disappointing when acting; others read badly

TRYOUT INFORMATION CARD

NAME (LAST NAME FIRST)		CLASS	AGE	PHONE
ADDRESS		SEX	HEIGHT	WEIGHT

PREVIOUS ACTING EXPERIENCE

WHAT VOCAL PART DO YOU SING? S A T B	WHAT MUSICAL INSTRUMENT DO YOU PLAY? EXPERIENCE:

WHAT DANCE TRAINING HAVE YOU HAD?

LIST YOUR CLASS SCHEDULE:

1	4	7
2	5	8
3	6	9

WILL YOU BE ABLE TO ATTEND ALL REHEARSALS ? YES ____   NO ____
IF NOT, WHAT CONFLICTS ARE THERE?

ARE YOU INTERESTED IN WORKING ON ANY OF THE FOLLOWING COMMITTEES?

MAKEUP	PROPERTIES	SCENERY CONST.
PUBLICITY	COSTUMES	STAGE CREW

ARE YOU INTERESTED IN BEING STUDENT DIRECTOR?

PROMPTER?   TECHNICAL DIRECTOR?   STAGE MANAGER?

DIRECTOR'S COMMENTS:

VOICE: PHYSICAL APPEARANCE —

   QUALITY —   IMAGINATION —

   PITCH —   ANIMATION —

   VARIETY —   STAGE PRESENCE —

PARTS CONSIDERED FOR:

who are excellent actors. In judging the tryouts, the director should sit a good distance away from the stage to check vocal quality and projection and physical appearance. Other members of the play committee should be scattered about the auditorium to encourage the candidates to project to the entire area.

Second Tryouts

After the best possibilities for all roles have been selected, second or perhaps third tryouts should be held for final selection of the candidates who might work together in regard to physical appearance, voice, and personality. By this time, any problems concerning rehearsal attendance, dependability, responsiveness to suggestions, and general attitudes should be determined as far as possible.

Perhaps the most important aspect of tryouts is that they be conducted in a friendly and relaxed atmosphere. Each student who tries out must know that he is being given a fair chance. Good tryouts can set morale at a high level for the rest of the production.

REHEARSING

If you are wise, you will attend every rehearsal, whether you are due on stage or not, in order to become a part of the play as a whole, appreciate the director's motivation for movements and tempos, and sense the satisfactory empathies he is establishing, to which the audience will respond later. You can also profit by his suggestions to the other actors and thus avoid their mistakes and profit by their achievements. One of the advantages of a school production is that the director has often had his actors in his dramatics class and knows what to expect of them in regard to stage techniques; much time is saved in avoiding explanations of his directions. As an onlooker, you can become conscious of the importance of developing a scene without needless interruptions by members of the cast who bring up personal problems of interpretation onstage. All discussion and arguments should be offstage during intermissions.

If you want to have fun realizing some of the disasters that careful rehearsing can forestall, read *All Wrong On The Night* by Maurice Dolbier. It is based on the stupid remark someone always springs after goofing in a rehearsal, "Oh, it will all come right on the night!" The book is a delightfully written account of actual incidents which have taken place on famous stages and which involve many of the great stars of yesterday and today.

Reading Rehearsals

The first rehearsal is most important. At it the director should expect all members — cast, stage manager, and crew; all understudies; the technical director; and the chairmen of committees involved in the back stage activities. He should make clear that the pleasure of play production lies in the efficient, happy, conscientious working together of everyone toward the objective of putting on the best production of that particular play with that particular group under the particular stage circumstances. He should point out what constitutes a fine performance — perfect timing, excellence of individual characterizations, coordination of human and technical material, all working toward a distinct climax and a gripping conclusion — during which the theme has been brought out and the spirit of the type of play maintained.

At this first rehearsal, some directors prefer to read the play themselves, thus setting at once the interpretation of the entire play and of individual roles. Others prefer to give the cast the opportunity to suggest their own characterizations by reading the parts assigned, while the director merely points out important details of phrasing, timing, and inflections. Whatever the method, the rehearsal must be kept exciting and inspiring and should build up a clear-cut conception of the play and of conduct during rehearsals. Careful notations should be made by all present.

In the first hours of work on the play, the director can sense the actors' ability to understand lines and project personality. He can also judge their willingness to respond to direction. He watches to see how much attention is paid by everyone present. If there is ample time, a number of reading rehearsals can "set" the characters and the lines. More reading rehearsals are necessary when dialects or excellent stage diction are imperative. In any case, a number of reading rehearsals makes actors feel more secure about interpretation when rehearsing on the stage.

Rehearsal Schedules

A time schedule for the entire rehearsal period should be worked out and copies made for participants to give their parents. This procedure helps parents understand how much time will be involved in the production. In making this rehearsal schedule, the director considers the time allotted for preparing the production, the length and difficulty of the play, and the availability of the cast. For instance, if

SEVEN WEEK TRYOUT—REHEARSAL SCHEDULE

Week 1:   Tryouts and first rehearsal (3 hours each)
  Monday   Tryouts
  Tuesday   Tryouts
  Wednesday   Re-tryouts (if necessary)
  Thursday   Cast posted
  Friday   Reading rehearsal

Week 2:   Blocking and line-check rehearsals (2½–3 hours)
  Monday   Blocking Act I
  Tuesday   Rehearse Act I
  Wednesday   Line-check Act I
  Thursday   Blocking Act II
  Friday   Rehearse Act II

Week 3:   Blocking and line-check rehearsals (2½–3 hours)
  Monday   Line-check Act II
  Tuesday   Run through Acts I and II
  Wednesday   Block Act III
  Thursday   Line-check Act III
  Friday   First run-through

Week 4:   Working rehearsals (full stage crew present — 3 hours)
  Monday ⎫   Special scenes — love, and so on —
  Tuesday ⎭   rehearsed privately
  Wednesday   Act I concentrated

the tryout-rehearsal-performance period has been set at seven weeks, after-school rehearsals should probably be planned for three hours a day, five days a week. The individual director can adjust the schedule to fit his own situation.

In such a schedule, the first week should complete the tryouts and the reading rehearsals. The second week includes "blocking" and "business" rehearsals and a line check for the first and second acts. The third week should complete blocking and business rehearsals for the third act, full line check, and initial run-throughs. The fourth and fifth weeks constitute working rehearsals of the entire play.

If the auditorium has not been available previously, a long Saturday rehearsal should be held at the end of the fourth week. At this time, whatever is technically difficult should be rehearsed. All avail-

Thursday	Act II concentrated
Friday	Act III concentrated
Week 5:	Working rehearsals (full stage crew present — 3 hours)
Monday	Acts I, II, III in sequence
Tuesday	Acts II, III, I — in that order
Wednesday	Acts III, I, II — in that order
Thursday	Problem scenes only
Friday	Final working run-through
Week 6:	Polishing rehearsals (all crews present — 3 hours)
Monday	Run-through and dress parade
Tuesday	Run-through with lights
Wednesday	Run-through with scenery
Thursday	Run-through with lights and scenery
Friday	First complete run-through
Week 7:	Polishing rehearsals and performances (4–5 hours)
Monday	Second complete run-through
Tuesday	Final run-through
Wednesday	First dress rehearsal
Thursday	Final dress rehearsal
Friday	Performance
Saturday	Performance

able sounds, lights, props, scenery, furniture, and costumes should be used. The sixth week is for polishing rehearsals, including stage-crew rehearsals and run-throughs with props and at least some costumes.

The dress rehearsals with full stage crew and the performances take place in the seventh week. On Monday of this last week, the staff should hold its last rehearsal in which interruptions can be made, problems discussed, final costumes and props checked, and all details settled.

If there is only one dress rehearsal, it should come on the Wednesday night before the Friday night performance. Tuesday may be spent in getting everything in final shape. It is wise to invite a few people to a dress rehearsal to accustom the cast to playing before an audience. It is sometimes wise to leave the night before the performance free for final adjustments.

Students involved in a production should be urged not to be absent from school because of their participation in a play. Much discrediting of school dramatics results from unnecessary cutting of classes and upsetting of routine when a play is being produced. With wise management and administrative cooperation, a big production can be put on without complicating the daily schedule. The auditorium should be closed to all other activities during the last three weeks, and ample opportunity must be given the technical director and crew to "hang the set."

Blocking Rehearsals

Blocking the movement and planning stage business follow the reading rehearsals. Work on the interpretation of lines should be delayed while attention is focused on movement and stage groupings. The director will have already worked out plans for using the stage area, emphasizing important groupings, and keeping effective stage pictures. However, in the early rehearsals he should be willing to discuss possible changes and incorporate spontaneous reactions of the actors. When the fundamental blocking of the first act has been set, that of the second should follow. The two acts can then be put together at one rehearsal. Following this, the third act should be set, and the first and second reviewed. As soon as the business of the first act is clarified, the lines may be memorized. It is better not to begin memorizing until the words and action have been correlated.

In planning stage business, the director must be sure that all gestures and movements are meaningful. In order to avoid later delay, he should try to eliminate tendencies of the actors to fidget, shift weight, and gesticulate ineffectively. If the actors have studied dramatics, they should understand that every gesture and cross must be motivated and definite and that the center of interest should be accentuated at all times. The director must adhere to fundamental directions when dealing with inexperienced people to avoid confusing them with too much detail.

If blocking rehearsals cannot be held in the auditorium, the assistant director should arrange a rehearsal area which has exactly the same dimensions as the stage. He should indicate the entrances and exits with chalk or tape and obtain furniture which resembles the pieces which will eventually be used.

During this period, a feeling of comradeship should develop. Both the actors and crew members should come to the director with their problems and suggestions and receive his considerate attention and advice. If the director remains poised and pleasant, many of the complications that attend school dramatics may be avoided. He is largely responsible for establishing morale, because his methods will be copied unconsciously.

The artistic principles prompting the director's planning for unity, proportion, and balance in the grouping of characters and furniture against the intended setting should be made clear to the actors at this time. It is often difficult to have them make the necessary movements an intrinsic part of the dialogue. Many directors then "give the actors the stage" and let them read their lines and move about as they please, and frequently their instinctive reactions are the right ones. Other directors have the actors improvise the scene without the script in their hands, and their natural reactions are often both pleasing and effective and can be incorporated into the planning. Such methods avoid the puppetlike following of directions, not felt necessary by actors, which ruin the immediacy of a scene.

Working Rehearsals

After all the action has been blocked out, the most creative part of rehearsing begins. Interpretation is developed, and words and action are put together. All the acting techniques previously discussed are brought into play and are coordinated with the director's carefully thought out plans. Some directors use the terms "essential" and "accessory" to describe action. The former is set by the director; the latter is worked out as a means of character delineation by the actor.

The interpretations of the roles are set during the working rehearsals. The influence of the Stanislavski Method has complicated this phase of early rehearsals, for some Method actors get too deeply involved in their own inner reactions. Always keep in mind that the director is in absolute control of the production, for he alone has planned the stage settings, action, and tempo to create an artistic whole of which the actors are only one part. He is also privileged to change his mind without question. However, individual and group discussions should be arranged, or encouraged informally offstage, where ideas can be exchanged and questions answered. Actors might find writing character sketches of their roles helpful, before such discussions, to clarify their thinking.

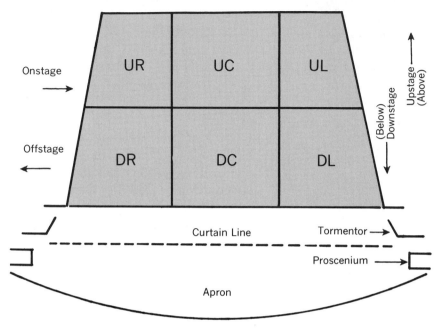

THE ACTING AREAS — SIX AREA PLAN

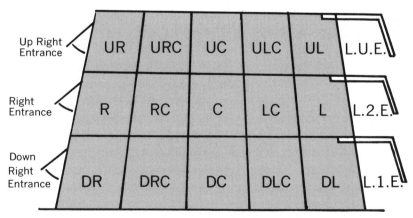

THE ACTING AREAS — 15 AREA PLAN

The upper diagram also indicates directions from the actor's point of view. The lower diagram shows entrance positions used with the old wing setting — L. F. E. (Left first entrance), etc., and early box sets — down right entrance, etc. These symbols are still used with many musical plays.

After the stage business has been blocked for the whole play, memorization should begin. Usually a date is set after which no scripts can appear on stage. Only then can real characterization begin. At this point actors should be left relatively free to move and speak; spontaneous physical and vocal responses frequently improve a scene. In fact, actors should be left as free as possible in their interpretation of lines, but they must not be permitted to fix a false inflection or swallow important words and phrases. Having the actor rewrite a passage in his own words often will make him appreciate the exact meaning of the lines. It is sometimes helpful if the director stops the actor suddenly and says, "Wait a minute. What are you saying? What is happening to your character in this scene?" As a last resort, the director may read the lines himself.

Speeding up or slowing down words and action to attain a certain mood or meaning is often difficult for amateurs. It is during the working rehearsals that the actors must develop tempo — learn to pick up cues rapidly, listen effectively, hold for a laugh or a pause, point lines, break up long speeches with action, and use appropriate body movement.

This phase of interpretation is especially critical; there is a tendency to revert to first inclinations under the pressure of performance, so no false inflections or moves, especially gestures, must become set. With troublesome lines, sometimes "bridging" is helpful; that means adding words before or after the difficult ones. Beginners must be helped to help each other by feeding cues properly, by listening effectively but not conspicuously, or by obliterating themselves entirely when necessary. Most amateurs have trouble in giving sufficient time on pauses; here it is frequently helpful to have them count, usually from three to five beats or even longer, for a desired effect. Restraining bodily movements in order to give a telling gesture or a glance a chance to register is very important.

The location of the director is crucial during working rehearsals. Most directors sit on the stage beside the prompter during early rehearsals and quietly interrupt to ask relevant questions and to give directions. Other directors place the prompter at one side on the stage and seat themselves about halfway back in the auditorium in order to check the entire stage area. Usually a combination of methods is preferable. If the director sits too near the actors, he fails to get a perspective on the stage pictures, the sense of unity of the action as a whole, and the clear and harmonious blending of the voices. On the other hand, if he is near, he can use the intimate question-and-answer to inspire the actor in trouble to think out his problem. A good procedure is to work intimately with a scene, bringing out details and correcting mistakes, and then retire to a distance and watch the entire action from different points of vantage, while he checks the clarity of key lines and words, the spacing of the actors, and the continuing effect of stage pictures. He can then have the difficult bits of action repeated correctly until they are set.

As soon as possible, mock costumes and props should be used, especially in period and stylized plays. Usually the assistant director is responsible for obtaining long skirts, proper shoes, coats, swords, hats, cups and saucers, cigarette cases — whatever the play requires — and for storing them after rehearsals.

In addition to the general rehearsal schedule, a second, specialized schedule should be worked out for actors who are together in a number of scenes. These scenes or fragments of scenes can be rehearsed separately by the assistant director. This schedule of simultaneous rehearsals avoids long waits and consequent boredom and restlessness. Important roles can often be rehearsed separately. Love scenes and other intensely emotional scenes should always be directed privately until the action is crystallized and the responses are natural and convincing.

Projection of lines is the means by which the play is heard and understood and is an absolute necessity, frequently disregarded by actors today. If you have taken seriously the exercises and text of Chapter 7 and have been practicing vocal exercises regularly, you should understand the fundamental principles. Your work now is to correlate the physical processes of correct breathing and articulation with the psychological consciousness of speaking to everyone in the audience. Remembering the last person at the farthest point in the auditorium, and at the same time considering everyone else as well, will enable you to project key words and sentences clearly. You should by this time be breathing correctly and relaxing your inner throat muscles from force of habit, while at the same time you are clarifying the important words with flexible lips and tongue.

Speaking intelligibly, not necessarily loudly, depends of course, upon the exact meaning of what you are saying. From the first rehearsal, you should have begun marking the words which must be heard and taking your breath in pauses to emphasize meanings; these pauses should also be marked while you are working out your characterization. The most common fault of amateurs is to drop the last words of every sentence instead of breathing between thought groups, for often the most vital words are at the end and must be heard.

Unless you are specifically told by the director to speak upstage, it is wise to speak front or diagonally front (three-quarter front), turning your head toward the person you are addressing on sentences of little consequence. Remember also that many small words like articles, prepositions, and minor adjectives and adverbs can be "thrown away," just as are the unaccented vowel sounds in many words. Too precise pronunciation of all words is a fatal mistake and should be used only in caricature for a definite effect.

Polishing Rehearsals

It is in the polishing rehearsals that the real joys of directing and acting are experienced. These rehearsals must be characterized by complete concentration, sustained discipline, and joyous participation on the part of all persons concerned. With lines memorized and action set, all phases can be brought together in an artistic whole.

From your standpoint as an actor, these rehearsals should bring the creative joy of developing the nuances of vocal inflection and pantomime which make your character live for both you and your audience; mannerisms of movement, distinctive physical attitudes, and subtle coloring of lines can only develop through identification with your role when you feel perfectly at ease in the environment of the setting.

Approximate costumes and accessories such as wigs and body padding should be worn at polishing rehearsals. The essential elements of the production should be in place. Exits and entrances, windows, staircases, fireplaces, and basic furniture should be onstage. Telephones and lamps should be in position, and sound effects necessary for cues should be set. Only then can the actors find themselves in the environment of the play and become a part of it. Once the mechanics of fitting themselves into the sets have been mastered, the actors can complete their search for identity with their roles in relation to the play as a whole.

From the director's standpoint, he must now make sure that the intangible quality with which every dramatist invests his plays permeates the production and that the proper atmosphere is sustained, without jarring tones, sudden movements, or inharmonious bits of

High school students in a scene from Once Upon a Mattress, *based on the old tale
"The Princess and the Pea."*

business cropping up. It is in these final rehearsals that subtle touches
of improvisation perfectly in accord with the entire production creep
into both acting and directing to enhance its appeal. These must be
absorbed and not lost by over-rehearsing; over-rehearsing occasionally results in a whole company's going stale. The director must
establish the tempo of the production as a whole while synchronizing
it with contrasting scenes. He should definitely speed up cues, eliminate irrelevant action, clarify speech while assisting the cast to point
their lines and hold their pauses. Voices, color, and lights must be
blended harmoniously. Even the music between acts, if there is any,
should be in accord with the type, mood, and period of the play.

If the play is dragging because of pauses between sentences, it is

386 helpful to have a rapid-fire line rehearsal, with the actors conversationally running through the play without any action or dramatic effects. To pace the timing and to make sure of clarity, some directors listen to difficult scenes without watching them.

The director's job at polishing rehearsals is to establish the tempo of the whole production. The rhythm of the play should be developed and maintained. Sound and light cues must be carefully timed. Telephones, lamps, fireplaces, and sound effects should function smoothly. A single extraneous sound, a slight motion, an unmotivated gesture, or a poorly timed sound cue can destroy the effect of a scene. The director must scrutinize every stage picture from all parts of the auditorium. Having worked with the cast onstage, he should then move back into the auditorium and observe larger, uninterrupted units of the play. He must be sure that all dialogue is clear and that the action is logical.

About ten days before the first performance, the complete play must be put together in rehearsal. When the actors make their proper entrances and exits, wear costumes, and use props, the director can see exactly what is still needed to make the play a success. From this time on, the rehearsals must be by acts, played through without interruption. Separate rehearsals for difficult scenes can be held as needed, however.

In the polishing process, some scenes are built up by having the lines "top" preceding ones, some are speeded up by rapid picking up of cues, and some are slowed down by effective pauses. It is possible to err in any of these directions. It is said that George M. Cohan's acting in his younger days was known for its overly brisk pace and rapid timing. However, once he discovered the effectiveness of the pause, he used it so often that it added eighteen minutes of playing time to *Ah, Wilderness!*

Members of the prop committee should have all props ready, and the wardrobe committee should have all costumes and accessories finished and on hand during polishing rehearsals. Curtain calls must be rehearsed, intermission time checked, and time allowances made for changes of costume.

Technical Rehearsals

During the weeks of rehearsal, the scenic artist and stage manager have designed and constructed the sets and planned the lighting. Fundamental units should be onstage as soon as possible in order that necessary adjustments can be made. Ideally the stage should be available for the three weeks before the performance, with entrances, exits, stairways, functional windows, doorways, doorbells, and practical sources of light all ready for use. As soon as possible, the cast and backstage crews should be working together in order that costumes, makeup, scenery, properties, and furniture can be considered simultaneously from the standpoint of color, light, and form. A sense of proportion must be established, with dominant elements made to stand out by position and lighting.

Stage plots must be made by the stage manager for each scene, showing exact positions and angles of flats and furniture. Each piece should be numbered and stagehands appointed to place and remove it and stack it backstage properly.

Crew rehearsals must establish a sequence of action and be carefully rehearsed in order that changes can be made in seconds rather than minutes. The same members of the crew should always handle the curtain, lights, and props, because exact timing must be established for every scene. Mistakes are disastrous and can ruin a whole performance.

Special lighting rehearsals are imperative; only experimentation can assure meticulous results. Stage lighting today is an art in itself; light is taking the place of paint, ensuring instantaneous effects. Any effect can now be achieved, but it takes hours of adjustment before shadows are removed, special areas highlighted, artificial sources of lighting made to appear natural, and exact moods established. Light must not be allowed to leak through flats or be reflected from mirrors on stage.

Only a stand-by cast need be called to help in the experimentation. Usually the crew can act as stand-ins for lighting placement and adjustment. School lighting equipment is often inflexible and the regulations concerning its use are quite stringent. If there is any question of overloading the circuits, it should be settled before a lighting rehearsal begins.

Dressing the stage is too often neglected in the later rehearsals when it should be done. It is often difficult to obtain the correct pictures, hangings, props, and household effects and to arrange them so that the stage looks "lived in" but not cluttered. It may take a week or more to locate just one article.

Securing curtains of the right color and texture is always a problem, but a good stage design demands that they be well chosen and properly draped. Backing for windows and doorways must be care-

Long Beach College Speech and Drama Department presents Shakespeare's Romeo and Juliet. *Note the effectiveness of costuming, scenery, and lighting.*

fully planned. Often shrubbery, garden walls, and skylines seen through the stage windows must be properly lighted to show the time of day and to create the mood. It also may be necessary to have backstage floodlights kill any shadows which would precede the actors onstage. Ample space must be allowed for the cast to get on and off the stage in character. The cast must learn a safe means of using any stage stairways and balconies, even in the dark.

These matters must be settled before the dress rehearsals. However, the planning is worth the effort if it avoids hectic dress rehearsals and a slipshod performance. "Eventually, why not now?" is an excellent motto for everyone connected with a play to keep in mind, for it is easier to attend to the inevitable details beforehand than on the day of performance.

Technical rehearsals are the first rehearsals on the stage with complete stage equipment. They are not always possible to arrange and the group sometimes has to go directly from the polishing to the dress rehearsals. Far too often the auditorium is not available until the final week before the first performance.

The first time the cast and technical crew work together with the set there is likely to be chaos. There will probably be confusion and delays in getting lamps to work, doors to open, curtains to come down exactly on time, and props to be in the right place at the right time. During these technical rehearsals, wardrobe people, callboys, and property people must get their performance duties clearly in mind and their materials organized. Actors should be trained to return props to the appointed tables backstage.

A long technical rehearsal on Saturday of the week before the performance is invaluable. All details of setting, costume, and makeup will not be ready but the essentials should be. A run-through of the whole play with changing of costumes, coordination of all effects, and curtain calls should begin fairly early in the forenoon. The assistant director, stage manager, and prompter work together to keep things going smoothly onstage. The director moves through the auditorium checking sight lines, acoustics, and total effects. The notes he takes should be shared with the cast after the final curtain. Every person involved will write down his suggestions.

In the afternoon, weak scenes can be redone, important scenes restaged, and all loose ends and details settled. If possible, photographs should be taken for the press at this time, with the leads in costume and makeup.

Dress Rehearsals

If possible, three dress rehearsals should be held, the last with an invited audience so that the cast can learn to point lines and hold the action if there is unexpected laughter or applause. An audience at the last dress rehearsal provides an occasion, too, for the house manager and ushers to learn their duties and familiarize themselves with the seating arrangement.

Usually photographs of the cast in various scenes are taken at a dress rehearsal. The picture-taking should be done either before or after the rehearsal so that the timing of the production and the establishment of moods are not interrupted. Every person involved in the dress rehearsals should have an instruction sheet listing the time actors are due for makeup, responsibilities for props, costumes, and stage equipment, and backstage regulations about outsiders who may wish to call or deliver flowers.

Note the use of masks in this production of Aristophanes' The Birds at the University of Miami. The staging and costuming are also worthy of note.

The final dress rehearsal should begin on time and go straight to the end without interruption. The cast and crew should be instructed not to correct mistakes obviously, but to go right along adjusting whatever is seriously wrong as best they can while the action continues. The main consideration is to avoid awkward pauses and the repetition of lines or action.

Backstage organization must be efficient. There must be a chain of command from the director down so that everyone knows what his responsibility is. The director is the final authority. He will usually check the makeup, costumes, props, lights, and stage before he goes out front. Then the assistant director acts in his place, receiving suggestions from or sending questions to the director concerning the lights, furniture, and other matters. Next in command is the stage manager, who has full responsibility for the backstage area. He checks the lights and stage before the curtain goes up, sees that the cast is ready, gets the crew members in their places, and gives the signals for lights, curtain, and sound effects.

The callboy must be sure that the actors are posted on curtains. He should notify them ahead of time and then check to see that they are at entrance points ready for their cues.

The prompter should not be interrupted once the curtain is up. He should have the pauses and lines clearly marked so that he will not be tempted to prompt during a dramatic moment of silence. He must be alert every instant that the play is in progress. Any prompting should be for the actors, not for the audience. The prompter should be not only inaudible but also invisible to the spectators.

When the final dress rehearsal is finished, the actors should leave the dressing rooms in perfect order, put away their makeup, and hang their costumes neatly. The wardrobe mistress can then check to see if any pressing or mending is needed.

After the curtain calls have been rehearsed, the cast should wait for the director backstage. During final rehearsals some directors sit at the back of the house and dictate notes which are written on separate sheets of paper for each performer. As these are given out, the director explains the correction and may ask the actor to run through the line or business. Other directors prefer that the cast write down the comments and remember them. Both cast and crew should feel encouraged and confident after a dress rehearsal. If there is continued cooperation, a good dress rehearsal should ensure a satisfactory performance.

Bibliography

Cartmell, Van H.: *Amateur Theatre: A Guide for Actor and Director*, Van Nostrand, Princeton, N.J., 1961.

Chilver, Peter: *Staging a School Play*, Harper & Row, New York, 1968.

Cole, Toby, and Helen Chinoy: *Directors on Directing*, Bobbs-Merrill, Indianapolis, 1963.

Dean, Alexander, and L. Carra: *Fundamentals of Play Directing*, Holt, New York, 1965.

Dietrich, John E.: *Play Direction*, Prentice-Hall, Englewood Cliffs, N.J., 1953.

Dolman, John, Jr.: *The Art of Play Production*, Harper, New York, 1946.

Gassner, John and P. Barber: *Producing the Play*, Holt, New York, 1953.

Gielgud, John: *Stage Directions*, Putnam, New York, 1966.

Heffner, Hubert, Samuel Selden, and Hunton Sellman: *Modern Theater Practice: A Handbook of Play Production*, Appleton-Century-Crofts, New York, 1959.

Nelms, Henning: *Play Production*, Barnes & Noble, New York, 1958.

Nuttall, Kenneth: *Play Production for Young People*, Plays, Boston, 1966.

chapter **13**

STAGE SETTINGS

An appreciation of the significance and beauty of stage settings should be one of the rewards of your study of the theater. The profusion of striking color and scenic effects in television productions and in motion pictures, as well as the spectacle of lavish musical plays, have increased the interest in scenic art on the part of performers and audiences alike. Scenery and lighting have become an integral part of contemporary play writing and production. No longer must the "set" be a platform with a nondescript background, or a drop with a poorly painted perspective of a locale totally unrelated to the play.

All students of drama should have a basic knowledge of stagecraft and design for four reasons: to develop an appreciation of the importance of scenery to fine productions; to better understand the relationship of each element of production to total theater; to introduce you to another realm of the dramatic arts in which you may **393** participate; and to provide knowledge that may enable you to share in further theater activities in college and community life. Wishing to act without knowing your theater environment is like wishing to sail without knowing the bow of a boat from the stern.

Even if you do not feel artistically inclined, you will find there are many things to be done backstage by those with a little knowledge, a lot of enthusiasm, and a willingness to learn. It takes many workers behind the scenes to make possible the bows of a few performers at curtain call. Backstage theater experience may bring you the satisfaction and joy of knowing that you have played a part in making a successful show possible.

PURPOSES OF SCENERY

The first and most important function of scenery is to provide a place to act — a place designed to emphasize action and conflict. The setting should define the locale of the play in terms of time — the era or historical period, the time of day, the season of the year, and changes in time which may occur during the play. The important environmental surroundings should be made clear — the climate and geographical conditions, the socio-economic situation, the cultural background, or perhaps the political-governmental system of the area. The set should also indicate whether the setting is an interior or exterior, rural or urban, real or imaginary.

A set should help inform the audience about the characters, particularly the effects of the environment upon them, and how, in turn, their personality traits affect the surroundings. We have all observed that the laziness, preciseness, carelessness, eccentricity, and so on, of a person is reflected in his home and its furnishings. In *You Can't Take It with You*, the strange conglomeration of mismatched objects found in the family living room clearly indicates the let-one-do-as-one-pleases attitude of the Sycamores.

A set often reveals the interrelationships between people, their rank, station, influence, or position in the family, office, royal court, or community. The audience can concentrate more easily on characters, symbolic elements, or a focal point of interest on the stage if the scenery is effectively designed. Scenery should provide a means for the actor to bring proper attention to himself. Elevating the actor on stairways and platforms gives him emphatic stage position; furniture may be arranged to facilitate triangular blocking; and well-placed doorways and other openings can dramatically frame the actor.

Mordecai Gorlik designed this expressionistic setting for Robert Ardrey's play Thunder Rock. *The action takes place in a lighthouse. Note the way the tower is framed and the effective use of a soaring stairway.*

In *Our Town*, Thornton Wilder brought about a strong concentration on the action and lines with a set design that has impressed most audiences as "having no design." *Our Town* has inaccurately been called "the play without scenery," but the experienced drama student will see that there *is* scenery — the scenery that Wilder felt necessary for the universality he sought. In fact, he used the most effective designer playwrights have called upon for centuries: the imagination of the audience. *Our Town* has been a most popular play for high school productions, unfortunately not because of its beauty and greatness, which are often missed because of what appears to be an obvious "simplicity," but because it "doesn't take any scenery." Many directors and their casts have failed to recognize that the concentration on the actors brought about by such a stage design demands an even stronger interpretation of the roles than in plays with conventional scenery.

Scenery should indicate the style of the production. A play is usually "presentational" or "representational." Presentational style "recognizes" the audience as an audience and the play as a play; **395** therefore, the actor may speak directly to them. Shakespeare's plays are presentational; so are many modern plays. Representational staging assumes the fourth wall and the actor is careful not to cross the curtain line. He "plays" as if the audience does not exist and as if he is unaware of their laughter and applause. A set may also reflect the style of a historical period. A number of theaters have been built with thrust stages, thus enabling the actor to apply the acting conventions of any era without seeming out of place.

One of the most important functions of scenery is a creation of mood and atmosphere. The tone of an entire production may be established by well-designed scenery. The reaction of the audience to the actors and the script may be determined to a great extent by the "mental framework" a set may create. For example, if the set is painted in bright yellows, oranges, and pinks, the audience will expect the play to be correspondingly light and gay. The emotional impact of a scene can be effectively heightened when the background is in keeping with the feeling of the action. The scenic designer utilizes the known psychological effects of artistic principles to arouse a subconscious emotional reaction from the audience. All sets should be aesthetically satisfying even when an atmosphere of fear, chaos, or mystery is to be created.

SCENIC DESIGN

Scenery must be in keeping with the author's intent and the director's interpretation. It must always serve the actor, never dominating him, swallowing him up, clashing with his costume, or becoming an obstacle course to his blocking. Scenery should never be distracting, inconsistent, or "pretty for pretty's sake." In addition, a set must be functional; it must aid the action of the play, never hinder it. It must fit all the needs of the play, yet maintain an essential simplicity — simplicity in design, construction, and shifting. REMEMBER: A basic rule for all aspects of theater from acting to stagecraft is "use the least to say the most."

Proper design adds the color and life to a production that makes theater an exciting experience for the audience. Costumes will seem more appropriate and attractive against a fitting background. A careful selection of stage furnishings makes the set and its people seem complete and correct. However, the scenic artists must always bear in mind that a good design can only be as elaborate or difficult as the talent and experience of the crew can handle well.

STAGE TERMINOLOGY

To help you understand the various phases of scenic design and the kinds of stage equipment which have been developed in the last 350 years, you should be familiar with the following terms.

act curtain: The curtain, hung just upstage of the proscenium, which opens or closes each act or scene.

acting area: The portion of the stage used by the actors during the play.

apron: The section of the stage in front of the curtain.

asbestos or *fire curtain:* A fireproof curtain closing off the stage from the auditorium.

auditorium: Where the audience sits.

backdrop: A large piece of cloth hung at the back of the stage setting.

backing: Flats or drops behind scenery openings to mask the back-stage area.

backstage: That part of the stage — left, right, and rear — which is not seen by the audience; also the dressing rooms, prop room, and waiting areas.

batten: A long piece of wood or pipe from which scenery, lights, and curtains are suspended, also used for bracing a flat or weighting a curtain or drop.

border: A width of material hung across the stage above the acting area to mask the loft from the audience.

box set: A two- or three-wall set composed of canvas flats representing an interior of a room, usually covered by a ceiling.

brace: An adjustable, polelike support for flats.

clout nail: A special, soft, self-clinching nail used in flat construction.

counterweight system: A system of lines and weights which gives mechanical advantage to the raising and lowering of scenery.

curtain: Playbook instruction to close the curtain.

curtain line: The imaginary floor line the curtain touches when closed.

cyclorama or *cyc:* A background curtain hung around the three sides of the stage, either smooth or in folds.

door stop: A molding on the door jamb to keep door from swinging through.

drop: Canvas cloth, fastened at top and bottom to battens, and hung from the grid.

dutchman: A canvas strip 4"–5" wide to cover the gap between flats.

A scene from Death of a Salesman. *In designing this set, Jo Mielziner selected details that would create the atmosphere of the Loman home but would not distract attention from the play itself.*

false proscenium: A frame built inside the proscenium arch to reduce the width of the stage opening and designed to be in harmony with the atmosphere of the play.

flat: A wooden frame covered with canvas used as the basic unit of structure of a box set.

flies or *loft:* The area above the stage in which scenery is hung so that the audience cannot see it.

floor plan: A drawing showing exactly how the scenery will be placed.

fly: To raise or lower scenery.

gauze or *scrim:* A large net curtain, which seems almost opaque when lit from the front and semitransparent when lit from behind.

grand drapery: A border at the top of the proscenium used to lower the height of the stage, usually of the same material as the act curtain.

greenroom: A backstage lounge used as a reception or waiting room for the actors.

gridiron or *grid:* A series of heavy beams or metal framework just under the roof of the stage, to which are attached the sheaves or blocks through which lines pass to raise or lower scenery.

grip: A stagehand who moves scenery.

ground cloth or *floor cloth:* A canvas covering the floor of the acting area.

ground row: A low profile of scenery which can stand by itself, used to mask the bottom of the cyc or backdrop.

jack: A triangular brace for supporting scenery.

jigger: A board used as a spacer in three-fold flats.

jog: A narrow flat, usually less than two feet in width, used to form such things as alcoves and bay windows.

lash line: Sash cord used for lashing flats together.

legs: Pieces of cloth, usually hung in pairs, stage left and stage right, to mask the backstage area.

masking: Any piece of scenery used to conceal the backstage from the audience.

parallel: A collapsible platform.

permanent setting: A setting that remains the same throughout a play, regardless of change of locale.

pit: The part of the auditorium where the orchestra may be located — often an area below floor level.

places: An order for actors and crew to get to their positions.

plastic piece: A three-dimensional article or structure.

practical-usable: Terms applied to such parts of the set as doors and windows which must open and shut during the action and stairs which must bear a person's weight.

profile or *cut-out:* A two-dimensional piece of scenery such as a hedge or bush.

proscenium: The arch or frame enclosing the visible stage, the opening between the stage and the auditorium.

rake: To slant or set at an angle. A raked stage is inclined from the footlights to the rear of the stage.

ramp: A sloping platform connecting the stage floor to a higher level.

returns: Two pieces of scenery set downstage right and left to mask.

reveal: A thickness piece placed in door, window, and arch openings to give the illusion of the third dimension to walls.

set piece: Individual pieces of scenery such as trees, rocks, and walls which stand by themselves.

sight line: A line for the side walls and elevation of the set established by taking a sighting from the front corners and upper balcony seats.

sky cyc: Smooth cloth hung at the back and sides of the stage and painted to give the illusion of the sky.

This imaginative set for The Teahouse of the August Moon *clearly indicates an oriental shack.*

sky dome: A quarter of a sphere built in plaster to make a permanent sky.

stage: Platform on which actors perform.

stagecraft: The art and craft of putting on a production.

strike: The stage manager's order to remove an object or objects from the stage or to store the set.

tab: A narrow drop.

teaser: A short drop hung behind the act curtain, regulating the height of the stage opening and masking the battens of overhead lights.

theater: A building used for the presentation of plays.

tormentors: Side pieces — flats or drapes — just back of the proscenium, used to narrow the opening.

trap: A door or opening in the stage floor.

traveler: A stage curtain which opens at the middle of the stage and moves to the right and left, rather than one which moves up and down.

trip: To double a drop for raising when there is insufficient fly space.

400 *wagons:* Low platforms on casters.

wing setting: A set made with pairs of wings on both sides of the stage, used with a matching backdrop.

wings: The offstage areas to the right and left of the set; also, one or more flats, usually hinged at an angle but sometimes parallel to the footlights, used as entrances but which conceal backstage areas.

SCENIC DESIGN AND THE STUDENT OF DRAMA

The basic high school drama course is concerned more with the principles of design and scenic construction than with the actual building of sets. However, a knowledge about the development of scenic design and some principles of construction are valuable whether or not you plan to take a course in stagecraft. You may want to work on backstage crews or on committees such as construction, properties, costumes, or makeup. Every performer needs to know the role and function of the director, scenic designer or technical director, and the stage manager and his crew in order to appreciate the contribution each makes and to achieve the *esprit de corps* essential to successful productions.

In bringing a play to life, the scenic designer is next to the director in importance. The aim of both is to create a world of illusion which will be accepted and enjoyed by theatergoers. The director works primarily with the bodies and voices of his actors; a designer works with mass, color, and line; together they create the proper atmosphere to express fittingly the meaning of the play. The scenic artist does not build real rooms, houses, or mountain tops. He usually does not even create pictures of great beauty in themselves. He uses his painted canvas, magic lights, and artificial effects to stir imaginations so that the audience is transported to the realm where the playwright's dream seems to become a reality. The scenic designer works with the four areas of scenery, lighting, makeup, and costumes to create satisfying empathic illusions; the more satisfying the empathies which are established, the better the production.

THE DEVELOPMENT OF SCENIC DESIGN

From primitive campfires to the modern theater house, devoted theater technicians have improved scenery and light design in the desire to convey meanings through visual sensations. The first important step was the "skene" building, which was subsequently enlarged by the Romans. Later came the "stations" of the miracle plays, with the special mechanical effect of Hell's Mouth.

Renaissance Designs

Stage design as we know it came into being in Italy in 1508 at the royal court of the Duke of Ferrara. The stage there was modeled after the ancient Roman theaters, solidly built and heavily decorated with elaborate niches, columns, and statues. One such Renaissance stage, the *Teatro Olimpico*, is perfectly preserved in Vicenza. It was the theater of the Olympian Academy and is sometimes known as the *Palladian*, after the architect Andrea Palladio, who made the initial designs. In 1585, Palladio's pupil, Vincenzo Scamozzi, created behind the entrances three streets in perspective from stucco and paintings. The streets were lined with buildings covered with statues of diminishing size. The amazing effect is that of a city stretching into the distance. Because there is no backstage lighting, the perspectives are illuminated in daytime by the light from the theater's windows. The whole auditorium looks like an ancient Roman theater roofed over and surrounded by immense columns and life-size statues. The space for the audience is in a crescent shape which joins the stage at the extreme left and right. The acting area is in front of the columned entrances.

In his fascinating book *The Theatre*, Sheldon Cheney traces the development of the proscenium arch from the large central entrance of the Palladian. The first real proscenium was in the Farnese Theater of Parma, where an elaborate architectural structure surrounded a frame with a curtain. Behind this frame, the actors performed against painted scenes. To facilitate scenery changes, "periaktoi" like the revolving prisms of the Greek theater were sometimes used.

Another Renaissance invention which spread to England and was still used in London early in this century was the raked stage. In a further attempt to make false perspective complete, the stage floor was slanted upwards toward the back of the stage. From this the terms "upstage" and "downstage" came into being; the actor was actually walking "up" or "down" the stage.

The tiring house facade of the Elizabethan playhouse emphasized simplicity and used a minimum of scenic effects, but the Renaissance masques were famous for their beautiful scenery. Some of the most extravagant masques were designed by Inigo Jones, an English architect, who introduced the proscenium to England. These elaborate productions, which extended into the seventeenth century, demanded detailed scenery quite different from the permanent setting of the Elizabethan theater house.

Drop curtains became very popular and large theaters were built to accommodate the extensive rigging needed to raise and lower the scenery. Wing settings were a continuation of the attempt to achieve perspective. However, the desire for perspective sets led to the fanning out of the auditorium and resulted in poor sight lines. The demand for many scenic backgrounds brought the introduction of shutters — flats which moved back and forth on tracks or grooves — and nested wings — several wings which were placed one behind the other to allow quick scene changes. Even revolving stages were tried during the Renaissance stage experimentations.

Restoration Stages

The Restoration period in England found most of the acting taking place on raked aprons, with little action behind the proscenium "in" the scenery. The proscenium at this time was a very thick wall compared to our picture frame stages — so thick that one or two doors were placed in each side wall of the proscenium to enable the actors to enter on the apron rather than in back of the frame.

The Eighteenth Century

In the Drottningholm Court Theatre in Stockholm, Sweden, built in 1766, you can see productions exactly as they were performed then in every detail. The architecture of the auditorium is carried through the proscenium arch to form an artistic unit with each of the thirty magnificent sets completely intact. More interesting is the backstage area. Underneath the stage the wooden scenery, including a giant windlass, functions perfectly, and overhead in the fly gallery are masses of ropes and wheels, rollers and pulleys, to hoist the amazing water and cloud drops and the painted wings for elaborate exterior and interior sets. Electric light bulbs of the same power and color as the original candles are in the same candlesticks, strung vertically behind each wing and manipulated as they used to be.

The Nineteenth Century

In the nineteenth century an effort was made to suit the scenery to the play. However, typical interior sets were still made of canvas drops and wings painted to represent walls, windows, curtains, furniture, potted palms, mirrors, and all the other details of a conservatory or a parlor. Exterior scenes were also painted. For example, the conventional garden and forests were replete with painted trees, shrubs, fountains, gates, and pathways. Street scenes had painted buildings, store windows, signs, and street lamps. Entrances were made through wings parallel to the back wall. These were often painted like the backdrop, with furniture and draperies for interiors and cut-out greenery for exteriors. Some of these sets are still used in isolated "opery" houses, and imitations are made for revivals of the old-fashioned melodramas.

One of the notable changes in the theaters of the mid-nineteenth century was the gradual shrinking of the apron and the subsequent addition of what are called orchestra seats in the space formerly occupied by the stage. The flapping canvas wings and backdrops with their painted doors and windows and illogical shadows were no longer satisfying to the designers, who were seeking greater accuracy in historical and realistic representation. The wings gradually "closed," forming "real" left and right walls on the stage. Thus, the box set came into existence and the beginnings of realism had taken root.

The Twentieth Century

The cry for realism was answered in France by André Antoine and in the United States by David Belasco. Their stage sets were so photographically accurate that their style of design was called naturalism. However, Belasco was so concerned with exact detail that his scenery distracted the audiences from the action of the play. Many stories have been told of Belasco's stress on accuracy, including individual selection of books and what-nots for shelves and the dismantling and reconstructing of real rooms. The important contribution of the naturalists was that their ultrarealistic sets worked toward making the realistic drama ring true.

Most stage sets today that are realistic are designed with selective realism. This modified form of realism developed because the many details of naturalism were confusing to the audience. An impression of actuality is considered better theatrically and artistically. The designer selects scenic elements which convey the idea of the locale rather than attempting to create an exact replica.

The modern realistic interior set in a proscenium theater has all essential entrances, doorways, windows, and so on, placed in a two- or three-sided room. The room is usually placed off-center and at an angle instead of squarely on the stage in the old-fashioned manner. The fourth wall is imaginary, of course, and its presence is only a suggestion. Furniture usually faces that fourth invisible wall, through

Note the details of this realistic setting for the Cornell University Theatre's production of A Taste of Honey, *by Sheilagh Delaney, which shows the top-floor apartment of the heroine. The skyline is especially effective.*

which the audience observes the action. There have been attempts, almost every one unsuccessful, to treat the fourth wall as a wall, placing a sofa with its back to the audience or having an actor look out an imaginary window. The selective realists for the most part have agreed that "a set is a set" and the audience must accept it as a room. Natural sources of light — windows, lamps, skylights — have helped establish the illusion of reality.

The properly designed stage set can become an ideal background for the author's theme, as well as a pleasing picture for the audience to enjoy. At the same time, it represents the actual living quarters of people, and discloses their tastes, financial status, cultural level, and habits of living.

Exterior sets are at best only suggestive. Plastic pieces (three-dimensional) and cut-outs (two-dimensional profiles) are placed against a drop or sky cyc. A "ground row" is used to break the line between the floor and the drop and to give the illusion of distance. As much as possible, the use of wings is avoided and some other means of masking the sides of the stage is incorporated into the set.

The twentieth century has seen many experiments in scenic design. Two European designers of symbolic sets rebelled against ultrarealism. Adolphe Appia concentrated on three-dimensional forms, **405** which he contended were essential for the performance of the three-dimensional actor. Appia emphasized the importance of the actor, and used dramatic lighting innovations to focus attention on the performer. The other designer, Gordon Craig, believed the essential message of a play could be conveyed most effectively by the scenic designer and even suggested eliminating the actor and replacing him with super-marionettes. If Craig's ideas had been implemented, the director-scenic artist would have become the god of all things theatrical.

The revolutionary ideas of Appia and Craig were carried out in this country in a modified form, especially in productions of the plays of the great American dramatist Eugene O'Neill. Flexible sets were made of screens, platforms, columns, and stairs. Psychologically, meaningful lighting and color schemes expressed the spirit and mood of the plays. The staging was in direct contrast to the lifelike physical detail of the realistic style.

MAJOR TWENTIETH-CENTURY STYLES

In twentieth-century Europe and America, the new ideas developed gradually into several major styles. You will want to know something about the distinctive qualities of these.

Symbolism

In scenic design, symbolism is the visualization of a play's idea or atmosphere through a visible sign of an idea or object. A symbol is a token of meaning; that is, it is one thing that stands for something else. For instance, a lone, twisted tree might represent a wasteland and also suggest barrenness in the hearts of central characters. Effective lighting can also be used in symbolism. For example, a lowering shadow can represent an approaching disaster — emotional or real. A shaft of light through a colored window can indicate a great cathedral. In *Riders to the Sea*, the white boards may seem like bleached bones, a fishing net may suggest the entrapments of life, the dying fire may parallel the death of the last son.

Expressionism

The exaggerated symbolism which strives to intensify the emotional impact of a play by distorting a major scenic element is called expressionism. For instance, in *The Adding Machine* one of the scenic pieces is a gigantic adding machine. Its size emphasizes the fact that it dominates the lives of the central characters.

Impressionism

This seeks to make the audience react and see as a character does when he is stirred by such intense feelings as anger, horror, and fear. Unusual rhythms, exaggeration of minor details, and violent contrasts of light and design are used. They enable the theatergoer to see through the character's eyes and actually realize the impressions he is receiving.

Constructivism

A technique which uses an architectural or mechanical skeleton as a background is known as constructivism. Originated in Russia by Vsevolod Meyerhold in the twenties, it has strongly affected staging ever since. The set often consists of a number of platforms connected by stairs, ladders, ramps, and arches, allowing the action to take place upon different levels. Although originally used as a background for plays which dealt with economic and social problems, constructivism has also been effectively used with other types of plays. It has

The Dallas Theater Center's production of Peter Shaffer's Black Comedy, *featuring members of the resident company and designed by Campbell Thomas. The cut-down scenery is set against a cyc. See also page 393.*

ANDY HANSON PHOTO

frequently been used in conjunction with other scenic styles; for example, Jo Mielziner's design for *Death of a Salesman* (page 398) used a modified constructivism in the roof line of the Loman house.

Theatricalism

Theatricalism is the term used to indicate a style of scenic design which makes no attempt to be realistic, but simply says "This is a stage set." Theatricalism may incorporate elements or techniques from other styles of scenic design, but stresses the illusory nature of the theater and the functional value of scenery. Any combination of props or scenic elements may be used if they serve the purpose. *Our Town* used ladders for rooms and a board placed across two chairs as the soda fountain in a drugstore.

Stylization

Stylization is a nonrealistic approach to design which strives to set a mood or pattern for the play. The designer often reveals his own artistic style through distorted shapes and colors or a motif repeated over and over again in the scenery, makeup, and costumes. Stylization has been successfully used in ballets, fantasies, dream sequences, and children's plays. The mood it creates is usually light, happy, quaint, or fanciful, such as is found in *The Bluebird* or *Chantecler*.

Formalism

Formalism is a style of design that has been with us for 2,500 years. It depends mainly upon an unchanging background that can become whatever the players suggest it might be. Formalism uses ramps, platforms, columns, and staircases against an unchanging facade or cyclorama background. It provides the actor with a dramatic place to perform but without elaborate scenery or distracting embellishments. The thrust stages such as the Tyrone Guthrie Theatre in Minneapolis lend themselves well to formal or theatrical design.

TYPES OF SETS

Box Sets

The box set has been the most common type of interior set since it replaced the old wings and drops of the nineteenth century, although it, too, has been replaced by other forms in recent years. The box set consists of two or three walls built of flats, often covered by a ceiling.

Unit Sets

The unit set is one which utilizes certain basic structural units to create several settings. Unit sets are quite practical for schools which wish to present multi-set plays or a program of one-act plays, or to build units for a little theater which can be arranged to fit the needs of almost any play. There are several kinds of unit sets. One type uses door or window units which may be completely rearranged for each scene change. There are usually two door flats, one or two window-bookcase flats, and sometimes, for variety, a wall with an arch-French door opening. These openings may simply be interchanged or may be "booked" together to form four- or five-unit walls; this can facilitate easy shifting and a variety of possible combinations.

A second important type of unit set is one which consists of many openings, some of which are quite large. Once the set is erected for a play, it is not struck, but doors, windows, arches, curtains, and backing units are placed within or behind the openings to simulate scene changes.

The Permanent Set

Another type of staging is the use of the permanent set, one which never changes during the play except in some instances when a set piece, stairway, or flown unit may be brought in. The Elizabethan playhouse was essentially a permanent set. Formalism works well for a permanent set. A simple doorway may serve as an interior or exterior entrance, a gate or a passageway; a platform may be used as a porch, a boudoir, a garden, or a sofa. Locale is determined more by controlled light than by scenic representation.

A modification of the permanent set is the multiple set which has several distinct acting areas, each of which may represent one or several locations. See-through walls, semipartitions, railings, and platforms can serve as dividers between acting areas. These strong dividers provide the main distinction between the permanent set and the multiple set. Flexible controlled lighting equipment is once again quite necessary.

Profile Sets

Screens and profile sets, sometimes called "cut-down" or "minimum" sets, provide further opportunities for scenic variation. Screens consist of two- and three-fold flats which are used either to form walls against a drapery background or to cover openings or furnishings as a quick means of changing scenes. Screens may be almost any height and width, but a height of 8 to 10 feet is usually the most satisfactory. Although screens may be hinged or lashed together to form solid walls, that is seldom necessary, since two- and three-fold units are free-standing.

Cut-down scenery may be constructed of screens, but the chief difference between the two is that the cut-down set is more like the box set in that it forms the entire perimeter of the setting. Its height may vary from a mere 2 feet to 8 feet, depending upon the stage openings and furniture. Colors suggesting changing moods and emotions may be aimed against the background cyc to bring about a strong identification with the action.

Prisms or "periaktoi" allow for fast changes with a minimum of equipment and space. The prisms are usually equilateral or isosceles triangles mounted to a wheeled carriage which can be pivoted. Each periaktoi is made up of three 6-foot or two 4-foot and one 6-foot flat. At least four periaktoi are needed, but for more variety in combination and position, and for more set possibilities, six or eight prisms may be used. Doorways may be created in several ways; the simplest method is merely the use of a space between two prisms. Another method is the hooking of a normal door flat between two prisms; a third method uses inserts, sometimes called "plugs," which may be hung between two periaktoi. The plugs may be shaped like ordinary doors or may be arched according to various architectural or stylistic designs. Window, bookcases, and fireplace flats may be used as one side of the periaktoi. The prisms are especially valuable for schools that lack fly space, have trouble masking the sides of the stage, or need quick changes but have limited equipment.

Curtain (Drapery) Sets

In many forms these have frequently been used as substitutes for constructed scenery. The typical school cyclorama rarely provides an adequate background for a play, but sometimes space, equipment, and budget force the director to use a curtain set which is not in some way modified. There are, however, many ways in which curtains can be used. A formalistic set with ramps, platforms, columns, and so on, may be at its best against a curtain set. The placing of a few flats such as doorways, windows, and fireplaces between curtains can often turn a "plain curtain set" into an acceptable theatrical set. Nevertheless, curtains can never be transposed into convincing realistic

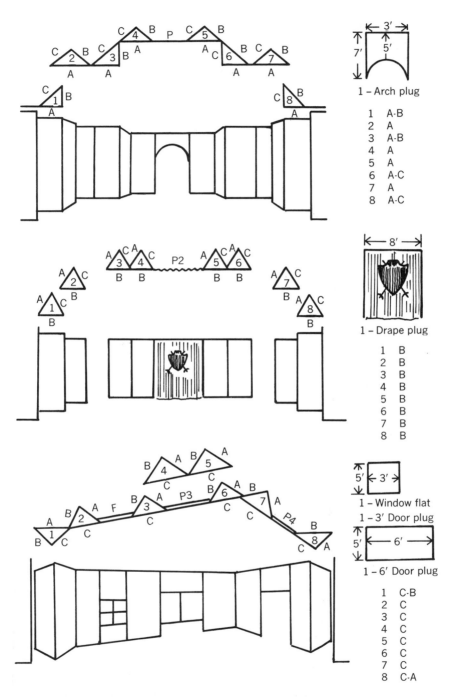

	1 – Arch plug	
1	A-B	
2	A	
3	A-B	
4	A	
5	A	
6	A-C	
7	A	
8	A-C	

	1 – Drape plug	
1	B	
2	B	
3	B	
4	B	
5	B	
6	B	
7	B	
8	B	

1 – Window flat
1 – 3' Door plug
1 – 6' Door plug

1	C-B	
2	C	
3	C	
4	C	
5	C	
6	C	
7	C	
8	C-A	

ROTATING PRISMS (PERIAKTOI) TO CREATE THREE DIFFERENT SETS

sets. One of the disadvantages of a cyclorama is that the acting area is always the same size and shape. Therefore, many designers who have had to use curtain backgrounds have ignored the cyc and have used free-standing set pieces and furniture to "shape" their sets within the frame of the cyc. See page 393.

An effective use of curtains may be employed by those fortunate enough to have a black cyclorama or a convertible cyc — black on one side and buff or gray on the other. Use of well-controlled lighting will make the actors and furnishings stand out sharply against the void of the "space stage." White furniture and clown white makeup can be particularly striking against such a background. A modification of the space stage which can be used with any cyclorama is the "skeleton" set, which consists simply of frames and openings, which may be left empty or filled by draperies, backings, doors, and so on.

NEW TECHNIQUES OF STAGING

The thrust stage (horseshoe staging) has stirred the imaginations of scenic artists to develop new techniques of set design. Many of the nonproscenium theaters are modified picture-frame stages without the nonlocalized permanent acting backgrounds of true thrust stages; one example is the Tyrone Guthrie Theater. Since the audience surrounds the stage on three sides, conventional scenery cannot be used without blocking the audience's view, unless it is placed deep on the stage. Designers have used cut-down sets and screens quite successfully, but one of the most effective innovations is the floating screen or multiple plane set. This technique employs single flats or narrow drops 6 feet or less in width which are placed at various depths parallel to the front of the stage. These floating screens provide concealed entrances for the actors and present a suggestive locale.

Arena staging, or theater-in-the-round, uses a different approach. Since the audience completely surrounds the stage, no scenery can be erected, for it will block the view of the audience. Objects normally placed on walls, such as pictures and mirrors, are often casually laid on tables. A set of andirons and a grate may serve as a fireplace. Furniture may be placed in natural groupings but must allow the actors to move constantly in "S" and circular patterns.

Designers

Every student of drama should know at least a few of the famous set designers — Adolphe Appia, David Belasco, and Gordon Craig have already been mentioned — but twentieth-century American theater has produced some of the most sensitive and brilliant scenic artists in the world: Robert Edmond Jones, Lee Simonson, Norman Bel Geddes, Jo Mielziner, Donald Oenslager, Howard Bay, Mordecai Gorelik, and Peter Larkin. Their chief aim has been to reflect the mood of the play by nonrealistic backgrounds of great simplicity which are thoroughly in keeping with the play.

Two European designers whose names you should be familiar with have strongly affected our modern trends. Antonin Artaud of France has been the inspiration of our theater of involvement, in which audience shock and participation and emotional engagement take the place of written scripts and carefully planned action. Erwin Piscator of Germany originated the idea of "total theater," in which all theatrical media can be utilized to bring out socially important problems humanity should solve. Working closely with Bertolt Brecht in the Epic Theater, he established procedures which culminated when he produced *The Deputy* by Rolf Hochhuth.

In Chapter 10 on the history of the drama, you can meet many phases of theater, scenery, and production which have developed through the ages and which you can actually see on stages around the world today.

Trends Today

Current practices incorporate a combination of styles, as seen in Jo Mielziner's design for *Death of a Salesman.*

However, experiments in the unlocalized backgrounds of thrust stages and the nonconventional settings of modern plays have introduced scenic techniques unfamiliar to many theatergoers.

Scenery has always been limited by the theme of the play and the author's stipulations of the essential props, entrances, and scenic requirements peculiar to the individual play. The fire escape and the dream-nature of *The Glass Menagerie* are two essentials to be recognized by the designer. The distortions of the antiplays have placed even more difficult challenges before the scenic artist. When experimental theater moved some of the actors out into the audience, a set design often became meaningless or changed meaning greatly during the course of the "happening." Consequently, some of the rules of design and their relationship to the drama have been challenged. Nevertheless, the interdependency of playwright, actor, and scenery have provided a total effectiveness that is beyond any challenge.

Theater Buildings

The "place to perform" has changed considerably during the 6,000-year history of theater. Campfires and dancing circles gave way to stone platforms and seats. Innyards, manor houses, and animal pits evolved into proscenium theaters, with raked stages that eventually changed to raked auditoriums. The picture-frame stage began to give way to arena theater and thrust stages in the middle of this century. You will probably see an entirely new form of theater building during your lifetime. The theaters in the cities, with shallow stages and cramped backstage areas, are almost all outmoded.

Because real estate in urban areas is so expensive, it is impossible to erect the kind of building envisioned by modern architects. It is on the university and college campuses and in many of the newest high schools that you will find the finest theaters. More and more schools are being equipped with small classroom stages, small auditoriums (connected with the backstage area of the large auditorium or having their own backstage areas), and large, perfectly equipped auditoriums and stages. There are frequently storage areas, and the latest equipment for moving and storing sets and costumes. Plays are being written especially for the new theaters, which are designed with the hope of recapturing the intimate contact so essential to the dramatic arts. The future scenic designer will undoubtedly have materials and equipment at his disposal undreamed of in the past, and canvas and wood may give way to plastics and synthetics.

PROCEDURES IN SCENIC DESIGN

The basic goal of scenic design is to enhance the production by creating a background for the action which does not intrude on that action. A set may have aesthetic appeal, establish tone and atmosphere, convey symbolism, and even aid in the expression of the theme, but if it does not help the actors move effectively, it has failed in its primary function.

Before making any plan, the designer reads the play carefully several times. Then he discusses the play and its style of production with the director, who will give him a foundation for design, including a basic floor plan. He then makes a pencil sketch or watercolor which scenically expresses the meaning and spirit of the play. After considering available equipment and material and the budget, he enlarges this sketch into a perspective drawing.

PHOTO BY BEN BLISS

A Long Island beach house is the scene for Red's My Color, What's Yours? *at the Cleveland Play House in 1970. The drawing shows the floor plan for the set.*

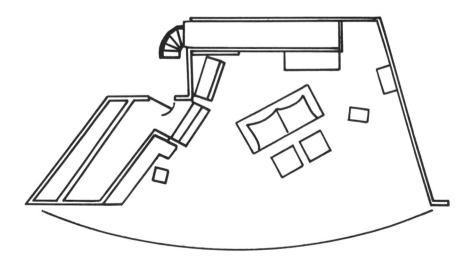

Next he works out a detailed floor plan — an exact diagram showing the position and size of entrances, windows, fireplaces, stairways, the backing for all doors and windows, and any pieces of plastic scenery or ground rows to be used. The furniture may be included in the original floor plan or in one made after rehearsals have started. At this point many directors and scenic artists build model sets as a basis for blocking and for a three-dimensional study of the design. Many directors have a model set viewer, often complete with simple lighting, in which the model can be tested. The final step in design is the drafting of an elevation and working drawings, which are detailed construction illustrations or blueprints.

If your classroom is not already equipped with an electrically wired model stage, one should be made. Plan your stage to scale — 1 inch to 1 foot is an excellent size, neither too small nor too large for practical settings. If possible, the model should be made in the school shops. The wiring should be properly checked, the curtain should function, and details should be worked out so that they are technically correct. Small strings of colored lights may be used. If possible, arrange to have three circuits of lights, one for green, one for red, and one for blue, so you can try out the effects of light on pigments and materials and gain some understanding of lighting problems.

In constructing your setting, first analyze the theme and mood of your play and settle upon the most suitable style of design. Then make your floor plan to scale, working out the necessary entrances, windows, and such structures as fireplaces and stairs. If you want to make figures to represent your characters, plan them in proportion to the set and furniture to be used.

You can make your setting out of cardboard, plastic wood, or actual wood or plaster. The setting should contain every detail of design and color, as well as the furniture, lamps, and props. Be especially careful to make the doors, windows, fireplaces, wall designs, and other such details to scale. Also be sure light can enter from backstage and overhead.

Predesign Considerations

Before designing a set, the scenic artist must obtain certain important information. First of all, he should know the size and shape of the auditorium, whether the floor is raked, and the type of seating arrangement. This is especially important in gymnasium-auditorium combinations and Little Theaters. He must determine what the avail-

The Arena Stage in Washington, D. C., has an acting space entirely surrounded by tiers of seats. For the play No Place to Be Somebody, *the setting for Johnny's Bar went below the stage level; otherwise it would have obscured playing levels for the audience.*

able space, including storage areas, will be for the production. He must know the dimensions of the apron and wings and the amount of fly space. He must also know what equipment is available or can be obtained and used on this particular stage.

If there is fly space, he must know if the flies are high enough to handle a drop without tripping and whether the system is manual, sandbagged, or counterweighted. In most school situations, the designer should determine how many flats are available, their height and widths, and how many drops and scrims are ready for use. In addition, he will want to find out how many special units such as platforms, ramps, and staircases are already constructed. And, finally, he must consider lighting equipment and its flexibility before designing the set.

The budget for the production may greatly affect the elaborateness of the design as well as the number of types of sets to be used. When several sets are called for, the designer must always be concerned **417** with the weight and mobility of scenic units, and the availability of a traveler or apron space for acting during scene changes — usually referred to as playing "in one." Two important factors to be faced whenever a shift in scenery takes place are time and sound. An audience can be quite distracted during a long wait while scenery is shifted; equally disconcerting is the profusion of noises too often heard coming from the stage during a scenery change.

Basic Principles

The first consideration of scenic design is the play itself — its theme, type, and style. The designer must be aware of important scenes and special effects essential to that particular play, including lighting needs. The functional aspects of the set provide the information necessary for a preliminary design — location of doors, windows, fireplaces, elevated areas, essential props, and so on. Since a set is the background for actors, their experience, age, size, costumes, and makeup must be considered.

Naturally, the designer must also consider the audience. Since they must see all important action, sight lines must be taken from the front corner seats and the highest balcony seats that may be sold. This means that the side walls must be raked (set at an angle) so that all entrances are visible to the entire audience; likewise, elevated upstage platforms must be carefully positioned in order that the upper balcony audience is not watching "headless" actors perform.

The designer must not forget that lamps, columns, and other set pieces can hide the actor unintentionally. This might seem to be an obvious problem that could be eliminated in design or early rehearsals, but most acting groups borrow furniture or build set pieces which are not seen upon the stage until a day or two before dress rehearsal — and then it is rather late to change blocking or obtain another prop.

After evaluating these essentials, the designer can determine what kind of scenery would suit the play and the director's purpose most advantageously.

Artistic Considerations

Unity and emphasis are the two most important design principles to keep in mind when designing a set. Unity demands that all elements of the set form a perfect whole, centering about the main idea of the play. All furniture and properties must be in keeping with the background, and, if possible, be a part of the stage design in period and composition. Emphasis focuses audience attention on some part of the stage, a piece of furniture, or an object on the set. This center of interest can be emphasized by placing it in a prominent position, by painting it a color which makes it stand out from all else, by making it the focus of all lines of interest, or by playing light upon it. Everything else on the stage should be subordinated to the center of interest.

Proportion and balance are also important artistic principles to be observed. Proportion takes the human being as the unit of measurement. In realistic plays, all scenic elements are scaled to a normal man, 6 feet serving as the common basis for design. Nonrealistic sets may make man appear dwarfed or engulfed by rocks, huge columns, or towering buildings. Except in stylized settings, asymmetrical or informal balance is preferable to symmetrical.

In any case, the central axis must not be forgotten. The central axis is the focal point in the design, usually the deepest point just off-center. The "halves" of the stage on either side of this axis should be balanced but not alike. The director and the scenic artist must work closely together because the position, number, and importance of people on stage form an intrinsic part of the scenic pattern.

For example, a strong character, who is to exemplify spiritual leadership and be the center of interest in a scene, can be placed on a height to one side against tall columns, a high arched doorway, or long drapes, with the other characters, perhaps a large crowd, below him. The importance of the strong character's influence in the minds of the audience will offset the number of the crowd, and the stage picture will balance.

The next three artistic values are those of line, shape, and mass. The use of lines alters the sense of proportion and affects the observer psychologically. Long vertical lines in draperies, columns, or costumes suggest dignity, elevation, hope, or spirituality and may be used for temples and solemn places. Horizontal lines are emotional levelers, bringing about calm, evenness, and tranquility. Diagonal lines may suggest a driving force, strife, uncertainty, or concentration. Curved lines may give the impression of ease, wealth, and expanse. Curves and angles, usually combined with strongly contrasted colors, give a sense of intense excitement. Crooked or jagged lines suggest chaos, shattered dreams, injustice, or pain.

Mass takes into consideration the concepts of bulk and weight, both of which are difficult to determine without testing under the lights. Dark objects usually appear heavier than light objects. Shape often influences both the concept of mass and the psychological reaction to objects on the stage. Remember that shape is outline, but mass is three-dimensional. Shapes may be geometric or free-form, natural or stylized, realistic or impressionistic. A circle may seem infinite, eternal, or feminine; a square or cube may appear staid or unimaginative; a triangle may seem uplifting or securely founded.

The Use of Color

Color is one of the most important elements of staging, for the various colors and their combinations produce very different emotional effects. The relationship between characters or scenes and the colors used may be determining factors in a play's success. On the stage, color effects are achieved by playing colored lights on the pigments used in sets, costumes, and stage furnishings. Because colored light makes very definite and often surprising changes in the appearance of pigment, it is necessary to experiment with both to get the desired result. Though this may be a long and involved process, it is fascinating to see what happens to fabrics and painted surfaces under different lighting.

Color almost always arouses an emotional response which can help establish the mood and atmosphere for each scene as well as for the whole play. Sets and costumes may be color-coded for both identification and emotional response. Color coding means that the emotional tone of a scene may be identified by its color dominance; for example, a "pink scene" may be that of romantic fantasy; a "red scene" may be one of anger and passion. Characters, too, may be color-coded in stylized productions; costume colors may identify romantic pairings, members of the same family, an army, or an ideological group, or simply the personality types of the characters.

In pigment, the primary colors are red, yellow, and blue. The secondary colors are orange, green, and violet. When dealing with light, the primaries are red, green, and blue. The secondaries are yellow, blue-green, and magenta.

Colors differ from each other in hue, value, and intensity. Hues are the various colors seen in the spectrum of a beam of light which passes through a prism; hue indicates the purity of color — the redness, blueness, and so on. Black is the absence of light and therefore is the absence of color. White is the fusion of all the spectral colors. As light falls on different surfaces, the colors are absorbed or reflected. A surface that absorbs all colors and reflects none is black. A surface that absorbs all the hues except green appears to be green because it reflects only that color.

The value of a color — its lightness or darkness — is determined by the amount of black or white mixed with it. Tints — light or pastel colors — contain a good deal of white. Shades — dark or deep colors — contain more black. The light colors are generally expressive of youth, gaiety, and informality. Dark colors suggest dignity, seriousness, and repose. Each color is said to have a value scale, running from white at one end to black at the other. If a costume or prop is to be emphasized, it should be placed against a background of different value or hue. If it is to be made inconspicuous, it should be shown against a background of its own value or hue so that it, in effect, disappears.

Intensity is the brightness or dullness of a color, often referred to as saturation. You can usually intensify a color by casting on it light of the same color. Intensity will be lessened if you add gray to the pigment or use a light of a complementary color. The complementary color for any one of the primary colors is achieved by mixing together the other two primaries. Thus, violet is the complement of yellow; orange, of blue; and green, of red.

A color wheel is an invaluable aid in designing, for it shows the relationships of the various hues. The colors next to each other on the wheel are said to be "analogous." For example, yellow, yellow-orange, and orange are analogous, since they all contain yellow. When analogous colors are used, a dash of complementary color will give a sense of balance.

Since neither pigments nor materials for coloring lights are likely to have pure color, endless experiments are required to get a desired effect. You can experiment with the effect of light on pigment on your model stage and on actual sets as they are built. Run through the color cycle of night to day — black, pale gray, light yellow, light red, deep red, orange, and full daylight. Then reverse this cycle and run from daylight to darkness through the sunset hues, ending with the green-blue conventionally used to simulate moonlight on the stage.

Colors are referred to as warm or cool. Red, orange, and yellow are warm colors. You see them in sunlight and fire. Blue, green, and violet are cool colors. You see them in deep pools and leafy shadows. Warm hues seem to advance, or move forward in space, because they attract attention quickly. Cool colors appear to recede because they are less noticeable. However, a stage background or set piece painted in warm colors looks smaller because it seems nearer, while one painted in cool colors looks larger. A warm-colored costume or object generally catches the eye at once and looks important. Objects or persons dressed in cool colors are generally less noticeable to the audience. The warm colors are stimulating and exciting, appropriate for emotional scenes and comedies. Cool colors give a sense of tranquility and are usually the predominant colors in tragedies. One should bear in mind that too much stress on warm colors can be very irritating and too many cool colors are depressing.

The psychological effect of color has been made the subject of interesting experimentation. It is an accepted fact that different hues of various intensity exert a definite psychological influence and produce emotional responses. However, authorities do not agree on the exact nature of the effects on different people. On the stage certain traditions are accepted, based on known reactions to color. Their use is an important means of getting satisfactory empathic responses in play production.

The following emotional values have been given to colors, and these color meanings are useful in stage design:

> Blue — calm, cold, formal, spiritual, pure, truthful, depressing
> Orange — exhilarating, cheerful, lively
> Red — aggressive, passionate, bloody, angry
> Yellow — cheerful, happy, youthful, cowardly
> Pink — fanciful, romantic
> Green — youthful, eternal, reborn, jealous
> Soft green — restful, soothing
> Purple — mournful, mystic, regal
> Gray — neutral, depressing, negative, somber
> Brown — earthy, common, poverty-stricken
> Black — melancholic, tragic, gloomy, deathlike
> White — truthful, pure, chaste, innocent, peaceful

In any stage set there should be a controlling color scheme which carries out the predominant mood and atmosphere of the production. The most effective are those which give a single impression, although other colors are often used for contrast.

Other Aspects of Design

Variety through contrast and subordination is necessary if a design is to be interesting. Too often high school stage settings seem to have every scenic element emphasized in equal strength and dominance. This is not to say that a single motif carried through an entire scene of a production will not effectively underscore the unity and harmony of design. The key word in good design is simplicity. Cluttered sets, "busy" walls, or too many colors are not found in artistic stage sets.

CONSTRUCTING THE SET

The most common types of sets involve draperies, flats, or drops. The flat is the basic unit of construction of box sets, screens, prisms, and cut-down scenery. Since the majority of plays require an interior set, you should learn the procedures in flat building, assembling, and painting.

The most satisfactory height for flats to be used on the high school stage is 12 feet, although 10-, 14-, and 16-foot flats are not uncommon. Large stages with high prosceniums may accommodate flats up to 24 feet. To determine the width of flats, we should consider two different approaches, each having definite advantages and disadvantages. One system includes the following as a basic number of flats:

Plain Flats		Special Flats	
WIDTH	NUMBER	TYPE	NUMBER
1'	2–4	Door flats, 5–6'	2–3
1½'	2	Window-bookcase flats, 5–6'	2
2'	2–4		
3'	6–8	Fireplace flat (optional), 5–6'	1
4'	6–8	Arch flat (booked), 8'	1
5', 5'9", or 6'	6–8	French door-sliding door (booked), 8'	1
	24–34		7–8

This system requires a total of thirty to forty flats, depending upon the size of the stage. One of the advantages of this system is that you would have matching flats for alcoves, bay windows, periaktoi, and columns. Another advantage is that it is easier to plan wall dimensions and designate flats accordingly. However, care must be taken that the set does not turn out nearly symmetrical.

The 5′9″ width is an arbitrary traditional figure which does not concern high school groups. Professional scenery did not exceed 5′9″ because that was the maximum width that could go through the doors of the old railway baggage cars. Also, it was the maximum width a flat could be made from a standard 72″ width of muslin.

The second system consists of twenty plain flats starting with a 12″ flat; each successive flat increases the width by 3 inches — 12″, 15″, 18″, and so on, up to 72″. Since there are no two flats exactly the same width, variety in the shape of the set is reasonably assured. Proponents of this system claim that the audience will not notice a 3-inch difference when flats are used for an alcove or bay window. There are many times, however, when flats are to be matched. Therefore, if this system is followed, it is wise to pair some flats. The special flats for this system are the same as in the first described.

Construction of a Flat

The materials needed to build a flat consist of lumber, fabric, hardware, and glue. The best kind of wood for stiles is 1″ x 3″ white pine because of its workability and light weight. The grade of the lumber may be "screen stock," "clear," or "#1." Although the cost of this grade of lumber may seem high, a properly built flat will last for many years. The boards used for stiles and rails should be absolutely straight and free of any but tight knots. The corner braces are made from 1″ x 2″ stock or may be ripped from any piece of 1″ x 4″ lumber. The corner blocks, keystones, and mending plates are cut from ¼″ plywood.

The best fabric is canvas, but its cost makes it prohibitive to most groups. The next best choice is unbleached muslin. The special stage hardware needed for a well-made flat includes three lash-line cleats, two tie-off cleats, and a stage-brace cleat. Corrugated fasteners are used at every joint. Clout nails (1¼″ soft nails that clinch themselves when a piece of heavy metal is placed under the stile or rail before hammering), three-penny box nails, or screws are used to attach the plywood to the frame. Staples or tacks and glue are used to fasten the cloth to the finished frame. Although gelatine flake glue, which must be cooked in a glue pot or double boiler, has been the traditional stage glue, diluted vinyl glue adheres nearly as well, does not run the risk of burning, and does not set up as rapidly.

The first step in the construction of a flat is framing. The most common joint used is the butt joint; however, mitre joints are better,

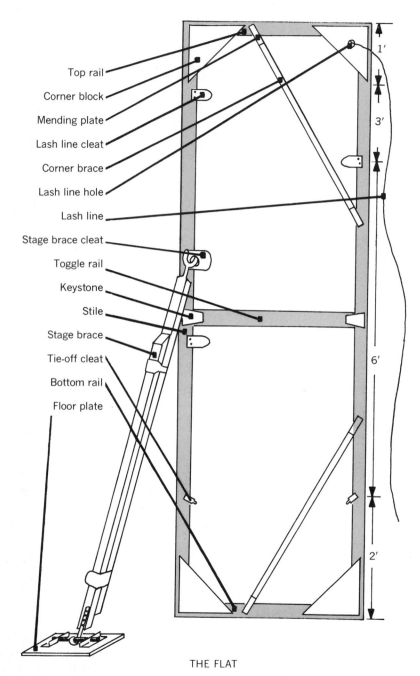

Top rail
Corner block
Mending plate
Lash line cleat
Corner brace
Lash line hole
Lash line
Stage brace cleat
Toggle rail
Keystone
Stile
Stage brace
Tie-off cleat
Bottom rail
Floor plate

1'

3'

6'

2'

THE FLAT

THIS DIAGRAM SHOWS A FLAT 12' × 4' HIGH AND 9' WIDE WITH ALL HARDWARE
AND PLYWOOD SET IN ¾'' FROM ALL EDGES.

since they are stronger and do not chip or split as easily. When using butt joints, the top and bottom rails are cut the exact width the finished flat is to be. This allows the flat to slide without splitting the stiles. This also means that the boards used for the stiles must be cut the desired height of the flat less the width of two rails. Bear in mind that widths and thicknesses of lumber are not what they are commonly called; that is, 1″ by 3″ (one inch by three inches) is not really 1″ by 3″. Always check exact lumber sizes with the lumber yard. Always measure carefully; then, check your measurements again before and after cutting. A board sawed too short can never be used.

When the top and bottom rails and two stiles are cut, the frame is assembled. The most important tool for scenery building is the framing square. Unless you have a template or can nail a couple of scrap boards at 90° angles to serve as a square, framing is easier when one person can hold the square while another does the nailing. Two corrugated fasteners are driven across the joint. Then, keeping the square in place, a corner block is nailed on with ten nails in the pattern shown. If you use a butt joint, the grain of the corner block must run across the joint.

REMEMBER: Whenever you attach anything to the back of a flat, it must be set back ¾ inch from the edge. A piece of scrap 1″ x 3″ will serve as a guide. This setting-back allows two flats to be joined at a right angle without a crack appearing between the flats. Place a corner block at each corner in the same manner.

Next, put in the toggle rail (*bar*). Toggle rails should be set at the same height so that keeper hooks may hold a stiffener board when the set is erected. Usually one toggle is sufficient for flats 12 feet or less but some scenery builders prefer two toggles. The toggles should be cut the width of the flat less the width of the two stiles. Do not measure the toggle by the space between the stiles. If you have to, force the stiles in or out as necessary so that the total width is exactly the same as the top and bottom rails. Nail in the corrugators and cover the joint with the keystones.

You can now install the corner braces. Notice that both are on the left side of the flat; if they were on opposite corners, the flat would torque (twist) diagonally. Corner braces need not be exact but are approximately the length of a rail and should extend from slightly past the midpoint of the rail to a point on the stile as determined by a 40–60° angle. Use corrugators and mending plates to secure the joint, and your flat is fully framed.

The hardware is screwed on as indicated in the drawing. All measurements for the hardware can be approximated except for the tie-off cleats, which must be exactly 2½ feet from the floor to facilitate lashing.

After flameproofing the frame, the flat may be turned face side up and covered with muslin. The muslin should overlap all sides unless there is a "finished" edge which may be placed ¼ inch in from the outer edge of one stile. Staples or tacks are spaced every 4 inches, ¼ inch from the inner edge of the stile. Fold the muslin back over the staples and spread glue on the stile. As soon as the glue is applied, fold the cloth back down on the glue and smooth down with a wood block. Carefully stretch the muslin across the frame, allowing it to "belly" to the floor in the center. Be sure the fabric does not pull or wrinkle. Repeat the stapling-gluing process until both stiles and the top and bottom rails are glued. Do not place any glue on the toggles or corner braces! Now, staple ½ inch in from the outer edge of the frame around all four sides. The cloth should be flameproofed with X-12 or the same formula that was used on the frame.

You are now ready to size — to paint on a glue-water mixture which seals the pores, provides a good painting surface, and stretches the muslin like an artist's canvas. Sizing is made from gelatine flake glue or from commercial cold water size to which a little whiting is added. Cold water size is easier for most schools to use, but needs more water than the directions on the box call for; the fingers should just tend to stick together when the sizing is properly thinned. After the sized muslin dries, the selvage (waste) is trimmed off ¼ inch from the outer edge of the stiles and rails.

All that remains to be done is to put a length of #8 sash cord or braided clothesline through the hole drilled in the upper right corner block, knot the end, and pull back tightly. Cut the rope 6 inches longer than the flat.

ERECTING THE SET

Flats may either be lashed or hinged together. If you plan to hinge all future scenery, every hinge should be matched, using loose pin hinges. Tight pin hinges are good only if the hinges are to be removed after the production. If only one set is required for the play, it is usually advisable to "floor block" — tack a small block of wood to the floor on both sides of each union where two flats meet. This keeps the walls straight and strengthens them. Stop cleats or stop blocks may be placed on the back of flats to prevent one flat from being pushed back of the other at sharp angle junctions. Walls that shake and rattle when a door is slammed have been identified with amateur theater far too often. Proper bracing will eliminate nearly all such distractions.

Adjustable stage braces provide support for the individual flat. One brace is used for all flats except door flats and occasionally window flats. The hook of the brace is inserted upside down and turned over firmly against the stile. It is very important that the brace be correctly installed; if it is not, a hole in the muslin and a wobbly flat will be the price paid by a careless grip. The brace may be anchored to the floor by stage screws or a floor plate. If stage screws can be used, drill a hole before inserting the screw. If the wood is reasonably close-grained, the same hole may be used over and over again for many years. (The dust from the stage will "fill" it sufficiently to secure the brace time after time.) If holes cannot be drilled in the floor, a wood block may be lightly tacked to the floor and the stage screw anchored into the block. Stage braces can be nailed directly to the floor, but this is seldom satisfactory, since it does far more damage than either of the other methods described.

However, when there are restrictions against the use of any nails or screws in the floor or when the wood is too soft to hold a stage screw, there is an easy solution which may be the best answer in almost all situations — the floor plate. The floor plate is simply a piece of plywood having a nonslip rubber pad on its under side and a special hardware adaptor which any school shop can make, bolted to the brace. Stage weights or concrete blocks are placed on top the floor plate to hold it in place.

Another type of bracing is the jack. A jack is a triangular wooden brace which may be hinged to fold out of the way or even placed on wheels to allow large units to be moved more easily. Jacks are often used with set pieces and ground rows. Similar in function to the jack is the foot iron. The foot iron is an L-shaped piece of strap iron which is attached to the back of the flat and anchored to the floor with a stage screw. Foot irons are mostly used when there is insufficient space for jacks or braces.

Another means of strengthening walls is the use of S or keeper hooks. Wherever there are two or more flats in a straight line, these handy pieces of hardware can be hooked over the top and toggle rails of each flat and a stiffener board dropped into the notch, making that

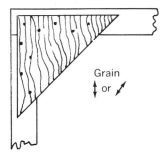

Nail pattern for corner block

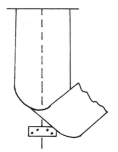

Applying a dutchman

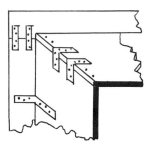

Rear view of door frame with "reveal"

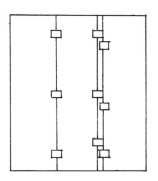

Booked flats with jigger

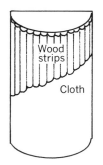

Wood strips

Cloth

Plywood cut to shape

Cloth

Wirecloth

3-Dimensional column and tree using wood strips, wirecloth, and muslin

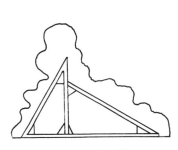

Rear view of profile

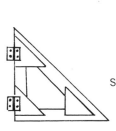

A jack for low cut-outs

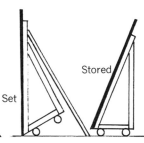

Set

Stored

Tip jack

SCENIC CONSTRUCTION TECHNIQUES

entire wall section one "solid" unit. Some technicians prefer hinged stiffeners, but keeper hooks are convenient, quick, and effective.

Once the set is assembled, the dutchman may be applied. A dutchman is a 4–5″ strip of muslin used to cover the cracks between flats. A dutchman is never used on a set that is to be shifted except on booked flats or screens. Depending on whether the flats were painted before set up or are to be painted after being erected, the dutchman may be dipped in either scenic paint or sizing, placed over the crack, and brushed down smoothly. If flats are perfectly matched, a strip of masking tape can sometimes be substituted for the dutchman.

PAINTING SCENERY

Painting the set is certainly one of the important steps in the completion of a set, but it should not be the chore it often seems to be. One of the problems faced by amateur theater is the handling of scenic paints and glue. It takes only one sour batch of scenery paint to strain the relationships between the drama department and the rest of the school.

There are four approaches which may be taken. The first is to mix dry scenic paint according to the old procedures: mix the dry pigments thoroughly, add water (always add water to pigments), and stir; heat this mixture and add melted glue sizing until it feels slick when rubbed between the fingers. Test the color and consistency, remembering that scenic paint will dry lighter than it appears while wet. One of the problems associated with scenic paint is the preparation of the glue; another is that scenic paint tends to bleed through new paint, and it is often necessary to wash old flats before applying a new coat of paint.

A second method uses one of the polyvinyl glues now on the market. There are polyvinyl liquid glues that require no cooking and there are polyvinyl alcohol resins like Elvanol which must be cooked, but once prepared, can be stored indefinitely without decomposing. Check with paint manufacturers for new developments in this area.

A third choice is the use of casein paints. Casein paints are made ready to use simply by adding water, but their cost is several times that of dry color and the color selection is not nearly so complete. Casein is more water repellent than dry color and can be used for scenery placed out-of-doors or in damp locations.

One other paint can be used, but in many ways it is the least desirable, although it can be the most convenient when shop space is limited or only a small amount of scenery is to be painted. This method uses premixed latex base paints or latex base paint and universal tinting colors. By shopping around, it is possible to buy fairly economical latex paint which can be diluted considerably for stage use. If the latex is purchased in pastels, the amount of tinting color needed can be decreased.

The advantages of latex, though few, are practical for many schools: it is readily available almost anywhere; it covers well and will not bleed through; it will not spoil; with universal tinting colors, the spectral range is possible; and you can have latex paints mixed to order at any good paint or hardware store. On the other hand, it is expensive to paint with latex; if the paint is applied too heavily, the muslin eventually "holds" so much that the fabric-life is shortened; universal tinting colors are very expensive in the deep tones; and when tinting colors are used at nearly full strength for special touches and accents, a dryer must be used or color rub-off is a problem.

The paint should be applied in random strokes or in figure eights. The base coat is usually better if uneven rather than a smooth, worked-out finish which is "flat" and emphasizes all the flaws in the set. After the base coat has been applied, the set should be highlighted and shadowed and then textured. The texturing process is the most important in securing a good paint job. The texture coat covers flaws, dutchman, patches, and so on, so that the audience is not even aware such flaws exist.

Spattering is the most common method of texturing. Use at least two colors, one a shade darker and the other a tint lighter than the base color. The complementary color may also be used to blend and harmonize the colors in the set. Dip a 4-inch brush into the paint and wipe it "dry" on the side of the pail. Stand about 6 feet from the set and strike the handle of the brush against the palm causing drops of paint to spatter the flats. This is a difficult technique to master, so you should practice on an old flat first. The dark spattering coat should normally be heavier at the top of the walls to make them appear shadowed.

Scumbling is a second method of texturing. A rag, a rolled-up piece of frayed burlap, or a sponge dipped in paint may be rolled over the walls to make them look like rough plaster. Some scenic painters use this same term to describe a texturing technique using two brushes, each dipped in a different color; the painter brushes first with one color and then cross-strokes with the other.

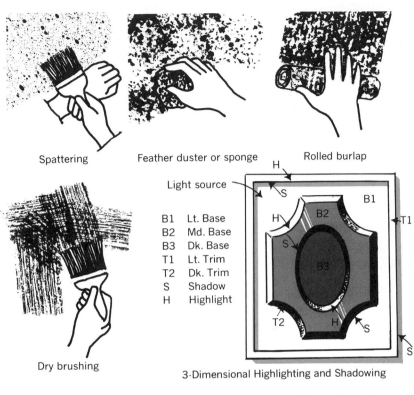

Spattering   Feather duster or sponge   Rolled burlap

Light source

Dry brushing

B1 Lt. Base
B2 Md. Base
B3 Dk. Base
T1 Lt. Trim
T2 Dk. Trim
S   Shadow
H   Highlight

3-Dimensional Highlighting and Shadowing

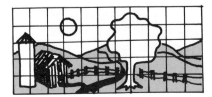

Transferring a backdrop design from the sketch to the drop through the use of a scaled grid.

SCENE PAINTING TECHNIQUES

Stippling uses a sponge, a crumpled rag, or the tips of a dry brush to gently touch the flat, leaving clusters of paint drops. The painting tool is constantly turned so that no set pattern is established.

Featherdusting is another popular and quick texturing technique. A featherduster is dipped into the paint, shaken off, and gently pressed against the surface to be textured. By turning the handle slightly, a different pattern is laid each time the duster is applied. Featherdusting is especially good for foliage effects.

Dry brushing may be used for wall texturing or for simulating wood grain. With a nearly dry brush, stroke in one direction with a light color and repeat with a dark color.

Highlights and shadows are essential if the scenery is to be convincing and alive. Before painting these realistic dimensional touches, the painter must consider the primary light source, that is, the direction and cause of the predominant light. Moldings, paneling, wainscoting, shingles, and siding, and bricks and rocks must be carefully painted, even when they are built in three dimensions. Stage lights often wash out natural shadows and all appears flat.

Profile scenery and drops are real challenges to the stage painters because such scenery almost always represents some three-dimensional object or a perspective scene. To make the enlarging from a sketch to a drop easier, the drop may be marked off into 1- or 2-foot squares and the sketch scaled proportionately. Then, the drawing, section by section, can be transferred to the drop.

One of the most frequent examples of careless painting seen on the amateur stage is the painting of rock walls. Strange "masses" randomly placed in an equal amount of gray mortar do not look like any wall. If only the painters would look at a real wall — how rocks are laid in mortar, how light causes highlights and shadows, and how the texture and color of the rock give the viewer the feeling of bulk and weight — they would have a practical lesson in "mass, line, color, and shape."

Scenery painting is an art that develops with time, experience, and experimentation. Watch what happens to colors and textures under various lighting effects and consider how you would represent them scenically.

SHIFTING AND SETTING

The most important requirement for shifting scenery is a well-trained crew who know what their job is and how to get it done efficiently. The stage manager "runs the show" backstage. His crews consist of grips — those who move flats, prisms, and set pieces; fly-men — those who raise and lower flown scenery and draperies; propmen — those who check properties in and out as they are set or struck; and the set dressers — those who are responsible for setting and striking the finishing touches on a set: pictures, scarves, flowers, and so on.

Changing Scenery

There are many ways to change scenery, including those discussed earlier: unit, permanent, prism, and screen sets. A "booked" set may be dropped inside an existing set. Screens can also be used for a "set within a set." Drops are the most frequently used type of flown scenery. Ground rows are usually brought in to mask the junction where drop meets floor, and wings or false prosceniums are used to mask the sides of the stage. Since most designers use wings sparingly, the masking of the wing areas is a real problem to the designer— the solution to which is often an even greater challenge to the crew. Masking the wings is a special problem associated with all exterior sets and, now, quite regularly with the musical play. Once again, a black cyclorama can help simplify the problems. Even a full sky cyc will close off the audience's view of the backstage areas; but a sky cyc may, in turn, make entrances and exits difficult.

Wagon sets are another means of executing scene changes. A set is placed on a wheeled platform which can be rolled out upon the stage. A type of wagon arrangement which often works quite well is the jackknife. The jackknife wagon is stored perpendicular to the curtain line on the side of the stage, usually behind the tormentor or false proscenium, and is pivoted out when needed. A second wall may be attached back-to-back to the wagon, making two sets possible for each wagon. Wagons require storage space in the wings, which may be lacking, but they are often the best solution when fly space is not available.

Some directors have complained that the elevation of the wagon destroys the illusion they desire and eliminates the use of the apron unless the actor steps down from the wagon. This problem may be corrected in one of two ways. First, you may treat the wagon as a natural elevation like a hallway above a sunken living room, or as a porch, with the apron as the lawn. The second method takes more work but the results are worth it. The apron floor is built up with a

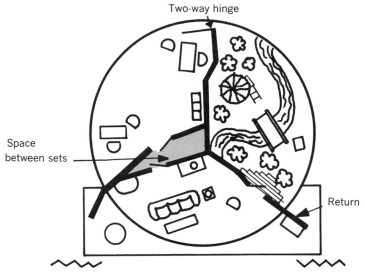

A revolving stage with an apron extension

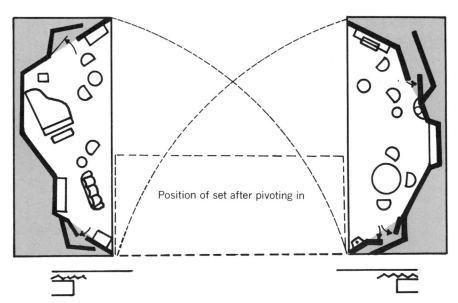

Jackknife staging using a false proscenium

TWO WAYS OF CHANGING COMPLETE SETS

gentle rake so that it is flush with the front edge of the wagon. The apron is treated as an extension of the wagon set. Hinged returns may be added to the side walls of the set to frame the apron acting area.

A revolving stage may be used if you have the budget, equipment, time, and skill. As many as three sets may be placed on a revolving platform. However, revolving stages are expensive to build and take special mechanical equipment to rotate smoothly. It is possible to build stages that can be moved manually. If this is to be done, however, it would probably be simpler and certainly more economical to bolt wagons together to make a "revolving square." Such an arrangement would allow four scenes to be placed on the platform. Of course, once a set is out of view of the audience, it may be redressed into a new setting.

Special Set Pieces

Set pieces are scenery units which may be carried or rolled upon the stage — benches, lamp posts, rocks, trees. Before designing and building set pieces, it must be decided how the unit will be used — is it only for appearance or must it support weight or operate? Those which operate — such as windows that will open, lamps that will turn on, or a tree that will allow an actor to sit on a branch — are called practical-usable. Because theater is illusion and time and expenses are always to be considered, few set pieces are built to be practical unless required to be so by the play. Columns, rocks, and trees may be plastic, that is, three-dimensional, or simply two-dimensional cut-outs. Three-dimensional pieces allow for more light and shadow effects, but cut-outs may better convey stylization and the feeling of illusion.

COMMON SCENERY PROBLEMS

One of the problems encountered on most stages, no matter how large, is that of insufficient space, particularly if the stage is shallow or lacks wing space. Many plays and most musical plays call for several sets and many changes. Sometimes the stage may be extended out into the pit area or built out over the front center seats. A runway may be built out from the center or may enclose the pit and, at the same time, the orchestra. Acting areas can often be added to the sides of the apron with platforms. Inadequate fly space may force the use of "trip" drops — doubled up for storage — or the use of short drops that can be raised as high as possible and concealed with

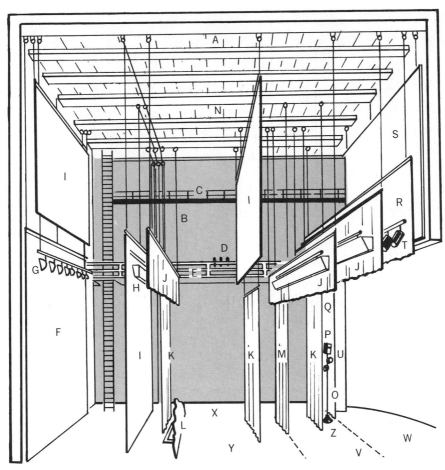

A	Gridiron	N	Spare Batten
B	Counterweight System	O	Tormentor
C	Weight Floor	P	Tormentor "Tree" or Boomerang
D	Pin Rail	Q	Act Curtain
E	Fly Deck (Gallery)	R	Grand Drape **(Valance)**
F	Sky Drop or Cyc	S	Asbestos Fire Curtain
G	Cyclorama Floods	T	Spot Light Batten (Bridge)
H	Border Lights	U	Proscenium Arch
I	Drop	V	Curtain Line
J	Teaser	W	Apron
K	Leg	X	Wings
L	Ground Row	Y	Acting Area
M	Traveler	Z	"In One"

CUTAWAY OF A STAGE

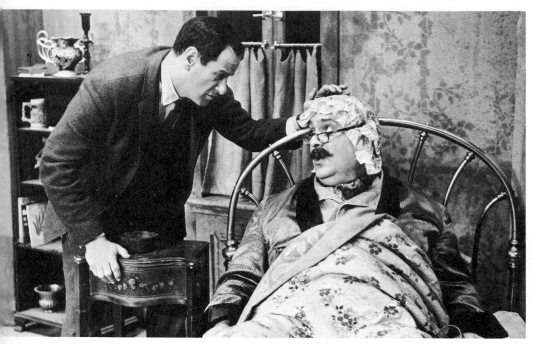

Eli Wallach and Zero Mostel in a scene from Rhinoceros. *They are both well known as versatile actors. Realistic details are used in furnishing the set.*

low-hung teasers. It may even be necessary, as in arena staging, to make changes in full view of the audience. In some instances, the "invisible" Chinese propman may be your only recourse.

Your stage opening may be too large to make a standard set look its best. Many auditoriums have prosceniums as wide as 40 feet, yet most sets average 27–32 feet in width. The grand drape can often be lowered to change the height of the opening. A false beam or ceiling can replace the first teaser. A false proscenium can decrease both height and width, as can teasers and tormentors.

Masking the side areas can be a serious problem in musical plays and exterior sets. A false proscenium or drops with tabs similar to a false proscenium work reasonably well. Screens, wings, hanging banners, and backs of double-walled wagons may also mask the wings. Of course, a sky cyc can meet this need quite well.

The acting surface in high school auditoriums often presents difficulties: stage and platform floors may be rough, slick, or noisy. A canvas floor cloth, especially one that is reversible — brown on one side and green on the other — covers the stage floor and replaces carpeting or "grass." Carpets are fine, providing they lie flat or can be tacked down. Carpets deaden sound and provide a realistic appearance to a room that otherwise may seem unnatural to the audience which can see the stage floor. Even wagons and parallels should be padded to lessen noise.

There are many problems associated with musical plays which are seldom encountered in a straight play. Most musical plays call for six to fifteen sets, with as many as twenty scene changes. Large stage areas are needed for big choruses and for the choreography. The scenic designer must take into consideration how to get such large numbers of people on and off the stage. Many scenes are played "in one." If too many are played in front of the regular traveler instead of one made for that production, those scenes might become ineffective. Dance sequences frequently require illusory backgrounds achieved through good lighting and the use of scrims. There are often some special scenic demands which are difficult to handle on any stage — fog or mist, flying apparatus, carousels, Wells Fargo wagons, and surreys. Sometimes it is better to "work around" such problems if you cannot treat them adequately on your stage. Rather than try a poor substitute, it is better to try another show.

THINGS TO REMEMBER

There are certain bits of information that come in handy to stage designers and crews. Among these are the common lumber measurements and nail sizes. These should be posted in the shop. "Clear" lumber is too expensive to be used for anything other than flats and parallels. Since muslin draws up when sized, the ends of drops should be tapered, or stretchers — boards installed vertically before sizing — should be used to keep the drop from pulling and wrinkling.

It is not necessary to accept a set that shakes every time a door closes. Determine what bracing is needed and use it. Remember that standard dimensions apply to most common scenic props: chair seats are 16″ from the floor; table and desk tops are 30″ from the floor; chests are usually about 16″ deep; stair treads are 10–12″ deep and the risers are 6–7″ high; finished door openings are 6′8″ high. Plywood comes in sheets 4′ x 8′ and may be 3/16″, 1/4″, 3/8″, 1/2″, 5/8″, or 3/4″ thick. Door knobs and light switches also have standardized heights.

Use different levels, ramps, and stairs as much as possible for interest and variety. Stage doors normally open offstage-upstage except in mysteries where it is important that a character be concealed. Fireplaces are more usable on side walls than rear walls. Watch the location of mirrors that they do not reflect lights or backstage areas into the audience's eyes.

Although most playbooks have a floor plan illustrated in the back, it is often foolish for schools to copy such a set. Most high schools do not have the time, budget, equipment, or space to build a "Broadway set." The essential entrances, furniture, and props must be provided, but the creation of a scenic design should not be stifled by another designer's concept. If the audience spends much time looking at the set and not at the actors, it is a poor design no matter how elaborate or attractive it may seem. Researching for a play is part of the fun and part of the learning; the library is usually the designer's best friend.

A SUMMARY STATEMENT

The student of drama should recognize that scenery is an integral part of modern play production but that scenic design has developed as a complement to the play and may lose its impact if looked upon as an end in itself. If scenery swallows up the performer, his costume, makeup, or acting; if the scenery is in poor taste or not aesthetically satisfying; if the mood of the play is lost by inappropriate surroundings; or if the set becomes a show piece for a talented designer or exhuberant art students, the purposes and intents of the playwright and director become distorted and meaningless.

Good scenery should add to and never detract from the overall merit of a production. Much of the scenery found in high school productions is inexcusably poor and ineffective when a little imagination, some inexpensive materials and equipment, and the youthful enthusiasm and talents of high school students might easily bring to the delighted audience a setting which enhances the total production and empathically brings audience and actor into that happy realm of the "everything-seemed-to-go-together" performance.

In order to accomplish this goal, high school directors, designers, and production committees should work hand-in-hand in the careful selection of scenic elements, emphasizing those they wish to convey to the audience and minimizing or eliminating those which would not make a positive contribution to the play. It is often the "little things" frequently overlooked that may make a realistic set look complete — the right number and kind of pictures on the wall; the knick-knacks on the shelf; the flowers in the vases about the room;

A Victorian room requires a careful choice of accessories in this setting for a scene in the play Victoria Regina. *Note how the window is made to reveal the outdoors.*

the choice of carpets, drapes, lamps, and furnishings; a flickering fire in the hearth; the shadow lines and texturing of the walls.

Conversely, it is usually the smallest number of elements with the greatest impact of identification and meaning which make a non-realistic set the most satisfying — a lonely, twisted cedar makes one think of barren wastes; three lofty, graceful poplars may suggest an Italian formal garden; six towering pines may take the audience into the heart of the Black Forest; the knothole eyes and mouths of frightening Tree-Monsters may make us want to run from the magical forest of Oz.

Selectivity, simplicity, and consistency are the guidewords of the stage designer. In addition, sets should be planned so that they may be set up and struck rapidly, carried easily, and packed away efficiently. Naturally, they should be built firmly enough to stand steadily. They also should allow the actors to move easily and safely and to be seen effectively.

Every student in a dramatics class should have the privilege of designing the setting of a play and seeing it under sunrise, daylight, sunset, and dark (with sources of illumination indicated). **441**

Stage Setting Projects

1. Select a play, study it carefully, decide upon style and type of scenery, and (1) draw a floor plan, (2) a simple perspective, and (3) an elevation.
2. Using your design, build a model set to scale.
3. Design a set for a fantasy, using a single motif or a one- or two-color emphasis.
4. Design a set using ramps, platforms, and staircases and only a few simple set pieces.
5. Design a set for an arena production.
6. Design a thrust stage and "facade" for your own school stage for a Shakespearean play.
7. Work out a scene-shifting schedule, including crew needs, for a multi-scene production.
8. Working in teams of two to four, build and paint a "practice flat."

Bibliography

Adix, Vern: *Theater Scenecraft*, Children's Theatre Press, Anchorage, Kentucky, 1956.

Buerki, Frederick A.: *Stagecraft for Nonprofessionals*, University of Wisconsin Press, Madison, 1955.

Cornberg, Sol, and Emanuel Gebauer: *A Stage Crew Handbook*, Harper & Row, New York, 1957.

Friederich, Williard, and John Fraser: *Scenery Design for the Amateur Stage*, Macmillan, New York, 1950.

Gillette, Arnold: *Stage Scenery: Its Construction and Rigging*, Harper & Row, New York, 1960.

Hake, Herbert: *Here's How: A Guide to Economy in Stagecraft*, French, New York, 1958.

Simonson, Lee: *The Stage Is Set*, Theatre Arts, New York, 1962.

STAGE LIGHTING

Stage lighting is the most rapidly expanding phase of scenic art. It is taking the place of paint in many productions; white backgrounds are transformed instantly by lighting in response to changes in mood, action, and location. In "total theater," projections and motion-picture films are integral parts of the action, and in musical plays, especially, dream sequences, dances, and tableaux are set apart by variety in lighting. Also, psychedelic effects combined with sound are affecting modern productions in varying ways.

With the improvement of the use of color in television, you have a constant source with which to study the use of light to influence emotional response as well as settings and people. The "now" films, frequently shown on NET, illustrate fantastic changes in light and shadow to create unique patterns and startling effects.

In such a a set as this, lighting is used to highlight the area of action. Compare this setting for Death of a Salesman *with that shown on page 398.*

There is no more intriguing phase of play production than working out truly effective lighting of different scenes, whether you have simple equipment or equipment which is the last word in flexibility and efficiency.

STAGE LIGHTING EFFECTS

Suppose, as the curtain opens, we look in upon an antiquated English manor house. The room is dark except for a flickering glow from the fireplace. A dim figure appears in the archway, silhouetted against the diffused light of the entrance hall. The room instantly comes to life as the young woman presses the wall switch and the two sconces over the fireplace together with the chandelier illuminate the right half of the stage. She presses another switch and the lamp by the chair at stage left brightens the rest of the room. The actress swiftly crosses upstage to the high window and pulls the drapery cord. Immediately, the stage is flooded by bright sunlight reflected off the snow-covered terrain outside. She crosses down right to the fireplace, places two more logs on the dying fire; as she stirs up the coals, a reddish-glow warms her young face. She turns, takes two steps toward the table, center, looks at her watch and utters the first line of the play: "I *do* wish Martin would hurry. It's been nearly three hours since he called."

The audience probably did not notice the room continue to brighten after the initial flash broke the darkness. It is unlikely, too, that they noticed the "sunlight" dimming slightly after the first rays had struck our heroine's face, nor would we expect them to question whether the fire continued to glow as brightly after she turned from the mantel toward the middle of the room into an area of strong light to say that first line. And, most assuredly, the audience never asked: "I wonder what lighting equipment was used for that effect?" All this an audience accepts as the effective illusion of modern stage lighting.

In the days of tribal ritual and primitive dance, the only lighting available was the natural light of the sun or moon and the artificial light provided by the campfire and torch. For hundreds of years, plays were performed almost exclusively in the daytime out-of-doors or in buildings open to the sky. The use of many candles and torches eventually made it possible to present plays in a completely enclosed structure, but it was not until gaslight replaced candles in 1803 that artificial light aroused much interest. By the 1820's Thomas Drummond, an Englishman, had developed one of the earliest spot-lights — an oxyhydrogen flame directed against a piece of lime. Actors soon learned how to play in the "limelight."

However, with the greater use of artificial lighting came the increased danger of fire. The history of theater has been blackened by the ashen shells of once gay playhouses. By the end of the nineteenth century electricity had revolutionized the lighting of the home and the stage. Today, we present well-lighted plays that may, with the proper equipment, be preset and computerized, although this creates problems of synchronization with the acting.

All students of drama — actors, directors, and crew — should understand the basic principles of light, its peculiarities, qualities, and effects on actor, audience, costumes, makeup, and pigments.

LIGHTING TERMINOLOGY

amperage: The strength of an electric current flowing through a wire.

arc or *carbon arc spotlight:* A very powerful spotlight having carbon rods as electrical conductors, used primarily as a long distance follow spot.

border light or *borders:* A type of striplight hung from pipe battens above the stage.

cable: Heavily insulated wire for joining instruments to electrical outlets or a switchboard.

circuit: The complete path of an electrical current.

color frames: Metal holders which fit into a lighting instrument to keep a color filter in place.

connectors: Devices for joining cables to each other, or cables to instruments.

dimmer: An electrical device which controls the amount of current flowing into a lighting instrument, thus increasing or decreasing the intensity of the light.

ellipsoidal reflector spotlight: A highly effective lighting instrument with a reflector shaped like an ellipsoid.

floodlight or *flood:* A high wattage (500 – 1,500 watts) lighting instrument having a metal shell open at one end, the inner surface of which is painted white, is polished metal, or has a mirror to reflect the nonfocused light.

floor pocket: A receptacle for stage plugs mounted in the floor.

follow spot: A long range high wattage (1,000 – 2,600 watts) lighting instrument capable of picking up or following a person moving on the stage with a beam strong enough to stand out against normal stage lighting. These instruments may be either the carbon arc or incandescent types.

footlights or *foots:* Striplights along the front of the apron to throw light up and back toward the acting area.

fresnel spot: A highly efficient spotlight featuring a fresnel or stepped lens, designed in a series of concentric circles, which projects a clear, strong light with a soft edge.

fuse: A protective device set in an electric current and destroyed by the passage of excessive current.

gelatin and *glass roundels:* Transparent color media placed on lighting instruments to produce different colors.

kill: Command to turn a light off.

light cue sheet: The lighting technician's guide for all dimmer readings and settings at act or scene openings and all lighting changes.

light plot: Diagram showing the placing of the instruments and plugging system, and where the beams from all the instruments fall.

linnebach projector: A lantern for projecting images from a slide onto a backdrop from the rear of the backdrop.

load: The wattage of lights and electrical pieces of equipment supplied by one circuit; an overload will burn out a fuse.

pin connector or *slip pin connector:* A special stage connector used for joining cables or instruments.

quartz lights: A new type of spotlight using a quartz filament. The bulb has a longer life and gives a much greater amount of light for the same wattage lamp than does an incandescent lamp.

spill: Light that strikes outside the intended area — as on the grand drape, proscenium, or upper walls.

spotlight or *spot:* A metal-encased lighting instrument having a lens and a mirror which gives out a concentrated light and can be directed specifically. It is used to light acting areas. In wattage, it varies from 250 to 1,500.

stage plug: A special male connector consisting of a wood or fiber body and broad copper contact. Its use is declining.

strip lights or *strips:* Lamps arranged in metal troughs.

switchboard: The panel which holds the dimmers, switches, and fuses. Ideally, all stage circuits are united in this one board so that they may be switched on and off by one operator. A board may have any number of circuits and/or dimmers. A portable switchboard is often the most satisfactory type for the school theater.

throw: The distance from a lighting instrument to the area to be lit.

tower: A platform on which lights may be hung.

tree or *tormentor tree:* A polelike stand having horizontal pipe (arms) for hanging lights, usually located behind the proscenium or tormentor.

twist lock connector: A type of stage connector which when inserted and twisted will not pull apart.

voltage: The force with which electric current goes through a wire.

wash: To bathe walls in light.

wash out: The drain (absorption) of color by light, leaving the actor, costume, or scenery lifeless.

wattage: The measurement of electric power; all lighting instruments, lamps, dimmers, and fuses are given wattage ratings to denote their electrical capacities.

NECESSARY EQUIPMENT

The ideal lighting equipment for the school stage is that which is flexible, efficient, and economical. Of these, flexibility is the most important consideration in the selection of equipment and the primary factor to be considered when facing budgetary limitations. Flexibility is determined by (1) mobility — how easily the instrument may be moved about the auditorium according to the needs of various productions; (2) control — how easily the amount of light can be controlled, usually by a dimmer panel; and (3) multiple service — the capability of a lighting instrument to be used for area lights, border lights, cyclorama lights, and so on. The type of instrument which meets these three requisites most effectively is the versatile spotlight, which provides the best control of light distribution.

When determining the lighting equipment needed, one must consider the availability and number of dimmers, the size of the stage, especially the depth of the acting area as well as of the apron; the height of the theater ceiling or the distance to the balcony rail, the availability of mounting locations and, of course, the budget. However, every high school should try to have the following minimum equipment.

The light panel is the first equipment of importance; its dimmer board allows the operator to choose which dimmer will control the brightness of the light of any given instrument. One of the best types

Note how lighting is used in this scene from Rashomon *as produced by the Drama Department of Hofstra University at Hempstead, Long Island, New York.*

COURTESY OF HOFSTRA UNIVERSITY

suitable for the high school stage has plugs, connected to each outlet or instrument in the auditorium, which may be inserted into a "patch-board," much like a telephone switchboard.

The stage cable and connectors are most important to the safe conduction of electricity. The danger of overloads, shorts, and fires is very great on the stage, and proper means of completing an electrical circuit are often overlooked.

The lighting instruments are as follows:

1. Ellipsoidal reflector spotlight of 500 – 1000 watts which provides the most important lighting. (These spotlights are mounted in the ceiling or on balcony rails.) Since these instruments normally operate in pairs, each pair lighting an area approximately 10 feet in diameter, six are needed for the normal set opening of 28 to 32 feet; but stages having 40-foot prosceniums should have eight ellipsoidals if the entire width is to be illuminated. The ellipsoidal spotlight gets its name from the shape of its special reflector, which enables the instrument to produce several times the light efficiency of the old box spotlights.

2. Fresnels — On a pipe just behind the grand drape a minimum of six to eight 500-watt fresnels should be located (250 – 400 watt baby spots may be substituted, although they are not as desirable).

3. Floodlights — Every stage needs at least two floodlights for special effects such as sunlight and moonlight. If a cyclorama is to be lighted, more floods may be necessary. Some stage aprons are efficiently lighted by a special flood called the beam light. Three to four beam lights would be sufficient to cover the apron.

4. Border lights — Three to four 3-circuit border lights are necessary for general stage use and for scenic color blending.

5. Follow spot — At least one follow spot is essential for every stage, although its use is rather limited in play production.

6. Portable strip lights — These are to be preferred over permanently mounted footlights. These may be used as footlights, backing or entrance lighting, or cyclorama lighting. Again, three circuits are necessary.

Other desirable equipment would include additional ellipsoidal reflectors for mounting on the side walls of the auditorium or just behind the proscenium; additional fresnels for the first batten, including two 3-inch fresnels; the previously mentioned beam lights; a second follow spot; possibly "black light" units and special effects projectors. (These special effects instruments create clouds, rain, flames, building, and scenic backgrounds, but are quite expensive.)

Also needed are pipe clamps for hanging the instruments, color frames for each spotlight and flood, and color media (roundels for striplights, gelatin or the newer plastic gels — Cinemoid and Roscolene). The best colors for the roundels in the borders and footlights are red, blue, and green. Amber is sometimes substituted for the green and this choice is wise if the light panel is one of toggle switches rather than dimmers or if a stronger overhead light is desired. The delicate colors are the most preferred gelatins in use today: DuBarry or flesh pinks, straws, ambers — especially bastard amber (light scarlet) — are some of the warm colors used; and special lavender, surprise pink, steel and daylight blue are some of the best cool color gelatins. Sometimes frost and chocolate are used for special effects, and green-blue makes a better night scene than blues or violets.

New types of lighting equipment are constantly being developed to meet the needs of the modern stage. One of the most revolutionary is the quartz-light equipment, which is initially expensive to purchase, but more than pays for itself by providing a most efficient light at far less cost than incandescent bulbs. A 400-watt quartz light will more than double the light output of a conventional 500-watt fresnel, with four times the bulb life. Another important advantage is that quartz lamps may be burned in any position.

Another development is that of the high wattage incandescent or quartz follow spot, which, at one-third the initial investment of a carbon arc spot, provides a brilliant light nearly equal to most arc spots at ranges up to 150 feet, without many of the problems often associated with the arc equipment.

Although financially not feasible for most high schools, highly refined electronic light panels have been developed which may be programmed to handle automatically all lighting changes in a production or series of productions.

BASIC LIGHTING PRINCIPLES

The most effective lighting takes into consideration the natural light sources on the set — the sun or moon, a window, a streetlight, lamps, chandeliers, fireplaces, TV's or radios, candles, lanterns. In order to avoid a pasteboard-figure effect, spotlights are usually operated in pairs, with warm colors coming from one side of the stage (the direction of the natural light) and cool colors from the opposite side (the diffused or reflected light). Each spotlight is aimed at a 45° angle toward the area to be lighted (see drawing). This results in the most

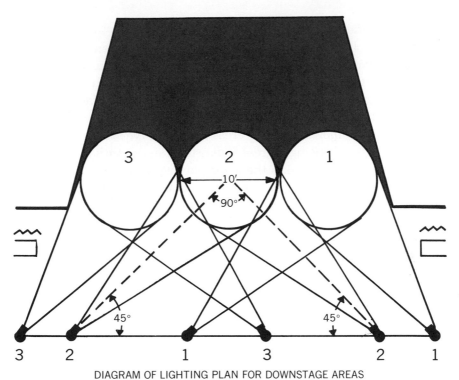

DIAGRAM OF LIGHTING PLAN FOR DOWNSTAGE AREAS

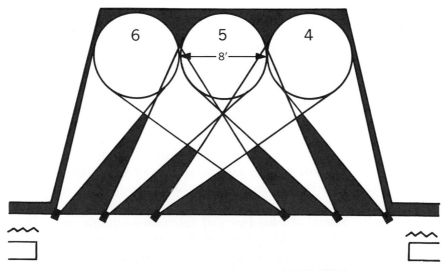

DIAGRAM OF LIGHTING PLAN FOR UPSTAGE AREAS

dramatic effect of highlight and shadow. Always to be avoided is straight-on lighting from centrally located instruments which wipes out all form and depth. Observe people around you under varying light conditions to note the natural highlighting and shadowing which bring interest, variety, and dimension to the human face. It is these qualities that the lighting designer attempts to recreate.

The most important acting areas need to have stronger concentrations of light. Bringing a greater distribution (quantity) of light into a given acting area makes the actor playing in that area stand out in emphatic contrast to the other actors and the set. The technical director and the stage electricians may help shift the focus of attention back and forth by the smooth flow of light from one actor or area to another throughout the play.

Without doubt, lighting is the most important element in scenic design, for it affects the creation of mood and atmosphere. The exuberant nature of a "bouncy" musical play is heightened by the gaiety of a brightly illuminated stage, and a mystery takes on a spine-tingling quality when the high walls and deep recesses of a deserted mansion are lost in the depths of shadow where undiscovered dangers may be lurking. An eerie fog, an iridescent liquid in a witch's cauldron, the ghostly whiteness of a full moon, the aura of intrigue and death in the shadowy alleys of the world of counterespionage, or the gay frivolity of the Mardi Gras—all of these may be created by the right distribution and brightness of light from carefully selected instruments; this is effective stage lighting.

As a general rule, tragedies and serious dramas emphasize cool colors, whereas comedies stress warm colors. However, the scenic designer should never allow actors to be lost in unintentional pockets of dark shadows. Nor should he try to eliminate all shadows by generalized bright light; the result of this is one huge flat glow of light — the most common lighting error of the high school stage. This problem stems from the incorrect notion that lighting a set means turning all border and footlights on full. This garish amber-white light makes the actor "dead" on the stage or makes him "disappear" into the set. Many of the most successful designers today use spotlights and floods exclusively; others add borders and foots for blending only. In any case, strong lights should be kept off the walls of a set; most designers would go so far as to suggest keeping the upper walls in shadow.

Most lighting changes should be a gradual blending by what is called a "cross-fade." This means simply that some lights are gradu-

Willowbrook High School in Villa Park, Illinois, used a stylized setting for their production of My Heart's in the Highlands. *Lighting becomes very important when a set of this type is used.*

ally "coming up" at the same time others are dimming down. The audience should not be consciously aware that a change is taking place. This necessitates light changes beginning far enough in advance that the technician can accomplish his desired effects smoothly.

There are some general considerations to remember when working with stage lights. Brightly-lighted scenes, especially of the type frequently found in musical plays, can cause serious changes in makeup and costumes. Strong amber can turn colorful fabrics into a drab brown; a strong red may wash the rouge out of the faces.

Night scenes are always difficult to light without having costumes and makeup turn black under a bluish light. When lighting scenes to be played in the "dark," it is always best to have some light even if no attempt is made to represent natural light sources. An unlighted stage is dead! Figures outlined against a moonlit window, a shaft of light through a window or skylight, a crack of light from under a door, or the glow of an old-fashioned street light may provide a realistic "source" for the stage light. However, if no other choice is left, a beam or two of colored light that is there solely for the reason that the actors must be seen may meet the requirements for light. The audience should never be left completely in the dark for more than a few seconds.

The effect of light on color is difficult to predict accurately because of the relationship between light and pigments and dyes, but there are some generalizations which may be made:

red light on red	—	red
red light on blue	—	violet
red light on green	—	gray
red light on yellow	—	orange
red light on purple	—	red
blue light on red	—	violet-black
blue light on blue	—	blue
blue light on green	—	green
blue light on yellow	—	green
blue light on orange	—	brown
amber light on red	—	brown
amber light on blue	—	greenish-orange
amber light on green	—	greenish-orange
amber light on violet	—	red
green light on red	—	black
green light on green	—	green
yellow light on blue	—	blue-green
yellow light on green	—	green
yellow light on violet	—	brown

Curtains, costumes, and furnishings also are affected by light. The smooth, shiny fabrics reveal light and shadows. The heavy, coarse materials, no matter how inexpensive, absorb much light and often appear quite expensive to the audience; outing flannel may look like expensive velour. The important consideration is the brilliance of the color of the material and the color of the stage lighting for the scene in which the material is to be used. Patterns and prints cause many problems, as do several colors in the same costume. Lighting of period plays is always difficult, for the mixture of lace, silk, velvet, wigs, and makeup is a technician's nightmare.

SPECIAL LIGHTING EFFECTS

Lighting is probably the designer's most versatile source of special effects, accomplishing such feats as pinpointing a face in a crowd, changing the stage into a blazing inferno, "suspending animation" as in the Soho Square scene of *My Fair Lady*, or creating the illusion of a silent movie by the use of a flicker wheel or strobe.

Douglas Campbell and Fredric March are shown here in Gideon, *a play by Paddy Chayefsky. Lighting is used effectively to reveal their faces.*

ZODIAC PHOTOGRAPHERS

One of the most striking scenic-lighting combinations is that of using a scrim (gauze drop). Lighting a scrim from the front makes it nearly opaque and lighting it from behind makes it semitransparent. Scrims, properly lighted, may help create fog, mist, or dream scenes. Actors and cut-out scenery may be silhouetted against the scrim by back lighting. In the Broadway presentation of *The Sound of Music*, the designer elected to represent the Austrian Alps by an outline silhouette of mountains and trees. Maria was nearly imperceptible as she reclined on a cut-out limb until both she and the lighting came to life with the song "The Sound of Music."

Painting or dyeing a scrim makes an impressive traverse curtain which provides a fine background for short scenes, especially in musical plays. Such a painted scrim can also create the illusion of "passing through." In *The Music Man*, for example, a scrim might be painted to represent the outside of the Madison Public Library. With front lighting, the scrim looks like any ordinary drop, but when the lights come up in the library (behind the scrim), the audience feels as if they have passed directly through its walls. **455**

In this production of The Changeling *by Thomas Middleton and William Rawley at the Cornell University Theatre, proper lighting is especially important.*

Another impressive use of a scrim and lighting has been used in the famous ballet scene of *Oklahoma!* Not only did proper lighting bring about the dreamlike quality of the dance, but the aiming of a spotlight down the fabric from directly above created a beautifully haloed "chapel of light" for the "wedding" sequence.

The Curious Savage has one of the most moving final scenes of plays frequently presented on the high school stage. By aiming a strong light from above and to the side, the "guests" of The Cloisters appear as figurines in the wished-for world of their inner dreams, where fantasy becomes reality and reality becomes unreal. It is only through lighting techniques that such illusions can be established.

One of the more unusual effects possible with light utilizes what normally is considered a negative effect of light. A standard makeup is applied, over which makeup using colors washed out under the normal stage light is placed. By changing the dominant lighting colors or by having the character move into the beam of a special spot, the actor may suddenly assume the mask of Death, the features of Satan, or the ugliness of a Mr. Hyde as the "invisible" makeup is seen.

When considering unique special effects, few techniques match the possibilities for the unusual which can be attained by the use of "blacklight." Many new colors of luminous paint, paper, and fabrics have been developed which have increased the flexibility and variety of "blacklight" uses.

PLANNING THE LIGHTING

The lighting for every production should be worked out carefully just as soon as the needs for costumes, makeup, scenery, and furnishings have been determined. Taking into consideration the information provided by the director and the scenic designer, the lighting technician works out the light plot and the lighting cue sheet (see illustrations). The light plot shows the location of each lighting instrument and the area or object each illuminates. Almost all important acting areas need paired spotlights. However, some locations, such as doorways and windows, may be adequately lighted by one spot.

Once the light plot is prepared, the lighting technician can work out the cue sheet. By carefully studying the script, he can indicate on the cue sheet how the light board is to be set up for each scene; what changes are to take place; which controls, which instruments, what setting to use; and the length of time each change is to take. These are listed chronologically as they appear in the play, including warning cues, execution cues, and timing cues, that is, how to count the time during a change. It might be mentioned at this point that the matter of timing is of great importance. One of the disadvantages of some electronic systems is that they are on timed settings and if the production gets off schedule, the lighting cues do not synchronize.

Lighting may be preplanned, but since the effects of light on any particular surface or color are unpredictable, the only means of properly lighting a production is by trying things out under the lights. A play can easily have its impact destroyed by poor lighting.

All lighting cues need to be worked out in rehearsals, although it saves the time and the patience of the director and his cast if most preliminary run-throughs and experimentations can be done in technical rehearsals held apart from the cast rehearsals.

The lighting technicians need to see that all equipment is in working order, that cables are not laid where they may be tripped over, that square knots or twist lock connectors secure each connection, that faded gels are replaced, and that any instruments which might

DIMMER	AREA	INSTRUMENT NUMBER	INSTRUMENT TYPE	STAGE MAIN OR STAGE MASTER	INDEPENDENT OR PROPORTIONAL	GEL	SETTING
M₁	#1 MICHAEL'S ROOM	—	—	—	–	——	10
H	" "	9,12 15,17	500 W FRESNEL	M	P	D.PINK SP.LAV.	6
2ₗ	" "	10,13 16,18	"	M	P	B.AMB. ST.BLUE	10
3ₗ	SKYLIGHT SPECIAL	11 19	500 W. ELLIP.	M	I	FLESH ST.BLUE	5
M₂	#2 HOTEL LOBBY	2,3 7,8	750 W ELLIP.	M	I	B.AMB D.BLUE	8
1₂	" "	14,19 23,25	500 W FRESNEL	MS	I	D.PINK SP.LAV	7
1₂	" "	2ₗ, 28	500 W NEL	MS	I	D.PINK SP.LAV	8

LIGHTING PLAN FOR:

LIGHTING CUE SHEET FOR:

CUE NO.	PAGE	CONTROL NO.	AREA	START CUE	RDG.	COMPLETE CUE	RDG.
1	3	M₁ M₂ M3	1,2,3	FOGHORN	0	BOATSWAIN'S WHISTLE	8
2	3	12,14	6,8	FRANK:"DO YOU THINK..."	0	PHIL:"I DON'T BELIEVE IT"	10
3	5	M₁ M₂ M3 12,14	1,2,3 6,8,	SCREAM (KILL)	8 10	(IMMEDIATE BLACKOUT)	0
4	8	M₁ M₂ M3 M4 M5	1,2,3 4,5	CAR COMING UP DRIVE	0	CAR STOP	10

have been accidentally moved by actors or crew during scene shifts have been realigned. The lighting crew needs to be alert to the dangers of reflective surfaces — mirrors, highly polished furniture, glass-fronted cabinets, sequins, jewels — anything which might throw a blinding light into the eyes of the audience or reveal backstage areas.

There are three problems common to schools and little theater groups which should be discussed. The first concerns the matter of cues. The ideal location for the light panel is in a booth at the rear of the auditorium where the technician may watch the action on the stage and see his effects as the audience sees them. However, most stages have the light panel at floor level or on an elevated platform stage right. Frequently the technician cannot see the actor and must listen for verbal cues, signals from other crew members in the wings or booth, or must depend on count-cues.

There are two ways to overcome the embarrassment of an actor standing with his hand on a light switch for five seconds waiting for the lights to change. One solution, of course, is to wire the on-stage lights directly to the power source so they are truly operational as in a home. A second method is to wire an on-stage switch to a pilot or cue light located on the wall directly behind the switch or, better still, by the light panel itself. When a switch is thrown, the pilot operates just like the on-stage lights, and the fraction of a second delay for the crew's reaction is imperceptible to the audience.

The second problem is more difficult to solve — that of the school having no dimmers or having the available dimmer linked directly to border or footlights only. An imaginative designer can devise various "tricks" by which he can get the necessary lights on by flipping toggle switches, but, after a short time, their uniqueness will wear off and he must return to "lights on, lights off." One can always use homemade dimmers, but a couple of small auto transformers would probably be the best low-cost investment. Several lights can be wired in a bypass system which uses the same dimmer. Unfortunately, good lighting effects demand a good dimmer panel and makeshift substitutes are only substitutes.

The third common problem faced by many schools and community theater groups is the limitations of a low budget. However, small spotlights and floods are not really too expensive, even for small schools; and their purchase makes fine money-raising projects for drama clubs, parents' groups, or class gifts. Still, some fine effects can be achieved by imaginative use of 150-watt PAR's or reflector floods which call for a very nominal cash outlay. It has been so widely acknowledged that good lighting is essential to modern theater that a series of good productions may soon pay for a large portion of the cost of new equipment merely as a result of increased ticket sales.

Summary

1. Effective lighting demands control over the distribution, brightness, movement, and color of light on the stage.

2. Highlights and shadows are essential for depth, interest, and variety.

3. Light has strange effects on dyes, pigments, textures, and materials; this fact necessitates testing under production lighting.

4. Lighting is the designer's number one source of special effects.

5. Lighting, more than anything else on the stage, indicates mood, atmosphere, and time most effectively.

Lighting Projects

1. Design the lighting plot for a play having an interior set, bearing in mind natural light sources (sunlight, lamps, fireplaces, and so on).
2. Design the lighting for an arena production to be presented in a lunchroom, gym, and so on.
3. Prepare lighting cue sheets based on the lighting design you have prepared.
4. Demonstrate the effects of different colors of light on different colors and textures of fabrics.
5. Set up a demonstration to illustrate the lighting color wheel by projecting overlapped patterns of red, blue, and green filters onto a large sheet of white paper.
6. Use lighting as the basis for a set design to suggest depth, time changes, or acting planes.

Bibliography

Fuchs, Theodore: *Stage Lighting*, Little, Brown, Boston, 1929.

McCandless, Stanley: *A Method of Lighting the Stage*, Theatre Arts, New York, 1954.

Selden, Samuel, and Hunton Sellman: *Stage Scenery and Lighting*, Appleton-Century-Crofts, New York, 1959.

15

COSTUMING

One of the integral parts of play production which suffers most on the high school stage is costuming. The actor must realize that his costume is not merely a means of characterizing his role as attractively as possible, but that in its color and silhouette it is a vital part of the stage design. One inharmonious costume, no matter how beautiful it may be in itself or how becoming to the actor, can ruin an atmospheric effect. The wise director will work out the costuming for the entire play well in advance of the dress rehearsal in order to avoid the necessity of last-minute changes. Because proper costuming is difficult and expensive, it is usually the first aspect of production to go under the "economy axe."

EFFECTIVE COSTUMING

A stage costume should express the personality of the character, revealing his social status, tastes, and idiosyncrasies. It should aid the audience's understanding of the actor's relationship to the other characters and to the play itself. The costume may be in harmony with others on the stage or in strong contrast to them. Color coding — matching characters by color or pattern — can provide a subtle **461**

In this production in the Children's Theatre of The Wind in the Willows, *the actors play the parts of animals. Note the type of costumes used. A back drop and side curtains set the scene.*

means of identifying members of the same family or group, a pair of lovers, or masters and servants.

Since costuming is a part of the total design, you will probably have little to do with the design of your costume. Too often, however, in high schools costumes are designed or rented only for period or stylized plays. When it comes to "contemporary" plays, the actors are frequently asked what they have in their own wardrobes. This is acceptable only if the student is portraying someone of his own age, personality type, social position, and so on, and this is rarely the case. For most plays the actor's personal wardrobe will never provide a suitable costume without some necessary modifications. Therefore, costumes should be designed for all actors in all plays. In any production, the effect of a costume on both the actor and audience is what counts upon the stage; the taste of the artist, not the actor, must govern the choice of material and color, and the meaning of the play must dominate all decisions. Valuable heirlooms, exquisite creations, and expensive fabrics are of no value unless they are appropriate in color, period, and design.

Amateurs are usually loath to appear anything but attractive on the stage, forgetting that the audience should react to the play, not the individuals. No director will ever deliberately insist upon unbecoming or ludicrous lines or colors unless they are imperative to the correct interpretation of the play. However, the psychological reaction of being comfortably, becomingly, and suitably clothed greatly assists an actor's work. It is for this reason that you should understand the theories of costuming in order to cooperate intelligently in wearing whatever is designed for you in your role.

COSTUME DESIGN

The first step in costume design, as with all phases of theater production, is to study the play carefully. The costume designer should then meet with the director and technical director to discuss costumes in relation to the theme, style, period, colors, scenery, lighting, and budget. Together they can suggest types of materials for costumes that will suit the play in question in texture, finish, weight, fullness, and stiffness. Then measurements of the cast are taken and preliminary sketches are made.

Fabric samples should be tried under the lighting planned for the show, remembering that the lighting may be changed and it is almost always the costumer who must make adjustments, seldom the painters or electricians. Once the fabrics are selected, the costumes may be sewn and fitted. It is wise to place the costumes under the lights again before making the final fitting and adding the trim. Once each costume is completed, it should be checked one last time under the lights before dress rehearsal.

Actors have a bad habit of not reporting lost buttons, tears, and other accidents to costumes. They should be reminded that such problems should be reported immediately so that the necessary repairs may be made before performance time.

An important point to bear in mind is that a historically accurate costume is not essential and might even have a negative effect on the production. An authentic costume may not look right on a particular actor, especially those which expose parts of the body, such as Egyptian, Greek, or Roman costumes. It is better to adapt the costume to the size, bone structure, and shape of the actor than to insist on historical correctness. Every historical or national costume has two or three indentifying characteristics which are sufficient to give the impression of that era or geographical region. A collar, cape, belt, or hat may be all the audience needs to accept the costume as being of a given time and place. The addition of a few little touches such as jewelry, handkerchiefs, or gloves will make the costume seem complete.

A "complete" costume is most essential. All accessories should be part of a properly designed costume and should be obtained early

Ancient Greek Dress. Costumes like these would be appropriate for any Greek play, dramatizations of Greek myths, and William Shakespeare's A Midsummer Night's Dream.

enough for some rehearsing. Neglect of such details as shoes, hats, purses, fans, and parasols can ruin the harmony of the design and mood. Masks, wigs, and hair pieces are part of both costume and makeup, creating the complete costume.

It is equally important that the actor have some substitute to rehearse with if the real accessories are not available for use. An actor needs to get the "feel" of a costume. For a hoopskirt a hoop alone may be used for rehearsing and will remind the actress that she will not be able to see her feet, that she may have difficulty maneuvering a 120-inch hoop skirt through narrow passages, and that she may have trouble getting close to a person or object without the back of the hoop tipping up embarrassingly. When accessories are added at the last minute, many beginning actors find they must change some of their stage business and even modify some of their blocking. It is a mistake to think that the addition of essential ac-

Medieval Dress. Appropriate for any play or pageant set in late medieval times, George Bernard Shaw's Saint Joan, *and Anatole France's* The Man Who Married a Dumb Wife.

cessories on the day of dress rehearsal is good because it may give the performers a "lift." Several weeks of rehearsal are necessary to develop the ease and naturalness essential to the use of a lorgnette, a monocle, a long cigarette holder, or a swagger stick.

The costume designer recognizes that clothing styles progress in definite patterns which may be applied to the characters in a play. In any era, someone sets the fashion — perhaps a clothing designer, perhaps a person of renown, perhaps the star of a movie. This fashionable apparel is first worn by professional models, then by the socially elite. Once accepted in elite circles, fashionable people everywhere follow the new style, until finally the general populace follows the trend. Then there are the people who are always outdated; they discard the previous style too late and consequently pick up the new style as it is waning. Finally there are those who wear styles of a time ten to fifty years prior to the play; these are usually the old-fashioned,

Elizabethan Dress. Appropriate for any Shakespearean play, George Bernard Shaw's Dark Lady of the Sonnets, *and Maxwell Anderson's* Elizabeth the Queen.

the eccentric, and the economically or socially deprived. Remember also that styles are often revived and that conservative and flamboyant styles occur in cycles according to the philosophical tone of the times.

It is usually safer to costume plays of the last two or three decades in present-day attire unless some aspect of the play hinges on authentic costuming. For example, the middies of the girls in *Cheaper by the Dozen* add to the humor of the play, but a long, straight-line dress of the twenties for Mrs. Gilbreth might seem ridiculously out of place.

Always consider the kind of action that will take place in the scene in which the costume will be used. A costume must be comfortable, easy to put on and take off, and strong enough to stand heavy strain. A skin-tight uniform may appear dashing, but may handcuff the actor completely in a fight scene. Costumes for dance sequences must be designed with the choreography in mind. If more

Restoration Dress. Appropriate for plays by William Wycherley, William Congreve, Goerge Farquhar, and Molière.

than one costume is to be worn, each costume must be designed in such a way that the actor can change costumes in the time allowed — it must be admitted that playwrights do not always consider carefully the time needed for costume changes. This is especially true in live television, where some performers have to execute complete costume changes in twenty-five to forty seconds.

The total design of the play determines whether the costumes may be stylized. Some period plays adapt well to modern dress — the wearing of contemporary clothing instead of authentic period costumes. Formal attire can be worn for many plays, particularly classical tragedies. Flowing robes, mosaic patterns, and variations in black and white fabrics may be used for certain stylized plays.

Appropriateness

Each historic period has its own distinctive line and form in dress. This is the "costume silhouette." Look carefully at the silhouettes

Eighteenth-century Dress. Appropriate for plays and pageants about the American Revolution, Richard Brinsley Sheridan's The Rivals *and* A School for Scandal, *and Oliver Goldsmith's* She Stoops to Conquer.

in this chapter and notice how each period has its own characteristics. If a costume does not recreate the basic silhouette of the period, it is not effective, no matter how beautiful or ingenious it may be. This is a very important principle.

In style, material, and cut, a costume must be appropriate to the social background and period of the play. On the stage certain problems of dress are intensified. Actors and actresses should study their full-length reflections at a distance to get the proper perspective on themselves in costume. The director should observe every costume from various parts of the auditorium.

Small details become important on stage. For example, long skirts are more graceful than short ones, especially when the actress is seated. Draped scarfs and stoles are very effective if they are skillfully handled. Trimming, to be noticed, must be somewhat conspicuous, but if it is overly so, it should be discarded.

Mid-nineteenth-century Dress. Appropriate for plays about the War Between the States, Rudolf Besier's The Barretts of Wimpole Street, *Robert Sherwood's* Abe Lincoln in Illinois, *and Ruth and Augustus Goetz's* The Heiress.

Costuming can cause more temperamental upheavals than any other phase of amateur production. Most people want to look their best when appearing in public, so costumes should fit well and bring out the best physical characteristics of the actor — unless a particular role dictates otherwise. It takes time in rehearsal to make a different style of clothing feel natural. The actor must lose his self-consciousness in the costume if he is to look right in it. Sometimes a high school performer "pulls back" in the role because he is uncomfortable in his costume — a girl may be embarrassed by a gown that is too "revealing," a boy may feel ill at ease in a Roman tunic. Often the student actors do not complain because they believe such a costume is what the director expects them to wear. But, if the feelings of discomfort cannot be overcome by a better understanding of the role and the relationship of the costume to it, then the director should consider modifying the costume slightly rather than send a tense,

Late Nineteenth- and Early Twentieth-century Dress. Appropriate for George Bernard Shaw's Candida, *Henrik Ibsen's* Hedda Gabler, *and Oscar Wilde's* The Importance of Being Earnest.

ill-at-ease actor upon the stage. In real life, clothes may not make the man, but on the stage they do. Fortunate indeed is the actor who has the knack of wearing clothes well and making them a part of the role he creates.

Color and Material

Costumes for comedies, farces, children's plays, and fantasies are normally made of light material, bright or pastel in color, and frothy in design. Restoration comedy calls for satins, laces, and brocades, which are usually as overconscious of style as the characters themselves. High comedy deals with persons of taste and social grace; costumes for fashionable characters require careful selection of color and material and also special attention to line. In realistic plays, almost any material which will create garments suitable for the character and for the stage picture can be used. Symbolic and allegorical

Dress in the 1920's. Appropriate for Edna Ferber and George S. Kaufman's The Royal Family, *Booth Tarkington's* Seventeen, *and Sandy Wilson's musical* The Boy Friend.

plays require even more thought concerning fabric, texture, and pattern, because the audiences will assume that the costumes used in such plays will help them interpret the inner meanings. Tragedies use grayed colors or dark tones in heavily weighted materials.

The personality of the character and the style of the play will determine whether a tailored cut or a touch of lace is needed. Even in plays in which we think the styles of costumes are much alike, there must be variety — in color, cut, line, material, and trim. The characters in every play must be treated as individuals to be identified in their stations of life, idiosyncrasies, or philosophies by some aspect in their costume design. At the same time, all costumes for the same play must "agree" with each other in basic design.

Lines in garments should harmonize with those of the human body without constriction or exaggeration. A stout person should cultivate long, vertical lines in costumes, hair styles, and hats. Tall, thin people should use horizontal lines, especially at the shoulder, and avoid long, clinging skirts, high hats, and V-necks. Black and dark colors are slenderizing, while white and light colors are broadening. Glaring colors, striking patterns, and lustrous materials attract attention and should be avoided by large persons unless they are especially appropriate to the characterization. Satin is a glossy material which in light colors makes a person appear larger, whereas velvet absorbs light, and dark velvet takes off pounds.

Prints must be carefully tested, for the stage lights obliterate small or light patterns into a grotesque effect. In general, blondes should cultivate the cool colors, with touches of warm color contrast, and delicate designs and materials are usually more becoming to them. Brunettes should cultivate warm colors, and they can risk brilliant fabrics and marked contrasts. Ordinarily red-haired actresses should emphasize their coloring, using yellow, orange, green, and golden brown. At all times good points should be stressed and defects minimized by a careful study of the principles of proportion, harmony, and emphasis as applied to dress.

Texture not only determines the outline of the costume, but also has much to do with the effects of a material under the lights. Heavy or soft materials such as velvet, burlap, cheesecloth, and flannel react well under stage lighting, and the more inexpensive materials often appear richer than many costly fabrics. Drapery material and even carpeting have been used for costumes for this very reason. Knitted materials drape beautifully and cling to the figure, emphasizing lines.

COSTUME PLOT FOR:							OUT	IN
CHARACTER	SCENE	COSTUME DESCRIPTION	MEAS. CARD	1ST FITTING	COMPLETE			
JULIE (CINDY PHELPS)	I, i	BLUE CHECKED GINGHAM PINAFORE w/WHITE BLOUSE AND WHITE APRON. WIDE BRIMMED STRAW HAT. PARASOL	✓	✓	✓	✓		
"	I, ii	LT. GREEN BLOUSE WITH PUFFED SLEEVES. PINK SKIRT w/BUSTLE. PURSE		✓	✓	✓		

Oilcloth, cardboard, plastics, rubber sheeting, felt, and other similar materials, including the special plastic molding materials now available, can be used for trim, accent features, and appliqués. All sorts of familiar materials can be utilized in creating bizarre or unusual outfits.

OBTAINING THE COSTUMES

Work sheets and costume charts should be made for every costume to be used in the production. The work sheets should describe the colors, fabrics, and all accessories for each design. Ruled columns, placed next to the items in the costume description, are of great value. As each listed task is completed, the item can be checked off. Such charts can facilitate matters so that the costumes are ready before dress rehearsals.

One of the first problems to be settled is whether the costumes are to be made, rented, or borrowed. This decision must be made in ample time for the costumes to be collected with a minimum of effort and expense.

Renting Costumes

If you decide to rent costumes, be careful. Rented costumes are always expensive! Many times the costume company will not have what you want or all that you need when you need it. Be particularly cautious when a costumer says he does not have quite what you request but will fix you up with something else. Even when costumes can be personally selected, the fitting and returning of costumes bring little for the effort other than a large bill.

If you send out of town for costumes, they seldom fit properly and frequently are in poor condition. Substitutions are common, accessories are seldom what you expect, and the use of interchangeables — such as using the same hat for several purposes simply by changing the identifying trim — can result in a sameness you did not anticipate. Many costume houses send "boot covers" to be worn over regular shoes; these are not too objectionable unless the performer must dance in them. Only when you deal with very large firms can you hope to get the color or pattern you desire; otherwise, you take what they have.

One of the chief drawbacks of rented costumes is that they are available for only one dress rehearsal or at most for only forty-eight hours prior to the first performance without additional charge. There is also an additional fee for each performance day after the opening night. Rental costumes are never available for publicity photos unless you rent them for that purpose; this can be done only if you are dealing with a local concern.

With so many reasons against renting, you may wonder why high schools should even consider renting. Formal evening dress, especially in period styles; uniforms and unusual national costumes; armor; and certain special properties are often unobtainable in any other way. If the budget is adequate, some of the leading costumes houses can provide you with the costumes actually used in the Broadway or other well-costumed production; these may have had a high enough budget to order the kind of costumes prepared which no high school could afford to make. The trim for such elaborate costumes is quite expensive, and only large productions or costumers can afford to trim the costumes properly.

When schools do not rent, there is always the temptation to take the "easiest, cheapest route," which means you may make even more substitutions than the costumer, or use some kind of apparel completely unsuitable for the play. Musical plays have sometimes lacked the sparkle and color so essential to their success simply because the costumes were "simple substitutions." If you do rent, often it is best to deal with a large firm or, better still, two reliable companies because the choice of costumes of each company for certain historical periods is usually limited; and you do not want your audiences to tire of seeing the same costume over and over again. If at all possible, the director, designer, and costume mistress should go to the costume company personally to select the costumes to be used.

Borrowing Costumes

Having the members of the cast and committee buy or borrow their own costumes may seem to be the simplest method of costuming a production — but it seldom is! It is very difficult to obtain garments which will achieve the planned and desired effect — even those which at first seem easy to get. In period plays, suitable costumes lent by generous friends are apt to be valuable and fragile, and no assurance can be offered that they will not be soiled or torn. Some young people have a rather careless attitude toward expensive articles of apparel, even though they have been borrowed and are often irreplaceable. Makeup stains that will not come out, delicate lace that is snagged, and materials which disintegrate under the strain of a performance are hard to explain to the owner of such treasured heirlooms. If you borrow costumes, treat them carefully!

Of course, when a student borrows or buys his own costume, it is obvious there is little or no budgeting cost other than the cleaning of the borrowed costume. As previously mentioned, it is not easy for a student to look older in his own clothes, and seldom would the wardrobes of character and actor match. Also, the actor may be more careful with a costume if he has paid for it or it belongs to a friend or relative. Since cost is always a major factor, most modern costumes are borrowed.

Making Your Own Costumes

To make your own costumes almost always outweighs renting and borrowing if you insist on good design, materials, workmanship, and a definite time schedule. The cost of making costumes is about the same as, and often far less than, the rental fee, but the major difference rests in the end result — an addition to the costume wardrobe, or a high bill with nothing to show for it.

Making the costumes serves several purposes. Those students who design and make them gain valuable experience and have the pride and satisfaction of seeing the effect a good costume plays in creating an effective stage picture. A more uniform pattern for the play in both color and line is possible, and the costume is made to fit the individual actor. Both the seamstress and the actor take a personal interest in this facet of production, bringing about a mutual respect for each other's contribution to the play. It is a thrill for the designer, as well as a relief to the publicity chairman, to have the actual costumes available for publicity photos, especially if the publicity chairman plans to set up a poster featuring "real" scenes from the play.

If the costumes are to be made, a well-stocked wardrobe room is essential. If your school does not already maintain a costume room where costumes, accessories, materials, and supplies can be stored and cared for, you and your classmates should get one started. You will find your supply will grow quickly when the need for costumes becomes known in the community.

When you are ready to make the costumes, individual sketches and costume charts and sheets should include notes on the kind, amount, and cost of materials. Dyeing makes possible a more satisfactory and unified costume scheme, but it requires skill in a complex activity, a place for the dyeing, and people willing to work until the job is completed. Before the dyeing is done, patterns should be cut to the exact measurements of the actors and be approved by the director, scenic artist, and actors. When all material has been dyed and checked under the stage lights, it may be cut from the patterns and sewed together.

The completed garments must be strong and firm enough to stand the strain of rehearsals and performances, but they do not need to have elaborate, ornamental sewing. Pinking edges and basting rather than stitching are quite acceptable for much of costume making. Details, such as a row of buttons, are usually nonfunctional or "dummied" in order to save sewing time and facilitate quick changes. The main emphasis in costume planning should be on the total effect as seen from the auditorium. The perfection of a costume cannot be judged by the design alone; it must be observed in action on the stage with the correct scenery and lighting. Costume design and construction are complex processes, but the effort is rewarded by the achievement of an original and artistic production.

Time is always the enemy in the production of a play; this includes costuming. A schedule for measurement, fittings, and completion should be established and adhered to. Sufficient time must be allowed for checking material under lights, for alterations and corrections, and for the costume parade. One of the great advantages of making your own costumes is that if they are completed on schedule — at least a week before dress rehearsal — you can test them under the lights, make final adjustments, and add a touch of trim, accent, or jewelry as needed several days before rental costumes would be available.

In the long run, a combination of renting, borrowing, buying, and making your own costumes is probably the only satisfactory way to meet all the costume requirements for your dramatic program, particularly if you present musical plays.

Never overlook the possibilities of making over old clothes or revamping old costumes. It is a good practice to save fabric remnants for trim or accessories or perhaps to add to a costume of the same material at a later date. Men's old suits can be cut and remade into cutaways without a great amount of work. Even beautiful hats — always a costume problem — can be made from a few materials, a little imagination, ten minutes in the library, and considerable patience.

CARE OF COSTUMES

After the costumes have been obtained, they must be cared for during rehearsals and performances. A competent wardrobe mistress should be chosen. She should have responsible assistants in all the dressing rooms. The assistants help the actors with their changes, hang up clothes, keep all accessories close at hand, and see that everything is returned in good condition after the performance. The wardrobe mistress sees that every costume is complete, in good repair, and identified by character and actor. Each performer should have a designated place for his costume, such as costume racks marked by tags or dividers. The wardrobe mistress checks with the cast for problems which might have developed with zippers, tears, and the like, keeping needle and thread and a few quick-need supplies like hook-and-eyes, buttons, or elastic on hand during all performances. All borrowed clothing should be dry cleaned or washed before it is returned to the owner. The wardrobe mistress also sees that all school costumes are cleaned, repaired, and stored carefully for future use, and that all rented costumes and accessories are returned promptly.

Dressing room floors should be covered with paper if long trains of fine materials are worn. The stage floor also should be kept clean; it should be vacuumed before dress rehearsals and performances. Protruding nails, unexpected steps, low ceilings, and other backstage hazards should be reduced to a minimum.

After almost every production, some things need to be replaced or repaired. The decision as to whether or not such expenses are to come out of the proceeds should be made at the beginning of rehearsals.

THE ACTOR AND HIS COSTUME

The actor must learn to wear his costume properly, bearing in mind the angle at which the audience will view him as he turns, bends over, or crosses his legs. He must also think of the other performers — that he does not jab them unintentionally with a sword as he turns; that buttons, medals, or jewelry do not snag or catch on another's costume; or that he does not step on another performer's cape or train. The actor must seem natural and at ease in his costume, learning how to make a turn in a flowing or trailing costume without meeting himself coming and going. Girls must learn how to sit gracefully while wearing a hoop or several petticoats; and boys must learn how a "man of quality" sits without pinning the tails of his full evening dress under him. "Snapping" fans, removing scarves and gloves, handling capes and "finger rings" must be second nature to the actor if he is to appear convincing in his role.

In addition, the actor himself should feel responsible for his costume and properties. He should remember that greasepaint, powder, spirit gum, and nail polish are almost impossible to remove and that torn fabrics can seldom be mended satisfactorily. Actors must personally see that every costume, accessory, and property is returned to the school, costumer, or friend exactly as it was received. But, above all, the actor should remember that the "total actor" is made up of a well-coordinated combination of voice, physique, makeup, and costume.

Studying the principles of costuming and makeup will give you valuable ideas about your own wardrobe and appearance. In playing a role in a social comedy dealing with well-bred people, you realize that the best dressed men and women wear simple, appropriate clothes of good material, cut along conservative but flattering lines; they also wear their clothes properly, with matching or contrasting accessories. By forming the habit of getting a perspective on your total appearance, which blends your hair styling and posture and carriage with your shoes, hose, and hats, you will always appear poised and at your best. Appropriateness to the occasion, suitability in the environment, and harmony with your own physique without exaggeration or restriction are as important in daily life as on the stage.

Costume Projects

1. Design the costumes for a play: (1) contemporary, (2) period, (3) fantasy, (4) stylized.
2. Design costumes for a children's play, using unusual materials such as boxes and paper sacks.
3. Color code the characters in a play by personality types or relationships.
4. Demonstrate the simple altering of a modern garment to represent that of an earlier historical era.
5. Demonstrate the use of a fan, cane, parasol, sword, night stick, monocle, or lorgnette.
6. Demonstrate how movements are affected by hoops, trains, tails, or capes.
7. Design costumes for a musical, consisting of coordinate units that can be interchanged or reversed — such as shirts, jackets, vests, skirts.

Bibliography

Barton, Lucy: *Historic Costume for the Stage*, W. H. Baker, Boston, 1961.
Paterek, Josephine: *Costuming for the Theater*, Crown, New York, 1959.
Walkup, Fairfax: *Dressing the Part: A History of Costume for the Theater*, Appleton-Century-Crofts, New York, 1950.

chapter **16**

MAKEUP

Makeup should be one of the most delightful phases of your dramatic experiences because it opens up a field of study that conveys the excitement, fun, and challenge of theater illusion and communication. Unfortunately, many students of drama do not fully realize that most actors must design and apply their own makeup. Makeup techniques cannot be mastered merely by watching a demonstration or reading about them. To help yourself acquire this skill essential to every performer, you should study faces to see how they show the effects of age and emotion. Observe portraits, cartoons, magazines, and photographs.

Better still, observe real people! Take special notice of differences in skin color and texture; where wrinkles occur, bones are prominent, and flesh hangs in folds; and the direction and patterns of hair growth. You will discover that the change that takes place in facial expression is related closely to the changes in personality, stature, and voice which occur when an actor develops an effective characterization. **479**

In the Hofstra University Drama Department's production of Shaw's Heartbreak House, *a student convincingly portrays an old man, thanks to the art of makeup.*

Bone structure is the key to facial makeup. Every student needs to know the bone-muscle relationship and how it alters with age and differs with nationality. It is essential that you study your own bone structure carefully before designing makeup for a role.

GENERAL CONSIDERATIONS

On the school stage, makeup must be handled with special care. Youthful faces do not always adapt themselves readily to older roles, and heavy makeup inexpertly applied looks "tacked on." Only the slightest amount of greasepaint should be used. It is much better to err by using too little than to use too much. For classwork, a mere touching up of the face and appropriate dressing of the hair can suggest age and nationality effectively. However, every student of the drama should study and practice elaborate as well as simple makeup.

When you are to design makeup for a large production, your makeup requirements change considerably. The larger the auditorium or the more lights to be used, the more makeup is needed. Stage lights can wash the color from the actor's face until it has a pasteboard effect. Too much light from above results in deep shadows under all the bony prominences. Bright footlights make the face appear flat

480

and lifeless. Many stages today do not have footlights; without them, unless there is proper lighting from the sides, serious shadows distort the actor's face; his eyes can appear lost in deep sockets, and the nose may take on strange shapes.

The techniques of makeup application are closely related to the portrait artist's approach: the face is made a blank mask and then the principles of chiaroscuro — the use of highlight and shadow — are applied to model the features into the desired effect. REMEMBER: Makeup does not make character, but it does help present the external appearance of the internally created role.

The Makeup Kit

A well-stocked makeup kit is essential to every drama department. However, since makeup is such a personal thing, many amateurs and all professionals prefer their own personal kits.

Makeup is very expensive and very messy. Proper care of the makeup supplies, the kit, and the makeup room is most essential. Materials should be carefully laid out; all containers and tables cleaned up after use; lids and caps replaced on the right containers; and all supplies put back in the kit or storage cupboards.

Before a rehearsal or performance, the makeup crew should place the supplies neatly on a covered table. When makeup is being applied by a crew, materials must never be carried off by individuals. An ample supply of cold cream and cleansing tissue is always important. Though not on the tables, the complete makeup supply must be readily available for emergencies. Only one or two experiences will teach the person in charge of makeup that if all the supplies are in sight, every one of them will be used, even if only slightly.

Makeup essentials are usually handled by a special committee, whose members are headed by someone experienced in makeup techniques, responsible for the makeup used during a production. This committee should obtain the following essentials:

Greasepaints: These come in tubes or cakes and are sometimes called foundations or bases. Shades ranging from light pink to dark sunburn are necessary for straight parts. For character parts such as sallow or florid old age, there are various mixed tones. For different nationalities, there are appropriate shades.

Face Powders: In shades to harmonize with the foundation or neutral.

Moist rouge: Light, medium, and dark.

Liners: Greasepaints in colors such as blue, brown, green, violet, yellow, and white.

Lipsticks: Use moist rouge.

Dermatograph pencils: Brown, maroon, and black eyebrow pencils.

Dry rouge: Light, medium, and dark.

Mascara: Black and white.

Cosmetic: Used for darkening eyelashes.

Cold cream, albolene, or makeup remover: Used for dissolving and removing makeup.

Powder puffs: Large and small.

Roll of absorbent cotton.

Baby brush or *special powder brush:* Used for removing excess powder.

Hair Whitener: Wheatcroft, cornstarch, clown white, liquid white shoe polish.

Color spray: Aerosol temporary hair color.

Liquid body makeup: Match foundation.

Round toothpicks, paper liners (stumps), and *sable* or *camel's hair brushes:* For making wrinkles, painting lips, and eyebrows.

Crepe hair: Gray, gray-blend, light brown, medium brown, black.

Spirit gum and *alcohol* or *acetone.*

Liquid latex: For attaching beards and building up features.

Nose putty, black tooth enamel, white tooth enamel, and *artificial blood.*

Collodian: Flexible and nonflexible.

Large mirrors.

Paper toweling: To protect the dressing tables.

Cleansing tissues.

Hand mirror, comb, brush, scissors, penknife, matches, needles, black and white thread, straight pins, hairpins, bobby pins, and *safety pins.*

MAKEUP PRINCIPLES AND PROCEDURES

Before beginning to make up, put on a smock, apron, or makeup cape. Carefully bind back the hair or cover it with a cloth. Allow ample time for the makeup — at least half an hour for a straight role and an hour or more for a character part. Men should be clean shaven, but should never shave less than a half hour before applying makeup. Men should never get a full haircut less than three days before the production because the back of the head and the temples may appear "skinned" under the lights. Also, to protect the collars of white shirts and blouses, a piece of adhesive tape may be placed over the fold of the collar.

Step One: Preparation for Makeup

Cleanse the face thoroughly, removing all cosmetics. Then moisten the fingertips with cold water and cool the surface of the face. Persons with oily skins may need to use an astringent to assure a dry surface before applying makeup.

Step Two: The Foundation

The second step is the application of the correct color of foundation. Soft (tube-type) greasepaint is preferable because of its economy and ease in blending, although pancake makeup has become increasingly popular. Do not use any cold cream before applying soft greasepaint! Use the charts available from the makeup companies as a guide to color choice. Generally speaking, men and boys use a darker base than girls, but foundation color is determined more by the age and health of the character, the hereditary background, and the environmental conditions. Careful character analysis will help the actor decide whether he should be sallow or ruddy.

Squeeze from ¼ to ½ inch of soft greasepaint into the palm and use the other hand to place dabs or streaks on the forehead, cheeks, chin, and neck. Use greasepaint sparingly. A thin, even coat is desirable; a heavy mask is not. Heavy greasepaint causes considerable perspiration and running makeup, lines are difficult to draw, and the makeup requires constant retouching. Remove the makeup from your hands, moisten the fingertips with water, and begin spreading the greasepaint smoothly over the face and all exposed parts of the head and neck area, including the ears. Work the foundation gently into the hairline to avoid a halo effect around the face that causes makeup to look like a mask. Also spread the base into the collar line, the back of the neck, and as far down the chest as is exposed or where body makeup will be applied.

Step Three: Shadows and Highlights

The application of shadow and highlight is really the most important aspect of modeling the face. Highlighting and shadowing are used for three purposes: (1) to bring out the features in order that they may be seen; (2) to correct the features; and (3) to change the features to indicate age, character, or physical impairments. For shadowing, use a greasepaint at least three shades darker than the foundation color, or use brown or reddish-brown lining color. Never

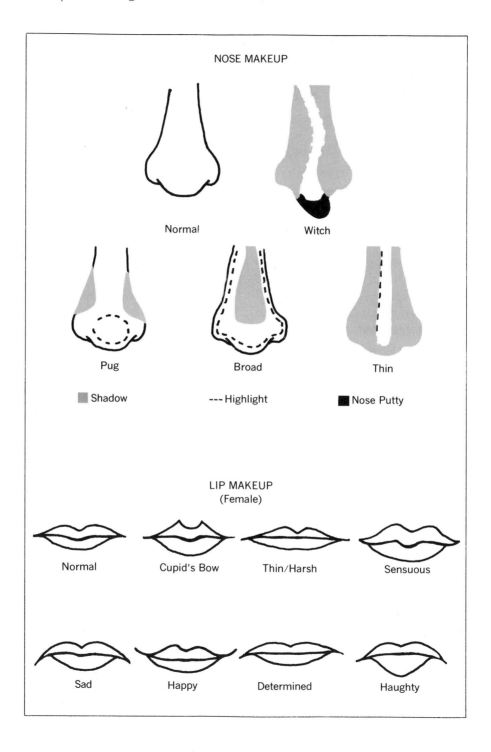

use gray except for extreme makeup; it makes the face look skull-like or dirty.

Every shadow has its highlight. For highlighting, you may use a greasepaint at least three shades lighter than the foundation, or yellow or white liner. White is usually the easiest to use because it will pick up enough of the foundation color to blend effectively without appearing garish. If your chin, nose, or brows are too prominent, blend a shadow over that part of the face.

If, on the other hand, some part of your face is not dominant enough, apply a highlight to that area. It is almost always necessary to highlight and shadow the nose a little in order for it to be seen under bright stage lights. The older the character, the more intensified the highlights and shadows. The eye sockets, the sides of the nose, the hollow of the cheeks, and all wrinkles and creases of the flesh must be lined or shadowed. As age comes upon the character, the cheek bones, bridge of the nose, eyelids, and chin stand out; folds of flesh appear on the brow, around the eyes and mouth; and the jowls and skin of the neck hang loosely. All such folds of flesh must be highlighted. A sable or camel's hair brush is the most satisfactory tool for lining, but a paper stump or round toothpick may work quite well if you are careful to make the lines thin and sharp before blending them out.

Step Four: Rouge

We now apply moist rouge to cheeks and lips. For a feminine straight part, select a color that blends with the complexion (foundation color) and costume. You should place the moist rouge where it will help shape your face to that of your character. If you have an oval face, apply the rouge in a crescent shape to the cheek bones and blend up and out. For a round face, blend the rouge along the cheek bone and then downwards next to the nose. For a long face, place the rouge high on the cheek bones and blend out toward the temples.

Blending is always important in makeup, but especially so in the application of moist rouge. You should never see where the rouge ends unless your character is a person obviously over-made up. Men and boys should use moist rouge sparingly — just enough for a healthy glow. Although rouge may be washed out under strong light, it often gives the same effect as shadowing. Use very little, if any, rouge for night scenes, since both blue and green lights will turn the red into a dark brown or black.

Step Five: Eyes and Eyebrows

The eyes and brows are made up next. The purpose of the eye shadow is to beautify the eyes, to make them seem larger, and to indicate character. Eye shadow is applied to the upper lids only, beginning with a heavy line next to the eye and fading out before reaching the eyebrow. The choice of color is determined by the color of hair and costume, the personality of the character, and whether the eyes are supposed to look "made up." Blue, blue-green, blue-gray, violet, or brown may be used. Brown is the safest and most flattering color and should always be used for corrective male eye shadowing. Violet is permissible only when a weepy appearance is sought or the character is a fragile old lady whose foundation color is a delicate pink.

Be certain that the eye shadow does not kill any highlight below the eyebrow. Men use shadow to deaden disfiguring highlights and to suggest age. The placement of the shadow can alter the appearance of the eyes to make them appear closer together or farther apart, or happy, sad, weary, suspicious, squinty. In all cases the shadow should be blended out so that no definite line is visible.

The eyes are enlarged and accented by lining. Makeup experts disagree sharply regarding both the technique and placement of eye lining. Brown or black lining color may be used, but black is acceptable only for a character who would use heavy eye makeup or for oriental eyes. If false lashes or heavy mascara will be applied later, the upper line is omitted by many actresses. Otherwise, you should use a sable brush or round toothpick to draw a line close to the lashes starting about two-thirds of the way in towards the nose and extending beyond the outer corner of the eye about ¼ inch. The lower line is drawn about one-third from the corner out to the upper line, fading out before it reaches the top line. Both lines should be softened by running the finger gently over them. The lower line should be about ¼ inch below the eye. If a dermatograph (eyebrow) pencil is used, it must be sharp or else the lines will be too heavy.

To add sparkle to the eye, some makeup experts suggest a small red dot in the inner corner of the eye; others recommend a touch of rouge just below the outer corner, or below the outer edge of the brow. The red dot, or "life spot" as it has been called, may help to serve another purpose: it can aid in determining how close or far apart the eyes seem to be; in oriental makeup, when latex lids or adhesive tape are not to be used, a dot placed below the inner corner may contribute to the illusion of a slanted eye.

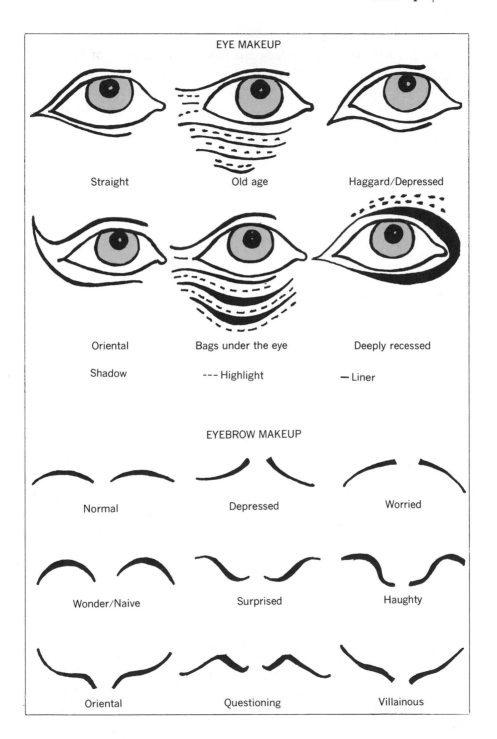

EYE MAKEUP

Straight

Old age

Haggard/Depressed

Oriental

Bags under the eye

Deeply recessed

Shadow   --- Highlight   — Liner

EYEBROW MAKEUP

Normal

Depressed

Worried

Wonder/Naive

Surprised

Haughty

Oriental

Questioning

Villainous

In straight parts the eyebrows should frame the eyes rather than attract attention to themselves. Again, brown or black may be used in hairlike strokes following the shape of the eye. Most natural eyebrows do not have identical arches; therefore, by matching them, makeup can greatly improve their appearance. In character makeup, many different effects can be achieved by changing the eyebrows. Close, heavily drawn brows appear villainous. Lifting the brows into a round, thin arch gives an amazed or stupid expression. Twisted brows or brows dropped at contrasting angles make a face seem plaintive, menacing, or leering.

Step Six: Wrinkles

There are several methods of applying wrinkles. Since wrinkles are quite often the deepest crease in a fold of skin, many actors prefer to draw the wrinkles over the foundation and then blend them out to make the shadows. There are two other methods of drawing wrinkles that are commonly used. The first method assumes you have already applied the highlights and shadows. If you have natural wrinkles, you can usually "mark" them in the foundation by raising the brows, squinting the eyes, smiling, and pulling the chin in. Then, while the lines are still visible in the greasepaint, draw the wrinkles on with brown liner. If you do not have natural wrinkles yet, you will have to follow the same procedure, but draw the lines while the muscles are still contracted.

The second method is used by those who like to draw the wrinkles before the foundation is applied. To use this method, spread brown liner over the areas where wrinkles are to be drawn. Form the wrinkles and carefully wipe off the visible liner before relaxing. When you relax the muscles, the natural wrinkles should be clearly marked by the remaining liner. Form the wrinkles again and apply the foundation grease paint; after this step, highlight the folds of skin, relax, and blend the wrinkles into shadows.

You must never draw too many lines on the forehead. You may discover that the lines on your forehead do not meet or are not straight. It is better to draw straight wrinkles than to follow natural lines that are disconnected or appear strangely slanted when the brow is relaxed. You should also be especially careful when drawing age lines at the outer corner and below the eye, for if they are too heavy, they will appear as smudges rather than wrinkles under the lights on stage.

Step Seven: Powdering

The most important step in the application of makeup is that of putting on the powder. Use a neutral shade or a shade one tone lighter than the foundation. The powder, when properly applied, sets the makeup, softens the lines and colors, and gives a "matte-finish" which removes the shine of greasepaint under the lights. Powder must be squeezed into the puff and the excess shaken off. Then the powder should be pressed into the makeup thoroughly but gently; be very careful not to rub or smear your makeup.

The pressing in of the powder holds the makeup in place and prevents its running under the lights. Some makeup authorities suggest patting the powder on, but beginners often find they get spots of heavy powder that are difficult to remove. Be certain you have powdered all exposed skin areas you have made up, including the eyelids, wrinkles, and lips. Brush off the extra powder very lightly with the powder brush, but do not disturb the lines or leave streaks and powder spots.

Step Eight: Lipstick and Finishing Touches

After the powder, you may apply the finishing touches. If the powder dulled the cheeks, dry rouge may be used to restore the color, but be sure no lines or spots of rouge are visible.

Girls should now apply mascara or melted cosmetic to the upper lashes. Use brown instead of black unless you are a real brunette. False eyelashes, put on with liquid adhesive and carefully trimmed to suit the character and lighting, are often very effective and in many ways preferred over mascara.

You should use moist rouge for the lips for with the many pigments found in lipsticks today, it is impossible to predict how they will react under modern lighting effects. Therefore it is dangerous to use your "street" lipstick unless you have tested it under the stage lights and the director has approved the color.

For sanitary reasons, it is best for the actor to apply his own lipstick. He may use his little finger or his own personal lipstick brush. Lipstick brushes may be used for group makeup provided they are wiped clean and sterilized after each use. Girls should remember that the shape of the lips is determined by the role and not by their ordinary street makeup. The lipstick should be blended on the inside so that a definite line is not visible when the mouth is open. It is also important that the corners of the mouth receive at least enough rouge to define the mouth against the foundation. If the lips are too full, the foundation may be extended over them and "new" lips created. If the lips are thin, the rouge may be extended beyond the natural lip line to any shape desired.

The line of the mouth can create many subtle expressions to heighten your characterization. For example, a full sensuous mouth can be made puritanical by blocking out the curves and using light, straight lines in their place. By turning the corners of the mouth up slightly, an actor may be made to seem happy or pleasant even when not smiling; by turning the corners down, the actor may be made to seem always bitter or doleful. Avoid making your mouth the center of interest in your face, however, unless the part you are playing demands it.

Step Nine: Removing Makeup

After the play is over, remove the makeup completely. Wearing makeup outside the theater marks you as an amateur and an exhibitionist. Use cold cream, albolene, or makeup remover to soften the makeup and cleanse the skin. Wipe off the liquified makeup with cleansing tissue or towels. Long strokes and a circular motion will prevent rubbing the makeup into the skin. Wash the face with soap and warm water and then rinse with cool water to close the pores.

SPECIAL MAKEUP PROBLEMS

Hair is an integral part of both makeup and costume. Well-planned and carefully dressed coiffures can help to transform high school girls into sophisticated middle-aged women, prim matrons, or exotic adventuresses. The use of easily removed hair tints can change a girl's stage personality. Hair whitener (wheatcroft), white mascara, liquid white shoe polish, clown white, or wash-out color sprays are used to gray or whiten the hair. The use of ordinary white powder is never recommended. Cornstarch is also used for turning hair gray. In small quantities it is rather satisfactory, but it has a tendency to deaden the highlights of the hair, and a cloud of white powder arises if anyone touches it. Costume changes over whitened hair are not difficult, particularly if the hair is covered with a protective scarf.

Wigs, hairpieces, and falls are quite helpful in changing hair styles to fit character types and historical periods. Only expensive wigs appear natural and effective. They should be individually fitted, if

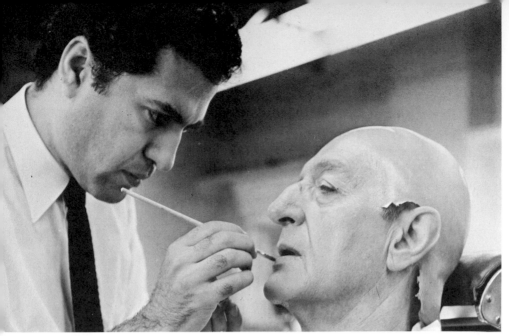

Note how the actor shown here is being made up for an older part. The nose has been enlarged and the hair covered with a "bald wig."

the budget permits, and they should be adjusted and handled with great care. Wigs are put on from the front and fitted back over the head. The real hair, if it shows, must be tinted to match the wig. A "bald wig" must fit perfectly, and the places where it meets the forehead and neck must be cleverly concealed by makeup. A piece of adhesive tape should be placed over the edge of the "blender" and foundation grease paint worked up over the tape onto the cloth.

For men, eccentric haircuts and hairdos are often more realistic than wigs. Boys' hair problems are important, for a perfect makeup and an impeccable adult costume can be ruined by a boyish cut. Two weeks before the performance, a good barber may cut the hair to suit the characterization. As a general rule the hair should not be cut after that time. Boys can easily change the color of their hair with mascara or wash-out sprays. White mascara is excellent for middle-aged parts. The hair should be freshly washed so that there is no grease on it. The mascara may then be applied with a wet toothbrush, brushing it back from the forehead.

Beards, mustaches, and sideburns require time and practice to apply realistically. Too many beards seem tacked to the point of the chin — probably because they were! Although professionally prepared beards and hairpieces are available, most are too expensive for school use. Wool crepe hair is used to create beards for the stage. **491**

Crepe hair comes in many colors, including grays, salt-and-pepper blends, blondes, light and dark browns, and black.

Crepe hair comes braided and is sold by the yard. It is curly when unbraided and must be straightened for most use. Dampen the crepe hair and tie it across the arms or back of a chair. After it has dried, usually overnight, the hair may be cut into lengths somewhat longer than the trimmed beard or mustache is to be. Several colors may be blended together for a more realistic appearance. Fan the hair between the fingers and thumb and apply to the adhesive-coated area.

Spirit gum is still a popular adhesive, although liquid latex is being used by many actors. One disadvantage of latex is that it must never get into the actor's natural hair or brows; but it does have a strong advantage for those who must wear beards and sideburns for several performances. A piece of nylon stocking cut approximately the shape of the beard can be glued to the face with latex; the hair is then applied to the nylon. The beard and nylon are trimmed to shape, but instead of discarding the beard at the end of the performance, the nylon-backed hairpiece may be carefully peeled off to be used for the succeeding performances.

When using crepe hair, always consider the patterns and directions of natural hair growth. Before applying the hair, be certain that the face is clean-shaven and that all skin areas to which hair is to be attached are free from makeup if spirit gum is to be used. Apply only a small amount of hair at a time, starting at the point of the chin and shingling upwards. When all the hair is in place, press it to the face with a towel. It can then be combed and trimmed to shape.

An unshaven effect can be created by stippling gray-blue or brown lining color on the foundation with a rubber sponge just before powdering. An even more realistic effect can be achieved by cutting crepe hair into tiny bits, spreading the shredded hair over the surface of a smooth towel, and transferring the hair to the face, which has been sparingly coated with spirit gum.

No makeup is complete if any exposed part of the body is ignored. Body makeup of the same color as the foundation should be applied to the arms, legs, back, and chest if they are visible. Hands clearly reveal age and should always be made up when you portray an older person. The tendons, knuckles, and other bones should be highlighted and the depressions should be shadowed. Extreme old age also may be suggested by strongly pronounced blood vessels on the back of the hands.

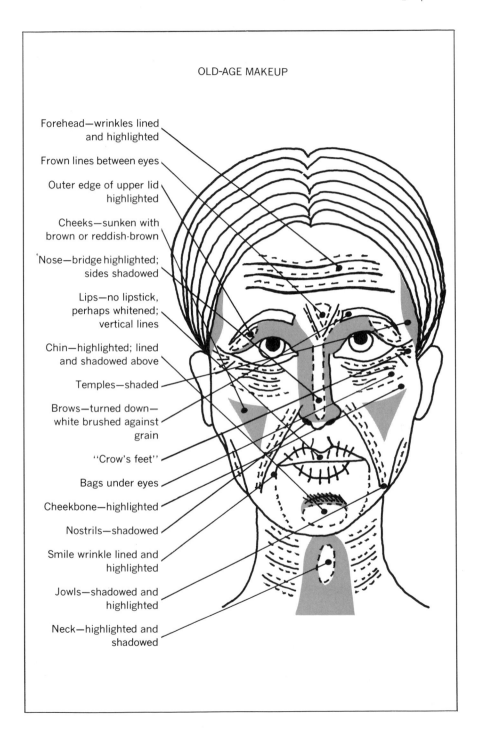

OLD-AGE MAKEUP

Forehead—wrinkles lined and highlighted

Frown lines between eyes

Outer edge of upper lid highlighted

Cheeks—sunken with brown or reddish-brown

Nose—bridge highlighted; sides shadowed

Lips—no lipstick, perhaps whitened; vertical lines

Chin—highlighted; lined and shadowed above

Temples—shaded

Brows—turned down— white brushed against grain

"Crow's feet"

Bags under eyes

Cheekbone—highlighted

Nostrils—shadowed

Smile wrinkle lined and highlighted

Jowls—shadowed and highlighted

Neck—highlighted and shadowed

A girl who plays the role of an old woman must be particularly concerned that she does not have the face of a seventy-year-old woman and the legs of a sixteen-year-old girl. Cotton hose may remedy the problem, but if the actress must wear dress hose, the legs must be aged. Girls should remember that highly colored fingernails are appropriate for only certain types of women and can often ruin an otherwise excellent makeup.

When you use nose putty, bear in mind that it must be kneaded into a pliable mass in the hands before being placed on the face. Adding a little greasepaint or cold cream will make it more workable, and a little spirit gum will add to its adhesiveness. Nose putty may be used for building up noses, chins, cheekbones, and ears; for creating warts, scars, and other blemishes; and for blocking out the eyebrows. Use alcohol or acetone to dissolve the spirit gum used to attach nose putty or crepe hair.

There are two types of collodion that are useful to the makeup artist — flexible and nonflexible. Flexible collodion is used for building up the flesh or texturing the skin. For example, a double chin may be built up with layers of cotton which have been coated with spirit gum. When the "chin" is as large as desired, the cotton is coated with diluted collodion (thinned with an equal amount of acetone), brushing outwards and extending the collodion about ½ inch beyond the cotton. Nonflexible collodion is used for making indentations, scars, and for drawing up the flesh. To form a skin depression, apply the nonflexible collodion with a brush and allow each layer to dry until the indentation is deep enough. To draw up the flesh, stretch the skin in the area to be painted, allow the collodion to dry; then, relax the skin. Collodion may be peeled off or removed with acetone.

Liquid latex, already mentioned, is one of the most effective makeup materials to be used in recent years. It comes in tan, flesh, and white. It can be used for building up the skin, especially for blemishes and rough textures. It is very important to remember that latex must not get into the hair, even the "down" of a young face. It can be stippled over a stretched skin area and allowed to dry; when the skin is relaxed, a wrinkled-textured face is ready to be covered with greasepaint. However, this rough surface is somewhat difficult to paint over smoothly.

Another method is used which for certain effects is even more satisfactory: the makeup, aged or character, is completed by the usual procedure. Then, a transparent layer of latex is spread over one section of stretched skin at a time until the face, neck, and hands have received a "latex skin." Powder is applied to all areas and the aging is complete. Latex can also be used for molding eyelids, cheeks, and other built-up features, attached to the skin with additional latex.

Adhesive tape can be a very effective aid to character makeup. Oriental eyelids may be created by placing tape over the lids; the lift of Oriental eyebrows may be achieved by a piece of tape that pulls the outer brow toward the temple. Tape may also "pull" parts of the face to suggest the effects of scars or paralysis.

Tooth enamel comes in black, white, ivory, or cream. The black enamel is used to block out teeth, to make teeth appear pointed or chipped, and to make large teeth seem smaller. The "white" enamels are used to cover discolored, filled, or capped teeth and braces. The teeth must be absolutely dry before the enamel is applied.

Some other techniques can be used which take time and practice to master. Bags under the eyes require careful highlighting and shadowing or the actor may seem to have two black eyes. Cotton or tissues may be placed inside the cheeks or jowls to increase the effectiveness of character makeup. It is sometimes necessary to block out part or all of the eyebrows. Foundation greasepaint is satisfactory if the brows are not too dark or heavy; otherwise nose putty may be required. Then draw new brows with an eyebrow pencil.

Bizarre makeup may be tried if it is in keeping with the type of play and style of production. Stylized makeup, including "white masks," clownlike faces, and mosaics, can be quite effective on the stage. Special makeup has been developed for use with ultraviolet light. Changeable makeup really involves two makeup designs, one visible under ordinary light and the other visible under special lighting. For example, place a character wearing a special red greasepaint under red light, and he will appear to be white or in straight makeup. Change to blue or green light and the red will appear to be black. Ultraviolet makeup can also be used for changeable illusions.

The dark-complexioned actor should use a matching foundation with highlights to define his character, and the base should not be too light. Flesh or yellow liner works better than white for highlighting; purple or lavender works well for shadowing, as will a dark brown in some cases. The eyes should be lined with dark brown or black. Since darker-skinned people often have oily skins, careful drying or use of an astringent is recommended.

MAKEUP AND LIGHTING

One must always be cognizant of the effects of light upon makeup. Amber light, which is frequently used upon the stage, causes the complexion to yellow, the rouge to fade, and blue eye shadow to gray. Under blue lights, blue is absorbed and red turns black. Be certain you know the lighting that will be used while you are on stage so that pigments can be selected or mixed in order that the light will reflect the proper colors. Finally, it is usually wise to plan a costume-makeup rehearsal to check the effects of light and costume upon makeup.

Remember that in both class and school plays it is the actor, not greasepaint and costume, who creates the real illusion. However, care expended upon a first-class ensemble of correct costume, make-up, hairdress, and accessories will give you an assurance which will help you create a convincing characterization. Makeup is an integral part of the actor's whole appearance. It is to be used and enjoyed as another tool in his craft.

Makeup Projects

1. Draw a "facial mask" of your own face, carefully indicating bone structure and features.
2. On the facial mask indicate the types and colors of makeup you would use if you were to make yourself up for a specific part in a play. Carefully show where each should be applied.
3. Design the makeup for a young woman in a night scene.
4. Design the makeup for all the characters in a stylized production.
5. Present a demonstration of some unusual makeup technique such as the use of latex, nose putty, or collodion.
6. Prepare a full beard and mustache on a nylon backing for yourself or a classmate.

Bibliography

Baird, John: *Make-up*, French, New York, 1941.
Corson, Richard: *Stage Makeup*, Appleton-Century-Crofts, New York, 1967.
Strenkovsky, Serge: *The Art of Make-up*, Dutton, New York, 1937.

EPILOGUE
Considering Your
Future in Drama

The stage and the school have a new relationship today in this transitional period of American drama, and you as a high school student of theater have greater opportunities and responsibilities than ever afforded other generations of young people eager to go into some theatrical field professionally.

REGIONAL AND REPERTORY THEATERS

Broadway and Hollywood are fading as the centers of creative activity; the whole United States is now a promising field for successful careers. In less than ten years there has swept across the country a movement opening careers in the newly organized regional, resident, or repertory theaters. These are now the centers from which agents and directors in all branches of the theater — stage, screen, and television — expect to get their actors.

Many of the new theaters have excellent training departments, sometimes labeled academies or conservatories, and it would be wise **497** to write for information concerning them. In them the established professionals and the newly accepted beginners attend classes regularly, learning the latest methods in vocal and bodily training, and studying and practicing the newest techniques in artistic development. The American Conservatory Theater (ACT) of San Francisco, for example, under the brilliant direction of William Ball, provides year-round employment for the entire acting company under "a double contract," one providing a performance salary and the other a weekly training stipend. The seventy-two "training sessions" include practical instruction and experience in every phase of theatrical techniques. The subject matter carries over into stage performance on the part of every member of the company. Mr. Ball favors high school graduates as theater enrollees in the ACT.

A promising development of the residence theater movement concerns company tours, for this means an interchange of productions and a broadening of experience for the actors, while building a unity in theatrical production not before existing here.

Never before in the history of education have opportunities for preparing for a theatrical career been offered as widely as in American colleges and universities today. Courses listed under various categories cover every phase of theater training; architecturally contrasted buildings provide auditoriums and technical equipment for every form of production; acting experience in every type of drama is afforded, frequently in traveling troupes playing before miscellaneous audiences. On many campuses there is contact with professionals in first-class repertory companies and with actors-in-residence who teach and act with students. A great advantage over strictly specialized schools is the accessibility of classes in allied subjects.

QUALIFICATIONS FOR A PROFESSIONAL CAREER

Very few people possess all the qualifications upon which success in the theater depends. Remarkable inborn talent is only one asset, although it is indispensable. Personal magnetism, currently called "charisma," is an intangible attribute more important than physical beauty. You should also have the adaptable physical appearance which will fit a variety of roles; height, weight, carriage are important. The faculty of dressing to accentuate pleasing characteristics and lessen defects both on and off the stage is of value, for an actor must be at his best all the time whether he is acting, rehearsing, or hunting an engagement.

Good health, both mental and physical, will enable you to take disappointments in stride and resist excessive bodily and emotional strain. Self-discipline is probably the essential element to cultivate at once, for there is a constant pressure from long hours, in which nervous tension builds up. Displays of temperament and hysteria are pretty well out of style for directors as well as actors today, but there are likely to be some unstable personalities upset by the confusion and innumerable details of backstage life. The temptations are usually exaggerated, but avoiding dubious means of getting ahead does often demand an unusual degree of moral stamina. There is not the opportunity for a romantic life for the average, dedicated actor who is kept busy with rehearsing, taking lessons in various techniques, and studying lines in any available hours in the too short twenty-four!

Sufficient funds must be available or obtainable for an indefinite period until you have a definite contract and Equity Card. In fact, you should have an assured income or the training to get other jobs during the emergency periods that may come up at any time in any profession based on entertainment that the public can do without when money gets tight. Few actors have not supported themselves at various times by ushering, typing, clerking, modeling, and retail selling. You should therefore prepare yourself to be efficient in some congenial field which is fairly certain to have openings when you need them.

MAKING GOOD IN NEW YORK

New York is likely to be the goal of every actor, and young people are far too often determined to get started there. There are many advantages in being there, in spite of the dwindling opportunities on Broadway. The dozens of more or less successful off-Broadway theaters offer experience but very little income — if any. Even getting a chance in them depends far more at first upon whom you know than what you know; "getting the breaks" in the theatrical profession is continually a matter of luck rather than of talent. Therefore, you should begin at once making contacts with first-rate theater people by every means possible. You can learn to act only by acting, and the more parts you play, the more flexible and adaptable you are. If there is a summer theater near you, try to serve as an apprentice; work as much as possible all the time with local youth theaters, community and church groups, and in television and radio studios.

Try to meet any professionals in road companies and see all you can of backstage life — you may decide you want no part of it!

Training in New York at the many first-class schools of theater is especially valuable, for you can be seeing the best actors and plays and enjoying all the other cultural advantages afforded on all sides. The public performances of such schools are attended by agents and managers looking for new talent, who usually make out reports concerning the work of promising performers for their own reference and for assistance to aspiring actors. The members of the faculties are also in touch with theatrical people and can make contacts for talented students. The subject matter and approach to acting in all the best schools and drama departments are kept up to date and the presentations of avant-garde productions in the off off-Broadway houses can help you to decide for yourself what is fundamentally of art value and what are passing fads in actual performance. Thus, studying in the fascinating city does afford special opportunities, but none of the schools can or will guarantee employment.

Among the professional schools offering the finest training are the following: The American Academy of Dramatic Art, the oldest firmly established school for the training of professional actors, where hundreds of stars have studied; Juilliard School, Theater Division, which is the newest department of the famous institution housed in the magnificent Lincoln Center of the Performing Arts and which upholds the traditions which have made its musical division representative of the highest standards in training in fundamental and advanced artistic styles; the Neighborhood Playhouse, whose charming theater holds an enviable record in advancing the careers of hundreds of successful actors in all fields of theatrical activity; New York University Theater Arts, which stresses the latest mediums of improvisation and imaginative contemporary theater trends; Columbia University Theater Arts, with highly selective courses in both professional and academic training.

Studying with private coaches in special fields is popular today. Whatever training you get should be carefully selected, for your future can depend upon it. Directors have neither time nor inclination to be dramatics teachers, and they expect you to be trained in using your voice and body effectively and to be responsive and intelligent in taking directions.

When you are studying, keep in touch with every means of making connections and, when you are ready, of attending auditions; these are listed in such publications as *Back Stage, Show Business, Variety,* and others. ANTA and the Theater Communication Group (TCG) can be useful. Inexperienced beginners have difficulty in making impressions with casting agencies and stage managers, and actually getting a contract with a reputable agent is about as hard as getting a job. If important agents can see you in a good part on a stage in a first-class school, you may be a type they are looking for and your luck begins. If your luck holds, you will be given a chance to read for a part. If you are given a part in a play, you must join the Actors' Equity Association at once.

Youth itself is an asset, and many young people get opportunities in television commercials, small roles on Broadway, and, if they can dance and sing well, steady engagements in musicals. If you have the temperament to meet continual frustrations and disappointments, New York can furnish a deeply satisfying experience.

The advantages of a dramatic career are obvious. They are a constant lure to talented people, both young and old. No profession offers more spectacular, profitable, and satisfying rewards to those who are physically and temperamentally equipped (and fortunate enough) to find them. The actor who is content to play average roles expertly, without striving to become a star, may possibly earn an excellent living after he once gets a foothold in any one of the mediums.

The disadvantages are financial and personal. The insecurity of making a stable living and the unconventional hours of employment create serious problems in daily living. Going on the stage depends upon self-exploitation, often with harmful psychological results, and because luck frequently plays a greater part than ability in getting ahead, frustrations and disappointments lead to emotional complications hard to cope with.

Success in a theatrical career is largely in the lap of the gods. Given talent and charm, sufficient funds, and a buoyant, optimistic nature, the stage aspirant may be sure of colorful adventure and a chance to get ahead in one of the most uncertain but alluring professions.

TECHNICAL CAREERS

The technical fields are less precarious than acting. Strong unions of theatrical employees ensure a good living for young people employed in backstage work, publicity, and other nonacting departments of the theater. Technicians are paid whether plays or programs succeed or fail, and new sets and scenic and sound effects have to be produced constantly. Television production affords more opportunities for young people to serve in technical capacities than do any of the other mediums.

GETTING INTO TELEVISION

Los Angeles and New York are the centers for television employment, but there may be local stations where you can get experience. Large networks give auditions, and many individual shows have casting directors. Advertising agencies which produce package shows have casting directors and so do many independent packagers. Your first step should be to file an excellent photograph and résumé with people or agencies that may be able to help you. The résumé should include your name, address, telephone number, age, height, coloring, professional and amateur experience, specialized training, and other significant information. Your photographs should show you with many makeups and your résumés must be kept up to date; many actors of all ages and races and background keep steadily employed.

GETTING INTO MOTION PICTURES

Practically all the old means of breaking into the motion-picture field have disappeared with the shrinking of the major studios and their highly organized casting departments, which were extraordinarily efficient.

If you should be fortunate enough to be selected by a scout or casting director, you will be given an expensive screen test; your future depends entirely upon whether or not you are photogenic. If your test is successful, you may be given a contract. In that case, you must of course become a member of the Screen Actors' Guild. Many members live in Hollywood and adjoining areas, and their photographs and résumés are on file in the *Players Directory*, compiled by the Academy of Motion Picture Arts and Sciences, from which casting directors may choose their casts. You may sometime wish to settle in Los Angeles, for, like New York, there are many opportunities there to work in repertory and other theaters as well as in pictures; and the climate, except for the smog, is pleasant and an advantage to many. You can arrange to be "on call"; you then report as directed and are paid by the day, according to your special assets. The daily pay is high, but a living wage over a year's period is not assured.

Young people are not encouraged to come to Hollywood, where Charlton Heston, for many years president of the Screen Actors'

Guild, says that prospects are bleak. The figures he quotes of low annual incomes and rising unemployment claims are appalling. He explains that agents are necessary but unwilling to take on new-comers, and unemployed experienced actors are always available. He advises seeking openings with independent directors on location or in regional theaters.

High school students interested in film making can take advantage of the expensive equipment and expert training now being featured in increasingly important college film departments without necessarily taking degrees. Openings for technicians and directors are becoming available in new-type studios springing up and in reorganized standard ones.

Thus, getting on the screen depends largely upon making good on the stage first, upon influencial connections, or upon an agent who is well known and resourceful.

CONSIDERING A TEACHING CAREER

Teaching all phases of drama in high school, college, and university is attracting thousands of young people devoted to the theater who want to enter a field where they feel they can be of vital and enduring service. More and more high school students are deciding, while they are enjoying the creative experience of the classroom and auditorium productions, that they want to be dramatics teachers.

If you are one of them, now is the time to learn all you can about class management, play planning and organization, and the relationship between the teacher-director and the student casts and backstage workers. Directing scenes and plays in class and serving as assistant director of at least one big production are your most valuable means of understanding what teaching involves. They are a practical means of determining whether you are temperamentally suited and physically equipped to stand the unending hours of nerve-racking work this entails. Now is also the time to familiarize yourself with theater departments and facilities which will train you for such work by visiting in person all the college campuses possible.

Attending a summer high school institute and workshop, usually open to juniors, is a splendid means of getting a background of advanced contact with a fine university. For example, one of the most distinguished is the National High School Institute in Speech of the Northwestern University Summer Session at Evanston, Illinois, one of the first to be established; it has served as model for many others.

Many teen-agers could succeed in both professional theater and in teaching, which equally demand dramatic talent, dedication, creative ability, and self-discipline. The capability of inspiring creative activity in others is, however, the teacher's chief asset, an asset which many actors do not possess. You can find out your own capacity by assisting other members in the class with their selections and, outside of school, by working in church and community productions. You can even form your own neighborhood group of players. You should also be starting a library of plays of all periods and books on theater and its techniques. A wide background of theatrical knowledge is a basis for the further education which you must have.

A college degree is an absolute necessity in the teaching field, with a Master's degree becoming more and more imperative at the high school level. However, it is sometimes wise for a young person to get his A.B. and then teach several years before getting his M.A. He may well find some particular phase of theater he wishes to specialize in or, in the present transition period, some entirely new interest featured at an institution where he might wish to go for advanced work.

At the college level, a Ph.D. is required for the important positions and best salaries. On the whole, salaries in large public high schools are higher than a young person can get in a college set-up, and there are far greater opportunities for rich teaching and producing experience. Many teachers much prefer high school students, whose energies, idealism, and concentration, if once aroused, can accomplish anything.

A sincere love of theater and of young people, plus the ability to draw their best creative power from them, are the essential requirements for the dramatics teacher, especially for a high school teacher. A sense of humor and infinite patience are almost as important. The ideal teacher-director is a rare combination of the artist and the pedagogue and the business executive. The multiplicity of details of both the classroom and theater activity can be overwhelming without the devoted cooperation of the students which, fortunately, most teachers of dramatics can inspire.

First-class training in all phases of theater is, of course, indispensable to teaching at the secondary level, where actually making the scenery and lighting equipment is necessary. Today there is a special need for a thorough knowledge and appreciation of the glories of the great dramatic periods of the past and a sane perspective on contemporary trends. A strong foundation in the techniques of vocal and bodily expression is necessary to help students overcome their youthful tendencies to fidget, mumble, chatter, and swallow important words and to help them gain poise, repose, and clarity of words and gestures.

Like all branches of theater, changes are taking place constantly in classroom methods. Therefore, membership in professional organizations is vital, particularly in the International Thespian Society and the American Theater Association (ATA) in which especially the *Course Guide* and other publications of the Secondary School Theater Association (SSTA), the division for high school interests, will be invaluable to the young teacher.

Advantages

If you have the inner urge to teach, combined with dramatic talent and aesthetic appreciation of all the arts, you will find many advantages in choosing the educational field. Today it is open from the elementary grades through the intermediate to the secondary schools and into the college and university; it even extends into many industries, welfare services, and governmental departments. If the improvisational activities of your classwork have appealed to you especially, creative dramatics in the grades and the therapeutic directions which modern theater has taken might interest you most. If personality improvement through bodily and vocal expressiveness, and the beauty and power of drama as an art, have a strong appeal for you, high school work will be a joy. Teen-agers usually love the course and enjoy doing work where they can check personal achievement and development and can experience emotional involvement. If you are a perfectionist and artist in performing and allied arts, the university will meet your needs most completely.

The inducements in the educational field are increasing all the time, especially for men. With the "cultural explosion" and the involvement of the government financially and idealogically in artistic activity to meet the needs of the growing leisure time in our American way of life, fellowships and scholarships and grants and loans for travel and study abroad are being extended. The great foundations are assisting promising artists in all fields and expanding regional and university theaters. Administrators are encouraging leaves of absence for professional experience outside the classroom, and broad backgrounds are being appreciated as never before. You should keep in mind, as a goal, studying abroad, particularly in England where, especially at the Royal Academy of Dramatic Art (RADA), invaluable experience can be gained.

Financial returns for teaching are improving, with overtime compensation becoming more prevalent everywhere. Most school principals are recognizing the values of dramatics and are more and more considerate in arranging the teaching hours, committee work, and extra-curricular demands in the preparation of assembly programs, public performances, contests, and festivals. The security of tenure and pensions has a definite appeal in comparison with the uncertainties of an acting career.

The Dramatics Club

It is in your school dramatics club, either as a student member now or as sponsor-director later, that you will find the deepest satisfactions. Working with a carefully selected group, you can experience the unique joy only the artist knows as he strives for the perfection he seldom reaches. Membership in a dramatics club should be based on superior talent and achievement in some form of theater, plus acceptable conduct and scholarship, and a sincere desire to serve the school and the community along cultural lines. Carefully planned and organized tryouts conducted on an unbiased and unprejudiced basis are usually necessary. Such a club should encourage regular meetings featuring stimulating programs and penetrating discussions concerning drama and related subjects; group attendance at local productions; the presentation of worthwhile one-act plays or programs of appropriate selections given for community organizations; and individual service in storytelling, creative dramatics, and teaching in welfare work for children.

The culmination of each year should be the production of a play — musical, drama, comedy, classic — representing your highest standards of achievement. A unified plan for programs, publicity, and every phase of the production should be imaginative, and every member of the club should have some important function to carry out.

An Alumni Association should be formed and one social affair held every year to establish a close link between actives and graduates. Thus members can keep in touch with each other as a practical means of bridging the generation gap, for a love of the theater knows no boundaries of age, race, creed, or background.

In the stage of the school the dramatics teacher continuously improves his own abilities in its two phases of classroom training and public performance. In addition, teaching affords opportunities to work with local amateur groups where he can enjoy the pleasure of acting without the professional hazards.

Thus the ultimate gratifications you should consider are threefold: the satisfaction of developing the full potentialities of young people as individuals and artists; the fulfillment of your own capabilities in creative activity; and the knowledge that you are having a vital share in influencing the theatrical taste of your community through students who enter all fields of endeavor.

THE STAGE AND THE SCHOOL

Today as a student of the drama you have a rare opportunity to encourage enduring values of fine theater. The seventies are witnessing a protest against the "non-plays about nothing" without meaningful themes, plots, characters, or dialogue, which characterized drama in the sixties. Voices are being raised demanding plays that bring real entertainment, inspiration, and enlightenment. When these appear on stage, screen, and TV, you and your student friends can be vocal in your appreciation and active in increasing financial returns to producers. You can encourage the new trends, bound to come, which will lift the drama out of the depths into which it has fallen. Surely playwrights with vision and producers with ideals will find means of expressing the high hopes and achievements of humanity instead of depressing them.

Theater in all its phases depends upon public taste and desires. You, as a student today and a teacher, professional, or intelligent playviewer tomorrow can play an important role in the expansion of this most influential of the arts.

CREDITS FOR PICTURES

We wish to thank all those who have furnished the pictures used in this book. For credits and other pertinent information, see the captions. Below is similar information for pictures without captions.

PERMISSIONS AND ACKNOWLEDGEMENTS

We wish to thank the following authors, publishers, and agents for granting us permission to include copyrighted materials:

ANDERSON HOUSE PUBLISHERS for the following: Excerpt from *Elizabeth the Queen* by Maxwell Anderson; copyright 1930 by Longmans, Green & Co. Copyright renewed 1957 by Maxwell Anderson. Excerpt from *Joan of Lorraine* by Maxwell Anderson; copyright 1946 by Maxwell Anderson. Excerpt from *Mary of Scotland* by Maxwell Anderson; copyright 1933 by Maxwell Anderson; copyright renewed 1960 by Gilda Oakleaf Anderson. For all excerpts: All rights reserved. Reprinted by permission of Anderson House.

WALTER H. BAKER COMPANY for the following: The excerpt from *Neighbors* by Zona Gale; the excerpt from *Riders to the Sea* by John Millington Synge. Both reprinted with permission of Baker's Plays, Boston, Mass.

BRANDT & BRANDT for the excerpt from *Golden Boy* by Clifford Odets. Copyright 1937 by Clifford Odets. Copyright renewed 1965 by Nora Odets and Walt Whitman Odets.

DODD, MEAD & COMPANY for the excerpt from "Work" published in *The Hour Has Struck* by Angela Morgan.

DBS PUBLICATIONS, INC. for the excerpt from *The Fantasticks** by Tom Jones and Harvey Schmidt.

ERNST, CANE & BERNER for the excerpt from Ketti Frings' adaptation of *Look Homeward, Angel*** by Thomas Wolfe; copyright, 1958, by Edward C. Aswell as Administrator C.T.A. of the Estate of Thomas Wolfe and/or Fred W. Wolfe and Ketti Frings.

*All rights, including the right of reproduction in whole or in part, in any form, are reserved under International and Pan-American Copyright Conventions. Published in New York by DBS Publications/Drama Book Specialists.
CAUTION: Professionals and amateurs are hereby warned that *The Fantasticks*, being fully protected under the Copyright Laws of the United States of America, the British Empire, including the Dominion of Canada, and all other countries of the Berne and Universal Copyright Conventions, is subject to royalty. All rights . . . and the rights of translation into foreign languages, are strictly reserved. Particular emphasis is laid on the question of readings, permission for which must be secured from Music Theatre International, 119 West 57 Street, New York, N. Y. 10019.

**This selection is fully protected by copyright. All rights in this selection, including professional, amateur, motion pictures, recitation, public reading, radio and television broadcasting, and the rights of translation into foreign languages, are strictly reserved.

509

SAMUEL FRENCH, INC. for the following: Excerpts from *Lilies of the Field* by John Hastings Turner; copyright © 1923, 1924 by John Hastings Turner. Copyright ©, 1951 (In Renewal), by John Hastings Turner. Excerpt from *Skidding* by Aurania Rouverol; copyright 1925 by Aurania Rouverol (Under the title of "Nowadays"). Copyright 1925 by Aurania Rouverol. Rewritten and revised, 1928, by Aurania Rouverol. Copyright 1929 by Samuel French. Copyright 1952 (In Renewal) by Aurania Rouverol. Copyright 1952 (In Renewal) by Aurania Rouverol. Copyright 1957 (In Renewal) by Jean R. Butler and William S. Rouverol. Excerpt from *Prologue to Glory* by E. P. Conkle; copyright 1936, 1938 by Ellsworth Prouty Conkle. Excerpt from *Lima Beans** by Alfred Kreymborg; copyright 1925 by Alfred Kreymborg. Excerpt from *The Hollow Crown*, entitled "Epilogue from 'The Morte D'Arthur," devised by John Barton; © 1962 by John Barton. All excerpts: Reprinted by permission of Samuel French, Inc.

DAVID GROSSBERG for an excerpt from *The Fabulous Invalid* by Moss Hart and George S. Kaufman.

HARCOURT BRACE JOVANOVICH, INC. for an excerpt from *The Antigone of Sophocles:* An English Version by Dudley Fitts and Robert Fitzgerald, copyright 1939 by Harcourt Brace Jovanovich, Inc.; renewed 1967 by Dudley Fitts and Robert Fitzgerald. Reprinted by permission of the publishers.

A. M. HEATH & COMPANY LTD. and the Estate of the late Patrick Hamilton for an excerpt from *Angel Street.*

HOLT, RINEHART AND WINSTON, INC. for excerpts from *Cyrano de 'Bergerac* by Edmond Rostand, Brian Hooker Translation. Copyright 1923 by Holt, Rinehart and Winston, Inc. Copyright 1951 by Doris C. Hooker. Reprinted by permission of Holt, Rinehart and Winston, Inc.

HOUGHTON MIFFLIN COMPANY for excerpts from Archibald MacLeish's *J.B.*, Copyright © 1958 by Archibald MacLeish. Reprinted by permission of the publisher, Houghton Mifflin Company.

*CAUTION: Professionals and amateurs are hereby warned that *Lima Beans*, being fully protected under the copyright laws of the United States of America, the British Empire, including the Dominion of Canada, and all other countries of the Copyright Union, is subject to a royalty. All rights, including professional, amateur, motion pictures, recitation, public reading, radio and television broadcasting and the rights of translation in foreign languages are strictly reserved. Amateurs may give stage production of this play upon payment of a royalty of Five Dollars for each performance one week before the play is to be given to Samuel French, Inc., at 25 West 45th St., New York, N. Y. 10036 or 7623 Sunset Blvd., Hollywood, Calif., or if in Canada to Samuel French (Canada) Ltd., at 27 Grenville St., Toronto, Ont.

MORTON L. LEAVY of Weissberger & Frosch, Counselors at Law, for excerpts from *Spoon River Anthology*, the stage version by Charles Aidman.

J. B. LIPPINCOTT COMPANY for an excerpt from "The Highwayman" by Alfred Noyes from the book *Collected Poems* by Alfred Noyes. Copyright 1906, 1934, 1947 by Alfred Noyes. Reprinted by permission of J. B. Lippincott Company.

ALISON P. MARKS for the excerpts from *The Piper* by Josephine Preston Peabody.

WILLIAM MORRIS AGENCY, INC. for the excerpt from *Come Blow Your Horn* by Neil Simon. Copyright © 1961 as an unpublished play by Neil Simon. For the excerpt from *Impromptu* by Tad Mosel; copyright © 1961 by Tad Mosel. Reprinted by permission of William Morris Agency, Inc.

THOMAS NELSON AND SONS, LTD. for the excerpt from *The Maker of Dreams* by Oliphant Down.

OXFORD UNIVERSITY PRESS, New York, publishers of the New York edition of Lady Gregory's *Collected Plays*, edited by Ann Saddlemeyer, for an excerpt from *Spreading the News* by Lady Gregory.

PUTNAM AND COMPANY, LTD. for the excerpt from *A Night at an Inn* by Lord Dunsany.

G. P. PUTNAM'S SONS for an excerpt from *The Teahouse of the August Moon* by John Patrick. Copyright 1952 by John Patrick. Reprinted by permission of G. P. Putnam's Sons.

RANDOM HOUSE, INC. for excerpts from *A Thousand Clowns* by Herb Gardner. Copyright © 1961, 1962 by Herb Gardner and Irwin A. Cantor, Trustee. For an excerpt from *A Man for All Seasons* by Robert Bolt. Copyright © 1962 by Robert Bolt. For an excerpt from *Barefoot in the Park* by Neil Simon. Copyright © 1964 by Ellen Enterprises, Inc. For an excerpt from *The Diary of Anne Frank* by Albert Hackett and Frances Goodrich. Copyright 1954, 1956 as an unpublished work. Copyright © 1956 by Albert Hackett, Frances Goodrich Hackett, and Otto Frank. For an excerpt from *Antigone* by Jean Anouilh, adapted and translated by Lewis Galantiere. Copyright 1946 by Random House, Inc. For an excerpt from *A Raisin in the Sun* by Lorraine Hansberry. Copyright © 1958, 1959 by Robert Nemiroff as Executor of the Estate of Lorraine Hansberry. For an excerpt from *Arsenic and Old Lace* by Joseph Kesselring. Copyright 1941 and renewed 1969 by Charlotte Kesselring. For an excerpt from *The Time of the Cuckoo* by Arthur Laurents. For an excerpt from *An Ideal Husband* by Oscar Wilde. For excerpts from *The Importance of Being Earnest* by Oscar Wilde. For an excerpt from *The King and I* by Rodgers

INDEX

*A starred page number indicates an illustration.

513